NATIVE AMERICANS AND THE CHRISTIAN RIGHT

ANDREA SMITH

Native Americans and the Christian Right

The Gendered Politics of Unlikely Alliances

Duke University Press   Durham & London   2008

© 2008 Duke University Press

All rights reserved

Printed in the United States of America on acid-free paper ∞

Designed by C. H. Westmoreland

Typeset in Warnock with Quadraat Sans display by Keystone Typesetting, Inc.

Library of Congress Cataloging-in-Publication Data appear on

the last printed page of this book.

ESPECIALLY FOR SUNJAY AND TSALI

Contents

Preface

SCENE 1

I am sitting in a Bible study session preceding church services at a conservative Southern Baptist church. The Bible study leaders, a married couple, are explaining the "biblically correct" pattern for male-female relationships within marriage, using their marriage as an example. The husband makes all the important decisions in the marriage, and the wife submits to his authority enthusiastically and unquestioningly. To illustrate: whenever the wife pays the bills she waits until her husband comes home so he can sign the checks. While listening to this lecture, I sense dissatisfaction from a young woman sitting next to me. She is a longtime and faithful member of the church. "Do you buy this?" I ask. "No," she replies, rolling her eyes. "Some people just are not enlightened on these issues."

SCENE 2

I am in another conservative Christian Bible study group. We are having a debate on abortion, with me defending the "pro-choice" position. While most members are strongly anti-choice, the male Bible study leader describes how he shifted from this position. A friend of his had an abortion, even though she thought it was murder. After this incident, he asked his female Christian friends, "If you had an unwanted pregnancy while single, would you have an abortion?" and they all answered yes. When he asked his male friends, they all said no. He concluded that a "pro-life" position is in a sense founded on male privilege.

SCENE 3

At an American Indian Movement conference, one of the speakers is describing how Christianity has oppressed Indian people. He charges the audience to turn its back on Christianity and follow traditional ways. The next day people are looking for him, but he is nowhere to be found. Finally, his wife reports that he went to church that morning.

SCENE 4

I ask a Native woman activist if she is pro-life or pro-choice. She says, "The fetus is a life, but sometimes that life must be ended."

SCENE 5

During a United Nations Conference on Racism held in Durban, South Africa, conflict arises between the indigenous caucus and the African descendant caucus over the issue of reparations. One member of the indigenous caucus states, "You can have the mule, but the forty acres are ours." Years later, however, members of both caucuses meet to develop a joint strategy for reparations for slavery and abuses perpetrated in Indian boarding schools.

SCENE 6

I am having a manicure when I get into a conversation with the manicurist about this project. She tells me how she became a staunch, born-again Christian committed to pro-life politics. However, she tells me, she voted for Ralph Nader rather than George W. Bush because she felt Bush could not really be pro-life if he supported the death penalty. She then explains why she supports same-sex marriage. Christians mistakenly believe that same-sex marriage will destroy the institution of marriage, when what is really at stake, she argues, is that gay couples need to be able to visit their partners when they are in the hospital. She informs me that she convinced her other evangelical friends and family members to change their position on this issue.

As someone rooted in both Native rights activism and evangelical Christianity, I have found that neither academic nor activist understandings of religion and politics have been able to account for the variety of social justice activisms that I have witnessed and participated in. As I read the scholarly and activist accounts of evangelicalism, which tend to depict evangelicalism as monolithically conservative, I see virtually no mention of the many people within these churches, including myself, who do not follow the Republican Party line. Similarly, scholarship on Native activism tends either to ignore contradictions and tensions within Native organizing or to dismiss it as unimportant. As a result, would-be allies join indigenous struggles with a romanticized view of Native resistance and quickly drop out when we fail to meet their expectations. They often have a particularly difficult time dealing with Native peoples who do not fit their image of a "traditional Indian"—for instance, Native peoples grounded in conservative Christianity. Christian Indians are generally seen as dupes for white supremacy, complicit in their own oppression. "True" Native activism is reduced to the politics and practices of a handful of prominent Native activists, generally males.

On the other hand, I have found that other sectors of "the Left" dismiss our movements as irrelevant to social justice. Native peoples are thought to be hopelessly mired in "identity politics," concerned only about cultural particularities. Social justice activists and scholars have particularly failed to consider the significance of Native women's organizing. We have nothing to contribute to social justice activism or theory in general, we are told; our struggles have no relationship to political economy. Consequently, the complexity and importance of Native organizing, particularly Native women's organizing, remains undertheorized.

My particular experience reflects larger trends within social movement theory. This theory, as it is produced in academic and activist circles, so strictly defines who can be thought of as an agent of political change that it has narrowed the options of those seeking political and social transformation. Today progressives in and out of the academy grapple with identifying methods of resistance and revolutionary change in an era dominated by multinational capitalism. In these difficult times, we might want to take a closer look at whom we have identified as potential allies and whom we have written off as unreachable adversaries. What groups have we identified as central to political organizing, and what groups have we dismissed as insignificant? In doing so, we might open ourselves to unexpected strategic alliances with groups across the political spectrum that further our politically progressive goals.

Thus, this book centers on questions about coalition building. Who can be allies and under what conditions? Which alliances matter? How do we carve alliances, not only with outside communities but internally within our communities (however we may define *community*)? In fact, how can so-called identity politics be reconceptualized as alliance politics? What are the ethical and political considerations involved in carving out alliances? What are the politics involved in refusing to work with potential allies? And how does a study of alliance politics force us to reconsider our conceptualization of left- versus right-wing politics?

In this work, I will examine religious and political configurations of

Christian Right and American Indian activism as a way of talking about the larger project of rethinking the nature of political strategy and alliance building for progressive purposes. I have chosen case studies in Native women's and Christian Right organizing in part because of my own history of organizing. In addition, these forms of activism provide interesting case studies because virtually no scholars see the Christian Right as a possible site for progressive organizing. The significance of American Indian activism also remains generally undertheorized. By comparing American Indian and Christian Right activism and analyzing their intersections, this study will explore the problematic nature of "resistance," "accommodation," and "acquiescence" to political structures of oppression within both progressive and conservative forms of organizing. More important, this study will open up new possibilities for political organizing that do not depend on uncritically held assumptions about what constitutes progressive politics and who is able to participate in them.

At first glance, Native American and Christian Right organizing appear to have an orthogonal relationship. But, by bringing into conversation with each other two such seemingly disparate constituencies as conservative evangelicals and Native activists, I am signaling that this book will disrupt some of the assumed notions we have about the logics of these organizing sites. I also hope to disrupt normative assumptions about their inevitable political distance from each other. As Rebecca Klatch notes in her study of left- and right-wing organizing in the 1960s, examining activist struggles generally seen to be on opposite ends of the "left-right" political spectrum demonstrates the "complicated and at times unpredictable nature of political commitments and allegiances" (1999, 5). These case studies also enable me to complicate views of religious and political identity that presume a simple and unchanging relationship between religion and politics. However, while I hope to carve out a space in which to think more creatively about Native *and* Christian Right organizing in particular, my primary purpose is to work with these case studies in order to shift the way we think about coalition building in general.

METHODOLOGY: CENTERING NATIVE AMERICAN STUDIES

Elizabeth Cook-Lynn argues that Native American studies is not understood as its own intellectual project that has broader ramifications: "It is as though the American Indian has no intellectual voice with which to enter into America's important dialogues." She writes, "The American Indian is not asked what he thinks we should do about Bosnia or Iraq. He is not asked to participate in Charlie Rose's interview program about books or politics or history. It is as though the American Indian does not exist except in faux history or corrupt myth" (1998a, 112). In essence, Native American studies is equated with projects that have Native peoples as their object of study rather than as a set of methodological and theoretical approaches that contest academic disciplinary formations with its own frameworks. I wish to differentiate between "studying Indians" and doing Native studies by centering Native studies as an intellectual project that can have non-Native communities as its object of study.

I also differentiate between *centering* and *including* Native American studies. As I have discussed elsewhere, projects that attempt to organize women of color have begun to reject the politics of "inclusion" (A. Smith 2005b). Instead they ask, if we recentered the analysis and organizing from the perspective of women of color, how would we see political issues differently? This approach differs from a politics of inclusion that seeks to include a marginalized voice within a preestablished politics or discourse —an approach that is generally the basis of the multicultural framework for organizing and analysis. Let us *include* as many voices as possible, the multicultural ethic urges us. Such an approach, while generally problematic, is particularly troubling for Native peoples and Native studies because the relatively small population of Native peoples always renders our inclusion less significant than that of groups with greater numbers. Furthermore, as Elizabeth Povinelli has so aptly demonstrated, the liberal state depends on a politics of multicultural recognition that includes "social difference without social consequence" (2002, 16). Thus, it becomes critical, as Kimberle Crenshaw notes, to focus less on *including* the apparent "difference" that Native peoples represent and more on *centering* the difference this difference makes (1996). As Povinelli further states, "These state, public, and capital multicultural discourses, apparatuses, and imaginaries defuse struggles for liberation waged against the modern liberal state and recuperate these struggles as moments in which the future of the nation and its core institutions and values are ensured rather than shaken" (2002, 29). This multicultural practice, as Sandy Grande asserts in *Red Pedagogy*, manifests itself within Native studies in terms of the constant imperative to represent Native culture and identity. She asks, "How has this preoccupation [with cultural representation] obscured the social and economic realities facing indigenous communities, substituting a politics of representation for one of radical social transformation?" (2004,1). In the concluding chapter, I will further discuss the theories and organizing strategies produced by Native women organizers that challenge the model of the liberal nation-state, which is the basis of multiculturalism.

Centering Native women in this analysis also helps us rethink how we constitute "community" or understand "the nation." As I discuss in chapter 4, coalitional politics often assumes stable communities or "nations" that come together for a common cause. However, Native women's organizing has called into question the heteronormative basis of this kind of coalition building. At the same time, as members of colonized nations, they have not dispensed with the goal of furthering "sovereignty" or nation building. Rather, they are articulating alternative notions of sovereignty that then speak to alternative understandings of coalition building. These visions of sovereignty demonstrate the extent to which identity politics is itself a politics of alliances, both internally and externally. This politic, constantly in flux, demonstrates that Native nations are distinguished less by an essential identity, than by what Justine Smith refers to as "ontopraxy." That is, Native peoples are fundamentally constituted by relationality and praxis (J. Smith 2005, 117).

The project of recentering entails a Foucauldian understanding of power and hence does not assume a permanent center or that the "center" is stable and monolithic. Rather, we constantly recenter the discussion to see if this illuminates our understanding of the issues so that we can build a more liberating framework, not just for the communities we center in the analysis but for all peoples.[1] And, as I discuss later, this recentering strategy is integral to the most successful forms of Native organizing because it allows Native organizers to *reframe* issues in order to garner broader support for their struggles.

Centering Native American studies as a starting point to articulate methodological approaches, however, does not suggest that these ap-

[1] To give an example of this approach in practice, when women of color decided to develop this approach of centering women of color in the analysis of domestic and sexual violence through the group INCITE! Women of Color against Violence, we saw that it did not make sense to focus our strategies on involving the criminal justice system in addressing violence because we were as victimized by the criminal justice system as we were by interpersonal gender violence in our communities. As an alternative, some people thought we should involve the medical system as part of an antiviolence strategy. However, when we *recentered* the discussion to focus on women with disabilities we saw that the medical system was as punitive as the criminal justice system and that we would need to work on developing alternative strategies. In the end, neither the criminal justice nor the medical system was going to solve the problem of violence for anyone, not just for women with disabilities and women of color. See INCITE! 2006.

proaches can be found only within the field. On the contrary, it provides us with an opportunity to see how the concerns of Native American studies intersect, overlap, and/or contradict other frameworks, demonstrating that Native American studies is part of a larger world that can inform and be informed by other intellectual approaches and methods. In fact, this work is an intervention against the parthenogenetic strictures that Native American studies sometimes finds itself in—the notion that it must create itself as if it exists completely uninformed by other discourses and practices. For instance I often hear, "Don't read Foucault or Marx, etc.; they are not Native," as if engaging non-Native scholars or thinkers within Native American studies contaminates it. I do not mean to suggest that there is no point in engaging projects in which we might almost exclusively use Native sources as part of our exercise of intellectual sovereignty. On the contrary, these projects are groundbreaking and critical to the growth of Native American studies (Warrior 1994; Wilson 2005; Womack 1999).

However, sometimes, in my experiences with both organizing and academic work, we do not engage others because we have actually decentered ourselves. That is, in reacting to our marginalization in the academy and organizing venues, which is the result of colonialism and white supremacy, we may fear that engaging in other discourses may continue our marginalization. But if we really want to challenge our marginalization we must build our own power by building stronger alliances with those who benefit from our work, both inside and outside the academy. When we become more directly tied to larger movements for social justice, we have a stronger base and greater political power through which to resist marginalization. When we build our own power, we can engage and negotiate with others from a position of strength rather than weakness. Thus, rather than fearing that engagement with the ideas emerging from non-Native communities will marginalize us, we can actually position Native peoples as intellectual and political leaders whose work benefits all peoples. The question, then, is not whether we should *include* Native studies in other discourses, such as American studies, ethnic studies, postcolonial studies, and so on, but what would happen to these discourses if we *recentered* Native studies within them. We might transform these discourses in ways that benefit all who partake in them. The last chapter in this volume reflects further on how the theory produced by Native women activists may benefit us in rethinking how we position Native studies within the academy.

In centering Native American studies as the framework for this book, I wish to employ three approaches I see as critical to Native Americans that inform its methodological approach. These concepts include (1) rearticulation, (2) intellectual ethnography, and (3) generative narratology and prolineal genealogy.

THE POLITICS OF REARTICULATION

The small numbers of Native peoples in this country have forced us to wrestle with the politics of rearticulation. Native peoples organizing on their land bases have to contend with the fact that they are often geographically situated next to white populations that are often hostile to Native interests. For reasons of pure political necessity, they are constantly forced to rethink how they rearticulate the politics of alliance in order to accomplish their political and economic goals. Yet, as will be discussed in the introduction and chapter 5, they have led some of the most successful organizing efforts through their use of unlikely alliances. These alliances were carved out through a politics of rearticulation, the process of transforming political allegiances to build movements for social change.

In this regard, they share Stuart Hall's analysis of rearticulation.[2] As Hall notes in his analysis of Thatcherism in Britain, the Right has often been successful because it has been creative in reconstituting its power base, frequently by redeploying conceptual frameworks of the Left for its own purposes (1988). In particular, it has developed popular support for cutbacks in the social safety net through appeals to "freedom" from state intervention.[3] It has mobilized popular support for repressive law enforce-

[2] For an explicit engagement with Stuart Hall within Native studies, see Valaskakis 2005.

[3] This rhetoric is evident in a critique of liberal politics articulated by Concerned Women for America, a Christian Right women's organization: "You see, liberals are looking for the silver bullet—but then, wouldn't we all think it grand if we could conjure up a government program that on a large scale effectively addresses societal concerns?" (Crouse 2000, 5). As Wilcox, Rozell, and Gunn further note, the New Christian Right has emphasized the development of political coalitions and underemphasized divisive religious doctrines in its organizing to build these right-wing hegemonic blocs (1996). Thomas Atwood, the former comptroller of Pat Robertson's presidential campaign, argues for the importance of developing alliances on the Right because the "major strategic error of the Evangelical Right has been the overestimation of its own strength: Thinking they had 'enough votes to run the country'" (1990, 45). He calls on white evangelicals to use issues such as privatizing public housing and educational choice for inner-city children to develop alliances with black evangelicals.

ment through its appeals to the racism of the white working classes. As a result, Thatcherism created a "hegemonic bloc" consisting of both corporate and working-class constituencies. The Left, by contrast, was unable to counter the rise of Thatcherism because it assumed that the working classes would naturally see their interests reflected in the Labour program. It made little effort to either create new alliances or challenge the ideological foundations of the Thatcher bloc. As a result, the Left spent the Thatcher years defending its ground rather than actively articulating an ideological framework that could create new strategic alliances. The problem with theorists and activists on the Left, according to Hall, is that they fail to realize that "interests are not given but always have to be politically and ideologically constructed" (1988, 167). Thatcherism was successful because it reshaped the public's notion of common sense. As Michael Billig further notes, "Common sense, which at one level seems to act as a force for conservativism, also contains the ideological resources that could be rhetorically mobilized by future social movements of critique" (1995, 77). According to Hall, however, the Left has not seen the refashioning of common sense as an important task (1988, 143).

Ernesto Laclau and Chantal Mouffe's *Hegemony and Socialist Strategy* is another helpful starting point for thinking about how to identify and mobilize resistance. The distinction they make between "representation" and "articulation" allows us to explore the inherent malleability of political alliances. They note that Marxists have traditionally relied on a politics of representation—that is, the view that actors for social change (proletarians, however they are defined) are historically given and political organizing depends on "representing" this historical reality to potential activists. They do not argue that it is illegitimate for the working classes to position themselves as key actors for social change, but they do argue that this position is not historically given. That is, if the working classes become central actors for social change it is because they have "articulated" this project rather than simply stepping into a predetermined historical role (1996, 65).

The politics of articulation has important implications for strategy. Laclau and Mouffe argue that Marxists who rely on notions of given agents of historical change ultimately advocate a conservative political strategy. That is, if the working classes are the natural actors around which other agents will naturally coalesce in effecting historic change, it is not necessary to actively forge strategic alliances that will enable the political project to go forward. Laclau and Mouffe cite Kautsky to illustrate the extreme limit of this position: "Our task is not to organize the revolution but to organize ourselves for the revolution; not to make the revolution but to take advantage of it" (1996, 22).

In addition, when activists assume universal values or common interests from which we struggle we have no incentive to *create* this common ground. The search for common interests constitutes what Laclau and Mouffe term the "hegemonic project"—that is, taking the political initiative to forge alliances on the basis of one or more political issues. It is true that political alliances are never completely stable, nor are actors involved in cultivating these alliances completely unitary. However, these facts do not impede political activism; rather, they force us to realize that, since the alliances are not given, we must constantly struggle to ensure that they thrive.

Many scholars have commented on the political fragmentation of the Left. When they speculate on the alliances necessary to form a reinvigorated movement, the prospective allies still tend to reside primarily within communities generally considered progressive. But might it not be possible for progressives to forge strategic alliances in new places? Given the Right's success in creating hegemonic projects that have attracted constituents previously seen as belonging to the Left, perhaps progressives can return the favor. We might even discover that the political division between Left and Right is itself a stumbling block in the creation of new political alliances.

Forging new alliances is difficult and, as Stuart Hall argues, while there is no fixed relationship between classes and ideologies, these relationships are not free floating either (1996b, 41). Consequently, reconstituting political positions is a Gramscian "war of position," requiring political actors to articulate a platform in light of the political and social forces that shape this war. "No ideological conception can ever become materially effective unless and until it can be articulated to the field of political and social forces and to the struggles between different forces at stake," Hall writes (42).

The case studies in this book also center the role of religion in social movements. As Christian Smith argues, social movement theorists have often neglected the importance of religion in building social movements (1996). To the extent that social movement theorists address religion, he argues, they see it as an epiphenomenon of the "real" motivations behind the social movement. It is important to take Smith's charge seriously by centering the theological content of these movements in the analyses. As he notes, while religious movements often adapt their theologies to fit changing political circumstances, at the same time theology can operate as an independent variable in shaping these movements.[4] Political progressives must therefore be watchful for possible theological interventions. Smith further contends that sociologists often emphasize the manner in which religious or spiritual practice functions to legitimize the political status quo and have not sufficiently analyzed its potential to disrupt and challenge power relationships (6). In this book, I argue that religious movements can be disruptive of the status quo, not only in explicitly liberative religio-political formations such as those found in indigenous peoples' movements, but even within groups that appear to support the status quo such as the Christian Right. Particularly in this era of "faith-based" organizations, it is important to analyze the complex ways in which religious and spiritual practices interface with political action.

This project aims to take up Stuart Hall's charge to rethink the politics of articulation and rearticulation in the age of ubiquitous multinational capitalism. What Native peoples often know by necessity all peoples need to realize—we cannot fundamentally ensure the well-being of our "communities" without rethinking who we can ally ourselves with in order to develop mass-based movements for social change. If we understand that current configurations of religious and political identity within Native and Christian Right communities are not givens, it is possible for them to be rearticulated into new configurations that favor progressive politics. I will explore these possibilities by focusing on sites of political and religious practice that do not neatly fit into categories of progressive or conservative.

In essence, this book is a Foucauldian political project. Both critics and proponents of postmodern thought often argue that Foucauldian analysis is inconsistent with articulating a politics of strategy or liberation. Nancy Hartsock, for instance, argues that Michel Foucault's analysis of power is not equipped to deal with social structures. Foucault "loses track of social structure and instead focuses on how individuals experience and exercise power" (1990, 169). In Hartsock's view, Foucault's analysis of power precludes the possibility of one group's domination of another: "Power is everywhere, and so ultimately nowhere," she writes (170). Foucault, she claims, is also pessimistic about social change and is content merely to describe power relations rather than engaging in political action. Hartsock invokes the eleventh Feuerbach thesis: "To paraphrase Marx, the point is

---

[4] See also Carol Maxwell and Ted Jelen's study of male pro-life activists, in which they conclude that religious theology is not an "epiphenomenal" explanation for their involvement in the movement (1995).

to change the world, not simply to redescribe ourselves or reinterpret the world yet again" (172). Craig Calhoun similarly complains that because all practices are implicated in power relations it is possible to talk of resistance but not possible to talk of emancipation (Calhoun 1996, 120; see also D. Smith 1999). Steven Seidman's work points to the flaws in these critiques. To say, for instance, that power does not issue solely from the state or other structures of domination is not to say that these structures do not *possess* a disproportionate amount of power. As he notes, "Foucault did not deny the social importance of the repressive power of the state or ruling social strata" (1998, 246). I would concur with this analysis. In fact, I would go farther than Seidman and argue that Foucault's analysis does not preclude talking about liberation or revolution, a perspective against which Seidman argues in his other works. As Foucault explains, "When I say that power establishes a network through which it freely circulates, this is true only up to a certain point. . . . I do not believe that one should conclude from that that power is the best distributed thing in the world. . . . We are not dealing with a sort of democratic or anarchic distribution of power through bodies" (1977b, 99). This framework does not preclude us from addressing hegemonic forms of power; it simply forces us to address the fact that struggles for state or economic power are not sufficient to shift prevailing power practices if we do not address how power relations are simultaneously enacted on the micro-level of everyday life.

Another argument frequently made by critics of poststructuralism is that its antifoundationalist approach renders the projects of identifying truth and adjudicating moral claims impossible (Bauman 1999, 126; Calhoun 1996, 116–17). In essence, poststructuralism is accused of moral and epistemological relativism. In actuality, a disavowal of foundationalism does not preclude us from taking stands, making arguments, or forming opinions (Bible and Culture Collective 1995, 3; Seidman 1998, 325). Relativism is really the flip side of universalist notions of truth. That is, claims to universalism and objectivity rest on the notion that individuals can transcend their historicity to decide what is eternally and cross-culturally true. Similarly, relativism rests on the notion that individuals can escape their grid of intelligibility, with its particular regime of truth, and see multiple truths. Foucault contends that all individuals live within regimes of truth that have their own logic and standards of truth, standards that allow individuals within that regime to adjudicate between truth claims. If a person's regime were to become destabilized, it would mean that he or she is in the grip of another (partially competing) regime, not living without one altogether. Because we know our regime of truth is historically conditioned, we know that it is flexible and given to change, but we are not capable of disbelieving its "truths" as long as we are living under it. That truth is historically conditioned, therefore, does not make it less true for us. As Stanley Fish argues:

> While relativism is a position one can entertain, it is not a position one can occupy. No one can be a relativist, because no one can achieve the distance from his own beliefs and assumptions which would result in their being no more authoritative *for him* than the beliefs and assumptions held by others. When his beliefs change, the norms and values to which he once had unthinking assent will have been demoted to the status of opinions and become the objects of an analytical and critical attention; but that attention will itself be enabled by a new set of norms and values that are, for the time being, as unexamined and undoubted as those they displace. The point is that there is never a moment when one believes nothing. (2005, 319)

Some might also argue that raising questions about "strategy" is hopelessly modernist and depends on a preconceived notion of a universal societal goal. As mentioned previously, a recognition that power is diffuse does not prevent us from seeing that power in many cases is also very concentrated. Consequently, concentrated forms of resistance are needed to address these concentrated forms of power. As Foucault says, "Like power, resistance is multiple and can be integrated into global strategies" (1977b, 142). Thus, a politics of liberation is not inconsistent with a Foucauldian analysis. Foucault, however, reminds us that liberation is not a once-and-for-all event but a continual and open-ended process (Lorentzen 1997, 145).

A Foucauldian analysis, while not precluding a discussion of "liberation," does force us to consider how political projects cannot escape reinscribing the power relations they seek to contest or possibly instilling new power relations, which can be oppressive. Consequently, my analyses attend not only to the possibilities of rearticulating political formations within Christian Right and Native women's organizing but also to the ways in which the discourses of these communities can discipline liberatory impulses and turn them into conservative political projects. The politics of rearticulation is a project fraught with danger at every turn, and this danger never ends. At the same time, if we understand identity as shifting and contingent, we also know that identities can change. Our political opponents of today could be our allies of tomorrow.

As a result, this project can be understood as a Foucauldian political project that assesses the possibilities of building alliances for the goal of political liberation "without guarantees." As I discuss in chapter 5, this type of political project resonates with the Native scholar Craig Womack's articulation of sovereignty politics as "an ongoing, dynamic process, rather than a fixed creed, . . . [which] evolves according to the changing needs of the nation" (1999, 60). It also echoes Reid Gomez's articulation of sovereignty as "a spiritual intellectual process of mobility" (2005, 163). The project of indigenous nation building, particularly within the context of genocide, the U.S. empire, and multinational capitalism, requires flexibility, strategy, and a commitment to a larger vision of a just world that is inclusive of all peoples. A politics of rearticulation is central to creating liberatory mass-based struggles committed to a revolutionary process that is unfixed and ever changing.

INTELLECTUAL ETHNOGRAPHY

Assessing the political possibilities of rearticulation requires alternative methodological approaches because I seek to answer the question of not "what is?", but "what could be?" This book will rely on a methodological approach that emerges when one centers Native American studies in intellectual ethnography. Native studies forces us to problematize the role of the academic and academic research in general. In their never-ending quest to "know" the Other, hordes of academics have descended on Native communities to procure their "tribal secrets" (Warrior 1994). As Philip Deloria notes, this ethnographic imperative correlates with Western imperial notions of the "vanishing Indian." "With the Indian past fading away, the documenting of it became a vital activity," he writes (1998, 80). He criticizes the ethnographic practice of "salvage ethnography"—"the capturing of an authentic culture thought to be rapidly and inevitably disappearing" (90). Much of this ethnography is concerned with what Mary Douglas terms "matter out of place." That is, Native peoples and other people of color who have survived centuries of genocide threaten the dominant culture's confidence that it will remain dominant. From the colonizer's perspective, Native peoples that continue to exist pollute the colonial body—they are matter out of place. To fully understand, to "know," Native peoples is the manner in which the dominant society gains a sense of mastery and control over them. As a result, researchers have not often asked such questions as "Do Native people want others to know about them?" and "Do Native communities find this research helpful?" Tired of these colonial investigations, tribal communities are placing increasing restrictions on what research they will allow (Fixico 2003, 133; Mihesuah 1998).

Western academia places a high value on procuring "knowledge" or "truth" as a goal in and of itself. In contrast, the Cree historian Winona Wheeler (Stevenson) notes that within Native communities the possession of knowledge does not confer the right to communicate that knowledge to outsiders:

> One of the major tenets of Western erudition is the belief that all knowledge is knowable. In the Cree world all knowledge is not knowable because knowledge is property in the sense that it is owned and can only be transmitted by the legitimate owner.... You can't just go and take it, or even go and ask for it. Access to knowledge requires long-term commitment, apprenticeship and payment. As a student of oral history, in the traditional sense, there is so much I have heard and learned yet so little I can speak or write about, because I have not earned the right to do so. I cannot tell anyone or write about most things because it has not been given to me. If I did it would be theft. So I'll probably be an Old Lady before I am allowed to pass it on. By then, I'll have learned all those rules of transmission and will probably feel impelled to keep it in the oral tradition and not write it down. (Stevenson 1998a, 11–12)

As Linda Tuhiwai Smith notes, the heart of the issue is that the research done on indigenous peoples has historically never benefited indigenous peoples themselves—rather, Native communities are seen as "laboratories" in which research is conducted for the benefit of the dominant society (1999, 118). As the work of Linda Tuhiwai Smith and Kamala Visweswaran illustrates, indigenous peoples have increasingly gained access to Western academic institutions and now have more opportunities to talk back to those who attempt to study them. As Visweswaran notes, the "subjects . . . have now become [the] audience" (1994, 9).

In my research, I seek to avoid the colonial "ethnographic imperative," which would strive to make Native communities more knowable to non-Natives. Rather, I seek to identify resistance strategies within Native communities that will be helpful in promoting Native sovereignty struggles in particular and social justice in general. In addition, rather than rendering Native people as objects of my study, I wish to position them as subjects of intellectual discourse about the relationships between spirituality, political activism, and gender identity. Robert Warrior describes this project as "intellectual sovereignty." He notes that Native communities are seldom seen by non-Native scholars as sites of intellectual discourse, and his work uncovers long-standing Native intellectual traditions (1994, 2). In centering Native American studies, I also wish to center the theories and approaches that emerge from Native women's organizing. Native American studies, while centering the intellectual production of Native people, often centers those in the academy. I seek to build on the work of Warrior and Cook-Lynn by broadening the application of intellectual sovereignty by identifying nonacademic activists as intellectuals. This work might be described as an "intellectual ethnography." Rather than studying Native people so we can learn more about them, I wish to illustrate what it is that Native theorists have to tell us about the world we live in and how to change it (Garroutte 2003).

As mentioned previously, Native American studies is not limited to intellectual projects in which Native peoples are the subject of study. Rather, its theories, methods, and questions have relevance to broad-ranging levels of inquiry. For instance, studies of the Christian Right have also been driven by the ethnographic imperative. Nonevangelicals rarely take conservative evangelicals seriously as contributors to theological, sociological, or political thought. Rather, they become larger-than-life enemies of freedom and justice or quaint eccentrics with inexplicably old-fashioned ideas about religion. While I do not see conservative evangelicals as oppressed communities, I think these ethnographic efforts have hindered our ability to more fully understand the significant role that evangelicals play in the spiritual and political life of the United States. An outgrowth of this tendency is scholarly neglect of the theology underpinning Christian Right activism. While a plethora of books analyzing the Christian Right have been published, few take seriously the theological content of Christian Right belief systems. This neglect of the theology of the Christian Right can distort analyses of its politics. For example, many activists and scholars of the Promise Keepers movement have argued that it is the "third wave of the Christian Right." They are not convinced by the group's leaders, who have staunchly argued that Promise Keepers does not wish to involve itself in politics or that its "Stand in the Gap" rally in Washington, D.C., in 1997 was intended simply to gather men to "pray for the church and the nation." Rather, they charge that Promise Keepers is essentially a stealth organization designed to increase support for conservative politics under a religious cloak (Conason, Ross, and Cokorinos 1996). These critics often fail to consider the theology of those involved in Promise Keepers: thousands of people actually *do* believe that praying is not just an empty gesture but a powerful act that can transform so-cial structures. As an example, the National Association of Evangelicals claimed that the killing of Saddam Hussein's sons during the Iraq War was the result of prayers by evangelicals (National Association of Evangelicals 2004). Meanwhile, *Charisma* magazine asserted that increased prayer has resulted in fewer abortions, less crime, and the collapse of the Soviet Union (Peterson 1999; E. Smith 1999). While I would certainly argue that Promise Keepers is political, the complex ways in which it is political have often been missed by critics, thereby hindering their efforts to mobilize against some of its problematic political stances. A greater understanding of the theological underpinnings of Christian Right politics would greatly enhance our analyses of what the Christian Right seeks to accomplish and what strategies would be effective in countering it.

In addition, because conservative evangelicals are not portrayed as thoughtful people who can change their minds, little attention is paid to the possibilities of articulating political platforms involving conservative evangelicals that might actually promote the goals of social justice move-ments. I will argue that these possibilities do indeed exist. This book, then, is not primarily concerned with making broad claims about the commu-nities that are its focus; rather, I investigate the possibilities and pitfalls of fostering resistance struggles in both Native and conservative evangelical communities. The approach of intellectual ethnography, while it emerged from Native American studies, is an approach that is also valuable in analyzing other communities, including the Christian Right.

GENERATIVE NARRATOLOGY AND PROLINEAL GENEALOGY

Justine Smith critiques the prevalent project within Native studies of re-placing Western epistemologies and knowledges with indigenous episte-mologies as a project unwittingly implicated in a procapitalist and Western hegemonic framework. She argues that the framework of "epistemology" is based on the notion that knowledge can be separated from context and praxis and can be fixed. She contests that a preferable approach is to look at indigenous studies through the framework of performativity—that is, indigenous studies focuses on Native communities as bounded by prac-tices that are always in excess but ultimately constitutive of the very being of Native peoples themselves (J. Smith 2005). The framework of perfor-mativity is not static and resists any essentializing discourse about Native peoples because performances by definition are never static. Today, much of Native studies is content driven, which leads to these essentialized notions of "what Native knowledges are," "what Native identity is," and so on (Turner 2006). This approach contributes to the previously mentioned problem of scholars always directing their energy toward "knowing" more about Native peoples. Furthermore, as Micaela di Leonardo argues, there is a tendency among academics to study Native people as a way for those in the dominant culture to learn more about themselves. Either Native communities have "ancient wisdom" to bestow on others or they represent the "savage" that proves the superiority of the dominant society. "Primitives," she notes, "are ourselves, or our worse or best selves, or our former selves, undressed: human nature in the buff" (1998, 147).

A Native studies approach that focuses less on a content-driven epistemological framework and more on a performative narrative would be a generative narratology. Such a methodological approach is evident in Audra Simpson's groundbreaking study of Mohawk nationalism (2003). What is significant in this work is the conscious refusal to reveal excessive ethnographic details about the Mohawk communities in which Simpson situates her work. This absence coincides with Justine Smith's analysis of indigenous texts as aporetic (2005). That is, what is significant about indigenous texts (*texts* understood in the broad sense of the term) is as much in what is *not* in them as in their positive textual content. We can see that the aporetic nature of Simpson's text serves several functions. First, it serves to decenter whiteness and the white gaze from her project. Furthermore, she further decenters whiteness in her approach by not signaling her methodological shift. In this sense, she echoes the work of Janelle White on black women in the antiviolence movement, in which one of her interviewees offers this analysis on the topic of decentering whiteness.

> It is okay to dislodge [white people from the center] . . . as long as you [explain it]. It's kind of like the way bell hooks appeals to white women because she talks explicitly about how we need to shift white women from the center and put Black women in the center. But if she had just done it? For example, if you think about Pat Parker compared to Audre Lorde. Pat Parker just talked about Black people. She was just into addressing Black people's lives. . . . Audre Lorde really addressed white women more. I mean, I still very much value what Audre Lorde wrote, but I think that's part of why Audre Lorde was heard of so much. (2004, 41)

White concludes: "Does acknowledging that white people are not at the center of academic discourses actually serve to affirm and sustain their perceived and/or material centrality?" (41). Similarly, Simpson does not engage a specific discussion in decentering whiteness and recentering Native peoples in her work; her aporetic text just does it.

Simpson's work is less a site for a voyeuristic look into the Mohawk community and more a project of generative narratology. That is, her text generates a praxis of nation building involving multiple narratives, including those of her interlocutors, herself, and her readers. This text does not simply describe Mohawk nationalism; rather, the narration itself becomes a moment of nation building. It is a text that invokes a collective participation in what could be rather than a description of what is. Hence Simpson's work can be described as a *prolineal genealogy* of the Mohawk nation. That it is, her focus is not just on writing "a history of the present" (Foucault 1977a, 31), an analysis of what nationhood has meant for Mohawk peoples today. Rather her prolineal genealogy tells a *history of the future* of the Mohawk nation, what nationhood *could mean* for Mohawk peoples specifically and Native peoples in general.

Inspired by the work of Justine Smith and Audra Simpson, I would like to frame this project as a prolineal genealogy of both coalition building and Native American studies, a project that centers not just on what coalition building and Native American studies are but on what they could be. As such, my proposed methodologies are not meant to be prescriptive for my purpose is not so much to convince people that Native American studies must use the specific methods of intellectual ethnography, rearticulation, or recentering. Instead of supporting a vanguardist approach for espousing theoretical frameworks or political strategies, this project aims to continue a conversation about how we can build Native American studies as its own intellectual project with its own integrity, which nonetheless has implications for other intellectual projects. In that sense, it is inspired by the work of Waziyatawin Angela Wilson's *Remember This!* In her generative narratology, she relies on indigenous oral history to demonstrate that it can stand on its own but has transformative implications for the world. She states, "With 300 million Indigenous Peoples worldwide with common histories of struggle against colonialism and neocolonialism, we have tremendous potential to transform the world. Sharing our stories and linking our voices is one step in achieving a different vision for the world" (2005, 13).

While at times this book may leave the impression that I am making totalizing claims about the theories produced by Native women or Christian Right organizers, or about what the project of Native American studies should be, my intent is to contextualize these ideas as a generative narratology, an invitation to be part of a conversation to develop Native studies centered on a praxis of liberation not only for Native peoples but for the world. My goal is less to argue what Native studies or Native organizing is or should be doing than to suggest what they *could* do based on what they are doing now. John Holloway's work speaks to the importance of theorizing from a prolineal genealogical rather than a vanguardist perspective. He writes, "Revolutionary change is more desperately urgent than ever, but we do not know any more what revolution means. . . . Our not-knowing is . . . the not-knowing of those who understand that not-knowing is part of the revolutionary process. We have lost all certainty, but the openness of uncertainty is central to revolution. 'Asking we walk,' say the Zapatistas. We ask not only because we do not know (we do not), but because asking the way is part of the revolutionary process itself" (Holloway 2005, 215).

SOURCES

My primary sources for this project come from archival material, participant observation, and interviews. My analysis of the Christian Right relies on an extensive survey of the conservative Christian periodical literature listed in the Christian Periodical Index under relevant subject headings, from 1971 to 2005.[5] In addition, I surveyed all issues of *Christianity Today, Charisma,* and *World* published between 1991 and 2005 to find articles that address these issues but are indexed under other subjects.[6] *Christianity Today* provides the widest coverage of issues in conservative evangelicalism generally, although it is rooted in neo-evangelicalism.[7] *Charisma* provides coverage of issues rooted in Pentecostal and Charis-

---

[5] The subject headings I surveyed include race, Promise Keepers, women, Native American, American Indian, African Americans, Asians, Hispanics, race relations, feminism, prisons, Prison Fellowship, Christian Coalition, Charles Colson, drugs, gangs, missions, and death penalty. The source materials cluster around different dates depending on the topic. The sources for chapter 3 cluster around the 1970s, when evangelical feminism first emerged, and the 1980s, when Christians for Biblical Equality was formed. The sources for the sections on Native peoples and race reconciliation focus on the 1990s, when the race reconciliation movement emerged but before it diminished in significance after 9/11. The sources for the section on prisons tend to wane around the late 1990s when Prison Fellowship, the primary Christian prison organization, began to decline.

[6] I began in 1991, when the race reconciliation movement developed.

[7] Around 2003, *Christianity Today* became a monthly magazine instead of one that published fourteen to sixteen issues per year.

matic Christianity. *World* provides coverage from an explicitly right-wing political perspective. (A more extensive map of conservative evangelicalism is provided in appendix 1.) I also surveyed periodicals not included in the Christian Periodical Index, material produced by Christian Right organizations such as Concerned Women for America, Prison Fellowship, and the Christian Coalition, as well as e-mail newsletters from Justice Fellowship. In addition, I draw from a number of books written by conservative Christian Right authors. My work is informed as well by the literature produced by a variety of evangelical Native organizations that are gaining greater prominence within white evangelical circles such as Wiconi International, Christian Hope Indian Eskimo Fellowship (CHIEF), *Indian Life*, and Eagle's Wings Ministry. All of the materials surveyed are cited in the text or footnotes. I draw primarily from these sources rather than the ethnographic data of particular evangelical communities because I want to focus on national discourses about these issues. As Sara Diamond points out, the frequent appearance of a topic in a community's periodical literature does not necessarily reflect that community's priorities. Periodical content depends on many other factors, including editors' and writers' particular preferences (1995, 409).[8] Nevertheless, this literature is very widely read by conservative Christians. So, while a prevalence of articles on a particular topic may not always reflect the interests of those at the grass roots, it certainly plays a role in determining the future shape of those interests. In addition, since this is a work of intellectual ethnography, I am not primarily interested in making representative claims about what evangelicals think about these issues. Rather, I want to look at some of the ideas in evangelical discourse that might signal new possibilities for political mobilization. In cases in which articles contradict what I find to be overall trends in Christian Right discourses, I provide references in the text or footnotes.

Because this book covers materials from hundreds of sources, it may be difficult to follow all the camps. Consequently, when the authors are relatively less well known, I usually cite them by magazine (generally *World, Charisma*, or *Christianity Today*) so as to provide a map of which ideas are being discussed in which venues. For prominent figures in the Christian Right, I provide brief identifying material when he or she is first

---

[8] Hence, I am not conducting the traditional "content analysis" of evangelical literature often used by scholars of the Christian Right to determine the beliefs of Christian Right activists as a whole since such studies do not necessarily reveal the beliefs of the larger community. For the problematics of such approaches, see Iver 1990.

cited. For additional background that might help orient the reader, I have provided a brief map of both Christian Right and Native American organizing in appendix 1.

I also draw on my history of participation in Native activists' struggles and Christian Right conferences and events. Observation helps supplement analyses of archival materials such as periodical literature because it provides a fuller sense of how ideas discussed in the literature are practiced in various contexts. The disadvantage of participant observation is that it can be difficult to obtain a critical perspective on the political work one is involved in. On the other hand, since my goal is to call into question the bifurcation between scholarship and political work, perhaps my participant research will provide a model for future scholarly activism. It is no secret that many scholars are divorced from the world of grassroots political work. At the same time, many activists live solely in the battle of the moment and often do not reflect critically on their struggles. I have come to believe that analysis grounded in political activism is helpful not so much because it is more true than other types of analysis but because it provides a model for encouraging social movement participants in general to develop a measure of critical awareness within their areas of political work. The unfortunate divide between academics and activists contributes to a situation in which academics produce theory that is not helpful to activists while activists produce theory that is not recognized as such, even by other activists, because it was not produced in an academic setting. In some cases, as the prominent human rights activist Loretta Ross notes, scholars often appropriate the intellectual work of activists who are not academically based, profit from activist work by publishing material that is not accountable to activists, and in so doing often damage rather than support social justice organizing (2000). As a result, activists outside of the academy often downplay the importance of critical analysis in their work. Both academics and activists sometimes celebrate "activism" in an undifferentiated sense without looking at how different activisms often reinscribe racism, sexism, and colonialism more than they resist them. In my experience of antiviolence organizing, for instance, those of us in the movement uncritically supported criminal justice interventions as the primary strategy for ending violence without considering how we may have been unintentionally supporting a racist criminal justice system until we took the time to critically interrogate and theorize about our work (A. Smith 2005b).

I also hope that my participant observation will produce some personal accountability for my research. If I continue to work with the same communities over a period of time, I will be forced (out of self-preservation if nothing else) to do research that is hopefully more accountable to them. Ethical issues arise, however, from my status as a non- or semiparticipating observer of Christian Right events whose ultimate political goals I do not support. Even when I am not engaged in research, I do not typically outline my political commitments to conservative evangelicals until I have established long-term relationships with them so that I can avoid excommunication. Since my observation of Christian Right functions was limited to one-time events in which I did not develop such relationships, I identified myself when asked (which was very seldom) as a Christian who is interested in the proceedings on a personal level and conducting research on a professional level. This approach did not resolve all of the ethical issues involved. Rather than pretending that I have developed a fully satisfactory resolution, I keep these ongoing ethical quandaries visible in my work, and as described in chapter 2, this approach did create problems for the subjects of my project. Given that I have yet to determine how to represent myself at the conservative evangelical events I attend in my personal life as a practicing Christian, where people assume that all evangelicals are Republicans, it is not a surprise that I have been unable to resolve issues of representation in my academic work.

I have supplemented participant observation with interviews and provide some data from thirty informal interviews of Promise Keepers members that I conducted while staffing the Promise Keepers Project for the National Council of Churches in 1997. These interviews were conducted primarily on the basis of convenience; I make no claims that they are representative. Nevertheless, they do provide some additional insight into the Christian Right discourse on gender and race politics. In my analysis of Native women's organizing, I found so little work published by and about Native women activists that I have supplemented my analysis of this work with interviews of sixteen Native women activists. Because I wish to position Native women activists not as objects of study but as producers of political and social theory that must be taken seriously, I have included their analysis in this work. Any uncited quotations come directly from these interviews. A brief description of the interviewees is contained in appendix 2.

OVERVIEW

The first chapter of this book explores prison organizing within conservative evangelical circles. I examine how the complicated relationships between the Bible and the state in evangelical discourse contribute to reactionary positions on issues such as gay civil rights, abortion, and so on while simultaneously supporting relatively progressive positions on issues of prison reform among some sectors of the Christian Right. While assessing the possibilities for rearticulating this movement into a more progressive politics, I also describe how evangelical prison organizing is fraught with complications and contradictions. By analyzing Christian "restorative justice" programs (terminology to be explained in that chapter) in conjunction with indigenous models of justice from which restorative justice programs explicitly borrow, I explore both the pitfalls and the possibilities of these programs. In particular, I explore the ways in which these programs both reinscribe and contest Christian imperialism, gender heteronormativity, white supremacy, and U.S. nationalist ideologies.

Chapter 2 explores American Indian activism with a particular focus on American Indians in the Promise Keepers and other evangelical movements. The first section looks at how American Indians figure in implicitly racially constituted notions of citizenship in Christian Right discourse, particularly as it is manifested in the race reconciliation movement. The second section looks at Native peoples who try to place themselves within this discourse. What impact does their vexed position have on Native and Christian Right identities? Native peoples within this movement often support Christian imperialism and perform "whiteness" in a manner that undermines Native sovereignty struggles. At the same time, however, they often use tenets of evangelical faith to undermine white supremacy and support Native nationalism. While the Christian Right articulates the Bible as a foundation for a "Christian America," Native peoples within these same movements use the Bible to undermine white Christian claims to a Christian America and to support tribal nationalisms. This project challenges the commonly held assumption that Christianization within American Indian communities is equivalent to assimilation.

However, whatever the progressive tendencies are within race reconciliation or evangelical prison organizing, neither movement contests a heteronormative paradigm for articulating the nation, the state, or the family. Thus, chapter 3 explores what interventions along these lines are made by evangelical and Native American feminists. Feminists within both Native and evangelical communities are often marginalized in feminist studies because evangelicalism is supposed to be singularly patriarchal and "Native women aren't feminists," as the mantra goes. By putting these feminist projects in conversation with each other, it is clear that even the way we conceive of coalition politics shifts. It also becomes apparent that Native identity and evangelical identity are themselves based on coalition politics. The chapter is divided into three sections. Because both communities often portray themselves, or are portrayed by others, in totalizing ways, both evangelical and Native feminisms have often been erased in the discourses within and about these communities. The first section explains the emergence of these feminisms, demonstrating that they do, in fact, exist. The second section focuses particularly on violence as a galvanizing force for feminist interventions within evangelical and Native communities. Antiviolence organizing is also an important site for investigating not only the successes of feminist organizing but also the failures of Native and evangelical feminists to coalesce. The third section assesses the interventions Native and evangelical feminisms make in their communities, how they trouble monolithic portrayals of both evangelicalism and Native struggles, and what the implications are for these interventions in developing coalitions within and between communities.

Since this work is in intellectual ethnography focusing on the theories produced within organizing circles, chapter 4 discusses how Native women and evangelicals themselves theorize about coalition politics and carving out "unlikely alliances" across political and religious divides. The first section focuses on how Native women and evangelicals theorize about the politics of coalitions. Under what contexts and through what ethical parameters are these alliances shaped? What is to be gained by such alliances, and what do these groups risk? The second section puts these communities in conversation with each other to suggest a model for alliance building on issues that seem to be hopelessly divided. In particular, I look at the possibilities for rethinking pro-choice versus pro-life abortion politics.

Explorations of coalition politics engender a question: coalition politics for what? In chapter 5, I conclude with a discussion of Native women's visions of sovereignty and nationhood that provides a framework for articulating struggles for self-determination that is based on a model of coalition building and interrelationships rather than on a heteronormative nation-state model that replicates the political status quo. These visions provide helpful critiques of some of the assumptions behind much Christian Right organizing, but they also call into question the logic of much of even progressive racial and national liberation struggles today. I will briefly conclude with a discussion of the implications of this work for the field of Native American studies.

CONCLUSION

Particularly with the depressing results of the 2004 elections, many progressives despair that the Christian Right has highjacked the Republican Party and the country. Some of the analysis tends to assume that there is a simple equation between evangelicalism and conservative politics. How can you reason with people whose politics are religiously motivated, ask many progressive thinkers. For example, Katha Pollitt argues, "If a voter wants Christian Jihad, he may not be willing to desert the cause for health insurance—especially with Republicans telling him 50 times a day that the plan is really a socialist plot to raise his taxes and poison him with Canadian drugs" (Pollitt 2004).

Contrary to Pollitt's analysis however, George Bush actually received widespread criticism in even the most conservative evangelical venues for his mishandling of the war and the economy. When one evangelical magazine, *Charisma* began publishing pro-Bush editorials, it was flooded with anti-Bush letters before and after the elections. Some examples include the following.

> I pray for President Bush and admire a clear moral vision grounded in Christian faith. But what are we to think when the outcome of that vision entails so much violence, and when it just happens to enrich his party's benefactors at places like Bechtel and Halliburton? And when the target of our latest selective liberation has oil (unlike Zimbabwe or Myanmar)? And when it buries other needs under a landslide of military spending and mounting debt? And when dissenting people and nations are bullied? Either this vision suffers from massive moral blind spots . . . or the administration is using God-talk to manipulate people for ungodly purposes. (Readers Write 2003, 10)

> I pray for our servicemen, and I agree that they are brave. But how does their service defend democracy or end terrorism? I don't think you can come to that conclusion without a PhD in convolution. I suppose it helps to have the faith of George W. Bush. He can invade a nation and say that it was somehow a just act of war. . . . I just don't see how Jesus Christ fits into all of this. (Letters 2004b, 8)

> When are we going to wake up and realize that American politics is based on money, oil and American dominion over the world? . . . In these last days, when the focus is on worldly treasures, a true Christian president would not be elected in America. Period! (Letters 2004a, 10)

Why should we Christians "stop bashing Bush" as some of your readers have asked? . . . Bush is the worst president since Richard Nixon. Our country is in the worse shape it's ever been, as we Americans are hated around the world! (Letters 2004a, 10)

I am concerned that *Charisma* consistently serves as a religious arm of the Republican Party. . . . You ignore the danger of proclaiming a human political party as God's party. (Feedback 2006a, 10)

Charisma is shocked at how Christians wrote angry letters about Bush. I am shocked there are Christians who think Bush really is a Christian. (Letters 2004a, 9)

These malcontents within conservative evangelicalism were not mobilized by progressives to significantly impact the elections, but they possibly could be. It is important to consider that the equation "conservative evangelicalism equals Republican politics" is socially constructed and the result of over fifty years of organizing on the part of the Right to articulate evangelicalism as a conservative political platform (Diamond 1989). Thus, it is important to consider how these religious and political alignments can be rearticulated to serve more progressive ends. In order to do so, it is important to look at fault lines within evangelical discourse that might provide opportunities for political interventions and grassroots organizing.

After the 2004 elections, Michael Moore felt the need to issue a communiqué to progressives entitled "Seventeen Reasons Not to Slit Your Wrists" (2004). After all, many progressives felt that the Left had done all it could to organize against Bush but lost anyway. I believe that the Left has done relatively little to change the political status quo in recent years. If we commit ourselves to grassroots organizing without sabotaging ourselves by clinging to outdated notions about who are our friends and who are our adversaries, we can build a truly progressive movement that goes beyond voting for the lesser of two evils. We can trace much of the ascent of the Christian Right to the overwhelming defeat of Barry Goldwater in the 1964 presidential election. Instead of despairing over the defeat, the Right took the opportunity to develop a mass movement, which we are now seeing the fruits of after four decades of organizing. Progressives can take this historic moment to either wallow in depression or build new coalitions that will transform our world.

Acknowledgments

Countless people have inspired me and assisted me with this project. I profusely apologize for anyone I might inadvertently neglect to acknowledge. Of course any errors and misrepresentations in this book are mine alone.

This book is inspired by the brilliant and courageous Native women intellectuals and activists who have taught me so much: Luana Ross, J. Kehaulani Kauanui, Audra Simpson, Justine Smith, Sherry Wilson, Loretta Rivera, Lakota Harden, Madonna Thunder Hawk, Judy Kertész, Christine Redcloud, Katrina Cantrell, Sharon Todd, Ellen Guttillo, Chrystos, Mona Recountre, Tonya Gonella Frichner, Sammy Toineeta, Mililani Trask, Haunani Kay Trask, Noenoe Silva, Jennifer Denetdale, Pamela Alfonso, Toni Sheehy, Rebecca VanVlack, Debra Harry, Kim TallBear, Waziyatawin Angela Wilson, Amy Lonetree, Dian Million, Michelle Erai, Yvonne Dennis, Sarah Deer, Lisa Hall, Mishuana Goeman, Val Kanuha, Eulynda Benally, Charlene LaPointe, Vera Palmer, Willetta Dolphus, Angela Morrill, Heather Milton, Sarah Deer, Renya Ramirez, Emma LaRocque, Eva Garroutte, Verna St. Denis, Val Napoleon, Priscilla Settee, Rosemary Gibbons, Pamela Kingfisher, Annie White Hat, Julia GoodFox, Debbie Reese, LeAnne Howe, Lee Maracle, Charlene Teters, Michelle Jacob, Leah Henry Tanner, Michelene Pesantubbee, Angela Gonzalez, Chris Finley, Angela Parker, Veronica Pasfield, Kiri Sailiata, Lani Teves, Joyce Green, and Peggy Bird. I must particularly thank Audra for reading the manuscript several times and encouraging me to continue the work when I became discouraged (by sending me off to get pedicures). J. Kehaulani Kauanui and Jennifer Denetdale inspire me with their amazing courage to speak the truth even when it is not popular, as well as with their fabulous selection of sovereignty shoes.

My colleagues at the University of Michigan in American culture and women's studies provided me with invaluable feedback on the manuscript. Tiya Miles, Gregory Dowd, Alan Wald, Carroll Smith-Rosenberg, Sarita See, and Nadine Naber read the manuscript several times. Philip Deloria, Julie Ellison, Elizabeth Cole, Peggy McCracken, Scott Kurashige, Maria Cotera, Damon Salesa, and Naomi Andre also reviewed and provide helpful feedback on my project. James Treat at the University of Illinois, Urbana-Champaign, provided additional support for my research.

This project originated as a dissertation through the History of Consciousness program at the University of California, Santa Cruz. The members of my dissertation committee—Angela Davis, Luana Ross, Herman Gray, and James Cone—were a pleasure to work with. In my master's program, James Cone and Jace Weaver encouraged me to pursue a PhD, and I have them to thank for even being in academia in the first place. Luana Ross is the most fabulous mentor on planet earth. And Angela Davis, my dissertation advisor, has been an exemplary role model for combining activism with a commitment to critical analysis.

Many people have provided me with political and intellectual inspiration along the way, including Dylan Rodriguez, Ruth Wilson Gilmore, Sora Han, Vince Diaz, Susan Najita, Joe Gone, Michael Witgen, Tony Clark, Glen Coulthard, John McKinn, Jennifer Harvey, Larry Fountain-Stokes, Alisa Bierria, Andrea Ritchie, Shana Griffin, Dale Turner, Julia Sudbury, Beth Richie, Clarissa Rojas, Mimi Kim, Paula Rojas, Simmi Gandhi, Isabel Kang, Paul Anderson, Penny von Eschen, Jayati Lal, Miriam Ticktin, Christine O'Brien, Tom Reisz, Debby Keller-Cohen, Matthew Countryman, Valerie Traub, Wanda Pillow, Liz Wingrove, and June Howard. Nadine Naber has been a constant support for me within the context of the academic industrial complex. Sarita See, Susan Najita, and Nadine must also be thanked for helping me with all my moving! Paula Rojas has been a complete inspiration in terms of political visioning and movement building. The women of INCITE! Women of Color Against Violence and the Boarding School Healing Project have provided me with much-needed direction and focus in my work. And Tom Reisz did extensive copyediting for the earlier versions of this manuscript.

Much of my thinking on the relationship between spirituality and political activism has been informed by members of U.S. EATWOT (Ecumenical Association of Third World Theologians), including: Benny Liew, Randy Bailey, Tink Tinker, James Cone, Jung Ha Kim, Dwight Hopkins, Linda Thomas, Ada Maria Isasi-Diaz, Rita Brock, Rosetta Ross, Michel Andraos, Jose Rodriquez, Rachel Bundang, and Teresa Sauceda.

Thank you to Terry LeBlanc, Randy Woodley, and Richard Twiss for holding me compassionately accountable for my work. I apologize for any misrepresentation of their ministries that might continue to exist in this book.

I received financial support to complete this project through fellowships from the Lannan Foundation and from the Native American House of the University of Illinois, Urbana-Champaign.

Of course this book would not have been possible without Duke University Press. My editor, Reynolds Smith, helped me through countless revisions and offered invaluable suggestions during this process. I particularly appreciate all the Snickers bars he bought me whenever I became discouraged. I would also like to thank Molly Balikov for the clarity of her direction during the copy-editing process.

Some portions of this book have appeared elsewhere in earlier versions. Parts of chapter 2 appeared as "'The One Who Would Not Break His Promises': Native Peoples in the Evangelical Race Reconciliation Movement" in *American Behavioral Scientist* (2006); sections of chapters 3 and 4 appeared as "Native Feminism, Activism and Social Change" in *Feminist Studies* (2005); and parts of chapter 4 appeared in "Beyond Pro-choice Versus Pro-life: Women of Color and Reproductive Justice" in *NWSA Journal* (2005).

Finally, this work could not be done without the support of my family who facilitated my "straight shot to the truth." The theological articulation of my then four-year-old nephew inspires this work: "God isn't a boy; God isn't a girl. God is a spirit. And if God had skin, it would be dark."

Introduction

Why Rearticulation Matters

My experience with Native activism as well as my findings from the research for this project suggest that not only is it possible to mobilize groups across "Left versus Right" divides but in fact these groups are mobilized on a frequent basis, particularly by Native activists. Because many Native communities are situated in conservative, white-dominated areas of the country, Native peoples have not always had the luxury to work in coalition with "progressive" sectors of society and have often had to find creative ways to work with conservative, even explicitly anti-Indian individuals and communities. In some cases, these coalitions have led to tremendous victories, allowing Native activist organizations with relatively small numbers of members and few financial resources to defeat the policies of multinational corporations. The political framework behind these successes is Native peoples' strategy of rearticulation. Rather than assuming who their political friends and enemies are, they have been able to rearticulate political alliances, thus transforming political allegiances to build movements for social change.

One struggle I was involved in revolved around the spearfishing controversies in northern Wisconsin in the late 1980s and early 1990s.[1] In 1989, the federal courts recognized the right of the Chippewa Indians to spearfish in ceded territory. A number of anti-Indian hate groups were soon formed such as Stop Treaty Abuse (STA) and Protect America's Rights and Resources (PARR). When the Chippewa attempted to spearfish, these groups would mobilize white people to flock to the boat landings and physically and verbally harass them. They would shoot at the Chippewa,

[1] For fuller accounts of this struggle, see Gedicks 1993; Grossman 2002; J. Smith 1996; Valaskakis 2005; and Whaley and Bresette 1994.

attempt to overturn their boats, and carry signs with racial slurs such as "Save a Fish, Spear a Pregnant Squaw." In order to deescalate the violence, Walt Bresette and others organized the non-violent witness program, which mobilized allies to stay at the boat landings with the Chippewa. These groups did not engage in acts of confrontation or violence, but their mere presence in large numbers helped deescalate the violence and create a safe environment for the spearfishers (Whaley and Bresette 1994).

The brilliance behind this program was the manner in which Bresette reconceptualized the struggle. In the beginning, it was easy to see the mobs of white sportfishers as the enemy. However, Bresette argued that Native peoples and their allies needed to look at this conflict in a broader context. During that time, it had recently became profitable for mining corporations to begin mining for natural resources in that area. However, the first attempts to begin mining were derailed by united Indian and non-Indian opposition. The courts' recognition of the Chippewa's right to hunt, fish, and gather posed an additional threat to these companies because if mining operations so degraded the environment that the Chippewa could not hunt, fish, and gather, then they were in a position to argue that such operations would be a violation of their treaty rights. Consequently, argued Bresette, it was entirely possible that these mining companies were funding the hate groups. The problem was not the sportfishers, who had every bit as much to lose if the mining companies destroyed their tourist economies. Rather, it was probably the mining companies that were promoting disunity in northern Wisconsin so there would be less political opposition to their operations.

As a result of this theory, nonviolent witnesses were instructed to conduct themselves in such a way that would help defuse the violence but would not create such hostility among the sportfishers that it would become impossible to build alliances with them in the future. The people who yell at us today, we were told, could be our future allies.

As it happened, Exxon and Rio Algom began the process of opening a sulfite mine in northern Wisconsin. The Midwest Treaty Network immediately began an educational campaign that reached over one thousand white residents of northern Wisconsin and informed them of the importance of siding with the Chippewa to stop Exxon. They and other organizations were so successful in mobilizing support among white people to stop mining in Wisconsin that the state's governor at the time, Tommy Thompson, who favored it, was compelled to sign a mining moratorium in 1997. Exxon withdrew from northern Wisconsin in 1998. Of course, racial conflict has not ended there. Nor have the threats posed by mining companies. Still, this effort was a very significant success in which the alliance building of a relatively small number of Native rights' groups was able to stop Exxon—a success not many groups can claim.

This success is not an isolated incident. Pamela Kingfisher, one of the interviewees, talks about how her organization, Native Americans for a Clean Environment (NACE), an even smaller organization, was able to force Kerr-McGee to close its nuclear conversion facility in Oklahoma and in fact to cease its operations in the United States altogether. Kerr McGee was Karen Silkwood's employer when she died under suspicious circumstances after making public Kerr McGee's lack of regard for the safety of its workers due to nuclear contamination.

Kingfisher became involved in this struggle while working for Indian Health Services. She noticed that many people coming in with cases of cancer were living near Gore, Oklahoma, where Kerr McGee was located. Consequently, she joined NACE on a volunteer basis. She describes how the key to her successful organizing was to demystify the nuclear process to community members, who became concerned about accidents occurring at the plant. "I guess I've just always been crazy enough to speak my heart and not be worried about looking stupid or mispronouncing a big word or standing up in a room full of suits and not having the alphabet behind my name that gave me the authority to come and say those things," she says. She also explains how their successful campaign relied on a number of strategies. On the legal front, they filed a number of lawsuits, the first of which stopped Kerr McGee from doing deep-well injections of their radioactive waste. In addition, their media strategy was successful in garnering support because their framing device was to argue that this was a human rights issue rather than a Native rights issue. This strategy of recentering and reframing is central to Native organizing; Native organizers frequently reframe and recenter issues so that non-Natives will understand that they impact not only Native peoples but all communities. Kingfisher describes how they focused on Kerr McGee's exploitation of its workers rather than the exploitation and contamination of Native lands.

[Kerr McGee] had a big break in a water line and had to dig up a big piece, and they hired contract workers to come in. And they put them in down in this water, and it was all mucky and they had to work on these pipes. Lance [Hughes, a member of NACE] was there with the Nuclear Regulatory Commission, and they were doing a tour because of our lawsuit. They had to invite us to everything they did. They were walking through. They were looking at these contract workers in the pit. And the water was real yellow, and one of the Nuclear Regulatory Commission guys said, "Why is that water so yellow?" And one of the plant workers said, "Oh, somebody must have pissed in it." And they laughed, and the workers are down there laughing. Later we found out that those men were all contaminated with uranium. It was yellow because of the uranium in it. . . . They got their sores in their mouths, and they had sores on their legs. They never told those contract workers what they were putting them into or that it was dangerous. So when we discovered that, we would just break these stories that were human stories. They weren't about Indians; they were about human beings. About people and about communities and about the animals. When we talked about the fish, that affected a lot of people. A lot of people there fished and ate that fish. And they understood what we [were] saying. We didn't have it just be Native; it was about everybody. This is an environmental issue, and we just attacked those *issues*.

Framing the issue as a human rights issue was particularly effective when NACE videotaped Kerr McGee spilling nuclear waste along highways when transporting it in their trucks so the company would not have to pay a fee for disposal. It also discovered that Kerr McGee was turning the nuclear waste into a fertilizer called raffinate. Kerr McGee bought cows that were fed on this radioactive fertilizer on lands it operated in conjunction with the Monsanto corporation. The beef and dairy products from these cows were sold at a popular ice cream franchise, Brahms. At first, it was not clear how dangerous this raffinate was because the company did not spray the outside grounds visible to the public. However, NACE was able to sneak into the grounds and document the level of contamination suffered by the cows. By publicizing this issue, its members were able to demonstrate how Kerr McGee's policies impacted not only Native peoples but anyone who might eat the beef or dairy products of cows that were fed raffinate. They also built alliances with white farmers, not always great allies of Native communities, who were subject to greater restrictions on how many cows in their herds could be allowed to die before their operations were closed down.

[Kerr McGee] had bought cows and put them on ten thousand acres with Monsanto Corporation, and they tried to turn their waste out of these sludge ponds into a fertilizer called raffinate. And they'd buy cows and put them on the land, and they were selling the cows to Brahms. And we protested Brahms and said they were selling contaminated cows, and we got them to stop buying the cows. When the Navajos had a severe winter and were losing all their sheep and cattle, Kerr McGee sent truckloads of hay out there. And we called the Navajos and said don't you dare feed that hay to your sheep. It's from this contaminated land where Monsanto Corporation and Kerr McGee Corporation have sprayed what they called raffinate.

And on the outside, [Kerr McGee] wouldn't spray [raffinate], so it'd be all green and happy. On the inside, everything was yellow and brown and dead. And one day we took video cameras and we went into the center, and we found their dead cow pits because the farmers started telling us every three/four months, all these trucks in the middle of the night would come in and unload cattle. What are they doing with all those cows? So we started poking around, and we found these dead cow pits with all these bones floating in these pits where they would dispose of all the cows once they died because they had ruined all this grass. Parrots that died off-site, anything that got sprayed, died, and we started interviewing all the neighbors and farmers. And the farmers stopped the raffinate trucks in the middle of the night with guns. They didn't talk to us. They didn't let anybody know. They just got out there, got their guns and stopped them. I can go on and on and on. The stories were incredible. The things they did and how we figured it out and tried to combat them. And then we'd get it in the news. They put that videotape of the dead cow pits on Channel 8. Our phone didn't stop for a week. Those farmers were so upset because they're regulated on how many cattle they can lose in their herd before they're shut down, and they were *mad* because they couldn't have gotten away with that, but Kerr McGee did.

The approach of attacking the issues, not people, enabled NACE members to address the suspicions of community members that they might be "outsiders" and also to build coalitions even with the workers in the plant who might otherwise oppose them. The key to carving out successful coalitions with unlikely allies, according to Kingfisher, was framing this struggle as a human rights and environmental issue rather than a Native rights issue. They publicized the extent to which Kerr McGee's operations threatened the well-being of people across the country. For example, they were able to get support from white farmers who might not otherwise support Native struggles. However, NACE eventually shifted its strategy to one of attacking the corporate leaders of Kerr McGee rather than the workers. This strategy was informed by collaborative efforts with Lois Gibbs, who became famous for organizing against the Love Canal contamination in 1978. According to Kingfisher,

We didn't attack people, but we attacked those issues. But then I started working with Lois Gibbs, and she was the first woman who organized at

Love Canal, twenty, thirty years ago, and Hooker Chemical Company had completely contaminated their community. They had chemicals leaking into their basements, scumming up the walls, and her kids got sick. And we started working with Lois, and she said, you make it personal. They're killing our children. You name their names. And we did. We took them on. And it really became a big piece of our strategy. And we talked on radio stations in their hometowns. And we wrote to their churches, and we wrote in their home. Because they come to our hometowns and contaminate us, and they don't live there. They go home to wherever they are with their nice homes. And nobody knows what they're doing. We wrote to the Rotary Club. We wrote the Lion's Club, and we named their names. We made it personal. You're killing us, and it's *you* who are killing us, and made it very personal.

And we thought, well, we've got media, we've got legal, we're organizing in the communities with our monthly meetings the last three years every month we were down with cookies and coffee and inviting the workers, the president of the plant would come. One night a woman sat down beside him and his wife, and she was right beside him on a picnic bench and turns to him and says, "Do you believe in God? How can you do this to our people if you believe in God?" He was *sooo* shamed; they never came back to another meeting. It was just a simple question, but it made him embarrassed, and all his workers against the wall were kind of looking at it. The community people there. . . . We never said, don't you come here. We always invited them. We sent him a flyer every time we had an event. We never protested the plant.

In addition, another successful media strategy that personalized the issue involved Kingfisher's attempt to have the head of the Environmental Protection Agency (EPA) arrested for child abuse. One woman who was a wife of a worker at Kerr McGee became ill while pregnant. The doctors conducted tests and concluded she was doing drugs and threatened to have her arrested. Eventually it was discovered that her sickness was the result of her visiting her husband while he was hauling raffinate for Kerr McGee. Kingfisher concluded that if this woman could be charged with child abuse why not also accuse those responsible for the contamination of child abuse?

[I went] down to the local health department and file a child abuse charge because I know you could go there and file child abuse charges. And I took a film crew—they came from Europe, and they were filming us for two weeks. The lady [at the health department] said, now you know, there's nothing I can do. And I said, I know it. I don't care. I just want this piece of paper to go to Oklahoma City. I want Bill Reilly's name on it of the EPA, the head of the EPA, and I want to charge him with child abuse. I want this baby's name on there as the child they abused. I made it very specific. And, of course, nothing ever happened. But I got a lot of news out of it. We did news articles in the newspapers, that there was a baby born that had been affected by what they did. And that we cared enough to call them child abusers. Because they were going to charge that mother with child abuse. And it wasn't that mother's fault; it was that company's fault, and it was the EPA's fault for letting it happen.

As a result of these kinds of strategies of rearticulation, Kingfisher notes, the community eventually supported their fight, contributing to their victory over Kerr McGee. On November 21, 1992, the company announced the decommissioning of the plant in June 1993. Says Kingfisher:

> We did a lot good and bad, but eventually we won. And when we won, we didn't celebrate it as a big win because we didn't want to rub it anybody's faces. . . . We were having a meeting that evening in the community, and about 8:30 a guy came running in. They said, they've shut the plant down. They fired everybody. It's over. And [workers from Kerr McGee] walked in and said, we're all fired. It's over. No warning. And then they [the workers] woke up and realized, you guys are right. They're not our friends. They're not going to take care of us and our families. We don't have health care now. We have nothing. Everything changed. Suddenly we were heroes because we had been speaking the truth all these years.
>
> We also got a whole bunch of workers calling us and saying . . . "Here's what they didn't tell you after they killed Karen Silkwood. They moved all those big heavy pieces of equipment that were contaminated at the plant she worked at, and they buried them in Gore, Oklahoma, at the site and never told anybody." So they just came out with all kinds of things. So we didn't go have a party. We didn't celebrate. We just put our head down, and just let the community recover from the shock. . . . Three years after the final shutdown, Kerr McGee sold all of its nuclear holdings in the United States and left town. To run Kerr McGee off, which I know that's what we did, I'm so proud of that. We hit them where the money counts, and that was key.

As Alex Ewen, an activist with the Solidarity Foundation in New York who was involved in the campaign to stop the James Bay Dam in Canada, says of this kind of political strategy, "When you have an 'us versus them' attitude, you unite them against you" (1996). Native peoples have, by necessity, used a politics of rearticulation to break this united front of "them" against Native peoples, and hence a politics of rearticulation emerges organically from Native struggle. Other organizing struggles stand to benefit from considering how such strategies might be helpful in rearticulating political formulations against seemingly intractable "Left versus Right" or "liberal versus conservative" divides. In the concluding chapters, I explore in greater detail the ethics and other considerations involved in formulating alliances with unlikely allies. But first I begin with a discussion of sites within Christian Right organizing that are helpful starting points for thinking about where possible unlikely alliances could and do occur.

1

Set the Prisoners Free

The Christian Right and the Prison Industrial Complex

The history of the prison reveals that this institution which has emerged as the dominant mode of punishment has been unable to solve the problem of crime, but rather has become a site for violence, assaults on human rights, and the perpetuation of racism. . . .

Ironically, forms of punishment designed to minimize crime—and especially their manifestations—themselves promote and perpetuate violence.

The whole system of punishment today is geared toward taking away people's dignity, putting them in an institution, and locking them up in a cage. Prisons are overcrowded, understaffed, dirty places. Eighty percent of American prisons are barbaric—not just brutal, but barbaric. . . . Prison as a punishment is a failure.

Mandatory sentences and longer sentences are counterproductive. . . . the tougher the laws, I'm convinced, the more lawless and violent we will become.

As for public safety, it can hardly be said that prisons contribute to public safety. . . . Prisons obviously are not deterring criminal conduct. The evidence is overwhelming that the more people we put in prison, the more crime we have. All prisons do is warehouse human beings and at exorbitant cost.

The first set of quotations comes from an essay by Angela Davis (n.d., 2, 34), a radical prison abolitionist. One might guess that the second quotation comes from a similar source. In fact, it comes from Charles Colson (1983), a prominent Christian Right activist and the founder of Prison

Fellowship (Fager 1982, 23; Forbes 1982, 34).[1] Colson, formerly an attorney with the Nixon administration, served time in prison for his role in the Watergate break-in. Colson recounts in his autobiography, *Life Sentence*, the vow he made to his fellow prisoners on his release: "I'll never forget this stinking place or you guys" (1979, 24). Colson is immediately challenged by one prisoner, Archie, who replies, "I've seen you big shots come and go. They all say the same thing. Then they get out and forget us fast" (24). But Colson's vow begins his involvement in prison reform and ministry, culminating in the formation of Prison Fellowship (Moreland 1982). Prison Fellowship started with a staff of six, but by 1998 it had programs in over eighty countries, a volunteer base of over eight hundred thousand, and a budget of over thirty-eight million dollars (Prison Fellowship 1998a). Its associated ministries include Justice Fellowship, which lobbies for prison reform; Neighbors Who Care, which provides assistance to victims of crime; and Angel Tree, which provides assistance to families of prisoners during the Christmas holidays. It also publishes a newspaper specifically for prisoners, *Inside Journal*. Prison Fellowship began Operation Starting Line, a coalition of thirteen ministries, including Promise Keepers, Campus Crusade for Christ, the American Bible Society, and the National Black Evangelical Association, whose goal it is to bring the Gospel to all U.S. prisoners over a three-year period (Christianity Today 1999a). In 2000, Prison Fellowship began to experience a budget crisis and was forced to close twenty offices and eliminate one hundred positions (Veenker 2000). By 2001, it had absorbed Justice Fellowship (Zoba 2001, 30). Still, over fifteen thousand inmates attend Prison Fellowship Bible studies, twenty-seven prisoners are connected to pen pals, and fifty thousand men and women enter prisons as Prison Fellowship volunteers.

The political positions often articulated within the site of evangelical prison organizing are positions not commonly associated with the Right. For instance, among the many platforms implicitly or explicitly supported by Prison and Justice Fellowship and other evangelical prison advocates are decarceration for drug offenders (Bruce 1997a; Colson 1977, 17; Colson 1980a, 52), minimum wage compensation for prison labor (Lawton 1988, 38), decarceration of all nonviolent offenders ("The first thing we have to do with prisons today is to get the nonviolent people out") (Forbes 1982, 33; Smarto 1993, 46), prison construction moratoriums (Colson 1985, 29; Justice Fellowship 2000; Mill 1999; Van Ness 1985), eradication of "zero tolerance" policies in public schools (Nolan 2004k), eradication of mandatory

---

[1] For a more extended biography, see (Veenker 2000).

minimum sentencing and three-strikes legislation,[2] decarceration of the mentally ill (Nolan 2004m), suffrage for convicted felons (Colson 1985, 34), expansion of community sentencing programs (Colson 1985, 29; Pulliam 1987; Van Ness 1985), and even prison abolition (Griffith 1993). In fact, Colson argues that 50 percent of people in prison today should be released immediately (Fager 1982, 23). While those involved in Justice Fellowship and Prison Fellowship are divided on their opinions on the death penalty, many are strongly opposed to it. As an organization, Justice Fellowship seemed to generally support the decision of Governor George Ryan of Illinois to commute the death penalty for all those on death row and establish a moratorium on the death penalty (Nolan 2003g). In addition, the DNA tests that led to the reversal of a number of death penalty convictions in the early 2000s seems to have tilted Justice Fellowship's position to a more explicit antideath penalty stance (Nolan 2003h). Pat Nolan (former Justice Fellowship president, current Justice Fellowship vice president) further critiqued the prosecutors of the D.C. Sniper case for aggressively pursuing the death penalty at the expense of victim concerns (Nolan 2003f).

Consequently, evangelical prison organizing is a helpful case study through which to investigate the possibilities of *rearticulating* the Christian Right to serve more radical political projects. While this chapter looks at evangelical prison organizing in general, it focuses on Charles Colson and Prison/Justice Fellowship since Colson is the most prominent figure in this field.

In an interview with *Eternity*, a now defunct neo-evangelical magazine, Colson discussed the seeming incompatibility between his more radical stance on prisons and the law and order sentiments of his conservative evangelical constituency, stating, "At first blush our position is one that would sound pretty radical to most conservative Christians. But then when you begin to examine it, it's not as radical as they think; at least, it's not another liberal reform movement that historically conservative Christians would turn away from. First of all, our whole appeal is based on the Bible. We say to conservative Christians, look, in the Bible prison is not used as punishment for crime" (Fager 1982, 23). Ironically, according to Colson, the same Bible that undergirds conservative positions on a variety of social and political issues—from abortion to multicultural education— also dictates a "pretty radical" position on the issue of prisons and incarceration (1988,1993).

[2] Bruce 1997a; Forbes 1982, 33; Justice Fellowship 2002; Nolan 2003a; Nolan 2004l; Nolan 2004n; Nolan 2006a.

The theories produced by Native women provide a helpful starting point to begin our investigation. First, in assessing one's apparent political enemy, one must investigate the "logics" of the opposition.[3] In doing so, one generally finds that this opposition comes not only from a retrenched position in support of patriarchy and white supremacy but also from material concerns, some of which Native peoples also might have. It is then possible to "reframe" the issue that speaks to the logics of the opposition. However, at all points of this process, it is critical to engage the dangers of coalitions, and assess to what extent we can be co-opted into logics we do not necessarily support. To investigate how communities grounded in a "biblical worldview" can rearticulate their political positions into more progressive politics, it is then necessary to engage the logics of these biblically based political articulations. Such an investigation will allow us to see how positions can be rearticulated but also the dangers involved in coalescing with these communities. To continue this investigation, I begin with the politics of the evangelical Bible itself.

THE BIBLE AND EVANGELICAL POLITICAL ACTIVISM

As the literary scholar Katherine Boone notes in *The Bible Tells Them So* (1989), evangelicalism claims to be a discourse unaffected by social realities. That is, evangelicals claim to speak only biblical truth, the inerrant word of God; biblical texts are thought to exist outside the boundaries of other social discourses. Consequently, political and social positions articulated from a biblical basis are considered ahistorical and unchanging. As David Barton, an evangelical revisionist historian, states, "The Bible has been transcendent across generations and cultures, and its guidance has remained timeless" (1994, 5). Boone analyzes how major fundamentalist commentators have been able to disguise their political interests from others (and even from themselves) by claiming that they are simply propounding biblical truth: "I am simply a servant of the text. You may think you are disputing me . . . but you are really disputing God, whose Word I faithfully and humbly expound" (Boone 1989, 70).[4] This understanding of

---

[3] This framework has been articulated by Dian Million (Athabascan) of the University of Washington.

[4] Boone subsumes evangelicals under the term *fundamentalist*. See also James Barr, who notes that fundamentalism sees no inconsistency between arguing that there is one "plain meaning" of Scripture while at the same time entertaining multiple interpretations of it (1977, 52).

evangelical political discourse, which is held not only by evangelicals but by nonevangelicals as well (Ponticelli 1993), is evident in a recent cartoon version of a U.S. map, circulated on the Web, in which all the states that voted for George W. Bush in 2004 are marked "Jesus Land." The assumption is that any constituency that follows Jesus will also vote Republican.

Although evangelical political discourse is taken to be transcendental, it has in fact been anything but static. Not only have evangelical political positions shifted historically on a variety of issues, from abortion to race and gender relations to the citizen's relationship to the state, but the same "transcendental" Bible has been used by evangelicals to justify competing political positions within the same historical period. Contestation over what the Bible has to say about crime, punishment, and incarceration is a case in point. I look at the various factors that play into the contested discourse on prisons.

An examination of evangelical discourse on crime and punishment has implications for how we analyze evangelical Christians as political actors. Many scholars of social movements have noted the political tenuousness of oppressed communities, which often lack the stability to act as collective agents for progressive social change. While progressive theorists and activists comment on the unstable nature of leftist political alliances, they often attribute a stable and unitary character to their opponents on the religious Right. For instance, Jacqui Alexander and Chandra Mohanty argue that fundamentalist movements are linked "to the failure of both capitalism and community to provide for people's material, spiritual, and emotional needs . . . [and to] the failure of the nationalist and socialist movements to bring about liberation from oppression. Fundamentalist movements are deeply heteropatriarchal in suggesting the control and regulation of women's sexuality as the panacea for all these failures" (1997, xxv). Similarly, Manuel Castells, quoting Martin Marty, argues, "Fundamentalists are always reactive, reactionary. . . . It is impossible for fundamentalists to argue or settle anything with people who do not share their commitment to an authority" (Castells 1997, 13).

While these analyses are important and will be explored later, scholars do not often investigate possible areas of resistance *within* fundamentalist movements. Following Gramsci, Hall notes that there is no necessary relationship between ruling classes and ruling ideas; rather, this relationship is the result of an articulation of a particular political platform by a particular class or community (1996b, 44). He further argues that this relationhship is never stable, writing, "Hegemony cannot be taken for granted—either by the state or the dominant classes. . . . The current use of the term, to suggest the unending and unproblematic exercise of class power by every ruling class, and its opposite—the permanent and finished incorporation of the subordinate class—is quite false to Gramsci's usage" (1976, 40).[5]

By extension, hegemonic power structures within fundamentalist contexts are never guaranteed either. Religious meanings and their significance for political and economic structures are constantly changing, despite the fact that fundamentalist discourse sees itself as anchored to the unchanging truth. The evolving fundamentalist position on race and slavery is just one case in point. Generally speaking, white evangelicals strongly supported race segregation in the 1950s and 1960s, or at least did not organize against it, but now they advocate the politics of "race reconciliation."

If we look at culture as "the signifying system through which necessarily (though among other means) a social order is communicated, reproduced, experienced, and explored" (Williams 1991,13), then the slippages in the reproduction of culture provide possible sites for transforming that social order. As Nancy Ammerman states, while fundamentalist cultures may represent themselves as closed systems based on obedience to models of hierarchical authority, "the opportunities for failure are legion" (1993, 185).

Sara Diamond, a scholar of the Christian Right, has critiqued the tendency of the Left to caricature the Christian Right as a unified right-wing conspiracy rather than to conceptualize it as an often fragmented mass movement. "The distortions inherent in the radical-extremist labeling effort," she writes, "blunted public awareness of how and why the Christian Right's millions of constituents became indispensable to the Republican Party. Instead some critics of the Christian Right promoted a view of conspiracies by small right-wing cliques to stage manage what was truly a mass movement" (1995, 6).[6] Nevertheless, she suggests that conservative

---

[5] Dick Hebdige further argues, "Hegemonic power, precisely because it requires the consent of the dominated majority, can never be permanently exercised by the same alliance of 'class fractions'" (1979, 16). See also Sassoon 1982, 107.

[6] For a similar analysis, see Jan Nederveen Pieterse's analysis of the Christian Right as an example of "Gramscism on the Right" rather than one of simple political manipulation by power elites (1992). Amy Ansell similarly uses a cultural studies approach to argue that "the political project of the New Right is interesting precisely because it has attempted to translate the neo-liberal economic project into a populist moralism and common sense" (1997, 17–18). For an example of the overly simplistic analysis of the Christian Right, see Janet Jacobs's description of Charismatic Christianity as a "cult" (1984).

evangelicalism and the Christian Right can be distinguished by a "consistent set of principles" (6)—particularly, "to be right-wing means to support the state in its capacity as enforcer of order and to oppose the state as distributor of wealth and power downward and more equitably in society" (9). If her definition is accurate, how do we make sense of Colson's efforts to take power *away* from the state in the arena of law and order? While she notes that the Christian Right is a mass and nonunitary movement, she still assumes a unitary conservative thrust to Christian Right politics.[7] She fails to theorize the resistances to right-wing political stances that exist *within* conservative Christian discourse.

This chapter demonstrates, using conservative Christian discourse on crime and punishment as an example, that not only are the Christian Right and conservative evangelicalism not monolithic but that their very own doctrines, while undergirding conservative political positions in some sectors, call these positions into question in other sectors. In particular, I focus on the work of Charles Colson and his associates involved in Prison Fellowship, as it is the most prominent evangelical organization working toward prison reform. I will show how Christian Right theological and political discourse contains the seeds of its own deconstruction. Contrary to the popular maxim, sometimes the master's tools *can* dismantle the master's house. Or, to quote the African theologian Emmanuel Martey, "Unlike Audre Lorde, who might be wondering whether the master's tools could indeed be used to dismantle the master's house, African theologians are fully convinced that the gun, in efficient hands, could well kill its owner" (1994, 46).

While this chapter analyzes evangelical discourse on prisons to demonstrate the political instability of conservative evangelicalism in general, I also discuss the implications of these political and theological contradictions within conservative evangelical discourse for mobilizing a "hegemonic bloc" against the prison industrial complex in particular.

CHURCH AND STATE

The varied and sometimes contradictory positions on prisons in evangelical discourse relate to the contradictory positions on the ideal relationship

---

[7] Charles Hall's study of the Christian Left versus the Christian Right further demonstrates that the political positions between these groups are not always sharply distinguishable (1997).

between Christians and the state. Christian Right organizing is undergirded by what the political scientist James Guth describes as a "civil gospel," which is a Christian Right rationale for political involvement: "This theology argues that the U.S. was founded as a Christian nation but has fallen from that status, and Christian citizens must take action to protect their own rights and restore the American constitutional system and buttress morality" (1996a, 160).

In the civil gospel, the state acts as the hand of God. Evangelicals have written, for example, that "the Bible clearly teaches that we are to be submissive to government, and it doesn't give any exceptions as to what kind of government" (Vernon 1991, 42) and "therefore, the State is the agent of God for justice" (Ellisen 1972, 102; Kamm 1972; McKenna 1973, 26).[8] Those who act as arms of the state are to be valorized (Doud 1991; Vincent 1987; Yamashita 1987). Strict adherence to the laws of the state is critical, for "government is ordained of God to enforce the law responsibly in order to keep sinful man from totally destroying himself" (Crabb 1976, 69; Powers 1982, 37; Taylor 1974). Deviation from these laws must be severely punished. Hence, many sectors of conservative evangelicalism advocate a tough law-and-order approach to punishment. The Moral Majority, for instance, was a strong advocate for the death penalty (Baker 1988). The Family Research Council issued a 1994 policy paper advocating longer prison sentences for sex offenders, sentencing repeat offenders to life imprisonment without parole, and establishing a national registry for sex offenders (Maynard 1995a; Newman-Provost 1997, 39). According to Stanley Ellisen, "The Noahic promise of no more great judgment by water was given in conjunction with the command for society to preserve order, even to the point of capital punishment. The power of the state is grounded in this divine command" (1972, 29). As the United States is the "New Israel," principles of Mosaic law as interpreted by the Christian Right remain central to preserving the state; "eye for an eye, tooth for a tooth" is the guiding principle of crime and punishment (Charles 1995, 435; Falwell 1982, 8; Maynard 1996a).

Christian Reconstructionism, a strand of Christian Right thought, takes these principles quite literally, arguing that U.S. laws should directly adopt Mosaic laws, including the death penalty for homosexuals, adulterers, and feisty children. The eschatological premise of Reconstructionist thought holds that Christ will return when Christians have reshaped the world so that it is governed under God's law as described in the Old Testament.

[8] The quotation source is listed first in all parenthetical citations.

Unlike mainstream evangelicalism, which often argues that the New Testament supersedes the Old Testament covenant between God and God's people, Reconstructionists hold that this covenanted relationship exists today. This relationship is not with Jewish people but with true Christians. Christian society, therefore, is judged by the extent to which it keeps God's Old Testament laws (Sandlin 1997b, 2). While human action is necessary to bring about the coming of Christ, God's providence ensures that Christians will be successful. Reconstructionists do not support violent revolution. Instead, they believe that through political activism and education citizens will eventually want to be governed under God's law (2). While the Reconstructionist movement is relatively small, it influences other sectors of conservative Christianity through the Coalition on Revival, a political coalition formed by Jay Grimstead to provide a theological rationale for evangelical involvement in contemporary politics (Frame 1989).

It is important to note, however, that while the civil gospel seems to suggest an easy marriage between biblical inerrancy and conservative politics this marriage is in fact a recent historical development. Until the rise of such organizations as the Moral Majority, conservative evangelicals and fundamentalists tended to be apolitical.[9] George Marsden notes that the rise in fundamentalism during the early 1900s was partly a reaction against the social gospel's emphasis on social activism. While the social gospel attempted to reform the social structures of the day, fundamentalism held that there was no hope that humans could change their inherently corrupt society. Fundamentalists believed that the only hope for "salvation" was on an individual rather than a societal level. In their view, "No longer was the goal to build a 'perfect society,' at best it was to restrain evil until the Lord returned" (Marsden 1980, 31; see also Wilcox 1987). The politicization of right-wing evangelical voters was engineered primarily by secular right activists, particularly Richard Viguerie and Paul Weyrich, who urged members of the clergy such as Jerry Falwell to found the Moral Majority in 1979 in order to help mobilize the previously apolitical conservative evangelical vote (Diamond 1989, 60; Guth 1996b, 15; Martin 1996; Oldfield 1996; Rosenberg 1984; Zwier 1982, 30–39). As the political scientist Michael Lienesch states, "At least at its inception, the New Christian Right, far from being a populist uprising, was an army organized from the top down by those New Right strategists who set much of the early agenda for their politically less sophisticated recruits"

[9] Clyde Wilcox points out, however, that the new Christian Right has historical antecedents such as the Christian Anti-communist Crusade of the 1950s (1987).

(1993, 8). And as Clyde Wilcox and his colleagues in the Moral Majority demonstrate, premillennialists still have cognitive dissonance over political involvement, which again shows that the links between religious and political positions are not fixed (Wilcox, Linzey, and Jelen 1991).

Despite the increased mobilization of the evangelical vote in favor of conservative causes, many conservative evangelicals remain suspicious of a marriage between conservative politics and conservative theology.[10] Tim Stafford tells evangelical Christians to learn a lesson from Hitler and look out for right-wing demagogues who can play conservative Christians "like a fiddle" (1989, 19). Similarly, Rick McKinniss writes in "Let 'Christian America' Rest in Peace," "It is time we recognize that communism may not be as great a threat to the American church as compromise with a nationalistic agenda. Attempts to save a 'Christian America' may well contribute to the church in this country losing its soul" (1986, 10). The Reconstructionist magazine *Rutherford* asserts, "It represented real arrogance when Pat Robertson named his political arm 'The' Christian Coalition, not a Christian Coalition. This arrogates to one group the claim of morality for all Christians" (Lynn 1996, 11). A U.S. Army chaplain wrote to *Christianity Today*, "I have served a tour in Iraq, and proudly wear the uniform of my beloved country. Yet I never felt comfortable participating in 'Patriotic Sunday' services around the Fourth of July. The mixing of the

---

[10] See Bock 2005; Briner 1996, 33; Bulletin Board 2001; "Christian as Citizen" 1985; Evearitt 1993, 190; Mattingly 2001; Mouw 1991, 38; Mouw 2001; Nickell and Conrad 1996; Palau 1990; Sider 1996, 48–50; Skillen 1990, 53; Stackhouse 2005; Thielicke 1985; Whitehead 1994, 1996; and Woodbridge 1995. Billy Graham has also criticized Jerry Falwell, stating that "it would disturb me if there was a wedding between religious fundamentalists and the political right. The hard right has no interest in religion except to manipulate it" (1986, 27). When Tim LaHaye commented that conservative Christians had been "legislated out of the possibility of a spiritual revival" ("Leaders of the Christian Right Announce Their Next Step" 1985, 65), he received a deluge of angry letters chastising him for excessively investing himself in the legislative process rather than trusting in God (Letters 1986). *Christianity Today* critiqued the movement to publicly display the Ten Commandments, arguing that they are not relevant outside their religious context and that using a symbol outside of its context runs the risk of that symbol being tokenized in a way that can oppress other peoples (Christianity Today 2000c). It also ran an op-ed piece arguing that Christians should divorce themselves from military involvement (such as military chaplaincies) because the church then becomes complicit in supporting U.S. imperialism (Gorman 2000).

Further, Wilcox, Jelen, and Linzey found in their study of the Moral Majority that the more doctrinally orthodox a member was the less likely it was that he or she would be politically active (1995).

symbols of God and country always remind me of the frightening photographs of German clergy proudly displaying the swastika in their churches and rending the Nazi salute during the Third Reich" (Readers Write 2005, 17). Christian Smith documents this ambivalent relationship between Christians and political activism in his study of evangelicals in the United States.

The belief that America was once a Christian nation does not necessarily mean a commitment to making it a "Christian" nation today, whatever that might mean. Some evangelicals do make this connection explicitly. But many discuss America's Christian heritage as a simple fact of history that they are not particularly interested in or optimistic about reclaiming. Further, some evangelicals think America never was a Christian nation; some think it still is; and others think it should not be a Christian nation, whether or not it was so in the past or is so now. It is a mistake, then, to presume that all talk of a "Christian nation" is a sure rhetorical indicator of the desire or intention to reestablish Christian domination of society, culture, and politics. The reality is more complex than that. (2000, 36–37)

Edward Dobson's and Cal Thomas's *Blinded by Might* (1999) sparked tremendous controversy in the Christian Right over the proper relationship between Christians and the political process (Associated Press 1999).[11] Dobson and Thomas, both former leaders of the Moral Majority, assert that the religious Right has fundamentally failed in its objectives because conservative Christians should not be focusing their energies on the political process. Rather, their primary focus should be on religious conversion and cultural change. Legislative changes, they argue, accomplish little if the public at large does not support these changes. They further contest the

[11] *Christianity Today* ran an issue that focused on the evangelical response to this book, with several siding with Dobson and Thomas (Eberly 1999; Shelley 1999; Thomas 1999a) while James Dobson, Ralph Reed, and Jerry Falwell did not (Dobson 1999; Falwell 1999; Reed 1999). Charles Colson weighed in with a moderate perspective. He called on Christians to continue their involvement but urged them to distinguish between church involvement in political issues and individual believer involvement. The church should speak to "moral issues" but resist being "seduced by political power" (1999, 59). *World* also held a forum to discuss the book ("Blinded By Might?" 1999; M. Olasky 1999b). In response to the various Christian Right responses, Dobson and Thomas specified that Christian individuals, but not churches, should be involved in the political process. For instance, churches should not be passing out voter's guides and Christians should not affix the name of Jesus to any lobbying group for "Jesus is not white, middle class, Republican or American" ("Blinded By Might?" 1999, 24).

notion that the United States is a Christian nation and argue that Christians should not strive to make the U.S. government more "Christian" because this goal leads to religious intolerance (1999). Even Paul Weyrich, a central architect of the rise of the Christian Right, wrote a letter to supporters saying that evangelicals should give up on the Right and separate themselves from a hostile culture: "I know that what we have been doing for 30 years hasn't worked, that while we have been fighting and winning in politics, our culture has decayed into something approaching barbarism. We need to take another tack, find a different strategy" (1999). It is ironic that, while progressives despair of the growing prominence of the Christian Right on the political landscape, significant sectors of the Christian Right despair over their own excessive involvement in politics and are calling for a retreat.

Of the many scholarly contributions to the debate over the relative success of the movement,[12] Sara Diamond's analysis of the political impact of the Christian Right seems the most compelling. Without overstating the Christian Right's legislative victories, she argues that it is an enduring mass movement despite the setbacks and failures it has experienced. The reason for its endurance is that the movement is based on a solid infrastructure of churches, parachurch organizations, various forms of media, Christian businesses, and so on that sustain it even through difficult times. As Diamond notes, political success can take place in a broader arena than just the legislative front; success can be simply the power to "shift the terrain on which other societal forces must pursue their goals" (1998, 18). An example can be found in Dobson's and Thomas's *Blinded by Might.* They argue that Christians should retreat from political activism but should not retreat from "moral" activism, which includes the issue of abortion rights (1999, 181). The extent to which the Christian Right has succeeded in transforming abortion from a political to a "moral" issue for many Christians is indicative of their success in transforming "the common sense" of evangelical Christians in the Gramscian sense of the term.

The Christian Right's ambivalent relationship with the state also affects

[12] Some have prematurely pronounced its complete demise (D'antonio 1989). Others argue that, while it still exerts some political power, the Christian Right has been relatively unsuccessful on the legislative front (Bruce 1988, 182–83; S. Bruce 1998, 164–75; Himmelstein 1990, 126). By contrast, Jeffrey Haddan argues that the Christian Right seems "destined to become the single most powerful political force in the United States (1988, 19). Tom Smith contends that Christian fundamentalism, while it is an enduring phenomenon, has not grown in popularity in decades (1992).

conservative evangelical positions on prisons. Insofar as prisons are instruments of the state, their legitimacy remains in question. One evangelical chaplain, Jerry Singleton, states, "More laws and more people to enforce them isn't the solution to our problems" (Singleton 1984, 3; see also Keiser 1997, 5).[13] Regarding the death penalty, Barry Hancock and Paul Sharp argue in *Perspectives on Science and Christian Faith*, "Perhaps we should consider not relinquishing the greatest portion of our socialness, with commensurate social bargaining, to political, judicial, and sectarian authorities who have a vested interest in usurping power, control, and death over others" (1994, 64).

Colson shares a similar suspicion about the state: "I don't trust our own government. . . . Government . . . remains a corrupt and basically sinful institution" (Fager 1982, 22). He notes how fear of crime can increase state power at the expense of individual liberty. Before 9/11, he prophetically stated, "If people feel order is threatened . . . then people will gladly surrender their liberties to achieve peace and security" (Colson 2001c, 73). In explaining his opposition to the death penalty, he wrote, "I don't want to give government that much power" (Colson 1983, 15). Although Colson's position on capital punishment has changed several times over the years,[14]

---

[13] Chandler Owens declares in *Christianity Today*, "Some legislators believe the solution to gang problems in the United States is more police officers, more prisons or longer incarceration periods for offenders. But those of us who know about life on the streets realize this is not the solution." The solution, according to Owens, is the power of God (1998, 48). Bettye Lewis writes in the militant fundamentalist *Christian Conscience* that the media hype over juvenile violence is basically a ruse on the part of the state to extend its control over youth (1998, 23).

[14] Colson reversed his position after interviewing the convicted killer John Wayne Gacy several years ago (Colson 2001b). He concluded that "Justice in God's eyes requires that the response to an offense (whether against God or humanity) be proportionate. . . . I now favor capital punishment, but only in extreme cases when no other punishment can satisfy the demands of justice [and] where there is no doubt about the offender's guilt" (Sillars 1998, 15). Prison Fellowship and Justice Fellowship, however, have not taken stands supporting the death penalty. At the Justice Fellowship forum, participants became embroiled in a debate over whether or not Justice Fellowship should take a stance opposing the death penalty. Many individuals strongly opposed the death penalty, but, according to President Pat Nolan, the Justice Fellowship board had decided that this issue was so contentious that it did not feel it could take a position without losing much of its backing. The Justice Fellowship's material on the death penalty is generally balanced but leans toward opposition. Also at this conference Justice Fellowship staffers mentioned that Colson had changed his mind several times on this issue and did not seem to be clear on his position at that point in time.

his suspicion of the government compels him and his associates, as well as many other evangelicals, to advocate many progressive positions regarding prisons under the rubric of "restorative justice" (Smedes 2002).[15]

RESTORATIVE JUSTICE AND EVANGELICAL
PRISON ORGANIZING

The basic principle of restorative justice (as compared to "retributive justice") involves restoring both offenders and victims to society rather than simply punishing offenders. Prisons, while sometimes viewed as necessary for the small minority of "hardened criminals," are generally at odds with the principles of restorative justice. In his book *Life Sentence*, Colson does not simply critique "inhumane" prisons; rather, he characterizes prisons as inherently inhumane. The inhumanity of prisons means that prisoners who are not dangerous offenders are more likely to come out dangerous. "The more people we put in prison, the more crime we have," he writes (2001c, 130). He is harshly critical of current drug policies, which he says "devastate human lives" (129). He describes how he was sued for slander for decrying conditions at the Fulton County Jail in Georgia. Many local residents, including the father of Martin Luther King Jr., took issue with him, arguing that it was a "good jail." Colson replied, "I have yet to see a good jail. It is terrible to herd men together like cattle. If you treat men like animals they become animals" (1979, 189). Unlike even many liberal reformers, Colson and his supporters question the relationship between prisons and crime reduction. Mainstream discourse about prisons tends to presume that they are necessary to reduce crime. However, a number of studies have demonstrated that more prisons and police do not lead to lower crime rates (Currie 1998; Donziger 1996, 42, 162; S. Walker 1998).[16]

[15] The concept of restorative justice is not exclusive to evangelical Christianity but is used by a broad base of constituents from diverse political and religious backgrounds. Justice Fellowship distributes a brochure called "Restorative Justice: Beyond Crime and Punishment," which explains its framework.

[16] The Rand Corporation found that California's three-strikes legislation, which requires life sentences for three-time convicted felons, did not reduce the rate of "murders, rapes, and robberies that many people believe to be the law's principal targets" (S. Walker 1998, 139). In fact, changes in crime rates often have more to do with fluctuations in employment rates than with increased police surveillance or incarceration rates (Box and Hale 1982; Colvin 1986; Jankovic 1977). Concludes Samuel Walker, "Because no clear link [exists] between incarceration and crime rates, and because gross incapacitation locks up many low-rate offenders at a great

The criminologist Elliott Currie finds that "the *best* face put on the impact of massive prison increases, in a study routinely used by prison supporters to prove that 'prison works,' shows that prison growth seems not to have 'worked' at all for homicide or assault, [and] barely if at all for rape" (1998, 59). Colson and other evangelical prison activists are clearly familiar with this research. Colson wrote, "I'm absolutely convinced that the principal cause of crime in America is the prison system itself" (1980a, 51; see also Colson and Van Ness 1989; Fager 1982; Heystek 1996, 6; McLean 1993, 21; Nolan 2005a; Skillen 1993, 131; and Smarto 1993, 56). Justice Fellowship asserts, "Research has shown little correlation between crime rates and the number of people housed in a state's prison" (1998). Daniel Van Ness, a former director of Justice Fellowship, contends that a study published by the Rand Corporation in 1986 found that offenders who were given prison sentences actually committed crimes faster and more often than similar offenders who were placed on probation (1987b, 9). He argues that as much as 80 percent of all people in prison should not be there (Colson 1980a, 52; Colson 1985, 34). *Charisma* ran an opinion piece that argued that prisons do not work. It particularly critiqued maximum security prisons, which are "further away from correction than they are from the moon. It is a tragedy" (Aikman 2000). *Faith Today* (a Canadian neo-evangelical magazine) opined, "More and more people are being locked up, yet public fear and outrage over crime are still growing. Victims are not being healed, and the rates of recidivism prove offenders are not being changed" (Harvey 2000, 36). At the 1999 Justice Fellowship Forum on Restorative Justice, Van Ness similarly deconstructed the "fear of crime," noting that it is greatest in communities with the lowest crime rates.[17] As Pat Nolan frames the issue, "It makes little sense to fill our prisons with people that we are not afraid of, but are merely angry at" (2003c). At this conference, speakers also addressed such topics as eradicating the death penalty, opposing mandatory minimum sentencing, decriminalizing drug use, addressing sentencing disparities between crack and cocaine use, and dismantling the "prison industrial complex" (DeCastro n.d.).[18] Not all speakers favored each of these measures, but each was discussed and

---

dollar cost to society, we conclude as follows: gross incapacitation is not an effective policy for reducing serious crime" (S. Walker 1998, 130).

[17] See also Harvey 2000; and Justice Fellowship 2000.

[18] An article calling for the decriminalization of drug use was also distributed at the conference, although many participants expressed disapproval of this position (Wink 1996).

debated seriously. In addition, while much of the literature on restorative justice does not question the categories of "violent" and "nonviolent" criminality, several speakers at the Justice Fellowship forum argued that the principles of restorative justice can be applied to so-called violent offenders. And *Missiology* published an article arguing that restorative justice should include support for reparations for communities impacted by unjust social policies (Petersen 2004).

Ironically, the basis for these progressive positions is the Bible. Van Ness argues that the form of punishment favored by the Bible is restitution. Biblical principles of punishment, as they would apply to contemporary society, dictate that drug offenders should be sent to treatment centers run on Christian principles and those arrested for other offenses should be involved in restitution and community sentencing programs— programs that do not remove offenders from the community but allow them to remain free while they make restitution to their victims. Colson takes a similar Bible-based position in denouncing prisons when he writes, "Prison is a relatively new invention, really only about 200 years old as a purpose of punishment. You'll find throughout the Bible that prisons are there for political reasons or for people awaiting trial, but not for punishment. Biblically, we are told to make restitution. . . . I believe in alternatives to incarceration for nonviolent offenders (1983, 14)."

Colson similarly uses the Bible to denounce the death penalty, arguing that if Christians are going to use the Old Testament to justify the death penalty they must also advocate Old Testament prerequisites for administering it—for example, that there must be two live witnesses to the crime. "There is not one jurisdiction in the United States today that meets the standard that God has set, he writes. "If we're going to take God's requirement that there be capital punishment, let's also take his requirement to be sure we've got the right guy" (1983, 16; see also Smarto 1993, 56). *Christianity Today* ran an article arguing that incarceration is incompatible with Christian values, declaring, "Prisons cannot stop crime. . . . There must be some alternatives—alternatives that are consistent with Christian values" (Jackson 1982, 34). Its basic argument is that restitution rather than punishment should undergird the criminal justice system (Balswick 1989, 225).

An article in *United Evangelical Action* (a now defunct National Association of Evangelicals periodical) goes so far as to argue that punishment itself is contrary to biblical principles and attempts to disarticulate the relationship between crime and punishment.

It is next to impossible to call the dogma of punishment into question, and to get Christians to consider seriously the way of the gospel. . . . Not to punish is thought to condone crime. And since punishment means prison, so-called "Christian America" ends up the most imprisoning society, next to South Africa and the Soviet Union, in the "modern" world.

Of course, we must take crime seriously. The trouble is, while we propose to take crime seriously, our way of punishing offenders through imprisonment is counterproductive. (Jeschke 1982, 23)

This article argues that prison may be necessary for very violent criminals but 90 percent of criminal offenses should be addressed through community-based reconciliation and restitution programs (23). Ironically, the same Bible that is used to support a strong law-and-order regime based on Mosaic law in some strands of the Christian Right is used in other strands to critique the criminal justice system, prisons, and the death penalty.

In examining evangelical prison organizing as a possible site for rearticulating Christian Right politics, it is essential that we assess how this site is also imbricated in the politics of racism, heteropatriarchy, Christian imperialism, and political quietism. Examining these complicated forms of politics will demonstrate the manner in which evangelical prison organizing can serve both politically reactionary and progressive ends.

RACE

Ann Stoler argues in *Race and the Education of Desire* (1997) that racism, far from being a reaction to crisis in which racial Others are scapegoated for social ills, is a permanent part of the social fabric. She writes that "racism is not an effect but a tactic in the internal fission of society into binary opposition, a means of creating 'biologized' internal enemies, against whom society must defend itself" (59). She notes that it is the constant purification and elimination of racialized enemies within the state that ensures the growth of the national body: "Racism does not merely arise in moments of crisis, in sporadic cleansings. It is internal to the biopolitical state, woven into the web of the social body, threaded through its fabric" (59).

The notion that the welfare of the nation is under constant threat from internal enemies is integral to the Christian Right's story of America.

America is tormented by a disease that threatens its covenant with God. Crime is an integral part of this story as it is the primary indicator of social disintegration. Regardless of whether or not crime rates are going up, the perception that crime rates are skyrocketing is central to the theological drama in which the United States is plummeting from God's favor ("Coping with Crime" 1975, 30; "Crime and Consequences" 1990, 8; Forbes 1982; Hunt and Raysar 1988, 23).

These internalized enemies remain racialized because the face of crime and social decay is colored. As I discuss in greater detail elsewhere, poverty, crime, and color are closely correlated in Christian Right rhetoric (A. Smith, forthcoming). Conservative articles on poverty, "illicit sex and drugs," urban unrest, and crime always locate these "vices" in, and identify them with, the communities of African Americans or people of color.[19] For instance, in an article that depicts African Americans running amok and threatening the lives of the police for no apparent reason, *World* posits that community policing cannot work in the inner city (Maynard 1993b, 13). Similarly, *World* dismisses activism opposing police brutality against people of color in its description of the torture of Abner Louima by police officers in New York, stating, "The case has been used by activists to stir up racial tensions in America's most ethnically diverse city" (No Comment Zone 1999).

At the same time that the rhetoric of the Christian Right conflates "poor" and "black," it obscures the relationship between poverty and violence, thereby suggesting that violence is the sad consequence of moral failure rather than a learned response to deprivation. It is only a short step to the conclusion that black people are by nature morally flawed: "I hear poverty this and poverty that. . . . But many of those people were frequent offenders who would have been arrested anyway. . . . These were not the people out looking for jobs" (Maust 1989, 40).

Christian Right ideologies trace the roots of poverty among people of color to their "welfare mentality" and a "mentality of . . . fatalism" (W. Stafford 2005) and ignore the effects of corporate downsizing and the

[19] See Bird 1989a; "Denominational Leaders Address Drug Crisis" 1990, 55; Frame 1997, 70–73; Lupton 1989, 11; Maxwell 1991, 36; Nash 1996, 187; Sherman 1996, 35–36; "Teen Sex" 1990; Wilson 1996, 55–62; and Wooding 1994, 24–30. Wooding, for instance, implies that no whites are involved in gang activity in Los Angeles. Passantino wrote an article that was part of a larger collection published in *Moody* on several churches in different communities in the United States. Unlike all the other articles, which focused on white communities, the names of the people mentioned in Passantino's were changed "to preserve their dignity" (1991, 36–38).

relocation of jobs to the Third World or the suburbs. So, the reasoning goes, if there are no structural reasons for poverty, poverty must be the fault of the poor. As Gary North states, there is a "right relationship between wickedness and poverty" (Lienesch 1993, 134), which of course means between wickedness and skin color.

Since poverty is the result of moral failings, crimes based on poverty are not the result of economic inequities but of immorality (Nolan 2004i). Not surprisingly, then, the face of both poverty and crime is colored: the drug trade is personified by murderous Latinos or urban black people; stories of crime generally focus on African Americans; juvenile delinquents are depicted as children of color; and prisoners, described as "criminals" in general terms, are people of color.[20] People of color are essentially the disease that threatens God's covenant with America. In Colson's collection of prisoner stories, *Changed Hearts*, people of color are quite literally the disease, spreading AIDS through contaminated needles or homosexual behavior (1989, 78–82). This drama is most acute in stories relating an individual prisoner's conversion.

While the face of crime remains colored, the face of the individual prisoner who transcends his or her situation (or was unjustly convicted in the first place) is usually white.[21] The ones who "save" prisoners are usually

[20] For Latinos, see Bird 1990; Dawson 2006; "Inside—and Out—of the Miami Drug Cartel" 1998; Johnson 1998; Miller 1995; Pearson-Wong 2000; Sherman 1995; Stertzer 2001; Whalin 1997; and Wood 2003. For urban black people, see Lawton 1991; Lawton 1998, 46; C. Owens 1998; and Richardson 2004. For crime stories, see Abraham et al. 2005; Alford 2000; Carnes 2001; Lawton 1991; Lawton 1998, 46; Lowe 2005a; C. Owens 1998; and Vincent 2005. For delinquents, see "100 Things Churches Are Doing Right" 1997, 14; Butcher 2000; "Hidden Children" 1995; and Thompson 1995. For prisoners, see Andrescik 2003; "Back to Prison . . . by Air" 2000; Carrasco 1993; Clapp 1989, 14; Conn 1994; Cox 1990, 15; Curry 1993; Doyle 1974, 45; Jackson 1982, 33; Larson 1975; McKenna 1971, 6; C. Owens 1998, 1987; Richardson 2004; Schonmaker 1978, 68; Spoelstra 1977, 31; Swank 1997, 12–13; Tunley 1978; and Zoba 2001.

[21] Andrews 1989; Baker 1999; Beane 2000a, 2000c; "Bible Student Convicted of Murder" 1983; Bird 1989a; Carothers 1970; Chandler 1989; Colson 1989; Courbat 1994; DeCastro 1998; Erler and Souter 1981; Frame 1985; "God at the Wheel" 1999; Hanson 1985; Isitt 1984; Johnson 1999; Kennedy 2002b; Lovato 2005; Maynard 1993a; Morris 1988; Preddy 1983; Shelton 1991; Spoelstra 1977; Thompson 1984; Tunley 1978; "Update" 1983; Van Domelen 2000; Yancey 1976a; Yancey 1976b, 26. James Dobson and Tim LaHaye ran an ad calling for George Bush to grant executive clemency to Bill Kennedy, "a dear friend of Dr. LaHaye and Dr. Dobson," who was serving a twenty-year prison sentence for a nonviolent offense and was supposedly the victim of "unethical federal prosecutors" (see www.justiceforkennedy.com; *World*, March 27, 2004). For people of color featured as changed prisoners, the

white as well.[22] These white "saviors" often have to pray "for the Lord's protection" as they bring their message to prisons or the inner city (Colson 1989, 31). In *Life Sentence*, Colson repeatedly uses anonymous black figures to legitimize his ministry and show that he can save black prisoners (18, 64, 85, 109, 248, 256). But the black prisoners are described as particularly threatening to him or as running away from Prison Fellowship's programs. And it is black prisoners who are always racially identified. The only African American Colson identifies as playing a significant role in Prison Fellowship is depicted as a troublemaker (1979, 84). Yet Colson, the white savior of black prisoners, proves himself when a black man tells him that he is "right on" (116).

A prominent race reconciliation advocate, John Perkins, notes that, even though almost half of the prison population consists of African American males, parachurch prison ministries are almost entirely white. African Americans in prison ministries, he states, are supported by white organizations ("Wanted" 1991, 36). Prison Fellowship volunteers are 90 percent white, although the majority of those they serve are people of color (Colson 1998). Thus, white people are saving society from the crime and decay caused by people of color.

Similarly, prisoner conversion stories are a microcosm of the larger story of Christian America; it is the white citizens of Christian America

---

exception to the rule, see Aldrich 1987; Beane 1998b; Bence 1998; Colter 2004; Duckworth 1984; Glanco 1987; Green 1986; "Inside—and Out—of the Miami Drug Cartel" 1998; Prison Fellowship 1988b, 5; and Shepard 1998. Generally, *Charisma* seems to be the magazine most likely to feature people of color as those who "save prisoners" or prisoners who transcend their lives of crime. As is discussed in the next chapter, this trend probably relates to Charismatic Christianity featuring race reconciliation more prominently than other strands of evangelicalism do. Also *World* ran an article on a repentant white prisoner that was unsympathetic, arguing that he should stay in prison on a murder conviction even though his church claimed he was a changed man (Vincent 2006b). *Indian Life* regularly features articles on Indian prisoners in its "Life in Prison" column, which is to be expected since the magazine is targeted toward Native peoples.

[22] See Bergin 2005b; Brewer-Smyth 2005; Bruce 1998a; Cox 2000; Hanson 1982; Jackson 1973, 36; Lawson 2000; Madsen 2006; Newman 2003; Richardson 2004; Scarry 1997; Sigler 1978; Vaughn 1985; Walker 2004; Wood 2003; Zoba 2000b, 45; and Zoba 2001. *Charisma* featured an article on William Bumphus, an African American evangelist who ministers to death row prisoners, but in a sidebar listed the most prominent prison ministries, all of which were led by white men—Charles Colson, Bill Street, Frank Constantino, Mike Barber, Chaplain Ray, Steve Walker, Kenneth Copeland, and Jim Bakker (Bruce 1997a).

who will rise above the miserable conditions of their lives and restore the country to its rightful relationship with God. The saga of Karla Faye Tucker, an evangelical white woman who was executed by the state of Texas on February 2, 1998, illustrates both the gender and racial politics of evangelical discourse on prisons. Tucker, who was convicted of murdering two people with a pickax, was sentenced to death. On death row, she converted to Christianity and became a cause célèbre among members of the Christian Right (Strom 2000). Staunch death penalty advocates such as Jerry Falwell and Pat Robertson called for clemency. Robertson claimed, "I am one who has supported the death penalty for hardened criminals. But I do think that any justice system that is worthy of the name must have room for mercy. And there are times for mercy. In the case of Karla Faye Tucker, she is not the same person who committed those heinous axe murders some fourteen and a half years ago. She is totally transformed, and I think to execute her is more an act of vengeance than it is appropriate justice" (1998, 1).

Meanwhile, the numerous men of color who are born again while in prison have not managed to capture the attention of the Christian Right. In his classic, *Evidence That Demands a Verdict*, Josh McDowell tells the story of a black man on death row who was born again. Nowhere in this testimony does McDowell suggest that this man deserved clemency after his salvation (1979, 344–45). Only white prisoners are "truly transformed" by Jesus and attain full citizenship in "Christian America." Prisoners of color, even when they are "saved," seem by virtue of their race to be unable to fully shed the sins of their past; there is no "room for mercy" for them in the criminal justice system. In this discourse, true Christianity is predicated on whiteness.

According to Stanley Ellisen, in an article in *Moody*, a now defunct evangelical magazine published by the Moody Bible Institute in Chicago, the right of the state to impose the death penalty on its citizens is integral to its right of conquest over other nations.[23] He notes, "The Moses' command to prohibit murder is in no sense an annulment of the Noahic injunction to execute murderers. It is rather an elaboration of that former command extending its range to a wider area of crimes. Furthermore, the God who gave the no murder command also gave the same people shortly thereafter the order to annihilate whole populations in East and West

[23] *Moody* magazine was initially called *Moody Monthly*. Citations in this book refer to the name of the periodical at the time of publication.

Jordan. Israel was commanded to act as God's executioner in destroying a cancerous society, as God Himself did" (1972, 29). Ellisen's exegesis illustrates Stoler's process of internal colonization.

> Power is no longer lodged in the sovereign right 'to kill and let live' but rather in 'the reverse of the right of the social body to ensure, maintain or develop its life.' . . . The more you kill and let die, the more you will live. . . . The more 'degenerates' and 'abnormal' are eliminated, the lives of those who speak will be stronger, more vigorous, and improved. The enemies are not political adversaries, but those identified as external and internal threats to the population. (Stoler 1997, 83–85)

Thus, the more the United States executes its deviants the stronger it will be in maintaining its global hegemony. Gary Gumpert and Susan Drucker make this connection explicitly in an article published in *Media Development*, a Christian media journal, in which they state, "Warfare . . . is an extension of the death penalty" (Gumpert and Drucker 1992, 17–18). This situation is complicated by the growing rhetoric of race reconciliation, which seeks to incorporate some communities of color, primarily middle-class African American males, into the Christian Right platform (Atwood 1990; A. Smith 1997). Nevertheless, the citizenship conferred on such sectors is a tentative one, easily revoked.

THE CARCERAL STATE

The evangelical critique of the criminal justice system resonates with Foucault's critique of the carceral state. Foucault argues that with the advent of capitalism, punishment changed its focus from a technology of the body to a technology of the soul. While physical penalties—confinement, forced labor, and so on—affect the body, such effects are an intermediary step toward reaching the soul: "The body now serves as an instrument or intermediary: if one intervenes upon it to imprison it, or to make it work, it is in order to deprive the individual of a liberty that is regarded both as a right and as property" (1977a, 11). Modes of punishment shifted from public displays of torture to institutions of surveillance and regulation that serve to normalize the prisoner into the social order.

This system of punishment is predicated on the existence of an individual with rights. As Foucault argues in *The Order of Things*, the existence of "man" (or the individual) as the primary site of philosophical investigation is a recent phenomenon: "Man is only a recent invention" (1970, xxiii).

According to him, the advent of the individual is related to a shift in ethical forms. The old form is predicated on an external moral code, whereas the new form is internally lodged within the individual (327–28). Thus, it would seem that the purpose of punishment "as spectacle" is to coerce people into recognizing and respecting the power of the sovereign, whereas punishment as "surveillance" entails producing subjects with internally derived ethics that conform to the social order. Foucault also argues that it is important to analyze the prison within a larger context of societal surveillance that is situated in other institutions, such as schools and hospitals, which have the cumulative effect of regulating and normalizing subjects. "The second process," he writes, "is the growth of the disciplinary networks, the multiplication of their exchanges with the penal apparatus, the ever more important powers that are given to them. . . . Medicine, psychology, education, public assistance, 'social work' assume an ever greater share of the powers of supervision and assessment" (1977a, 306). This larger context Foucault terms the carceral system.

Many conservative Christians have offered similar critiques about the quiet expansion of the carceral system, particularly into the medical fields (Griffith 1993). C. S. Lewis's "The Humanitarian Theory of Punishment" is quoted widely in evangelical circles and is often credited as a foundational text for contemporary evangelical prison organizing (1970, 287–300).[24] Lewis argues that the reform impulse within prisons, while seemingly humanitarian, actually expands the state's control over its citizens. "The things done to the criminal, even if they are called cures," he writes, "will be just as compulsory as they were in the old days when we called them punishments. If a tendency to steal can be cured by psychotherapy, the thief will no doubt be forced to undergo the treatment" (1970, 288). He argues that under this theory of "humanitarian" punishment offenders are assumed to be socially or psychologically deficient and should remain under state control until properly cured. The assumption behind these practices is that citizens are not entitled to challenge the ideologies of the state; they must be caged until they conform: "If crime and disease are to be regarded as the same thing, it follows that any state of mind which our masters choose to call 'disease' can be treated as crime; and compulsorily cured. It will be vain to plead that states of mind which displease the government need not always involve turpitude and do not therefore always deserve forfeiture of liberty" (293). In addition, Lewis argues that

[24] See, for example, Babbage 1972; Balswick 1989, 223; Bube 1981, 108; Crabb 1976; Ellisen 1972, 29; Van Ness 1986; and Wennberg 1973.

what the state considers "normal" is often contrary to what the church deems normal: "We know that one school of psychology already regards religion as a neurosis. When this particular neurosis becomes inconvenient to government, what is to hinder government from proceeding to 'cure' it?" (293).

According to Lewis, humanitarian punishment is not under the control of officials who are in some way accountable to the public but to "experts" who alone get to decide whether or not an individual is "normal." As a result, punishment in this system becomes interminable. No longer does one serve a finite sentence; one remains under state control until "cured." "The first result," he notes, is "an indefinite sentence terminable only [on] the word of those experts . . . who inflict it" (1970, 290). Followers of Lewis similarly contend that rehabilitative approaches incorporate more people into the carceral system for longer periods of time. According to the evangelical writer Richard Bube, "Since the introduction of rehabilitative, behavior modification prison programs in California, the median term served by 'felony first releases' has risen to twice the national average, incorporating the evils of an 'indefinite' system as a natural outgrowth of this perspective" (1981, 108; see also Crabb 1976, 69). This analysis coincides with critiques of reform by prison abolitionists, who contend that reform tends to strengthen rather than challenge the foundations of the prison industrial complex (Davis 2003; Rodriguez 2005; Ross 1998a).

This "humanitarian" form of punishment runs counter to the basic evangelical concept of the inherent sinful nature of humans. The notion of rehabilitation presumes that people are deviating from a virtuous standard to which they must be taught to conform. Evangelical theology presumes, by contrast, that people are inherently evil. The only escape from this evil is to begin a personal relationship with Jesus Christ (Crabb 1976, 68). Consequently, any rehabilitation program based on secular principles is doomed to fail. As Jerry Falwell's journal opines, the true model should not be rehabilitation but "regeneration" through Christ ("Liberty Prison Outreach" 1988, 27). One possible consequence of this theology, however, is that Jesus's power to "save" also obviates the "lock them up and throw away the key" mentality that buttresses the dominant discourse on prisons. Says evangelical prison activist Don Smarto of the Billy Graham Center, "Prison ministry shows the church that no one is beyond God's mercy" (1993, 192). And the former crime victim-cum-prison activist Richard Grayson complains, "We often shoot our wounded—society locks offenders up with the attitude 'keep them in prison and let them suffer'" (Colson 1989, 43). Instead, Grayson says, we must give offenders a chance to make restitution.

Ironically, the "rehabilitative" penitentiary system was itself founded on religious principles, as many evangelical Christians note (McGowen 1995; Schlossman 1995). However, they sharply repudiate this history. In his discussion of the religious basis of the U.S. penitentiary system, which he claims originated with the Quakers, Randall Hekman declares, "Although they had the best of intentions, the Quakers produced an expensive system that in the minds of many (including modern day Quakers), is more cruel than other methods of punishment" (Hekman 1985, 20; see also Bergman 1986; Colson 1989, 85; and Van Ness 1986, 74).

This critique of the "humanitarian view of prisons" in evangelical Christian discourse inspires a wide variety of policy suggestions. Some theologians argue, as did C. S. Lewis, that prisons should punish and nothing more (Bergman 1986, 36; Hekman 1985). Some go so far as to argue that society should reinstate what Foucault would refer to as punishment as "spectacle" through the institution of torture and corporal punishment.[25] Writing for *Christian Scholar's Review*, Robert Wennberg is sympathetic to the notion of prisons as punishment and suspects that rehabilitation programs are no less punishing than prison. But he feels that Lewis fails to offer safeguards against abuses of prisoners within his framework. On the other hand, he notes, "If our approach to handling the criminal is that we send him to prison *as* punishment (the punishment consisting in his forfeiture of freedom of movement for a period of time) but not *for* punishment (he is not to be maltreated in prison as part of his punishment), then we can advocate punishment as a means of handling criminal behavior without committing ourselves to banishing convicted offenders to dark and comfortless cells where they are to be abused and cruelly treated" (1973, 110).

Richard Bube takes an interesting approach to prisons in the *Journal of American Scientific Affiliation*, a journal that focuses on science from an evangelical perspective. He all but advocates prison abolition in favor of restitution *and* capital punishment. "Except for the rare case where a person is a constant danger to others and himself, he notes, "efforts to involve the offender in acts of restitution are likely to be far more beneficial than seeking retribution alone by locking him up in prison" (1981,

[25] "Why put a person in a cage for years, subject to homosexual rapes and other satanic influences? Is that really more humane than a limited number of lashes or paddles on one's backside?" (Hekman 1985, 20). Borrowing Foucault's notion that "the public execution is to be understood not only as a judicial but also a political ritual, Gumpert and Drucker suggest that executions should be publicly televised (1992, 18).

110). He goes on to argue, "Any alternative to prison seems desirable . . . [as] prisons all too often offer only bitterness, loneliness, hate, vengeance, sexual frustration and abuse, sexual perversion, and futility. . . . The argument that imprisonment for many years or for life is more humane treatment than capital punishment can be questioned directly on its own merits" (110). However, while he advocates capital punishment in principle, he does not favor its implementation in our current society with its racial and economic inequities.

FROM THE CARCERAL STATE TO
THE CARCERAL CHURCH

While there is a strong critique of the carceral state in evangelical prison discourse, this discourse often simply replaces the carceral state with the carceral church. This tendency is evident in the policy suggestions of many evangelicals to support a mix of punishment and rehabilitation as long as rehabilitation programs contain the "Jesus factor" (Biddle 1973; Crabb 1976, 70; Mack and Craft n.d.; Maynard 1994; Strang 1995, 116; Wilson 1971, 84). Programs that incorporate the "Jesus factor" do not attempt to rehabilitate prisoners to the norms of a corrupt society but rather provide them with the opportunity to develop a saving relationship with Jesus Christ that allows them to live moral lives. Christianity is seen as the only hope for dealing with social unrest. Colson argues that only Christianity can provide the "transformation, the redemption" needed to stop crime (2001c, 91). As Charles Watson, a former Charles Manson follower and now a born-again Christian, states: "There's a lot of lip service about rehabilitation, but I don't really think penal officials, even social activists, really believe it deep down inside. How can they? How can anyone who doesn't understand what Christ did for us truly believe in the transformation of an individual?" (Bird 1989b, 26).[26] Smarto argues, "I believe that the church, more than any other segment of society, especially government, is uniquely equipped to help those the world treats as garbage" (1993, 87).

One of the goals of these Christian-based rehabilitation programs is to turn prisoners into law-abiding citizens. Evangelical prison advocates sell Christian prison ministries on the promise that such ministries can help

[26] See also Nolan 2004.

stop revolutionary sentiment (Colson 1990, 6). This concern about political organizing in prisons was particularly prevalent during the early 1970s. The prisoner "is fair game for an advanced education in either crime or revolution. There are those who believe that Attica was just a skirmish for a forthcoming revolutionary campaign in the society at large. Self-preservation alone should prompt us to support prison reform" (McKenna 1971, 7; see also "What Can Christians Do to Fight Crime" 1973). In his review of George Jackson's *Soledad Brother* in the neo-evangelical magazine *Eternity*, now defunct, John Goodwin similarly warns that unless Christians proactively reform prisons more revolutionary prisoners will emerge from the criminal justice system (1972, 15). Charles Colson stated after 9/11 that there should be a ban on Wahabbite prison chaplains because "If we do not stop them, radical Islamists will use prisons, packed with angry and resentful men, to put an evil twist on [an old] message: Give me your tired, your poor, your huddled masses—yearning to get even" (Quotation Marks 2002).[27]

The conversion to Christianity of Eldridge Cleaver, a leader of the Black Panther Party, is portrayed as an example of how Christ can save people from destructive revolutionary fervor. Cleaver states, "You see, it's not by accident that my appreciation of democracy coincides with my conversion" (1977, 28) and further notes, "I've reached another progression where I now recognize the limitations on the political and economic solutions and I've now isolated the spiritual and moral dimension as being the fundamental aspect of the whole problem" (37). Social change is no longer necessary, and with its demise prison reform will become less necessary: "Be not deceived into thinking that by changing the prison regime you're going to change behavior" (41). Cleaver's story also plays a prominent role in Colson's autobiography. Prior to his conversion, Colson remembers Cleaver as a thuggish sexual predator filled with hate. His sharpest memory of Cleaver was a statement he made at a rally: "Kill the pigs, rape the white woman" (Colson 1979, 170). The basis of Black Panther politics escapes Colson. Fortunately, from Colson's viewpoint, Cleaver realizes that the horrors of communism are far greater than "even in the worst of American ghettos" (170). When Cleaver returned from exile, his reading of Colson's *Born Again* was supposedly central to his conversion to Chris-

---

[27] See also *World's* complaint that prisons have been overwhelmed by a "racist cult called the Five Percent," which came out of the Nation of Islam (Prison Disfellowship 2998).

tianity and his allegiance to the ideals of "America" (172). In this narrative, Colson's version of prison ministry promises to save America from the black militancy that is promoted by prison repression.

While groups such as Prison Fellowship organize against the prison industrial complex, they also offer a Christian package designed to quell prisoner resistance to prisons. It is significant that while articles often talk of the need for prisoners to have visitors, very rarely is the brutality of prisons mentioned—unless the prison is located in a country at odds with the United States such as Cuba (Alford 2004; Colson 1990, 7; Conawa 1984; Yancey 1988).[28] The Abu Ghraib prison scandal has not compelled Prison Fellowship to critique U.S. policies in Iraq or make the links with prison abuse at home. This disarticulation between Abu Ghraib and domestic prison abuse is interesting given that Justice Fellowship often publicizes abuse within U.S. prisons (Nolan 2004c). However, the case of Abu Ghraib seemed to concern Justice Fellowship more because of possible damage to the reputation of the U.S. empire than because of what it signifies in terms of the inherent violence of the prison industrial complex. Justice Fellowship seemed to minimize the horror of the scandal more than other evangelical venues, which unequivocally condemned it, coinciding with Colson's support for a preemptive war on Iraq (2002b).[29] Similarly, Prison Fellowship's involvement in prisons around the world has not

[28] Alford's article on Colombia's prisons featured a country not at odds with the United States. However, Colombia is generally thought of as a country that persecutes Christians through government paramilitary and revolutionary groups. These articles, including the one cited, never mention that these paramilitary groups are supported by the United States (Alford 2004).

[29] Pat Nolan complained about the coverage of the scandal, saying the media should have emphasized the horrors of Saddam Hussein's regime instead (2004a). Meanwhile, editorials in *Christianity Today* and even *World* (usually an apologist for U.S. imperial policies) were more condemnatory. See Christianity Today 2004; Jackson 2004; and Seu 2004. *World*, for instance, opined that it is not sufficient to argue that Hussein also abused prisoners; the United States must be held accountable for its actions (Belz 2004b). Harry Jackson's op-ed piece in *Charisma*, while clearly supporting the war, more holistically critiques U.S. policies in Iraq. He contends that the abuse was a result of Justice Department lawyers maneuvering to avoid the Geneva convention. By setting it aside, the United States set the conditions that let the abuse get out of control. The United States must ask "forgiveness for inappropriate actions in the war. . . . We are not disgraced, but we are wrong" (2004). Incidentally, while he had supported Bush's war on terror, Colson began to question it when news broke of an Afghan, Abdul Rahman, who was facing the death penalty for converting to Christianity. According to him, "If we can't guarantee fundamental religious freedoms in the countries where we establish democratic reforms, then the whole credibility of our foreign policy is thrown into serious question" (Olsen 2006).

contributed to its critique of Western policies in the countries that contribute to the oppressive conditions giving rise to prisons (Morgan 2004).
In the end, the Prison Fellowship message is that prisoners need only
Christian fellowship, not advocates, to assist them in resisting oppressive
conditions. As Diana Garland (a former dean of Southern Baptist Seminary who was fired in 1995 during the fundamentalist takeover of the
Southern Baptist convention) states in the journal *Social Work and Christianity*, "The purpose of volunteer Christian ministry is not necessarily to
make changes but rather to be with another. After all, Christ's service
to humankind was not effective in the sense that he brought an end
to confusion or political turmoil. In large part Christ's service was his
incarnation—his coming to be with us to take on our sufferings as his
own, to stand with us and to go through with us whatever it is we are going
through" (Garland 1985, 23)[30]

A central reason for the political quietism in prison ministries is that
they depend on the approval of prison administrations for their success.
Those involved in prison ministries are specifically asked not to become
involved in prison reform (Pederson 1979, 111). As Stephen Patterson
observes in his guide to prison ministry, "Your credibility as a volunteer
who supports the administration, by obeying rules and regulations, is
extremely important to your work relationship" (1984, n.p.).

Consequently, Colson answers the question "What do prisoners need
most?" not with prison abolition, prison reform, or any amelioration of
oppressive conditions but with "the Gospel message" (Colson and Vaughn
1987, 26). Consequently, in 2004 Prison Fellowship distributed one thousand copies of the film *The Passion of the Christ* to prisons.[31] After one
accepts Christ, one becomes "free from the only prison that matters" (Bird
1989b, 24). The reformed thief John Hall notes that while he is still in
prison the important thing is, "I've made friends with Christians from
the church I burglarized. I'm thankful they've forgiven me just as Jesus
has" (1989, 51; see also Larson 1975, 6; and McGinnis 1991, 4–5). Morry
Eghbal, an Iranian sent to prison in part because of Arab racial profiling,
drops the discussion of racism to conclude, "God turned my life to good"
(2005, 28). The evangelical prison reformist Don Smarto ends his book
on prison reform by retelling the story of Pope John Paul II touring a

---

[30] See also Hall and Sanders 2001, which focuses on ministering to those on death
row with no critical analysis of the death penalty.

[31] Charles Colson, fundraising letter for prison fellowship, Merrifield, Va., December 3, 2004.

maximum-security prison. His advice to the prisoners: "Don't lose hope. This is not the worst prison. The worst prison is a closed heart" (1993, 205). Colson describes a testimony from a man on death row in Zambia: "The fear of death had held me in bondage. [But] Jesus Christ annulled death." Colson concludes, "From Death Row comes the glorious message: He lives. And because of that fact, we can live as well" (1986, 16). That a man will be killed is irrelevant in light of his salvation, and actually liberating prisoners from prison is unnecessary.

This theme is particularly prominent in the 2004 movie *Woman, Thou Art Loosed*, which is based on an enormously popular novel by a prominent Pentecostal pastor, Bishop T. D. Jakes.[32] *Woman, Thou Art Loosed* began as a T. D. Jakes sermon and later evolved into a play, a book, a conference, and eventually a movie, which was financed by Danny Glover, Oprah Winfrey, and Spike Lee Jones (Andrescik 2000a; Tiansay 2004). This movie focuses on the story of Michelle, an African American woman who lives at the intersections of race and gender oppression. The movie depicts the way her history of sexual abuse "compels her to crime" (Richie 1996). While spending time in prison for a number of crimes, she ends up on death row for killing her primary abuser. The movie does point to the inherent racism in the criminal justice system. For instance, during a sermon in the movie, Jakes (who plays himself) criticizes what he calls the Just Get over It Generation: "They fire you after twenty years of working for the company. They say, 'Get over it.' They lock you up in jail for twenty years and then find out you're the wrong person and say, 'Oops, get over it.'" Yet, while the movie points to the interlocking racial, gender, and class oppressions the protagonist faces, in the end her redemption comes from developing a personal relationship with Christ. The call at the end of the movie is not a call to change the prison system or the prevailing economic, racial, or gender systems of oppression but to become a Christian.

This sentiment suggests the possibility that evangelical reformers might begin to support the privatization of prisons, particularly if they can be run by religiously affiliated organizations or companies. In fact, Prison Fellowship operates prisons in Brazil and Ecuador. In 1997, it also began

[32] Jakes is a very popular but controversial pastor. He has been accused of heresy for his association with the Pentecostal oneness movement (Lowe and Grady 2000). His MegaFests which bring together hundreds of thousands of people that fuse his Woman Thou Art Loosed and Manpower conferences are also criticized for featuring secular entertainers (the 2005 conference was criticized for featuring Gladys Knight in a tribute to Coretta Scott King) (Lowe 2005b). He is also known for preaching a "prosperity" gospel and living an extravagant lifestyle.

the first faith-based prerelease program, called InnerChange Freedom Initiative, in Houston (M. Olasky 1999c). The state provides the guards, food, and clothing, but Prison Fellowship supplies the program, directors, volunteers, and church-based support system for up to two hundred prisoners. Prisoners volunteer for the program. They do not have to be Christian, but the program itself is explicitly Bible centered. Prisoners follow a strictly regimented schedule of Bible study classes, life skill classes, lessons in Christian values, and mentoring by church leaders. The mission is "to create a personal environment that fosters respect for God's law and the rights of others, and to encourage the spiritual and moral regeneration of prisoners" (Zoba 2001, 34). According to Jack Cowley, a program administrator, "We're there to save souls" (Cowley 1999). After a prisoner is released, he is guaranteed a job, given a local church to attend, and assigned a mentor. Inmates are also trained in technical fields such as computer technology (Webb 1999). Apparently the state of Texas waived the requirement in its request for proposal process that programs receiving money through it be "faith neutral" (Maynard 1997, 14). The Dallas chapter of the American Civil Liberties Union (ACLU) contends that the program does not violate church-state separation, although its Fort Worth chapter has filed suit against InnerChange's Christian Bible study wing, calling it the "God Pod" (Jones 1998). More than six hundred men are currently enrolled. States only fund about one-half of the six hundred thousand dollars needed to run each program (Zoba 2001). InnerChange programs have also opened in Iowa and Kansas. Americans United for the Separation of Church and State filed suit against the program in Iowa on February 12, 2003, with the complaint that this program gives preferential treatment to prisoners based on their willingness to undergo religious conversion and indoctrination. At issue is the fact that these programs receive 20 to 50 percent of their funding from the state, whereas the Texas program is funded completely by private donations (Bergin 2005b). In addition, while Prison Fellowship provides jobs for inmates in Texas, in Iowa the state provides halfway houses ("Iowa IFI Program to Begin in September" 1998). The volunteers have access to private bathrooms and keys to their cells. Prison Fellowship argues that state money does not support the religious programming part of InnerChange, that participation is open to all, and that religious conversion is not a requirement (Religious News Service 2003). In June 2006, a federal judge in Iowa, Robert Pratt, struck down the InnerChange program as unconstitutional (Colson and Morse 2006; Nolan 2006b). Pratt ordered Prison Fellowship to refund $1.5 million that the state of Iowa had paid to fulfill its contract over the past four years. However, he further opined that even if Prison Fellowship had used no public money he still would have ordered an end to the program. Currently, the decision is on appeal to the Eighth U.S. Circuit Court, and the effects of Pratt's decision have been stayed until the appeal is resolved (Belz 2006a).

Since this program's inception, evangelical magazines, Prison Fellowship, and the White House Office of Faith-Based and Community have all cited a study from the University of Pennsylvania's Center for Research on Religion and Urban Civil Society reporting that InnerChange graduates have been rearrested and reimprisoned at dramatically lower rates than was a matched control group (Richardson 2004). These venues have not mentioned the critics of these studies, who argue that they are invalid because they only include people who successfully complete the program. They argue that if the studies had included everyone who started with InnerChange, the program would have been shown to be *less* successful that normal prison programs (Kleiman 2003).

Nonetheless, this program, which is widely applauded in evangelical circles (Jackson 2005a), could signal the expansion of faith-based pre-release programs and potentially of Christian prisons as well.[33] In 2003, the governor of Florida, Jeb Bush, opened a Florida prison entirely dedicated to faith-based programming. The Florida prison offers programming to inmates of all major faiths and is not specifically Christian based, unlike InnerChange (Nolan 2004b). The High Impact Leadership Coalition has made prison reform, in the form of Colson's model, one of its primary tenets (Jackson 2005a). It is also conceivable that George W. Bush's federal faith-based initiative was sparked by the success of Inner-

---

[33] At a business meeting at the Justice Fellowship Forum, Pat Nolan announced that Prison Fellowship would begin educational campaigns among private prisons. I asked him if that meant Justice Fellowship supports privatization of prisons. He said it did not have a position on this issue but in his experience prisoners are treated better in private prisons. The reason, he argued, is that prison guards in private prisons own stock in the company and are vested in ensuring that there are few lawsuits filed by prisoners for abuse or neglect. However, he staunchly opposed relocating prisoners to prisons outside of their communities. After he expressed his thoughts on privatization, another Justice Fellowship staffer whispered to me that, while prisoners may be treated better in private prisons, they are also kept there longer. He also posited that private prison corporations would be less likely to support community-based restorative justice programs that did not involve incarceration. Another Justice Fellowship policy analyst mentioned that they are still trying to research this topic and would like information on this issue in order to develop their talking points.

Change, which he supported as governor of Texas. In fact, his support for these programs developed soon after the evangelical outcry resulting from his execution of Karla Faye Tucker. These faith-based programs may have the tendency to co-opt the more progressive tendencies within Christian Right prison organizing and reroute their organizing efforts against prison buildup into the buildup of Christian prisons and prison programs.

An example of this tendency is evangelical praise of Warden Burl Cain's infamous Angola prison of Louisiana. Cain, a Southern Baptist, took over as warden in 1995 and started a program that emphasizes obedience to God. He also started an onsite college to produce ministers. These prisoners have been sent as missionaries to other prisons across the state. These programs are credited with changing Angola from a hotbed of violence into an orderly prison. According to Cain, "it helped the prisoners accept they're in prison and that it's God's will that maybe they don't get out—and that while you're here you do your best for him" (Fink 2004, 36). The evangelical portrayal of Angola contrasts sharply with more progressive representations such as the movie *The Farm*, which features Angola prisoners who are clearly not guilty of their crimes. Another inmate, who is depicted as a model prisoner, is eligible for release but his request is still turned down (African American model Christian prisoners do not seem to become the cause célèbres that white women such as Karla Faye Tucker do). These representations have also called into question many of Cain's practices that seem to profit from prison labor and squash dissent (Bergner 1998). However, in an evangelical-produced video on Angola that was presented at the 2005 Promise Keepers Awakening gatherings, the prisoners in Angola are depicted as content to be in prison because Angola is one happy Christian community where "there is no crime." So the emphasis shifts from challenging the system of unjust incarceration to building Christian prisons.

As yet another example, the work of evangelical prison organizers was clearly influential to the thinking of John Dilulio, who is actually a Catholic Democrat but also a prominent political scientist who writes for conservative papers and speaks at evangelical events. He was a major advocate of get tough on crime policies. He argued that prisoners should not be paroled and increased imprisonment would reduce crime. But at the 1999 Justice Fellowship Forum he announced he had been incorrect in his thinking and now advocated a moratorium on prisons (Colson 2001c, 131; Nolan 1999). He also proposed a number of strategies for garnering political support to reduce incarceration, including repealing mandatory minimum drug laws and releasing drug-only offenders (1999). However, his work soon became subsumed in advocating for faith-based initiatives, including those in prisons, and he was appointed by Bush to the White House Office on Faith-Based and Community Initiatives (he was forced to resign six months later) (Stafford 1999).

FROM THE CARCERAL CHURCH TO
THE CARCERAL FAMILY

Within the carceral church, the family rather than prison becomes the primary site of social control. Louis Althusser argues that the family is in fact an ideological apparatus of the state. Even though the family is often seen as part of the private rather than the public sphere, Althusser contends that it is nevertheless a site where the dominant classes ensure "a reproduction of the submission to the established order" (1971, 127). Using Gramscian analysis, Stuart Hall points to the fact that Althusser tends to conflate civil society with the state and ruling-class interests (1996a, 429).[34] To call the family an ideological state apparatus is problematic because it fails to account for how the family is shaped by forces other than state power. While Hall's analysis is sound, it is interesting to consider the ways in which the family *is* explicitly tied to the state and does function as an ideological state apparatus in the Althusserian sense of the word.

Evangelical discourse traces the origins of crime and the breakdown of the state to breakdowns in the patriarchal family. "The events within the family can make or break the individual and, collectively, civilization. This fundamental unit is the building block and was the building block of all social organizations" (Olford 1982, 8; see also Grady 1991; Greene 1973; Norfolk 1975; and Ogle 1995). Colson and others similarly state that family breakdown is a major source of crime (Fagan 1997). According to Colson, "We ought to be addressing it by helping out children to understand their moral responsibilities at an early age and keeping that family unit together" (1983, 16). Programs to instill in youth "a respect for authority" are advocated as prison prevention techniques (Blackley 1993,

[34] Althusser says that the state is "the machine that ensures bourgeois domination" (1971, 131). However, at the same time he argues that a party cannot continue to rule the state for long if it does not control the ideological state apparatuses, which assumes a disjuncture between the state, ruling class interests, and civil society (139).

79). *Christianity Today* suggests that the solution to the problem of crime is stronger class discipline in schools (Tennant 2002), and *Fundamentalist Journal* says the solution is stronger discipline in the home (Graham 1987).[35]

Women prisoners are rarely mentioned in evangelical venues, but when they are their incarceration is seen as the result of their inability to deal with patriarchal control, even abuse, properly ("Overcoming a Past of Pain" 1998).[36] Fran Lance, a jail ministry worker in Seattle, explains the roots of women's imprisonment with the fact that women prisoners have faced everything, "from incest to rape to wife beating to verbal abuse. That's their rejection. . . . We should be dealing with the rejection. We've got to get the inmate to recognize her hatred of those rejecting her. In her mind, that may include God. Until this release, she will always hate and rebel. We must help her realize, as Jesus did on the cross, that those who are rejecting and abusing her do not know what they are doing. . . . Forgiveness brings healing" (Kelley 1984, 57).

In this analysis, it is rebellion from the family structure, and from God as the ultimate patriarchal father, that causes women to becomes social deviants. (A sure sign of female deviance is the reluctance to perform domestic chores [Norris 1979, 70].) Fatherless families also increase women's vulnerability to rape opines *World* (Maynard 1999). Faith in Christ restores them to their natural place in the nuclear family (Beane 1998b; Kolplen-Bugaj 1988, 7). For instance, *Changed Hearts*, Colson's collection of prisoner stories, describes how Linda Bowman, a former heroin addict, fell into trouble because of her relationship with her father. Fortunately, she was saved when John and Alex Wickstead began ministering to her in prison and taught her her proper role as a woman. According to Colson, "Alex Wickstead, a woman equally at home serving tea or leading a bible study in prison, taught Linda a self-esteem and gracefulness she had never known. Alex also gave Linda practical advice, coaching her in good nutrition. John counseled her with fatherly wisdom. Like her heavenly Father, they proved love to her over and over again. In response to the Wicksteads' love, Linda learned to love her parents" (1989, 49).

By learning to love her "heavenly father," Linda learns to love her biolog-

[35] As a counternarrative, *Campus Life* featured three youths in the criminal justice system, and their stories demonstrated that their engagement in crime was a result of violence in the home or poverty rather than a lack of discipline (Cryderman 1991).

[36] One article on a women's prison ministry, Prison Alpha, did not particularly differentiate between the needs of male versus female prisoners (Alford 1999).

ical father. She is then able to marry her husband, Frank, and live her life in obedience to both him and God, the Father. In fact, prison ministries often use married couples as evangelists to demonstrate "model marriages" to prisoners (Colson 1989, 16–19). The nuclear family is the key to encouraging offenders to live by societal norms.

Quoting Chief Justice Warren Burger, Colson suggests that it is the emancipation of women that is causing increases in crime: "Now 46 percent of our work force in the U.S. is women, resulting in too much freedom for the child. So many parents have defaulted. If a family can be strengthened, the problem will go away" (Colson 1980a, 23). Concerned Women for America traces the increase in the number of women prisoners to abortion, claiming that "The emotional impact of abortion often drives women to destructive, sometimes criminal, behavior" (Concerned Women for America n.d.). One article on Programmed Activities for Correctional Education (PACE), a Christian rehabilitative program based in Chicago during the 1970s, portrayed the men's and women's programs side by side. A picture of the men's program featured vocational training; the women's program featured manicures. The captions read, "Fred Majors (*center, above*), vocational educational teacher, goes over blueprints with students. And in the women's division (*right*) beauty culture is a favorite subject" (Sigler 1978, 31). Another ministry favors employing women prisoners in domestic work (Smarto 1990, 20).

The Karla Faye Tucker story illustrates this notion of female criminality. Prior to her conversion, Tucker was a prostitute operating outside the boundaries of respectable womanhood. Her downfall is traced to the fact that she was the product of her mother's extramarital affair (Meeuwsen 1998). But Tucker was able to redeem herself by accepting Christ and marrying a prison ministry worker. The fact that she and her husband could never have sexual relations proved that Tucker was safely within the bounds of patriarchal sexuality and thus redeemed by Christ: "The fact that she and Dana [her husband] can't touch each other is the reason she knows God called them together.... 'Dana and I—physical things actually never got in the way to begin with, and so what we came to know wasn't flesh,' says Tucker" (Chiero 1998b).

In *Life Sentence*, Colson uses his family situation to illustrate the forces that threaten to disrupt society. Because Colson was a poor role model as a father, his son became involved with drugs and was arrested on drug charges (Colson 1979, 33). His wife, by contrast, fulfills her proper feminine role by supporting Colson's vocational choices. Although she does not want him to go into prison ministry, she tells him, "Well, I just want you to know that if that is what you want, I'm with you all the way" (153). In this narrative, Colson sees little need to make these major decisions in collaboration with his wife, as he does not seem to take her concerns seriously. He writes, "It may have been unfair of me but I sloughed off all of Patty's concerns. Wives worry about security and finances" (43).

In contrast to Patty, Colson's security-obsessed wife, there is Jennifer, whom Colson describes as a sexual temptress who joined Prison Fellowship at its inception and threatened to single-handedly destroy its work. "Men in prison have plenty of difficulty restraining their normal sex drive," he writes. "This group would have temptations enough just being out of prison for two weeks without having to cope with a seductress in their midst" (Colson 1979, 87). In another story, a young woman asks Colson to have his picture taken with her. Because she is pretty and big breasted, he assumes she wants the picture taken for blackmail purposes. A friend warns Colson, "It could be blackmail. There are newspapers that would love to run a picture of you and some bosomy chick" (192). The responsibility for maintaining proper relations between women and men resides with the woman in Colson's narrative. Sexual temptresses constantly threaten the work of godly men. While Jennifer's powers of destruction seem unlimited—keeping her in her place "was like corralling a wild horse" (90)—the program is saved by another woman, Jackie. Jackie was a bank officer who rebelled against the gender differences in salaries at her company and attempted to adjust these differences through "creative accounting." Her struggle against sexism only landed her in jail, but fortunately, with the help of the prison ministry, she repents of her sin and also monitors Jennifer's behavior closely to ensure that Jennifer's sexual assertiveness will not destroy the program (89).

Perhaps an even bigger threat to the patriarchal family than female sexual autonomy is homosexuality.[37] Much of the evangelical opposition to prisons comes from the view that prisons are a breeding ground for homosexuality and therefore threaten the Christian family order (Patterson 1984, chap. 6; Smarto 1993, 57). Colson argues that homosexuality is a "pervasive problem" both in prisons (Colson 1979, 26) and in society at large (196). Van Ness argues that one of the primary harms prisoners suffer is that they "lose the opportunity for heterosexual contact. They live

[37] For further analysis of the relationship between homosexuality and the carceral church, see Didi Herman's and Christy Ponticelli's analyses of "ex-gay" ministries and antigay organizing in evangelical communities (Herman 1997; Ponticelli 1993, 139–44).

in an environment which does not offer the balance that comes from having both men and women around" (1986, 52). Consequently, prisons turn men into sodomites, rapists, and gender deviants, learning sexual practices that damage the social fabric.[38] *World* contends that the lack of attention to prison rape is the fault of human rights groups, which are "dominated by feminists" who are interested in "politically correct prison assaults" that involve male guards and female prisoners (Morse 2001). It seems that this issue is one of the few in which *World* takes a more sympathetic perspective than its otherwise "get tough on crime" approach to prisoners. In this article, it noted that a poll in the *Boston Globe* found that 50 percent of respondents said that prison rape is part of the price criminals pay for breaking the law. *World* critiques this attitude, citing Charles Colson, who declares, "Prisoners have a right not to be brutalized, and we should not tolerate it (Morse 2001, 23). However, this article seems less focused on prison reform than on critiquing racial justice and Lesbian Gay Bisexual Transgendered (LGBT) organizations, which, *World* claims, do not support the issue of stopping prison rape because they fear this issue will promote racism and homophobia.[39]

As previously mentioned, since these prisoners are also usually depicted as people of color, the evangelical discourse on prisons evokes images of sexually predatory men of color threatening the white nuclear family. In fact, a *Charisma* article on T. D. Jakes's prison ministry describes it as particularly focused on "curing" prisoners of color of homosexuality (K. Walker 1998). *World* magazine featured the story of John, who was put in prison for eight years. He was a white man who was gang raped by black inmates in Texas. White supremacists, who had asked guards to put him in the black section, encouraged him to join them, and he later was

[38] See Colson 1977, 13; Colson 1989, 71; Gonzalez 1997; Green 1986; Hekman 1985, 20; Larson 1975, 5; Nolan 2004f; and Pulliam 1987, 28. *World* further implied that the media was covering up stories of homosexual rapists and murderers to present the image that gays are only victims of crime rather than perpetrators of it. And at a 1993 Moody Bible Conference on sexuality a guest speaker, a Chicago police officer, contended that he can always tell when a crime has been committed by a homosexual because it was committed in a particularly sadistic fashion.

[39] One exception to the narrative of prison rape simply being an outgrowth of homosexual deviance is Justice Fellowship's report on a woman who won a conviction against the prison guards who raped her. Pat Nolan noted that her case helped gain support for the passage of the 2003 Prison Rape Elimination Act (2004g). Colson argues that we should organize against prison rape, not "because we fear the spread of disease will affect us" but "because it is the human and Christian thing to do" (2001d).

responsible for the 2003 lynching of James Byrd, a hate crime that received national attention. This article concludes that prisons are breeding grounds for violence, "especially [among] men who are young, slender, and white" (Morse 2001). Ironically, this article suggests that black people were ultimately to blame for Byrd's lynching.

Charles Colson makes the link between homosexuality and the nation-state in his analysis of the war on terror. One would think that the scandal in Abu Ghraib would provide an opportunity for Justice Fellowship to make the links between it and prison abuse in the United States. Instead, this crisis prompted a call for compulsory heterosexuality. Colson explains that one of the causes of terrorism is same sex-marriage.

> Marriage is the traditional building block of human society, intended both to unite couples and bring children into the world. . . . There is a natural moral order for the family. . . . The family, led by a married mother and father, is the best available structure for both child-rearing and cultural health. Marriage is not a private institution designed solely for the individual gratification of its participants. If we fail to enact a Federal Marriage Amendment, we can expect, not just more family breakdown, but also more criminals behind bars and more chaos in our streets. It is like handing moral weapons of mass destruction to those who would use America's decadence to recruit more snipers, highjackers, and suicide bombers. (Colson 2004)

> When radical Islamists see American women abusing Muslim men, as they did in the Abu Ghraib prison, and when they see news coverage of same-sex couples being "married" in U.S. towns, we make our kind of freedom abhorrent—the kind they see as a blot on Allah's creation. [We must preserve traditional marriage in order to] protect the United States from those who would use our depravity to destroy us. (Colson and Morse 2004)

Pat Nolan similarly links homosexuality to terrorism: "These photos (which could well be mistaken for homoerotic art funded by the National Endowment for the Arts) appear to validate the propaganda of the radical Muslims, who portray Western civilization as sexually perverse" (2004d). *New Man* (an evangelical men's magazine formerly linked to the Promise Keepers) asserts that what causes Muslim resentment of the United States is not foreign policy but the fact that America "has embraced immoral ways of living such as homosexuality . . . divorce and prostitution" (Penemaker 2005, 51). The Heritage Foundation explains that breakdowns in the patriarchal family erode U.S. sovereignty and create crime and social unrest (Fagan 2001). Implicit in this analysis is the assumption that heteropatriarchy is essential for the building of the U.S. empire. Similarly, other articles opined that, in addition to sexual deviance, feminism contributed to the Abu Ghraib scandal by promoting the inclusion of women in the military (Grady 1991; Greene 1973; Norfolk 1975; Ogle 1995; Olford 1982). When women do not know their assigned role in the gender hierarchy, they become disoriented and abuse prisoners (Belz 2004b; Olsen 2004; Veith 2004a). The Traditional Values Coalition opined that "Homosexual activists are exploiting the terrorist attack upon our nation by quietly promoting passage of pro-homosexual legislation in Congress" (Sheldon 2001). And *World* described gay and lesbian organizing within the United Methodist Church as a "gay jihad" (Plowman 1998a).

According to Anne McClintock, in the colonial imaginary, "global history is imaged as a universal family (a figure of private, *domestic* space), while domestic crises are imaged in racial terms (the public figure of *empire*) (McClintock 1995, 43, original emphasis). Thus, as Ann Burlein argues in *Lift High the Cross*, it may be a mistake to argue that the goal of Christian Right politics is to create a theocracy in the United States. Rather, Christian Right politics works through the private family (which is coded as white, patriarchal, and middle class) to create a "Christian America." She notes that investment in the private family makes it difficult for people to invest in more public forms of social connection. In addition, investment in the suburban private family serves to mask the public disinvestment in urban areas that makes the suburban lifestyle possible. The social decay in urban areas that results from this disinvestment is then construed as the result of deviance from the Christian family ideal rather than the result of political and economic forces. As the former head of the Christian Coalition, Ralph Reed, states, "The only true solution to crime is to restore the family" (1990, 231) and "Family break-up causes poverty" (1990, 231, 89). Concludes Burlein, " 'The family' is no mere metaphor but a crucial technology by which modern power is produced and exercised" (2002, 190).

It is important to note, however, that the danger inherent in positing the carceral church and its nuclear family structure as the solution to societal problems is not unexamined in the evangelical community. For instance, in response to Colson's analysis of the relationship between homosexuality and crime or terrorism, Gary Roth of St. Andrew Lutheran Church wrote a letter to *Christianity Today*, declaring that, "Blaming gays for broader social problems is like blaming a lesion for our illness when there is cancer throughout the entire body. 'Gay marriage' needs to be judged on its own merits (or demerits)—not on fear and suspicion, nor as a scapegoat for idolatries we would rather have go unchallenged" (Readers Write 2004a). *Christianity Today* admits that strong family ties are not necessarily the solution to crime because "in spite of the public's fear of criminals, most violent crimes occur between acquaintances, often family members" (Jackson 1982, 35). The fact that even evangelicals have admitted that the presence of religious fundamentalism is the second-best predictor of sexual abuse in the home indicates that Christian family values do not protect society against criminal violence (Heggen 1993, 73). Recently, Pat Nolan has also addressed sexism within criminal justice sentencing, noting that many women receive longer sentences because their partners, who are usually involved in the drug trade, offer testimony against them. Meanwhile, women often do not have information to trade to get shorter sentences (Nolan 2006a).

The carceral church is also critiqued within evangelicalism. Richard Bube, for example, addresses the dangers of enforcing Christian values in society at large, arguing that "acceptance of beliefs, if they are to have any value, must not be coerced. For Christians in the minority to attempt to legislate beliefs is not only inappropriate but also foolhardy, for it gives approval to all other conflicting minorities to proceed in the same way. It is sometimes difficult to affirm that we should protect the freedom of speech of all, no matter how offensive, obscene, or disruptive, but it is much easier to defend the free speech of all on the grounds that Christians are included in that 'all'" (1981, 111).

Charles Riggs, the chief of chaplains for the U.S. federal prison system, while proclaiming his evangelical faith, also argues, "Unless all are free to believe in any religion—Islam, Sikh, Hare Krishna, whatever—then none are free to believe. If I can watch the beliefs and customs of others being overridden and unregarded, if I fail to safeguard others' freedom to choose their religion, how can I expect to have my freedom guarded?" (1993, 100).[40] In fact, the Prison Fellowship helped draft the Religious Land Use

[40] I recently called the Justice Fellowship office in Sacramento to inquire if it would be willing to support religious freedom for Native prisoners and was informed that it would be willing to provide technical assistance and support for Native prisoners wishing to practice traditional spirituality in prison. I also talked to a Justice Fellowship staffer at the Justice Fellowship Forum who was collecting stories of prisoners who have been denied religious freedom in prison in order to draft religious freedom legislation. I asked him if he was only collecting stories from Christians. He informed me that he believes it is *more* important to protect non-Christian religious practices since they are often under greater attack. He argued that Justice Fellowship recognizes that if any religious practice is under attack Christians will eventually suffer as well. See also Colson 2001f.

and Institutionalized Persons Act (RLUIPA), which was ruled constitutional by the U.S. Supreme Court on May 31, 2005. This statute stipulates that the government cannot, without a compelling cause, limit the religious liberty of prisoners in federally funded institutions. Ironically, this case reached the Supreme Court when members of the Satanist, Wiccan, and other non-Christian groups sued Ohio's corrections department. This case was supported by Prison Fellowship and Americans United for the Separation of Church and State. According to Colson, this court decision "protects our ability to practice our faith in the prisons. It has a downside because it also protects Wiccan and other wacko religions. But that's the price of freedom, isn't it?" (Banks 2005). Brian Fahling of the American Family Association Center for Law and Policy said that the decision would benefit Christians, "but the oddity about this, again, is the fact that we have religious freedom being protected through the agency of a Satanist and a witch" (Liberty Watch 2005).

The difficult relationship between restorative justice and Christian imperialism was quite apparent at the 1999 Justice Fellowship Forum on Restorative Justice. On one hand, some speakers argued that restorative justice is not possible "without Christ." Colson's keynote speech at the conference was primarily dedicated to explaining why Christianity is the "natural law" and superior to all other religious traditions. He then credited Daniel Van Ness, a Christian restorative justice advocate, with inventing the principles of restorative justice. On the other hand, many speakers, including Van Ness himself, do not see restorative justice as inherently Christian. Van Ness informed me that he needs to correct Colson's assumption that he (Van Ness) started the restorative justice movement. He and many speakers credited indigenous models of justice as being one of the primary sources of the restorative justice movement.[41] Those individuals who see restorative justice as a much broader movement are aware that communities of diverse religious and political allegiances have an interest in supporting restorative justice, and consequently Christians in this movement need to develop ways to work in strategic alliances. In fact, many non-Christians attended the Justice Fellowship Forum. Pat Nolan, the current president of Justice Fellowship, opened the conference by apologizing to non-Christians if they felt oppressed by the Christocentric

[41] A *Media Development* article also credits Native peoples with creating the sentencing circle process for addressing crime, which can serve as a model for alternatives to the mainstream criminal justice system (Restoule 1997).

language of the conference. He said that Justice Fellowship means no disrespect to non-Christians but argued that if Justice Fellowship is to persuade evangelicals to give up their support for the "prison industrial complex" and support principles of restorative justice instead Justice Fellowship must use biblical language to articulate its agenda: evangelicals will support restorative justice only if they think it is biblical. When one non-Christian audience member expressed some feelings of marginalization at the conference, a number of Justice Fellowship staffers tried to reassure her that people of all faiths were welcome to work with Justice Fellowship. Because this issue is of interest to so many diverse communities, evangelical advocates of restorative justice may find themselves forced to adopt positions and rhetoric that are more sensitive to issues of Christian imperialism than those of other sectors of the Christian Right. It is also important to note that the promotion of the carceral church is not exclusively the domain of Christian Right discourse; even progressive Christians and liberation theologians support this model. For instance, when Congress scaled back welfare support, many progressive churches became involved in organizing Call to Renewal conferences in response to Christian Coalition organizing efforts. At these conferences and in other venues, progressive churches declared that *they* should be the ones to administer welfare programs through state block grants (Sider 2001). The religious Left also offers Christian prescriptions for the rest of society. Jim Wallis, of the Sojourners community, rightly denounces the racism of conservative Christians but then unwittingly reinscribes their racism and Eurocentrism by proclaiming that the two-parent family "*is* the norm in this society and every other one" and calling for the poor to take "more personal responsibility" for their condition (1994, 129, 157).

THE INDIVIDUALIZATION OF CRIME

Within evangelical discourse, crime is rarely given the social context accorded to poverty, institutionalized racism, and so on. In fact, some evangelicals go so far as to argue that there is no social context for crime. One author has stated that "Material deprivation is not a sufficient explanation for hostile behavior. It might almost be said that the more the material state of the American people is improved, the worse crime gets" ("Coping with Crime" 1975, 30). Colson and Van Ness contend, "There is only one taproot of crime. It is not some sociological phenomenon; it is sin" (Colson and Ness 1989, 57; see also Colson 2000; and Colson 2001c).[42] This attitude is reflected in a letter to the editor of *Charisma* that criticizes racial justice critiques of crime: "Though African-Americans do face injustices in America today, rather than focusing on how unfair things are—for example, that white people get away with crime and black people are punished—we should focus on the fact that no one should be committing crime at all" (Feedback 2006b). Similarly, the *Journal of Christian Reconstruction* explains that prisoners are just "lazy" (Ahmanson 1983).

As a result, evangelical prison reform frequently operates with an individualized understanding of crime. Prison Fellowship argues that the criminal justice system should not define criminal offenses as "crimes against the state" and should focus instead on developing restitution and reconciliation programs between victim and offender. The offender should cease paying his or her debt to society and pay the victim back directly (Nelles 1990a, 28; Nelles 1990b; Redekop 1990; Tarr 1990; Umbreit 1982, 36).

This individualization of crime has consequences for other social policies. Colson's suspicion of the state, which contributes to his "pretty radical" views on prisons, also contributes to his lack of support for public schools, public assistance, and other state programs. Colson explains that the increasing support for his positions on prison reform within evangelical communities is part of their growing suspicion of government programs in general. "A few years ago," he wrote, "if I talked about these kinds of things, you'd feel a chill go through a lot of churches. I think that's part of the maturing process—a growing awareness maybe that government social programs aren't really meeting needs, and that the church has a responsibility in this area" (1983, 14). He further contends that "As Christians we believe changes in people—and thus in society—come not through political, exterior structures but through changes in the heart" (Colson and Vaughn 1987, 23). *Charisma* contends that "the sure cure for crime . . . [is] the gospel of Christ" (Bruce 1998a). An article in *Eternity* asks, "Can law enforcement and rehabilitation programs really achieve what are actually spiritual goals?" (Hitt 1986, 10). This rhetoric is identical to evangelical rhetoric on race relations. We do not need to effect institutional or political change to address racism, the story goes, because what we suffer from is a "sin problem, not a skin problem" ("Christian Coalition

[42] Van Ness similarly asserts that "criminals are the major cause of crime, not society" (Van Ness 1986, 87). See also Charles 1995, 438; Mawyer 1982, 30; Pile 1987; and Uttley 2001.

Official Says Ending Sin Will End Racism" 1996, 4; Boone 1996). (I discuss this logic of race reconciliation in more detail in chapter 2.) Similarly, the social conditions that produce prisons are elided in some of the "prosperity gospel" emphasis of the T. D. Jakes prison ministry. As mentioned previously, Jakes is very prominent Pentecostal pastor who enjoys a flamboyant lifestyle and preaches capitalist economic development as the solution for African American prisoners. He says he offers "hope for people who think the only way to get a Mercedes is to do a drug deal" (Winner 2000b, 59).

Christianity Today ran an editorial supporting the expansion of prison labor in private industry. While it quoted Colson and other advocates within Justice Fellowship, it failed to advance one of the tenets of Colson and Justice Fellowship's stance on prison labor—that prisoners should earn at least the minimum wage and have jobs that are challenging and interesting (Colson 1989, 88; Lawton 1988, 38). Colson argues that to crush someone you "need only give [that person] work of an absolutely, completely useless and irrational character," which is what most prison labor is likely to be (1989, 88). This editorial rebutted charges that prison labor was taking jobs away from workers outside prison by claiming that "when private industry contracts for prison work, American jobs are saved, as low-skill, low-wage tasks are retained in our prisons instead of being shipped outside of the country" ("Let the Prisoners Work" 1998, 15). The author seemed to miss the point that prison populations are essentially our country's Third World labor force—unregulated, exploited, and underpaid. The author also failed to question why, regardless of whether the jobs go to the Third World or prisons, private companies are laying off workers, particularly unionized workers, and using prison labor instead.

In fact, not only do evangelicals often ignore the social context of crime, but their programs often depend on oppressive social conditions to succeed. Missionaries are often explicit about the fact that the worse off people are the better targets they make for mission work. Juvenile centers, for example, make excellent "harvest fields" ("Hidden Children" 1995, 14). Prisons are "a new mission opportunity with an exciting future" (Jackson 1973) and "represent one of the great unharvested mission fields" (Smarto 1993, 165). John Dearing argues in *Churchman* (an evangelical Anglican journal) that the death penalty is good because it brings convicts to Christ, offering "the possibility of repentance in the face of imminent and certain death" (Dearing 1994, 357). In fact, Dearing goes so far as to claim that the execution of the innocent is not entirely bad because if the innocent were to go free they would have no incentive to accept Christ. Their unjust execution becomes their eternal salvation. He writes, "I cannot help but think that the self-righteous anger with which many of those victims of faulty verdicts have greeted their release is hardly likely to have benefited their immortal souls" (357). Dearing notes with approval that the widespread use of the death penalty for relatively minor crimes in the 1700s advanced the cause of evangelism, as "The very cheapness of life in that age served . . . only to render the gift of salvation to eternal life even more precious to men" (363). Karla Faye Tucker's biography also ends with the message of God's redeeming love rather than a call to eradicate the death penalty (Strom 2000).

This individualization of crime creates a critical contradiction in the development of restorative justice programs. Restorative justice typically requires intact communities to hold offenders accountable for their deeds; however, the communities most in need of restorative justice programs are also typically those that have been fragmented by colonialism and the inequitable allocation of society's goods and resources. Some of the most successful programs are those developed by small indigenous communities. In a model developed by the Sandy Lake First Nation, when a crime is reported a working team talks to the perpetrator and gives him or her the option of participating in the program. The perpetrator must first confess his or her guilt and then follow a healing contract or go to jail. The perpetrator can decline to participate completely in the program and go through normal routes in the justice system. These indigenous models involve everyone touched by the abuse; the victim, perpetrator, family, friends, and the working team are involved in developing the healing contract. Everyone is also assigned an advocate throughout the process. Everyone also holds the perpetrator accountable for his or her contract. One Tlingit man noted that this approach was often more difficult than going to jail for "First one must deal with the shock and then the dismay on your neighbors' faces. One must deal with the daily humiliation, and at the same time seek forgiveness not just from victims, but from the community as a whole. . . . [A prison sentence] removes the offender from the daily accountability, and may not do anything towards rehabilitation, and for many may actually be an easier disposition than staying in the community" (Ross 1997, 18).

Since the Hollow Lake reserve in Saskatchewan adopted this approach, forty-eight offenders have been identified. Only five chose to go to jail, and only two have repeated crimes (one of the reoffenders went through the program again and has not reoffended since). This approach has been successful in addressing a wide variety of "crimes," including crimes of violence.[43] However, since the key to the success of these programs is an intact community that can hold "criminals" accountable, these models work particularly well for tribes that are small, close-knit, and geographically isolated. In larger communities, we bump up against the capitalist imperatives to create and maintain a mobile and unstable workforce. Larger intact communities require a major restructuring of the global economic system, a project that seems to hold little interest for evangelicals.

There are, however, some exceptions to the individualization of crime within evangelical discourse. As Fred Thompson writes in *United Evangelical Action*, "Systemic violence is committed by rich and powerful nations against millions of their own people by supporting economic policies that permit the wealthy to prosper at the expense of the poor. . . . And their supposedly peaceful laws, which maintain this spurious kind of order, are in fact instruments of violence and oppression. . . . Internally, nations resort to violence coated in 'legality' whenever crisis situations of a threatening nature develop" (1982, 15; see also Burrow 1992, 87). A *Christianity Today* article similarly points to a

> failure to examine how crime, deviance, and victimization are constructed in the public imagination. How do we define crime, and whose purposes do these definitions serve? Why do we assume that the main threat to our safety and well-being comes from below—rather than above—us on the socioeconomic ladders? For example, why does the victims' rights movement not include the concern of white-collar crime and industrial pollution? And if, as some studies show, poverty increases the pressures to commit property crimes, why do we not work to eliminate our nation's criminally large income gap rather than simply deploring the high crime rates of impoverished neighborhoods? (Weaver-Zercher 2000, 104)

As Jack Balswick states in *Perspectives on Science and Christian Faith*, "a biblical view of punishment calls for restoration at the societal level. . . . Social structures, for example, which allow a few to accumulate vast wealth, while others are left poor and destitute, are by their very nature structures which encourage criminal activity. Such social structures are

---

[43] It should be noted that many Native feminists are critical of the proclaimed success of these programs, arguing that they sacrifice safety for women and children who are victimized by abuse. See Emma LaRocque, "Re-Examining Culturally Appropriate Models in Criminal Justice Applications," 85.

evil and most undergo restoration" (1989, 225).[44] Lee Griffith, in *The Fall of Prison*, directly critiques Colson's claim that "criminals, not society, are the cause of crime," arguing that "At the most fundamental level, it is *only* society that creates crime, by empowering elected representatives to define what is or is not crime" (1993, 181). Even Colson implicitly admits the social context for crime when he states, "But everyone of us, I believe, is nine meals away from being a criminal, because if you go without food for nine meals you begin to think criminal thoughts" (1980a, 54). He further states that prison organizing is important because "the compassion and decency of a society is measured by the way it treats people on the bottom of the ladder" (2001d). Consequently, prison advocates do not always ignore the importance of community in platforms for prison reform. "You cannot just take a guy and ship him off to the state pen and forget about him, because when he comes back, he's going to be a real menace to your society. We have to deal with them in the community" (Colson 1983, 16; Coote 1972, 38; Nelles 1990b, 29; Nikkel 1990; Van Ness 1986, 121; "What Can Christians Do to Fight Crime?" 1973, 15). In a recent op-ed piece, Colson took a more moderate view of the causes of crime. On the one hand, he critiqued what he terms the liberal notion that poverty causes crime. But he then critiqued what he terms the conservative view that prisons stop crime, a view he blames for the exponential growth of prisons, which has done nothing to lower crime rates. Neither liberals nor conservatives are correct on the issue of prisons, Colson argues. Crime must be punished, he contends, as dictated by the Bible, but the Bible also states that the Israelites "were told to leave gleanings at the side of the field for the poor, maintain honest scales, feed the hungry, and clothe the naked" (2005).

Finally, while Prison Fellowship was relatively silent on the issues of prison abuse in Abu Ghraib, there was a widespread critique of these abuses in other evangelical venues. While some articles claimed the abuses

[44] See also Van Ness, who argues that the primary goal of Christian-based prison ministries is to restore "shalom." "What is shalom?" he writes. "It is wholeness and completeness in the community. It is reconciled relationships, harmony, and concord," (1993, 78). John Redekop further states, "There is more to a criminal act than the act itself. . . . Because crime has roots in a community, any solution to crime must also involve the community" (1990, 22). And James Skillen argues, "To limit ourselves as Christians to a narrow range of questions about prisons, police, and due process while ignoring all the unanswered questions about injustice is to close our minds to the wider context of our responsibility for promoting a just society" (1993, 134).

were not that extreme, most, even in Republican-apologist *World* magazine, were sharply critical of them (Belz 2004b, 2004c; Carter 2004; Grady 2005; Jackson 2004; Readers Write 2004b, 12–14; Seu 2004; Veith 2004a). However, none of these articles linked the abuses to prison abuses within the United States. Generally, as mentioned previously, they were linked to other, disparate phenomena such as women in the military, homosexuality, using civil contractors to run military facilities, and pornography (Colson and Morse 2004; Dawson 2005). While Justice Fellowship did not take the opportunity Abu Ghraib provided to frame a message about the abusive structures of prisons, immediately after 9/11, when even many liberals were clamoring for war, Charles Colson did call for a more restrained response to the problem of terrorism.

> If [Bush] orders an all-out assault on the terrorists and those who harbor them, it could provoke extreme elements in moderate Muslim countries to topple their governments. This would have the net result of turning our allies into rogue nations who are willing to aid and export terrorism. Enormous wisdom—nothing less than God's wisdom—is required. We can also pray that the "quiet, unyielding anger" of the American people of which Bush spoke, an anger that is both natural and appropriate, does not spill over into rash demands. The President knows he must act swiftly. But for the rest of us, this is a time when our anger must be tempered with patience and restraint. May God have mercy on us. (2001a).[45]

THE LIMITS OF RESTORATIVE JUSTICE

Native women have much to say about the limits of the restorative justice model because many look to indigenous models of justice for inspiration. The relationship between restorative justice and indigenous peoples is complex. On one hand, Christians, such as Colson, often appropriate justice models based on indigenous forms of governance without crediting indigenous peoples. On the other hand, many Natives, particularly antiviolence advocates, complain that restorative justice programs have been foisted on them by the state under the claim that they are "indigenous." These programs often prove inadequate when addressing issues of

[45] Daniel Van Ness also called for "forgiveness" for the terrorist attacks based on the principles of restorative justice (2001). Unfortunately for Colson, his call for restraint quickly ended when Bush began calling for a preemptive war in Iraq, which Colson supported (Colson 2002b).

sexual and domestic violence (Green 1998; A. Smith 2005b; Strang and Braithwaite 2002). To illustrate these controversies, the Aboriginal Women's Action Network (AWAN) and Native American domestic violence advocates have critiqued the uncritical use of "traditional" forms of governance for addressing domestic violence. Native communities, AWAN argues, have been pressured to adopt "circle sentencing" because it is supposed to be a "traditional" indigenous practice. According to AWAN, there is no such traditional practice in its communities. Moreover, it is concerned that the process of diverting cases outside a court system can be dangerous for survivors. In one example, Bishop Hubert O'Connor (a white man) was found guilty of multiple cases of sexual abuse of aboriginal women, but his punishment under the restorative justice model was to participate in a healing circle with his victims. Because his crimes were against aboriginal women, he was able to opt for an "aboriginal approach" —an approach, AWAN argues, that did little to provide real healing and accountability for the survivors. At the same time, members of that community (Alkali Lake) complain that AWAN dismissed the healing circle when in fact it was what the survivors wanted.[46]

The Native sociologist Luana Ross further critiques the limitations of such models. Because of their semisovereign legal status, indigenous nations have more flexibility in setting up alternative programs (Nielsen and Silverman 1996). The majority of these programs, however, still fall under the purview of the federal government. Some tribes have even attempted to design their own prisons based on indigenous models. Ross argues that these attempts to marry indigenous and white models of criminal justice fail to take into account the fact that prisons are "white by design." Consequently, whatever good intentions go into the establishment of Native prisons, they generally devolve into the same oppressive structures that constitute white prisons (Ross 1998b). Hence, her analysis should be instructive to those who feel they can build more humane "Christian" prisons. According to Ross, it is important to challenge not only our current

[46] Information drawn from talks given at the "Color of Violence: Violence against Women of Color" conference, University of California, Santa Cruz, April 2000; and the Generation Five Strategy Session, San Francisco, June 2004. Green reports that some programs attempt to address these issues by ensuring that survivors of gender violence have their own support team, ensuring that survivors and perpetrators do not meet unless the survivor requests it, and calling for all the facts of the situation to be addressed before sentencing begins (1998, 76, 81). For evangelical coverage of the O'Connor case, see Aldred 2000; and Harvey 2000. These articles position aboriginal peoples as leaders of the restorative justice movement.

models of punishment but also our models of criminalization—that is, who is defined as "criminal" and why. In the United States, acts of Native resistance have generally been categorized as criminal. Meanwhile, "genocide against Native people was never seen as murder. Indeed, in the Old West the murder of Natives was not even a crime" (Ross 1998a, 15).

These critiques provide a helpful place for dialogue with activists and scholars in the prison abolition movement. The prison abolitionist and scholar Dylan Rodriguez notes, "Turning attention away from conventional notions of 'crime' as isolated, individual misbehavior necessitates a basic questioning of the conditions that cast 'criminality' as a convenient political rationale for the warehousing of large numbers of poor, disenfranchised and displaced Black people and other people of color" (2000a). Thus, some of the more radical models adopted by tribes are those that circumvent the U.S. system completely. One California tribe, for instance, recently asserted its sovereign right to banish a tribal member for incest regardless of what the U.S. government claims as its jurisdictional rights (Luana Ross 2000). The Native anti-violence activist Eileen Hudon, formerly from Clanstar, reports another radical act of sovereignty from a Native community in Alaska.

> In Alaska, there is a struggle against acknowledging sovereignty. But one tribe was asserting that authority without the justice system. They sent out a letter when they heard about a domestic assault and said to the men that it has come to our attention that you have been involved in a domestic assault. We want you to know there are resources. We also want you to know there are resources outside the community. And here is the date we want you to come before the tribal council to tell us what you are going to do to ensure you can still live here. (2000, 93–94)

As Dylan Rodriguez notes, one of the problems with religious progressives on prison issues is their tendency to advocate for alternative sentencing programs rather than prison abolition (Rodriguez 2000a, 2000b). The result is that restorative justice programs become just another reform movement *within* the system, augmenting rather than replacing it (Barker 1985; Bianchi 1985; Brown and Hogg 1985, 57; Cohen 1985). Stanley Cohen, a prison abolitionist, argues that alternative models are typically co-opted to serve state interests, increase the net of social control, and often lose their community focus as they become professionalized (1985, 129). Indeed, the history of prison reform indicates time and time again that minor reform programs actually strengthen the prison system and increase the number of people who fall under its purview (Foucault 1977a;

Rotman 1995, 152). The fact that some programs require the perpetrator to make a guilty plea to be eligible for sentencing, for instance, could lead more people, particularly people of color without legal representation, to plead guilty and find themselves in the criminal justice system (Green 1998, 77). For instance, women religious reformers in the 1800s advocated reforms for women prisoners kept in the same brutal institutions as men. These reformers imagined women prisoners not as criminal, fallen women deserving harsh treatment, but as sick or wayward women in need of a cure or proper retraining. They fought for the establishment of sex-segregated "reformatories" rather than prisons to provide women the guidance they needed to fulfill their domestic roles. As a result, great numbers of women in the criminal justice system suddenly found themselves receiving domesticity training. Women "were sentenced instead to new reformatories whose ostensible purpose was not to punish but to cure or redeem. And yet the effect of this tacit decriminalization of women was in fact to extend control over women by replacing short sentences for petty offenses in local prisons with indeterminate terms in these new specialist institutions. Women were liable to be held until they were considered to be reformed or cured" (Zedner 1995, 316; see also Freedman 1981).

Echoing C. S. Lewis's critique of "humanitarian punishment," Luana Ross points out that the outgrowth of this ideology is that women often find themselves in prison longer than men because have to prove they have been "cured" (1998a, 118). As mentioned previously, the penitentiary system itself is a product of Quaker reform efforts to move prison systems away from a model of physical punishment and toward a model of spiritual penitence.[47] The result of these reform efforts has been the fortification of the prison system through the implementation of mandatory minimum sentencing. Simply adding restorative justice to the present criminal justice system is likely to strengthen the criminal justice apparatus, particularly in communities of color that are deemed in need of "restoration." As Rodriguez argues, "Penal abolition implies a principled and uncompromising commitment to opposing, disrupting, and ultimately erasing those historic structures and institutions of power that reproduce themselves through the systematic incarceration, punishment, and elimination of those populations and bodies rendered deviant" (2000b, 5). In *Policing*

[47] Ironically, Quakers today are often at the forefront of the prison abolition movement, which historically called for an end to indeterminate sentencing as part of its abolitionist programs (Knopp 1983, 89).

the Crisis, Stuart Hall and his colleagues argue that when the fear of crime, particularly in certain sectors of society, grows out of proportion to the actual levels of crime, this phenomenon can be described as a "moral panic." They note that moral panic is the ideological weapon used by ruling classes to gain popular consent for repressive state policies (Hall et al. 1978). Criminalization is a process by which communities of color generally are scapegoated for social ills, thereby enabling the ruling classes to escape accountability for social policies that are detrimental to the poor and working classes.

It is important to note that there are abolitionist strands *within* evangelicalism. For instance, Griffith writes:

> Focusing on the political, racial, sexual, and economic scapegoats of the prison system entails a danger of creating the impression that what is wrong with prisons can be fixed with some judicial or political tinkering—that what is needed is kinder and gentler politicians, judges, police or prison guards. . . . The fundamental problem with prisons is not bad police or bad guards. These people act at our behest and, more often than not, they are victimized and brutalized by the same system that victimizes and brutalizes prisoners. (1993, 85—86)

> God's good news in Jesus to the prisoners calls us to the reality that Jesus means *freedom*, not *reform*. (1993, 201)

In engaging the critiques of the restorative justice movement and the prison system made by the prison abolition movement, it then becomes necessary to engage a more sustained critique of the nation-state model of governance, as many Native theorists have done. As Charles Colson's writings suggest, a critique of prisons can lead to a critique of the state since the prison is simply a logical extension of the nation-state form of governance. In chapter 5, I more thoroughly discuss these critiques in an analysis of Native women's articulations of nationhood and sovereignty.

IMPLICATIONS FOR MOBILIZING EVANGELICALS AGAINST THE PRISON INDUSTRIAL COMPLEX

Evangelical prison organizing, with all its problems, is important because it challenges the support for the prison industrial complex within conservative circles. Prison Fellowship and Justice Fellowship are willing to work with all sectors involved in opposing prison expansion. They have been very successful in dominating the Christian periodical literature on this level, even though it is Prison Fellowship's ministry rather than Justice Fellowship's political activism that seems to receive the greatest praise and attention. For instance, a right-wing *World* staffer, Roy Maynard, praises Prison Fellowship in one article (Maynard 1997; Kadlecek 1994), but in others he opposes many of Justice Fellowship's platforms by advocating mandatory minimum sentencing, increased application of the death penalty, reducing appeals available to those sentenced to death, and increasing the prison sentences of nonviolent offenders (including drug offenders) and youths (Maynard 1996b, 17).[48] This work has also impacted the right-wing Heritage Foundation, which is marked more by its political conservativism than its attachment to evangelicalism (Loconte 1998). Christian periodical literature is a faulty barometer of grassroots evangelical sentiment about prisons because people involved in prison ministries are the ones most likely to write articles about prison. These writers are more likely to hold progressive views on prisons than are the magazine's readers. This disparity is evident in many of Colson's statements regarding the difficulties he faces in garnering evangelical support for prison reform. He notes how evangelicals are much more interested in his conversion story than his prison work. In *Life Sentence*, he describes how his declaration of faith in an inerrant Bible earned him a chorus of amens at a conservative church. But when he spoke passionately about the importance of visiting prisons the sanctuary was silent.[49] "I knew my conversion had won me many new friends," he writes, "but did they care at all about the terrible conditions in our prisons? I was trying hard to alert people to a real need. Was anyone listening? Sometimes I thought not" (1979, 116).

Similarly, at the Justice Fellowship Forum the participants and speakers were clearly not in complete accord regarding the importance of restorative justice. According to Colson, by restorative justice, he means "teaching that we must go beyond punishing wrong doers by reconciling criminals and victims, asking criminals to make restitution, and restoring offenders to the community. That is why, when inmates are released, Christians should be there to help them find a job, a home, furniture and friendships . . . assistance that will restore the wholeness of the commu-

[48] Interestingly, however, *World* ran another article arguing that the war on drugs was a bust and noted that the war on drugs was racist in its application (Maynard 1995b; Veith 1996).

[49] To even be able to move the headquarters of Prison Fellowship to Reston, Virginia, the organization had to promise that no inmates would stay there ("Prison Fellowship Moves Ahead on New Headquarters" 1985).

nity" (2005). Another participant at the conference who spoke out as a victim of crime claimed to be a proponent of restorative justice, but what she advocated was not recognizably different from the standard "get tough on crime" policy. Her notion of restorative justice seemed to be limited to allowing victims to make victim impact statements (Beane 2000b). In fact, one speaker who develops community policing programs in Washington, D.C., argued that, although we now hear more talk about community policing and restorative justice coming from bureaucrats within the criminal justice system, the principles and models of restorative justice have been warped and co-opted by the system to serve punitive ends. It appears that many evangelicals who become involved in restorative justice are not always attracted to it in its purest form. For them, restorative justice involves little in the way of decarceration and greater justice for offenders; in fact, it involves nothing more radical than increased attention to victims' rights. At the 1999 Justice Fellowship Restorative Justice Forum, I asked Daniel Van Ness, the former president of Justice Fellowship, what he thought the level of support for restorative justice was among evangelicals. He said that Justice Fellowship had spent so much energy trying to pass various forms of legislation it had not done the work necessary to build support for its programs at the evangelical grass roots. Justice Fellowship then reorganized its program priorities to emphasize grassroots education. Since evangelicals are not known for their support for prison reform, the work of Prison Fellowship and Justice Fellowship, however flawed, is an important starting point for mobilizing evangelical support for prison reform and possibly prison abolition.

Faith Today ran a series of articles on prison accompanied by a reader's poll. The sentiments expressed in the poll were much more conservative than those expressed in the accompanying articles (Meed 1990). Of the poll's respondents, 75 percent felt that prison conditions were too comfortable. However, the majority of people who thought prison conditions were inhumane had visited a prison while the majority of those who thought prisons were too comfortable had not (32). It appears that articles in the evangelical periodical literature with the strongest law-and-order sentiments are written by those not involved in prison ministries. I did not find one article advocating a "punishment only" model that was written by either an ex-inmate or someone involved in prison ministries. All of these individuals speak of the need for programs that attempt to reform and not simply punish prisoners (Larson 1975, 7). These findings suggest that exposing people to prisons is an important step in transforming their consciousness about them. As Colson himself notes, he would never have become involved in prison reform had he not served time. "Over and over in the months ahead," he observes, "I was to discover the pleasant indifference of men who had the fate of thousands of prisoners in their hands. They pass laws, provide the money, express appropriate horror about the rising crime rate, but beyond that, they don't care. But then, I reminded myself, I had possessed this kind of power once and I hadn't cared either" (1979, 42).

The impact of his prison experience is most telling in Colson's view of the 1971 Attica prison uprising in New York before and after his incarceration. In the prologue to *Life Sentence*, he recalls President Richard Nixon praising Governor Nelson Rockefeller's brutal repression of the prisoners at Attica after the uprising.

> "Rockefeller did the right thing, Chuck," Nixon continued. "He'll catch it though from all those liberal jackasses in the press. But he's smart. The public wants no more nonsense from criminals. The public will cheer him on. 'Gun 'em down,' they'll say."
>
> "No doubt about it, Mr. President. Our people out there have had enough of being soft on criminals. . . ."
>
> For the next several minutes, as we sipped coffee, the President talked about our anticrime program. I took notes profusely so I could relay his instructions. "Must get tough," I underlined at the bottom of one page. It was good politics. We believed that long sentences, increased police powers and tough prisons were the answer to the crime problem.
>
> Neither of us mentioned the 31 prisoners who had been killed, but I suggested that the President send personal letters to the families of the nine slain guards. A nice gesture. (1979, 14–15)

Colson's perspective on Attica shifted sharply after his prison experience. In recounting his visit to Attica, he identifies with the prisoners and the "slaughtered inmates." He criticizes the prison officials for denying the prisoners a monument to honor the inmates killed during the uprising. During his talk at Attica, the officials refused to allow him to meet with the prisoners. Despite these orders, Colson jumped off the speaker's platform and entered the audience. In summing up these disparate experiences, he writes, "September 13, 1979 . . . April 3, 1978: two worlds, and journey traveled, some things learned" (1979, 19).

From my observations at the Justice Fellowship Forum, it appeared that many of the prominent members of Justice Fellowship were conservative Christian Right Republicans who, for one reason or another, found themselves in prison. Justice Fellowship's former president, Pat Nolan, was a former conservative member of the California assembly before he was caught in a sting operation and sentenced to prison for racketeering. At the Justice Fellowship Forum, he noted that prior to his incarceration he was a strong proponent of "get tough on crime" and "victim's rights" legislation. When he was in prison, someone sent him a Justice Fellowship brochure that convinced him he had been addressing issues of crime and punishment from the incorrect paradigm. He now believes, for instance, that the Victims Rights Act (Proposition 15, California) he sponsored has done nothing to help victims but has served only to strengthen prosecutions. In an interview published in *Jubilee* (Prison Fellowship's magazine), he states: "During my time in prison . . . I learned that all those things that I supported as a legislator, while they were justifiable, didn't get to the root cause of the problem and weren't really solutions. For all the prisons we built . . . our communities weren't any safer. . . . So it really caused me to think, *There has to be a better way*" (Peck 2000, 16).

Ernest Preate, another Justice Fellowship staffer, was a former attorney general of Pennsylvania who successfully argued for the constitutionality of Pennsylvania's death penalty before the U.S. Supreme Court. He, too, ended up in prison where he became aware of the racism endemic in the criminal justice system. Through this experience, he was born again, and he stated at the Justice Fellowship Forum, "If Christ can forgive me, I have to forgive others." Now he is a staunch opponent of the death penalty, a major critic of the "war on drugs," and particularly concerned with ending racism in the criminal justice system. The evangelist Jim Bakker was sent to prison following the Praise the Lord scandal. There he concluded that prisons should refrain from imposing harsh punishments on inmates. Following his release, he declared, "We should not keep hurting the hurting" (Bruce 1997a, 56). In Britain, Jonathan Aitken, a Tory minister of defense, went to prison for perjury in 1999. He began working with Colson when he was released (Mastris 2001). It appears that the most effective way to dismantle the prison industrial complex is to incarcerate as many conservative Christian Republicans as possible.

Despite their problems, prison ministries give many people exposure to prisons, a factor that appears to be critical in changing public sentiment about prison conditions. In fact, Colson uses this insight to alter public policy on prisons by organizing prisoners to visit legislators on Capitol Hill.

Gradually each class which visited Capitol Hill was changing the stereotyped image of prisoners as evil, violent and dangerous individuals. In place of reading cold statistics and impersonal reports about prisons, members of Congress were meeting real human beings they could touch, talk to and often identify with. Many congressmen offered for the first time to visit a prison, others began corresponding with inmates. Their personal concern, which is growing, is the major hope for long-overdue, much-needed, reform in the system. (Colson 1979, 232)

Colson's final advice to readers of *Life Sentence* is to "go in your thousands into prisons across the land" (301).

Prison ministries also publicized the case of Karla Faye Tucker, which has caused many conservative Christians to waver in their support of the death penalty. The following if from a transcript of Kathy Chiero's interview with Tucker on Pat Robertson's show, *The 700 Club*.

> Kathy: I think one of the reasons your case has often [garnered] so much attention is that [it] really puts us in a quandary, because we cannot be pro-Karla and pro-death penalty. In this case, what do you think the Karla Faye Tucker case, as they call it, has done for our thinking about the death penalty?
>
> Karla: My prayer is that it would make [people], most especially the body of Christ, realize that God can redeem any life He wants to. . . . And that's my prayer—that they would begin to see people who have sinned, but can be redeemed. . . .
>
> Kathy: You know, Karla, I did an interview last week with a radio station and one of the questions they asked me was why shouldn't we care about the anonymous men and women on death row, or in the general population who also love the Lord, who also are born again? Why just Karla? And I said, "Well you are probably right. We should care, and one of the things that is Karla's legacy is that she has put a face on death row." (Chiero 1998a)

Tucker's execution was so troubling to Christians that even *World* felt compelled to write something approximating a balanced article on the death penalty (Sillars 1998). *Christianity Today* ran an editorial arguing that "evangelical instincts against her execution were right, but not because she was a Christian." Instead, the editorial suggests, the lesson of Tucker's case is that the death penalty is indefensible because it discriminates against the poor and people of color, disrespects the humanity of those convicted of crimes, and fails to deter violent crime ("Lesson of Karla Faye Tucker" 1998, 15–16). The magazine also ran an article by Virginia Owens, a resident of Huntsville, the town where Tucker was executed. Over one-third of the executions in the United States take place in Huntsville. Owens notes that the town is financially dependent on the prison system: "If Texas felons suddenly reformed . . . the Wal-Mart superstore out by the Interstate would have to shut its automatic doors" (1998, 46). Yet the Tucker case forced Huntsville residents to question their complicity in the brutality of the system. Owens writes, "Huntsville has always been the location for executions in Texas, yet until Karla Faye Tucker's execution we had never felt our imputed guilt so keenly" (46). William Bumphus, the death row evangelist and former inmate, concluded that "Jesus would never pull the switch on anyone" (Bruce 1997a, 59).

Of course, whether or not prison ministries are beneficial to prisoners is another story. Assessing the impact of these ministries is beyond the scope of this chapter, but it is certainly important to make this assessment before advocating the expansion of these ministries in the criminal justice system.

Although evangelical reformers often ignore the social context of crime and punishment, their work points to the importance of addressing social injustice. For example, in an article on prison ministries, *Christianity Today* published a large graph showing that not only did the United States have the highest per capita incarceration rate in the world but it incarcerated black people at a per capita rate four times higher than South Africa under apartheid (Maxwell 1991, 35). *Charisma* ran articles stating, for example, that "we must improve racial inequalities in the 'three strikes you are out' [prison] system" (Jackson 2005b) and critiquing racist antidrug policies (Daniels 2005). One article went so far as to argue that "prisons have replaced plantations in America as a place of bondage for the black man" (Daniels 2005, 122). Articles on the death penalty routinely point to the racism endemic in its application (Bube 1981, 110; Hobbs and Hobbs 1983, 253; Llewellyn 1975, 11; Shelley 1984, 16; Van Ness 1987a, 24–27). In *Perspectives*, a Christian Reformed journal, Al Heystek wrote a critique of the racialization of the war on drugs, noting that "In relationship to cocaine, Black Americans are statistically less likely to have used this drug than whites, yet they are many more times likely to be punished for it and to get longer sentences." He concludes, "It's quite evident that incarceration for drug using or selling does nothing to improve the socio-economic factors that are part of the problem in the first place" (1996, 6). *Charisma* featured a story on Mark Olds, who was the first person to be ordained a minister while incarcerated. According to this article, he preaches "liberation theology" through his Righteous Men Ministries, in which, through Christ, people must find not only spiritual liberty but also "social and economic freedom" (Colter 2004). In Van Ness's succinct formulation: "The rich get richer and the poor get prison" (1986, 43). Particularly since the Rodney King riots in Los Angeles, the topic of racism has found its way into discussions about all aspects of law enforcement (Harvey 2000; Mackey 1989, 46; Nolan 2004e). Don Smarto argues that "we must not tolerate authority figures, especially frontline police, who practice racial prejudice, abuse the rights of those arrested, or commit crimes in the name of justice" (1993, 45) and also notes the economic injustices inherent in the criminal justice system (124). Richard Crow wrote an article for *Eternity* sympathetic to the Attica uprising in which he exhorts Christians to "be the vanguard—advocating, demanding and effecting change" (1973, 19). James Skillen (an evangelical philosopher and head of the Center for Public Justice) argues that evangelicals concerned with prison reform must link this cause to other social justice issues: "We must also work for a just education policy, for just health care policies, for economic justice, for environmental justice" (1993, 137). In Smarto's volume on evangelical prison organizing, Gordon McLean implicitly critiques the exponential growth of the prison industrial complex: "In not too many years, if we keep up the present trends, half our American population will be in jail and the other half will be prison guards!" (McLean 1993, 160). At the Justice Fellowship Forum, issues of institutional racism and classism within the criminal justice system were widely discussed. Participants even used the term *prison industrial complex* to describe the system they opposed.

Colson and company also critique the media hype over crime and prisons and specifically the venal uses to which law-and-order rhetoric are put: "Do we dare say we ought not to be putting more people in prison? Politicians have played this tune so long, and it always gets applause. But how long does it take you to educate the public and get over that?" (Colson 1983, 15; see also Smarto 1993, 199; and Solomon n.d.). Colson has been outspoken about his opposition to the "get tough on crime" rhetoric of presidential candidates and was particularly critical of George Bush Sr.'s use of the Willie Horton case in his presidential campaign (1980b, 28; Lawton 1988, 39; McLean 1993, 161; Smarto 1993, 175). In one story, he angrily denounces a judge who blithely purveys this "get tough" rhetoric.

> "Lock 'em up, I say, and throw away the keys. . . ." He pressed on. "In my district, I sentence everybody to the big house at Atlanta, not to any of those country clubs like Eglin and Maxwell." [Colson served his time in Eglin.]
> . . ."Have you even been there, Judge?" I asked.
> "No, but I know all about those places. They're too good for criminals."
> The food had lost its taste; I prayed silently for self-control. (Colson 1979, 115)

In *Convicted*, Colson and Daniel Van Ness implicitly critique the prison industrial complex (the economic system that keeps the prison system in place), writing, "It's hard to think of anyone who benefits from our current system of justice and punishment—anyone, that is, except the politicians whose campaigns feed on this crisis, and the architects and builders who construct the walls and bars of our nation's concrete monument to failure" (Colson and Ness 1989, 33). *Life Sentence*, in its attention to the horrific conditions in prisons such as Attica, Stillwater, Georgia's Fulton County Jail, Atlanta Prison, and Lorton, makes it quite clear that prisons are not country clubs (Colson 1979, 18, 57, 85, 188, 292). In the case of Stillwater, Colson's advocacy led to the closing of its solitary confinement facility (279).

In the course of his prison reform advocacy, Colson has often confronted prison officials, in some cases leading to their dismissal (Colson 1985, 29). His ministry has also not balked at advocating for the release of certain prisoners and for the amelioration of living conditions for others (Colson 1979, 117). He writes, "Many Christians I knew, believed our sole task was to point others to salvation; that is, to preach the good news. But what is the news? Jesus forgave sin and fed the hungry. They aren't mutually exclusive. He did both" (151). At Atlanta Prison, Colson describes an evangelistic message he gave to prisoners that resulted in widespread conversions. However, this success did not satisfy him: "What torture, I thought. These men come back from the spiritual high of this meeting and then live in this hell. But this too will change" (300). He also points to the economic incentives for the proliferation of prisons: "Some states are blindly spending billions for new prisons. That's good news for the architects and builders who are generous contributors to the campaigns of local politicians. But it's bad news for the public" (1987, 11). He further states, "We have a philosophy that gives us a larger answer [to the problem of crime] than merely arresting more people and building bigger prisons. An effective strategy against crime must start by asking fundamental philosophical questions: What makes a good community?" (1997).

It is nearly impossible to become involved in prison work without eventually having to confront the evils of capitalism, racism, and other forms of social injustice.[50] Even when prison ministries focus on converting indi-

---

[50] As William Boggess, an evangelical former inmate, notes, while conversion to Christ was central to his change in life, the system still conspired to prevent him from changing the lives of other prisoners: "I ran afoul of 'the system' which is set up to punish and not to rehabilitate" (1981, 77).

viduals to Christ rather than changing the system, they often find themselves forced to confront the system in order to do conversion work effectively. These tensions suggest that prison ministries may be a starting point for evangelical activists hoping to pursue prison reform and other social justice issues.

The nature of this issue puts evangelical prison activists in dialogue with individuals of more radical persuasions. Some participants I talked to at the Justice Fellowship Forum had also attended a more radical conference, Critical Resistance: Beyond the Prison Industrial Complex, in 1998. Pat Nolan mentioned that he had worked with the feminist lawyer Gloria Allred on prison issues. Speakers talked at length about the need to develop relationships with mainline denominations, non-Christian groups, and even leftist organizations. Just as support for the prison industrial complex has been bipartisan, so, too, has opposition to it. Consequently, Justice Fellowship is often linked with many progressive groups that support antiprison legislation, including the 2004 proposed amendment to California's three-strikes legislation. Pat Nolan also stresses Justice Fellowship's bipartisan work as central to its organizing (2003b, 2003c, 2003d, 2004h, 2004j). According to him, "If we . . . keep our partisanship secondary to our obedience to Christ, there is much that we can accomplish together. It is not just the lamb and lion that shall lie down together, but Democrats and Republicans, too!" (2003e). This emphasis on bipartisan organizing stands in contrast to the activities of many other Christian Right organizations, such as the Christian Coalition, which are often criticized even within evangelical circles for being a "wholly owned subsidiary of the Republican Party" (Reed 1990, 245). Consequently, it is often at odds with other sectors of the Right, which espouse the "get tough on crime" approach.[51] This issue may be unique in its ability to bring evangelical Christians into dialogue with groups they would normally avoid.[52] In fact, Nolan regularly highlights Justice Fellowship's alliances with people across

[51] In response to the charge that Justice Fellowship is supporting "soft on crime" legislation, Pat Nolan responds, "Those who do nothing to change this system are the ones who are 'soft on crime.' Certainly their policies lead to more of it" (2004h).

[52] Phillip Hammond and James Hunter argue that the processes of education tend to shift the religious beliefs of evangelicals, noting that even the process of education in *evangelical* institutions generally tends to convert evangelicals into nonevangelicals (1984). Of course, this study was conducted before the full force of the fundamentalist takeover of the Southern Baptist Convention was felt, in which many of the more liberal professors in these prominent evangelical educational institutions were fired and replaced with hardcore fundamentalists.

political and party divides. According to him, "Justice Fellowship is in a unique position to forge political alliances across party and racial lines" (Nolan 2000, 2).

These relationships *could* prove significant in pushing evangelical politics to the left. By hinting at this possibility, I do not mean to suggest that such an outcome would be easy to achieve or even likely. As Stuart Hall notes, while political alliances are never stable they are not free floating, either. They have histories, which make some hegemonic blocs easier to form than others (1988, 140). Nevertheless, as I demonstrate in this book, even more unlikely alliances have been built around progressive issues, so it is still worth considering how evangelical prison organizing could be interpellated (in the Althusserian sense) into more progressive discourses.

CONCLUSION

The complexities of the politics of articulation are exemplified by the racial politics of Charles Colson. He describes in *Life Sentence* how his work in prisons has made him sensitive to racism. In attempting to collaborate with an African American leader in prison ministry, John Staggers, Colson's self-described condescending attitudes led to major conflicts between the two men. Colson also tells of how he referred to African American men as "boys" eleven times in a lecture he gave to African American prisoners at Lorton prison: "How could I be so insensitive, so blind to the obvious? My poor relationship with John Staggers, and my clumsy efforts at Lorton, made me realize how little honest effort I'd made to understand black attitudes and concerns. Half the nation's prison population is nonwhite" (1979, 86).

Colson notes that his work on prisons (not to mention his own imprisonment) has sensitized him to other areas of social injustice as well. "The more I mingled with the poor, the disadvantaged, the mistreated people of our society, the more I saw the raw evil of injustice," he writes. . . ."My contempt for the 'fuzzy-headed liberals' who have marched so often to protest discrimination and injustice was lessening. In fact, although it was painful, I had to admit that on occasion I even felt some grudging admiration for their courage in taking unpopular positions" (1979, 281). However, while prison work clearly sensitized Colson to the racism endemic in the prison system, his work has not been sufficient to challenge his Eurocentric standpoint regarding multicultural history. He complains that "revisionist history" now depicts "Muhammed-inspired Muslims and the pantheistic Native Americans [as] the real good guys" (1992, 72). He also complains that Christians have been falsely implicated in the Spanish Inquisition and the genocide of Indian people.

In another story, Colson tells of how his interaction with prison reformers in Europe challenged his viewpoint that the United States is a Christian nation blessed by God.

> I often concluded speeches with stirring appeals to restore America as the Christian nation its founders intended, discovering that those words invariably brought the crowds to their feet. They were as surefire as some of the slogans I'd found so effective in politics. In the introduction to *Born Again* I wrote, "How magnificently has God honored the covenant of our forefathers"—words, I now admitted to myself, which were intended to arouse the same emotions in the book's readers. Indeed there were covenants, but was it presumptuous to assume God was party to them? . . . Yes, I could only conclude, I had been wrong. (1979, 145)[53]

However, renouncing his allegiance to "Christian America" has not stopped Colson from supporting the Christian Coalition or declaring that those who challenge the religio-moral superiority of the United States "eviscerate the Christian faith" (1992, 72). And after 9/11 he called on Christians to "go ahead—get out that flag" (2002c). Without further organizing efforts on the part of progressives, these tensions within Colson's politics will not add up to a platform for progressive political change. Nevertheless, the sites of contradiction and contestation in Christian Right discourse suggest the possibility that these multiple resistances "can be integrated in global strategies" (Foucault 1980, 142). While Colson does not seem to be tending toward more progressive politics, other sectors of this movement might. The Right has been very successful in mobilizing previously apolitical evangelicals who believed that Christians should stay out of politics because all social problems would end with the second coming of Christ. This "hegemonic bloc" created by the Right has been revolutionary in its ability to implicitly transform the eschatological framework of thousands of evangelicals to accommodate political activism.

If the Right can be so successful in using tensions within evangelical discourse to garner support for its political platforms, political progressives should think about the possibilities of doing the same. While the

---

[53] See also (Colson 1994)

tensions within evangelical discourse do not add up to a comprehensive program for social transformation, they indicate points of strategic inter- vention that progressives might seize on to create hegemonic blocs not only against the prison industrial complex but against other forms of social and political oppression as well.

2

"The One Who Did Not Break His Promises"

Native Nationalisms and the Christian Right

Religion is never just the opium of the people.
—ALAIN TOURAINE

On May 18, 2004, the city council of Eureka, California, voted to return 40 acres of land to a local tribe, the Wiyot, which had been trying to regain control of it since the 1970s. Whom did activists in the tribe credit with this successful campaign? They credited a constituency not generally known for supporting Native land struggles—the evangelical churches in the area. Earlier the Humboldt Evangelical Alliance had invited Wiconi International, a Native charismatic organization, to facilitate a reconciliation between evangelical churches and the Wiyot tribe in California (Wiconi International 2001, 4). After taking part in a three-day event, the churches donated a thousand dollars to help the tribe purchase land on Indian Island. The tribe bought 1.5 acres of land before the city council gave the Wiyot another 40 acres. The Wiyot claimed that this reconciliation meeting had paved the way for the city council to return the land in 2004 (Uttley 2004b).

This story illustrates the increasing participation of Native peoples within the "race reconciliation" efforts of conservative evangelicalism. This movement began in the early 1990s with the goal of fostering racial unity among evangelical Christians. Since its inception, most prominent white evangelical organizations have issued statements and passed resolutions on race reconciliation. A plethora of books on the topic have been published in the past five years, and there has been a significant increase in the number of articles in the conservative Christian periodical literature that focus on people of color or racism. The purpose of race reconciliation, as Tony Evans puts it, is to "establish a church where everyone of any race or status who walks through the door is loved and respected as part of God's creation and family" (1990, 157).

As with evangelical prison organizing, the race reconciliation movement has the potential to shift the politics of the Christian Right, although it is not necessarily clear that it can push white evangelicalism to the left or communities of color to the right. In a forthcoming book, *The Christian Right and Race Reconciliation*, I address the politics and history of the race reconciliation movement more generally. In this chapter, I focus specifically on Native peoples within the movement. If, borrowing from Judith Butler's analysis, we understand Native identities as performative rather than always already constituted (1990), it is important to examine the kinds of Native identities that are performed in white-dominated evangelical venues. Does the presence of Native peoples within the Promise Keepers and other white-dominated evangelical groups indicate that Natives have forsaken their identities in order to "assimilate" into white evangelical culture? In this chapter, I look at the ambivalent relationship between Native peoples and the new charismatic movements, particularly the Promise Keepers. The performances of Natives within the Promise Keepers movement seem to be at odds with Native sovereignty struggles. But, as Foucault warns us, power is never enacted unilaterally for "Where there is power, there is resistance" (Foucault 1980, 95). Even in disparate power relationships between subjects, there continues to be resistance among those who apparently accede to these relationships. Foucault writes, "We must make allowance for the complex and unstable process whereby discourse can be both an instrument and an effect of power, but also a hindrance, a stumbling-block, a point of resistance and a starting point for an opposing strategy" (1980, 101). The relationship between Native and white evangelicalism is simultaneously one of reinscription and contestation. Consequently, both the potential for shifting evangelicalism to more progressive positions vis-à-vis treaty rights and the potential to push Native communities farther to the Right exist simultaneously within this movement. In fact, as I will discuss later in the chapter, this potential is even more significant than I had realized when I first began this research.

There's no question that white evangelical Protestants, especially in the South, were not only on the sidelines but were on the wrong side of the most central struggle for civil justice of the twentieth century, namely the struggle for civil rights. . . . Until the pro-family, religious conservative movement becomes a truly biracial or multi-racial movement, it will not have moral resonance with the American people, because we were so wrong at that time. I want the Christian Coalition to be a truly rainbow coalition. I want it to be black, brown, yellow, white. I want it to bring Christians of all faith traditions, all denominations, and all races and colors together. I don't think that's going to happen over night. It's going to take years, but we're committed to it. (Martin 1996, 365–66)

This quotation by Ralph Reed, a former director of the Christian Coalition, reflects a growing concern among members of the Christian Right: race reconciliation. His description of "black, brown, yellow, white" peoples within race reconciliation also speaks to the exclusion of Native peoples when this movement first began. The race reconciliation movement presumes that both communities to be reconciled are essentially equal partners in the church. Native peoples, by contrast, were generally depicted in evangelical literature as inassimilable pagans who should be objects of Christian mission activity rather than partners within the church. While evangelicals are critical of slavery, even if they overemphasize the role they played in ending the institution, they remain blithely ignorant of the destructiveness of mission work among Indians.[1] They also seem to be unaware that in some regions of the country Indians are largely Christian. For instance, an article in *Charisma* contends that there is only one church in Tulsa, Oklahoma, that works with Indians, even though there are several in the area. The article also states that less than 1 percent of all Indians are Christian, whereas most statistics place the number between 25 and 50 percent (Grady 1994, 25–32). *World Christian* describes Indians as "Unreached Peoples," despite decades of enforced attendance in Christian boarding schools (Stewart 1985). *Moody* referred to Indians as "savages" even in the late 1980s (Scalberg and Cordell 1987),

---

[1] Barnes 2006; Daigle 1999; Fiero 1988, 22–23; Goolsby 2004; Hageman 1988, 6–7; Hoyle 1994, 3–11; Hughes 2004; "Indians Hold Historic Crusade" 1988; Justice 2000; Owens 1987, 12–17; Saint 1998; Scalberg and Cordell 1987, 55–57; Simpson 2005; Wood 2005. *World* even called the expulsion of missions from Venezuela in 2005 anti-indigenous (Dean 2005a).

and even today *World* refers to some indigenous peoples as "morally depraved" (Veith 2006a). *World* suggests that we should celebrate Andrew Jackson Day despite his Indian-hating policies of removal (Olasky 1998). George Jennings, in *Evangelical Missions Quarterly*, denounces even Navajo Christians as being under the thrall of "Satan," who continues to "work through cultural features" such as peyote (Jennings 1990, 64). As reflected in *America's Spirituality Mapped* by the charismatic megachurch pastor Dick Bernal, evangelicals are reluctant to embrace Native cultural practices because they fear such practices are "a clever scheme of Satan to seduce the naive" (Bernal n.d., 94). And according to *Faith Today*, "murder [is] a practical means of dealing with jealousies and revenge" in these Native communities (Fieguth 2002a).

Native peoples who have attempted to integrate Native culture into evangelical worship have often met with resistance. For instance, Art Begay of Warriors for Christ says that his use of Native dance in worship contributed to "one pastor's wife ask[ing] if she could cast an Indian spirit out of him" (Grady 2000b, 22). *Faith Today* ran an article that proclaimed, "Accommodation to the native belief system is not the answer. It will not bring native people to a total commitment to Jesus Christ. When people are fully liberated from the old ways, they don't want to go back" (Barnes 1989, 59). *Charisma* reports that at one Native Christian conference in Branson, Missouri, the conference brochure stipulated "no drums or feathers" (Grady 2000b, 22). Evangelicals often regard Indians as not truly Christian because as tribal peoples Indians "continue to be influenced to some degree by the animistic world view," in other words, Christian one day, primitive the next (Mumper 1986, 21).[2] *World* complained that indigenous peoples are portrayed inaccurately by liberals as suffering from "imperialism" when in fact the problem is that "Satanic spirits . . . have long gripped the primitive tribes in a web of fear, filth, witchcraft, and death," mandating that they must become "civilized" (Bomer 1996, 21). Except as the object of mission work, Native America has been almost completely invisible to the Christian Right.[3]

---

[2] See also Ankerberg and Welson 1996, 532–52; Fieguth 2002a; Larson 1989, 106–9; Maust 1985, 48–50; Maust 1992, 38; J. Moore 2004; and Newman 2004.

[3] On mission work, see Augspurger 1995; Lutes 1991; Owens 1987; and "Preschool in the Andes Highlands" 1987. In 1973, *Eternity* published a series of articles in response to the Wounded Knee takeover by the American Indian Movement (AIM). (For a description of the incident, see Appendix 1.) These articles were largely unsympathetic to AIM but did acknowledge the valid complaints Native peoples have of American colonialism. They also approvingly cited Vine Deloria's work

The major exception to the exclusion of Native peoples within race reconciliation programs is the Promise Keepers, a prominent evangelical men's ministry (Promise Keepers is discussed in more detail in chapter 3). Native people have had a fairly prominent role within Promise Keepers and are represented on its board and among its staff. The organization's rallies have consistently featured Native speakers, and a contingent of Native men opened its 1997 national gathering, the Stand in the Gap rally, with a blessing. According to Jon Lansa, the former liaison between Native communities and the Promise Keepers, over eighteen thousand Native men were formally associated with the organization as of 2000. The work of Promise Keepers in turn sparked growing visibility of Native peoples and organizations—including those that are *not* charismatic— within the new charismatic movements. Examples of charismatic and non-charismatic groups that have newfound visibility include CHIEF, Red Sea Ministries, Wiconi International, Warriors for Christ, Wesleyan Native American Ministries, Inuit Ministries International, Eagle's Wings Ministry, the World Christian Gathering of Indigenous Peoples, *Native Wind*, the Two Rivers Native American Training Center, and many others. To encourage the proliferation of these groups, the North American Institute for Indigenous Theological Studies (NAIITS) was launched, which grants masters and doctoral graduate degrees for Native leaders in the area of contextualized evangelical missions. In addition, NAIITS creates forums for dialogue and engagement with other emerging indigenous theological streams including the variety that are emerging in Native North America. NAIITS has developed partnerships with Asbury Theological Seminary in Wilmore, Kentucky as well as several denominational and non-denominational organizations, colleges, and seminaries ("A Perilous Venture" 2006).[4] Many prominent Native leaders are either involved in these programs or earning graduate degrees thorough Asbury Semi-

---

(Jones 1973; "Who Are the 'Indian Givers'?" 1973). In a forum on Wounded Knee and the future of Indian missions, *Eternity* did not include any Native peoples. Some of the participants were more sympathetic to Native peoples than others, but one participant, Glen Bradford, the former director of Indian missions for the American Baptist Church basically supported termination policies for Indian reservations: "Traditional Indian missions will last only as long as the present reservation structure pertains, possibly another generation and a half, or two generations in some areas. Ultimately, these traditional ministries will be done away with, because our Indian people will eventually merge with our society" (Phipps et al. 1973, 23).

4 See also NAIITS website at http://www.firstnationsmonday.com/NAIITS/about .htm.

nary, including Richard Twiss of Wiconi International, Randy Woodley of Eagle's Wings Ministry, and Terry LeBlanc (Uttley 2005).

The Promise Keepers has gone through many ups and downs in its history. Participation in Promise Keepers rallies peaked in 1996, and at the 1997 Stand in the Gap rally it brought close to one hundred thousand men together in an event that prominently featured race reconciliation (Bruce 1997b). Promise Keepers expected to raise enough money from Stand in the Gap to support its ministry through 1998, but its donations barely covered the cost of the rally itself ("We're in This Together" 1998). It also attempted to reach out to unsaved men by not charging admission to their rallies, but this failed to attract new constituents while catastrophically decreasing Promise Keepers' revenues (Christianity Today 1998; Kellner 2000; Plowman 1998b). In 1998, the organization downsized from a staff of four hundred and a budget of 117 million dollars to a staff of ninety-six and a budget of 30 million dollars (Maxwell 2000, 27). Promise Keepers also canceled plans to hold rallies at state capitals in 2000 (No-Comment Zone 1999). According to one prominent evangelical pollster, George Barna, despite the popularity of the Promise Keepers movements in the 1990s, church membership among men actually dropped (Andrescik 2000b; Morley 2000).

Judging from my participation in the 2004 and 2005 Promise Keepers conferences, race reconciliation, particularly among non–African American men of color, figures significantly less prominently than it did in the late 1990s, and so Native peoples seem to figure much less prominently in the Promise Keepers.[5] However, the space it has created for Native peoples within primarily charismatic Christianity remains. For example, *Charisma* now regularly features articles on Native peoples. Of course there are many Native conservative Christians within the Southern Baptist and other noncharismatic evangelical and fundamentalist denominations, but

[5] In 1996, Promise Keepers prioritized race reconciliation, and 30 percent of its staff members were people of color (1 percent were Native American). At a 1996 New York gathering, 25 percent of attendees were African Americans (Olsen 1997). The organization still holds rallies across the country with smaller numbers of participants and now charges admission, but the theme of race reconciliation does not figure as prominently as it did prior to 1998 (Guthrie 2003). In fact, the organization's founder Bill McCartney suggested that Promise Keepers has already accomplished race reconciliation (Horner 2002). For a more extended analysis of the Promise Keepers and race reconciliation, see my *The Christian Right and Race Reconciliation* (forthcoming).

they figure much less prominently in white-dominated fundamentalist or neo-evangelical venues. To the extent that they do appear, charismatic Native peoples are usually shown participating in a broader neo-evangelical event. For instance, in 2004 many Native leaders were featured prominently for the first time at the Fifty-Seventh Urbana conference (Uttley 2004a), the Intervarsity-sponsored conference that brings together tens of thousands of students every three years. Also, some non-charismatic Native leaders such as Tom Claus have gained increasing prominence through charismatic venues such as Promise Keepers. Billy Graham and his son Franklin featured a Native American night at their 1998 crusade in Albuquerque (Gardner 1998). Native peoples have also broken into the world of televangelism. God's Learning Channel features a Native-oriented show hosted by Jay Swallow and Negiel Bigpond from the Two Rivers Native American Training Center. Together they have begun a project to put a direct-to-home satellite system in every Native American Community Center on every reservation in the United States and Canada.[6] Testifying to the increased prominence of Native pastors, particularly within charismatic venues, *Charisma* published an article on the Assiniboin pastor Dobie Weasel, who became the first Native American to lead a multiethnic Assemblies of God congregation (in Omaha, Nebraska) (Meers 2000). Within more charismatic venues, Native peoples have recently begun to figure much more prominently as spokespersons rather than simply as objects of mission activity. However, as James Treat's *Around the Sacred Fire* demonstrates, this trend has precursors such as the organizing of Native Christians to work with tribal traditionals in order to stimulate cultural revival and unity among Native nations through the Indian Ecumenical Conference of the 1970s (Treat 2003).[7] The work of these groups and individuals generally predates that of the Promise Keepers. Tom Claus, for instance, began preaching in the 1940s, began collaborating with Billy Graham in the 1960s, wrote books in the 1970s (including *On Eagles' Wings* [1976]), and founded CHIEF in 1975. Yet today the new Charismatic movement has given him greater prominence that ever before. It is also important not to *overestimate* the influence of Promise Keepers. Many of these groups that had previous affiliations with

[6] See www.godslearningchannel.com.

[7] Prophetically, *Missiology* ran an article on this movement, documented by Treat, which called on evangelicals to begin paying more attention to Native Christian movements. It also contended that all Native Christian movements have "deeply anti-imperialist ideologies at their roots" (Starkloff 1985, 98).

Promise Keepers no longer do, and some never did affiliate with Promise Keepers. Still, its popularity as a movement rooted in New Charismatism provided a space for increased visibility for many Native groups, including those that are not charismatic.

Before examining the theoretical production of Native peoples in the race reconciliation movement, I must stress the diversity of thought within this movement. In fact, many of these ministries are in ideological conflict with each other. While there are common positions often espoused by these evangelical leaders, one cannot assume that they all hold the same position. Thus, in this intellectual ethnography, I am presenting many of the ideas that are circulating within this movement, broadly speaking, without attempting to assess the work of any particular individual or ministry.

NATIVE PEOPLE WITHIN THE NEW CHARISMATIC MOVEMENTS: PERFORMING WHITENESS

The Promise Keepers movement is rooted in the New Charismatic movement, particularly since its leaders are associated with the Vineyard Church. Key Vineyard characteristics that are shared by the Promise Keepers include engagement with the Holy Spirit, emphasis on the experiential transformation of individuals, and avoidance of large, bureaucratic structures (Maxwell 1997). The result is that sometimes it does not have the support of traditional African American denominations since its African American leadership does not come from them (Maxwell 1997). But its base in the Charismatic movement does help explain why it is one of the more multicultural organizations.

Donald Miller sheds some light on why Native peoples are prominent within the new charismatic denominations in particular. He notes that a defining feature of these movements is the adaptation of Christianity to the surrounding culture. He quotes the prominent charismatic leader Greg Laurie, who explains the strategy: "If they [nonbelievers] are going to reject the message I preach, let them reject it, but let them reject the message and not all the peripheral things that are secondary" (Miller 1997, 66). Thus, music at church services tends to feature popular rock rather than old-time hymns. Congregants and even pastors wear casual clothing rather than their "Sunday best." These movements attempt to distinguish between what they see as the central message of Christianity and the

outward forms Christianity might take. As a result, the majority of recruits into denominations such as Vineyard come from nonevangelical
backgrounds (Perrin, Kennedy, and Miller 1997; Perrin and Mauss 1991).

This strategy has provoked much criticism from other evangelical and
fundamentalist denominations, which charge that New Charismatics have
sold out the gospel message to secular culture. Many Native evangelicals,
however, see an opportunity for intervention in these New Charismatic
movements. If it is legitimate to incorporate the secular "white" culture
into worship, then it must be acceptable to incorporate Native culture
as well. Leaders attempt such incorporation in a variety of ways: holding Christian powwows, adapting ceremonial songs by adding Christian
words, using the drum in services, wearing regalia during services, and so
on (Dixon 2006; Francis 1997; Grady 2004a; Gruszka 1997; Huckins 2000;
Steinken 1998; Stewart 2000; Suuqina 2000; Twiss 2000b, 2000c; Woodley
2000). *Indian Life* publishes Red Eagle comic books, which are designed
to teach Native youths how they can retain their Native culture while
remaining faithful to Christ. In one issue, a character named Dawn is
crushed by the suicide of her brother. His last words to her are, "Indian
things don't matter anymore." Dawn descends into alcoholism until her
cousin rescues her and shows her that "Indian things" do in fact matter and
are in harmony with the saving power of Jesus Christ (Opops'kan and Dog
1991). Warriors for Christ organized a dance troupe that tours on the powwow circuit, spreading the gospel message through powwowlike dance
(Warriors for Christ 1996). Working in collaboration, these ministries
host Culture, Christ, and Kingdom seminars throughout the United States
and Canada to promote the synthesis of Native cultural practices and
Christianity. Their argument is that these Native "forms" do not alter the
basic "message" of Christianity (Twiss 1996).

To avoid charges of religious syncretism, these Native leaders appeal to
white Christians for inclusion by arguing that Native culture can be separated from spirituality. That is, it is okay to incorporate Native cultural
practices to the extent that these practices do not import "pagan" or
"antibiblical" spirituality into the Christian message.[8] (Of course, Native

[8] Bledderus 1997; *Indian Life* 1993; Cowan 1991; Enns 2000; Fuller 1996; Goolsby
1999; Jacobs 2000a; T. LeBlanc 1997; Ward 1995. One exception to this mandate to
separate pagan from Christian spiritual practices is an article published in *International Review of Mission*, which espouses a "two-path journey" that rejects "the
polemic of syncretism" and "affirms the spirituality and identity of aboriginal culture." It also "challenges the Western essentialism and universalism that seeks con-
sistency and does not tolerate apparent contradiction" (Ferguson 1998, 385).

evangelicals are not in consensus about which practices are acceptable.) Richard Twiss explains.

> We must guard against syncretism and not allow the blending of native religion and historical Christian faith. We must make a crystal clear distinction between theological and cultural blending or mixing. Theological syncretism is in direct contradiction of Biblical truth, and cultural blending is a normal fact of everyday life. . . . As Native leaders it is we who must be careful that we do not allow an emphasis on subjective personal experience and not solid biblical theology, to lead us to an unfounded fear of "syncretism" among ourselves. . . . When we try to artificially separate Native believers from their cultural practices and traditions, we are actually denying God's creative handiwork in us. (1998, 16–17)

At the 1999 Culture, Christ, and Kingdom conference, a position statement by the Native American Fellowship of the Assemblies of God (written October 31, 1998, Albuquerque) was distributed that stipulates which Native practices are acceptable. The following are some excerpts.

> To attempt to mix Native religion with Christianity is contrary to scripture, and therefore is to be avoided. Native religious practices that are contrary to scripture must be renounced and forsaken. It must always yield to the authority of scripture.
>
> Cultural practices must be separated from practices that stem from Native religion. All Native religious cultural practices must be avoided.
>
> Dances, instruments, songs, regalia, and language may be used to express praise and worship to the Lord.
>
> Names given by parents should be accepted and honored. No one should be discouraged from giving their children Native names.
>
> Pow-wows, and Indian celebrations. The purpose for attending these events must be evangelism.
>
> Medicine men and other so-called spiritual guides. Jesus Christ must be kept as the prominent figure in life. . . . All "mediators" must not be consulted in spiritual matters.

The problem with this rationale is that it is simply not true to either Native culture or spirituality; the two cannot be separated (Deloria 1992; Weaver 1997). Within Native communities, they are always inextricably linked because spiritual practices are not separate from everyday life. The habit of "respecting" Native culture while simultaneously condemning Native spirituality contributes to a spiritual-cultural practice that inevitably pits Native Christians against traditionals. First, while aspects of Native culture are incorporated into Christian practices, Native religions in general are condemned as "animistic" or "pagan" (Anonymous 1992; Indian Life Ministries 1999, 60–61; Craig Smith 1997, 21). One selling point of New Charismatic traditions in comparison to other Christian denominations is that New Charismatics emphasize gifts of the spirit and spiritual warfare, thereby acknowledging the power of Native spiritual traditions. As Craig Smith, a pastor with the Christian and Missionary Alliance, notes, not all spiritual practices are used for good; they can also be used as bad medicine against someone. Rather than dismissing the fear that might result if someone were the object of bad medicine, Charismatic traditions in particular do not question these spiritual powers but contend that the spirit of Jesus Christ is superior to the power of any traditional spiritual practice (Salway 1990, 58; Craig Smith 1997, 21; Ward 1994, 133–66). For instance, a Native evangelical, Gordon Thayer, from Lac Courte Oreilles, said he was harassed by dark spirits until he accepted Christ and burned "his Native American spirit paraphernalia" (Piper 2001). Attendees at the World Christian Gathering of Indigenous Peoples, held in the Black Hills of South Dakota in 1998, took a "strong stand when they came against the strongman of native religions such as shamanism, animism and totemism" ("Christian Indigenous Peoples Gather to Worship the Greatest Chief" 1998, 8). Furthermore, because worshipping Jesus is the only appropriate strategy for spiritual battles, even traditional practices that are healing are condemned as demonic or idolatrous (Dixon 2006; Indian Life Ministries 1999, 39). Native evangelicals, while embracing some aspects of Native culture, also wholeheartedly condemn many practices that are fundamental to Native community life such as peyote and sun dances (Indian Life Ministries 1999). They do not all agree on what is acceptable; some condemn sweat lodges and naming ceremonies, for instance, while others do not. Some take part in such ceremonies as a regular part of their spiritual practice. But they are all clear on this principle: "A line must be drawn on what is permissible and what is clearly defined in Scripture as against the principles of the Kingdom of God" (Indian Life Ministries 1999, 42–43, 55; see also Craig Smith 1997, 124).

It is important to note, however, that in a follow up meeting I had with Richard Twiss and Randy Woodley (May 9, 2007), they pointed out to me that some Native evangelical writings that critique syncretism are strategic. That is, they are written to be persuasive specifically to evangelicals who might reject the inclusion of *all* Native cultural practices within Christianity. In fact, some Native evangelicals do not separate Native spirituality and Native culture and do not see the practice of traditional Native spirituality as a contradiction to Christianity. Evidence for this argument can be seen in Richard Twiss's revision of his previous statement on syncretism. Now, the revised version of the same document states, "As native leaders, it is we who must be careful that we do not allow biblical ignorance to lead us to an unfounded fear of syncretism among ourselves. We must prevent . . . syncretism from becoming an emotionally defined standard for a type of modern day inquisition to root and burn out of Native Christians any ties to their culture and tradition. When we do this we are basically denying God's handiwork in us. It says we cannot see the design or plan of God in our cultural identities as First Nations people" (Twiss 2002, 71). Here his concern has shifted from the fear that Native cultural and spiritual practices might be syncretistic to the fear that the charge of syncretism is policing Native spiritual and cultural practice in Christianity. In this revision, he identifies the problem, not with Native spirituality, but with the racism of Eurocentric versions of Christianity.

The stated rationale for the incorporation of cultural practices into Christian worship is to facilitate the missionization of Native peoples (Barnes 1989), a process that ultimately erodes the spiritual and cultural foundations of traditional Native communities. One letter written by a Native reader of *Charisma* asserts that racism must stop or else "Native Americans will not get saved" (Letters 1999a, 10). George Kallappa, of the Assemblies of God Native Christian Resource Center in Mesa, Arizona, drafted a document for his denomination in 2000 that endorses the use of Native culture "for purposes of worship and evangelism," not because Native culture has value of its own (Grady 2000b). Craig Smith suggests that Native peoples in the United States and Canada need to be incorporated into Christianity in order to facilitate the missionization of indigenous peoples in other parts of the world. Native peoples, he contends, more easily evade the "imperialist American" label and thus more successfully convert other indigenous peoples (1997, 106). Interestingly, this logic underpins a *Charisma* article on Judy Shaw, a black Pentecostal who started a mission outreach program on the Crow Creek Sioux reservation in South Dakota with the thought that Indians might trust her more than white people since they have both "endured hardship at the hand of the white man" (Lowe 1997, 24). Ironically, Native peoples (and other people of color) are used in the service of U.S. imperialism to missionize other indigenous peoples, who belong to "the most vicious and horrible tribes on earth" (Kikawa 1994, 27). The mission of the Two Rivers Native American Training Center in Bixby, Oklahoma, is to support "a Christian military training base camp for the purpose of dealing with occult and territorial enemy strongholds on the reservations."[9] Richard Twiss notes that "no other people group is as uniquely positioned for world evangelism" (2001). This "colonizing trick" promises Native peoples the ability to be equal partners with white Christians in the Christian civilizing mission. Paradoxically, however, the special vocation proffered Native peoples in evangelizing other indigenous peoples is premised on fundamental racial and cultural difference. Borrowing from David Kazanjian's analysis, the "universal" subject of evangelical Christianity is necessarily constituted through both national and racial differentiation and subjection (2003).[10]

Randy Woodley goes so far as to say that missions to Native peoples should adopt the "Muslims for Jesus" and "Jews for Jesus" approach to mission work (Berger n.d.). These ministries try to assert that one can "follow Christ" without being a Christian and hence can still call oneself a Muslim or Jew. In the Native context, Woodley asserts that "the term *Christian* is not the good news we intend it to mean. Rather, it is the bad news of colonialism, oppression and even genocide" (2001, 53). He recommends that, rather than embracing Christianity, Native peoples simply "follow Jesus" (52). Similarly, *Native Wind,* a newspaper focused on missionizing to Native peoples, holds that we should avoid terms such as *Christianity* and focus on Jesus (De Marco 1997). This mission work seems to disavow its own project; one can missionize Native peoples without admitting that this is what one is doing. Similarly, Bonnie Sue Lewis, a missionary to Native communities in the Presbyterian Church, advocates that Christians abandon "white missionary privilege" without abandoning missions (2004). If white people train Native peoples to do mission work, it is possible to disavow missions as a project of whiteness. However, it is worth noting that this appeal to mission work can also be strategic, as I will discuss later in the chapter. In addition, some of these evangelical leaders, such as Randy Woodley, Richard Twiss, and others, would argue that their ministries are *not* mission-based. Rather, they are an attempt to demonstrate to Native peoples that there are alternative ways to express Christian faith that are not so complicit in colonialism.

With the adoption of Christianity comes the adoption of male supremacist and heterosexist ideologies based on biblical mandates to condemn

[9] See http://www.2-rivers.com/2Riv—Staff.htm.
[10] Kazanjian analyzes the African colonization movement in particular, but his analysis applies to evangelical Native peoples as well.

homosexuality and support male headship in the church and home (Indian Life Ministries 1999, 19; Parker 1999, 14; Craig Smith 1997, 136; Ward 1994, 33–64). A particularly disturbing story illustrating this point involves the testimony of one Native woman who had problems with her second husband because he was abusive to a child she had by another man. Because she felt that the Bible required her to stay with her husband and submit to his headship, she gave away her son, as she believed was mandated by the Bible. This testimony is described not as a tragedy but as a sign of God's love (Ward 1994, 76–77). Furthermore, as many scholars have noted, Native communities were generally not structured on a strict binary gender system or male dominance prior to colonization. Christian missionization has oppressed Native women and Native peoples who do not fit into heteropatriarchally prescribed genders (Allen 1986; Anderson 1991; Jacobs, Thomas, and Lang 1999; Medicine 1993; Perdue 1999; Pesantubbee 2005; Shoemaker 1995). Ironically, evangelical discourse often asserts that Christianity liberates rather than oppresses Native women, making issues of gender oppression within a Christian context even more difficult to challenge (Zoba 1997). The recent bans on same-sex marriages passed by several tribal councils certainly speak to the dangers of a heteronormative religious ideology within Native communities.[11] Interestingly, the Native response within this discourse to a heteronormative, white, Christian America has sometimes been a heteronormative Native nationalism. It is important to note, however, that not all Native evangelicals support heteropatriarchal ideologies. Within evangelical discourse, there is often not space to directly critique homophobia, but one cannot necessarily presume from this silence that all Native evangelicals oppose homosexuality and support patriarchy. I explore these issues—particularly alternative articulations of Native nationalisms—more fully in chapter 5.

Because Native Christians are forced to say that the practices they are willing to embrace have no spiritual content, they are not obligated to

[11] On April 22, 2005, the Navajo Tribal Council passed the Dine Marriage Act of 2005, which prohibits same-sex marriage in the Navajo nation. However, on May 1, Navajo president Joe Shirley Jr. vetoed the act, saying that while he "strongly supports family stability," it "said nothing about domestic violence, sexual assault and gangs on the Navajo Nation—problems that are rampant" (Associated Press 2005). In turn, the tribal council voted to override the veto on June 3, 2005 (Aguayo 2005). The Cherokee Nation of Oklahoma also passed a ban on same-sex marriage on June 13, 2005, after a lesbian couple obtained a marriage license from the Cherokee tribe (Previch 2005). These policies are being challenged by Native organizations such as the Two-Spirit Press Room, headed by Richard LaFortune.

respect traditional protocols for engaging in them. For instance, because Indian names are not generally given to non-Indians, many traditionals would be horrified to witness naming ceremonies, common in these circles, in which non-Natives are given names by Native people. The process of naming is inextricably linked to histories of kinship; it is not a random process and not appropriate for non-Indians, who are not part of these histories. As Betty Cooper complains in the film *White Shamen, Plastic Medicine Men*, "Indian names come from a very honored place, from a family carrying on its tradition through its name. We don't just pluck names out of the sky" (Native Voices Public Television 1995).

In addition to the problem of bestowing names on non-Indians, Native leaders often do not concern themselves with whether they have the proper "credentials" to perform these ceremonies in a traditional context. Legitimacy that might be granted within a traditional context becomes unimportant; any Christian leader who receives an insight from "God" is entitled to perform these ceremonies because they are devoid of spiritual content anyway. Sammy Toineeta, a Native activist and interviewee, describes the tensions between traditionals and Christians who appropriate traditional practices in the service of Christianity.

> Christians now think that they're more understanding, more tolerant, and more accepting of our ways. They're not. . . . It's really a kind of spiritual racism. It's kind of condescending, but they don't see it. The struggle is always going to be there. The Christians are always going to think that their God is the real God. That all the rest of them are idols or copies or cheap imitations. . . . Even the work I do with other Indians who are Christian. And they're trying really hard to be more accepting. They don't want to get into it. They want to stand on the edge, and say we're accepting. They want to stand on the edge and say we believe the same you believe with the sacred pipe. Or believe the same you believe about the sweat lodge, or we believe the same you believe about the water. But they don't really want to immerse themselves or involve themselves in it. So, they think they've done it. I see a lot of ministers who've done it. But it's never quite right. . . .
>
> There's a minister in Oklahoma, and he has a drum in his church, and he uses cedar for smudging. . . . He thinks he's doing a big thing, and at the end he takes the blanket and spreads it on the floor and asks people to drop their tithe, and then he brags that the offering has gone up from $500 to $1200 a month. That's not the purpose of doing those things. So you have this man who probably grew up as a white man, and suddenly found he was an Indian when he was in seminary or something. And he's using these things, and he

thinks he's being respectful. He thinks he's not charging people, but he is. His expectation of how much they're going to give to the church has grown. That's charging. That's a different way of charging.

George Tinker, a Lutheran pastor and theologian (Osage) similarly argues, "The gospel of this christianizing process is not Jesus but the euroamerican Christian cultural value of individualism with its embedded capitalist propensities" (2004, 63).

To further illustrate the conflict, several Native evangelical organizations came together to hold a Christian powwow in conjunction with a Christ, Culture and the Kingdom seminar held in Pasadena, California on July 25, 1999. In response, one attendee wrote an angry letter to *News from Indian Country* denouncing the powwow as akin to the New Age appropriation of Native culture. This complaint seems justified as today white evangelicals have even begun appropriating Native spirituality. *Charisma* reported on one event in 2000 where a white man, Charles Schmidt, began a service in fringe and moccasins, beating a drum, and saying "I am not a white man" (Grady 2000b). Another *Charisma* article reported on a white pastor, Frank Armistead, who utilizes the sweat lodge, smudging, and "Native designs" in his workshops. "I use what enriches my faith," he asserts (Armistead 2000). And the 2004 Promise Keepers rally evoked the ideology of the vanishing Native by appropriating a Maori dance, the *haka*, which all participants were asked to perform. A video showed Maori people doing the haka while a voice-over declares, "That was *then* [as if Maori people have disappeared]. This is *now*," at which point the video switched to a football game. This is not to suggest that Native evangelicals support non-Native appropriation of Native culture and spirituality. In fact, many, such as Randy Woodley, explicitly condemn such appropriative practices. Still, it is possible that these performances can potentially and unwittingly encourage appropriation, even if that is not the intent of Native evangelicals themselves.

This kind of multicultural practice carries with it the problems of liberal appropriations that often take place under the rubric of multiculturalism, specifically, obliviousness to the colonial power relations that structure the interaction of cultures. Lisa Lowe sheds some light on additional problems of this kind of multicultural practice. She argues that multicultural performances tend to sever these performances from their histories and communities. The result is that these performances become tamed and homogenized. "Each performance tradition [is] equated with every other," she writes, "and its meaning [is] reduced and generalized to a common denominator whose significance [is] the exotic" (1996, 89). In another performance of Native culture identity, a tipi was erected at the Promise Keepers Stand in the Gap rally held in Washington, D.C., in October, 1997 (Bruce 1997b). The tipi was to be representative of all Native cultures, despite the fact that it is not used by most Native tribes. After singing a Muscogee hymn, Huron Claus (Tom Claus's son) seemed to minimize the importance of indigenous languages by assuring white attendees that we all speak "one language." Much of the literature produced by various ministries is geared toward providing detribalized "Indian" versions of various Christian prayers, Bible verses, and so on. The Indian version of the Lord's Prayer, authored by Tom Claus, reads, "Our Father, up in the sky, your name is the most Holy of all. Gather your tribe from the four winds and come be our Chief here on earth like you are in the sky. Give us corn to make bread each day. Have pity on us when we do wrong and help us to pity others when they do wrong to us. Lead us away from enemy territory and deliver us from his attacks. Keep your tribe by your great power and lead us into our shining presence forever. Amen" (Gowan 1997, 96).

Woodley adopts a pan-Indian Christian approach by attempting to paraphrase the Bible into Indian slang. The promotional material for this project that was handed out at the 1999 Culture, Christ, and Kingdom conference states, "For the first time portions of God's Word will be available in a vernacular that many Native Americans can understand. It is a combination of English with common Indian phrasiologies and colloquialisms—in other words 'Rez talk.'" This project gives the impression that all Native peoples live on the same reservation and speak the same language, which sounds remarkably like English. Here is a sample "rez talk" translation of Genesis 1:1–3: "Before anything else was—Great Spirit created the world above and mother earth. Mother earth had no shape and had nothing to give, it was dark over the great waters, and the Sacred Spirit of Creator was flying over the waters. And Great Spirit said, 'Here is light,' and there was light."

This kind of gesture toward inclusion of Indian culture erases the distinct cultures of each indigenous nation, undermining claims to specific nationhood. Such performances of Native identity are problematic because Native tribal cultures generally come from specific land bases. Cultural preservation has a material dimension. When Native cultures become homogenized into Indian culture, there is no need to maintain the land base from which specific Native cultures issue. In their defense, some

Native evangelicals might argue that pan-Indian performances might provide an entry point for urban-based Native peoples to learn more about their specific tribal traditions. In addition, they might contend that because of the processes of urbanizations, there may well be a pan-tribal culture to which those Native peoples who did not live in their home communities relate.

As Lowe notes, when exotic signifiers become homogenized through multiculturalism, whiteness inevitably remains in the center (1996, 90). Similarly, the performances of race reconciliation within Promise Keepers events are always between white people and people of color. There is never a discussion of the relationships between communities of color. White people remain central in this project. Furthermore, the politics of multiculturalism tends to separate cultural representation from material realities. The power dynamics between dominant and marginalized cultures are obscured in this discourse of pluralism (86).

A similar analysis can be made of the Native "performances" at Promise Keepers events. While the Promise Keepers apologize for broken treaties, they make no reference to continuing treaty claims. A plethora of rituals are enacted in which white people apologize at length for various past genocidal acts committed against Native peoples. Examples include the Cherokee Prayer Initiative, which involved Native and white Christians visiting Cherokee massacre sites and praying for repentance and reconciliation (Harmon 1999); an Arkansas City, Kansas, meeting to "heal the land," which focused on Cherokees who were displaced from their homes during the infamous Cherokee Land Run in Kansas and Oklahoma (Bonham 2005); the Operation Restoration prayer expedition of 1996, in which participants repented for massacres of American Indians and southern slavery (Blair-Mitchell 1997); and the campaign to apologize for the "unjust killings of Mohawk Indians" in upstate New York (Greco 1997). In these events, one sees little discussion of how white people can act in solidarity with Native struggles today. They seem to offer an easy resolution to the continuing legacy of genocide: in return for apologies for past atrocities, Native evangelicals tacitly promise not to bring up current acts of genocide, not to become adversarial, and not to significantly alter the terms of white evangelical discourse. In short, they do not say anything that significantly challenges the political or economic privileges of whites or makes them very uncomfortable. This focus on racism at the micro-rather than the macrolevel also shifts evangelical discourse on social ills in Native communities from a focus on colonialism to a focus on the supposed inherent dysfunctionality within them. Native communities are depicted as having inexplicably high suicide and substance abuse rates that are not connected to colonialism. Accepting Christ then becomes the only solution to these ills (Dean 2005b; Fieguth 2000a; Huckins 2000; Tiansay 2005).

One Promise Keeper. Jeff King, declares his allegiance to America and Christianity in his essay "The American Indian: The Invisible Man." He describes himself as an assimilated child of a military family. He says that he does not know his language and was called "white boy" by his Muscogee relatives because his father is white (1995, 80). He calls on all American Indian men to model Christ by forgiving and reconciling with their white Christian brothers and to let go of the bitterness incurred by five hundred years of genocide. Craig Smith, while arguing that white Christians need to back up their apologies for genocide with action, suggests that the first thing whites need to do is more aggressively evangelize Native peoples (1997, 59). *Indian Life* typically advises readers to forgive abusers and the perpetrators of racism unconditionally, regardless of whether the abusers express remorse for their actions (Indian Life Ministries 1999, 11, 94–95; "Native Americans Find Peace in Promise Keepers" 1997). In fact, the magazine explicitly states in one article that the point of forgiveness is to "let them off the hook" (Indian Life Ministries 1999, 15). The evangelical James Skeet suggests that the proper response to the continuing history of broken treaties and stolen lands is not restoration of the land to Indian peoples because reconciliation does not take place on "a socio-economic level but on a spiritual level" (2000). Tom Claus stated at one Promise Keepers rally that he would "rather have Jesus than all the land in the U.S." (Clarkson 1996, 16). At Stand in the Gap, he declared, "I'm proud to be Indian by race, I am *more* proud to be Christian by grace." At the same event, Ross Maracle (Mohawk) stated that while he used to raise his hand for Red Power he now says "without anger" that he has been saved by the power of the blood of Jesus. In an article for *Faith Today*, he decries the colonial practices of Canada that resulted in the Oka crisis of 1990. But his solution to the crisis is increased Native-led missionary work in Native communities (1991). Tom Bee, the founder of the 1970s music group XIT,whose music supported the Red Power movement, defended the repressive policies of Israel against Palestine on the July 16 episode of *Light of the Southwest* on God's Learning Channel.

The history of genocide is often articulated problematically as well. In many conversion stories, the destructive legacy of Christian boarding schools is attributed to Roman Catholics or nonevangelical Protestants, who are defined as not really Christian, leaving Christian evangelicalism unaccountable for this history (Salway 1990, 23; Tanis 1996, 55).[12] Daniel Kikawa goes so far as to argue that Native Hawai'ians followed the Christian God until they were colonized by other Pacific Islanders. White missionaries did not colonize Native Hawai'ians but liberated them to follow their original spiritual practices. Native Hawai'ian spirituality thereby becomes colonial and Christianity becomes indigenous (1994).

Another problem with these acts of reconciliation is that they are always bilateral: while white peoples repent for genocide, Native peoples must also repent for their bitterness about genocide (Aldred 1997; Rascher 1995; Craig Smith 1997, 39). In fact, Native representatives from twenty tribes gathered at Plymouth Rock to "repent for their peoples' unforgiveness of white Americans for hundreds of years of oppression against them" (Hutchinson 2002b). Jay Swallow (Southern Cheyenne) said, "I repent for myself for my people for every tribe for turning our back on Your Son, Jesus Christ. Our people turned our backs on the gospel that the white man brought to America. We have used broken treaties and broken promises and so many other excuses. Today, we have come to repent, to start the healing today" (Hutchinson 2002b). This dynamic suggests that both communities are equally to blame for the conditions of white supremacy. In essence, racism becomes articulated as a problem of personal prejudice from which both parties suffer rather than as an institutional set of practices from which one community benefits at the expense of the other.

In addition, as I discuss elsewhere, there appears to be an inverse relationship between the political focus of evangelical writers and organizations and the depth of their race analysis (A. Smith, forthcoming). That is, the more involved an individual or organization is in the political process the less likely it is to call for sweeping social responses to racism. A group such as the Christian Coalition, which is heavily involved in the political process, never discusses institutional racism. Promise Keepers does—at least it did in its early history—but it is not explicitly involved in the electoral process. Consequently, the evangelical rhetoric concerning race reconciliation that does exist inevitably depoliticizes issues of race so that they become personal rather than an institutional.

One example is a *Christianity Today* article on the involvement of

[12] *Christianity Today* did not frame residential schools in Canada with such a distanced perspective, but then it was also not that sympathetic to the movement for restitution for Native residential school survivors (Simpson 2005).

ministry groups in the campaign over five hundred missing Aboriginal women in Canada, particularly Vancouver. Native women's organizations in Canada have been campaigning to call attention to hundreds of murdered Native women, many of whom are sex workers, as well as the failure of the police to address these murders. This article never mentions that the murdered women were aboriginal, simply that they are prostitutes in need of services, thus erasing the gender and racial politics of the campaign (Fieguth 2002b).

Finally, as Craig Smith notes, it is important to understand how Native ministries replicate the colonial structures of the United States and Canada. That is, much more than other racial or ethnic "minority" church or parachurch organizations, Native ministries are controlled by non-Indians (1997, 41). Indian Life Ministries, for example, which publishes many of the works by these writers, is run primarily by white people. The writings are filtered through non-Indian authors. The audiences of two of the gatherings I attended in Southern California were dominated by non-Indians who seemed primarily interested in acquiring tips on how to more successfully missionize Indian peoples. As a result, untangling the agenda of Native evangelicals from their non-Indian benefactors is a difficult job.

NATIVE PEOPLE WITHIN THE NEW CHARISMATIC MOVEMENTS: CONTESTING WHITENESS

While Native charismatics seem to "perform whiteness," they resist it as well. As R. W. Connell notes, hegemony is never complete (1995, 37). And, as Lowe argues, the introduction of the Other into a national or religious discourse does not necessarily lead to the Other's embrace of the fiction of inclusion (1996, 47).

According to the art historian Carolyn Dean, attempts to assimilate Native peoples within Christianity both consecrate inequality and carry the threat of disorder for the dominant culture (1999, 50). That is, the inclusion of racial or cultural Others in European forms of Christianity fundamentally threatens to reshape the nature of Christianity.

As was mentioned in chapter 1, the literary scholar Katherine Boone argues in *The Bible Tells Them So* that evangelicalism claims to be a discourse unaffected by social realities. That is, evangelicals claim to be speaking only biblical truth, repeating the inerrant word of God (1989, 89). If this were so, then all peoples interpellated into evangelical culture would share similar religious understandings. However, as Steven Seidman notes, "Because the self is always interpellated in many discourses and practices, she is said to occupy contradictory psychic and social positions and identities—in principle, making possible opposition to dominant ideologies. . . . The self is assumed to be socially and historically produced and positioned in contradictory ways to structures of domination and hierarchy" (1997, 73).

The result of people of color being integrated into white evangelicalism while simultaneously being rooted in nonwhite cultural practices is that this reshapes the terms of evangelical discourse. Many evangelical writers anxiously note that the result of bringing people of color and people from the Third World into the "Christian nation" is that "whites comprise only about 40 percent of all Christians, and . . . the center of Christianity . . . has shifted to the Southern World, to Asia, Africa and Latin America. . . . The third millennium will be shaped largely by the Southern Church" (Greenway 1989, 4). This anxiety underscores the social construction of white evangelicalism: if evangelical discourse were simply grounded in eternal truth, then it would not be affected by the inclusion of people of color. However, threatened by possible discursive shifts, evangelicals argue that Western missionaries train indigenous missionaries to eschew the dangers of "syncretism, cults, and false teaching" (Kendall 1988, 221).[13]

Consequently, evangelicals are constantly on guard against racial Others who threaten to shift the meanings of evangelicalism. For instance, one Promise Keepers rally featured a naming ceremony, to the great chagrin of many fundamentalists: One article opined, "In keeping with the spirit of paganism, Promise Keepers has a group of Cherokee Indians walk 168 miles from North Carolina to perform a name-giving ceremony. Since the highest honor that an Indian can receive is a name, the Indian's Chief conferred names on Randy Phillips and Bill McCartney. . . . Both were honored with an Indian Headdress, a poem was read called 'No More Broken Treaties,' and a former Indian Medicine Man, Peter Gray Eyes,

[13] This perceived threat may explain the huge controversy over Chung Hyun-Kyung's presentation at the World Council of Churches in 1991, where she was charged with exhibiting "a tendency toward syncretism with non-Christian churches" (Padilla 1991, 4). A recent call for papers in the western region of the Evangelical Theological Society (ETS) on the topic of racial and ethnic diversity was titled, "How Far Is Too Far?" The theme of the national ETS conference in 2001 was, "The Boundaries of Evangelicalism." However, the conference focused primarily on the "heresy" of open theism (the notion that God does not have foreknowledge of all future events).

prayed over Phillips and McCartney. What will PK come up with next?" (BDM 1997, 9).

Similarly, an anti-charismatic fundamentalist Web site, Deception in the Church, denounces this entire movement and the people involved in it, including Richard Twiss, Terry LeBlanc, and Daniel Kikawa.

> When you mythologize religion and ignore the clear teachings of the Bible, as above, in order to make people feel better about themselves and their cultures, you are effectively preaching another gospel. If what Richard Twiss and Daniel Kiwawa and a host of others teach is true, then there was no need for Jesus Christ to die on the cross for sin. According to them all cultures, and even religions, already had ways to redemption built in by God Himself. But they forget that without Christ every man will be judged by their works, and therefore they cannot be saved. (Simpson 2005)

It then asserts that the Native peoples in this movement "will be punished with everlasting destruction" (Simpson 2005). What Dean says about the missionization of the Incas holds true for evangelical Natives in American society, for these performances "established the colonizers as inherently and naturally superior, properly and necessarily in control. And yet, of course, the things they could never control—especially hearts and minds—would continue to provoke anxious moments" (Dean 1999, 47).

Ironically, while these Native Promise Keepers seem to reject their tribal cultural practices in favor of evangelical practices, they often use evangelical language to fight for the maintenance of some indigenous practices. Given the continuing history of evangelical attempts to destroy all forms of indigenous cultural and spiritual practice, this resistance, however limited, is significant (Enns 2000; Williams 1993). As Joseph Elkerton complains, "When a Native person becomes a Christian, it seems he's expected to give up everything of his culture. White people still keep their wedding ceremonies and holidays like Thanksgiving. Natives are expected to assimilate into white culture" ("A Tough Task" 1993, 11). While he refuses to take part in many traditional practices, such as the sweetgrass ceremony, he notes that some aspects of traditional spirituality are healing. "I'm not sure that's a threat to Christianity," he writes, for "We can still live out our Christianity and still be Native" (11). It is also interesting that Native evangelicals are often able to find biblical support for the cultural practices with which they most strongly identify. For instance, Herman Williams notes that the Bible concurs with many traditional spiritual beliefs that owls are "abominable" and possess "demon spirits" (Indian Life Ministries 1999, 51). These efforts are becoming common in non-Indian Christian venues, particularly *Charisma* magazine, signaling to white Christians that they can no longer define the terms of Christian practice.

Indian people, including conservative ones, are particularly unwilling to give up their languages (Berkman 1999; Careless 2001; Fledderus 1999; "Jesus Speaks Ojibway" 2002; Moore 2002). In fact, at a conservative Southern Baptist Mississippi Choctaw church in Chicago, whenever there was a conflict in translation between the English and Choctaw Bibles, Bible study leaders would unhesitatingly state that the Choctaw translation must be the correct one. However, as Joy Anderson notes, "in the United States . . . we find much opposition to the Bible's being in the Indian language. Whites feel Indians should use the English Bible since they can read it" (1988, 242). The Native desire to maintain language also runs counter to campaigns in certain sectors of the Christian Right to support English-only laws. When we consider that language is the means by which culture is articulated, the maintenance of an indigenous language is of no small political significance. Missionaries have historically complained that indigenous languages were unable to communicate Christian concepts. From their perspective, Indians not only lack the Scripture, but they lack the language that would allow them to comprehend God. Complained Jonathan Edwards, "The Indian languages are extremely barbarous and barren, and very ill fitted for communicating things moral and divine, or even things speculative and abstract. In short, they are wholly unfit for a people possessed of civilization, knowledge, and refinement" (1998a, clxxx). Missionaries also complained that indigenous languages were unable to communicate the concepts of "Lord, Saviour, salvation, sinner, justice, condemnation, faith, repentance, justification, adoption, sanctification, grace, glory, and heaven" (1998b, 426). It is not sufficient, therefore, simply to have Scriptures; the Scriptures must be in a suitable language—and that language happens to be English. After all, if Christianity is couched in languages that do not have concepts of Lord, Savior, salvation, sinner, and so on, are Native peoples practicing the Christianity of English-speaking cultures? For instance, as Justine Smith notes in her analysis of the Cherokee Bible, because that Bible is a translation of the Greek and Hebrew versions rather than the English versions of the Bible, the Cherokee Bible is not simply a replication of the texts of the dominant culture; it serves as an oppositional text to the English Bible (2000).

In addition, while Native Christians often argue for the inclusion of Native cultural practices only to the extent that they can be safely incorporated into Christianity, this concession to Christian superiority is actually used, somewhat paradoxically, to contest Christian missionization of Native peoples. That is, within evangelical circles, developing mission work is often seen as a sign that a group "has arrived" (Maust 1993; Smith and Maracle 1989, 32, 37). Testifying to the "successful" conversion of African Americans to Christianity, *Christianity Today* reported on one African American church in Oakland, California, that set up a mission in Castro Valley to reach Caucasians ("Man Bites Dog" 1990). Consequently, Native evangelicals contest notions of religious inferiority by arguing that Native peoples should be doing the missionary work rather than being the objects of missionizing. Craig Smith contends that U.S. churches should stop seeing themselves as "sending" churches and recognize that they are themselves a mission field. Christianity originated in Jerusalem, after all, not the United States. Smith writes, "I have often told Anglo churches that you can't get much farther from Jerusalem than the United States of America! In the biblical sense, we are actually the end of the earth, the boondocks, and the foreign field! I have also said to them, "Have you ever thought that you should be the ones on the slides, rather than the ones watching the slides of foreign fields when missionary conference time rolls around?" (1997, 88). Similarly, Richard Twiss argues:

> After 500 years of missionary activity, many Native people today view Christianity as the religion of the oppressive white government. God, however, is a covenant-keeper. He is starting to pour the oil of His Holy Spirit into the wounds of First Nations people today. And as He is, He is raising us up to be His voice to other nations all over the world.
>
> As we near 500 years of missions among the tribes of North America, it is critically important for the church to stop viewing Native people solely as a mission field. As a people we have enormous needs and tremendous challenges to overcome. But that is not the way God made us, and neither is it the identity we claim.
>
> The Spirit of God has issued a prophetic call for non-Natives in the body of Christ to find ways to partner the First Nations peoples. (1999)

In another article, Twiss jokingly suggests that U.S. white churches should be the mission field of Native churches, not the other way around: "We won't make them wear our feathers and buckskin. We will let them have their music and their culture. But we will give them the gospel!" (Grady 2000b, 22). So, while on one hand evangelical Natives seem to be "mimicking" their oppressors by attempting to join the missionizing project, on the other hand the attempt to begin missionizing is also a strategy to stop white Christians from continuing their mission work in Native communities (Jacobs 2000b; T. LeBlanc 2000a). Craig Smith calls on white people to turn the leadership of denominations and parachurch organizations over to Indians (1997). Ironically, his proposal for Indian-white relations in the church echoes Vine Deloria's proposal of developing a Native denomination supported by the other Christian denominations but led and controlled by Native peoples (81). While he does not address racism as a set of power relations in society in any detail, he is clear about how racism is institutionalized in church structures, going so far as to argue that Christian missions are the most racist institutions in the country (66). As we have seen, this analysis could certainly be extended to a discussion of institutionalized racism in society at large.

While Native evangelicals generally posit a political quietism, it may be helpful to look at the reasons why some activists who were involved in groups such as AIM abandoned this form of politics to become evangelicals. Twiss's description of his conversion experience from AIM to Christianity echoes many others. "Since I truly surrendered my life to Christ, I have been at peace with myself and the world around me," he writes. "Many Indians are filled with hate and rage at the way their lives have gone and how the world seems so unfair. I know, because I was one of them! But now I have learned that in Jesus Christ, native people can have a new life that replaces anger with divine love" (Ward 1994, 197).

Tom Bee similarly describes how his allegiance switched from Red Power to Christianity during the July 16, 2006, episode of *Light in the Southwest*, a God's Learning Channel television program, because he recognized that there was nothing at the time that could disrupt his patterns of self-destruction that were hurting him and his family—other than Jesus. In *Indian Life*, he recounts how Christianity helped him combat alcoholism and mend his relationship with his family (2001). What these individuals seem to suggest was missing in the activist struggles they were involved in was a sense of "divine love," a sense of community wholeness and well-being of which they felt they were a part. These testimonies speak to the manner in which Native spirituality and political activism have been influenced by Western, masculinist notions of resistance that emphasize aggressive, publicity-driven resistance at the expense of community restoration. In the past few years, evangelical magazines have been reporting on widespread Christian revivals among the Inuit and other indigenous peoples living near the Arctic (Bruce 2000; Fieguth 2000c). What the testimonies consistently report is that these revivals have helped reduce alcoholism and suicide rates in Native communities, something the more obviously political movements have failed to do (Fieguth 2000b,

2002a; Newman 2004; Parker 1999). In my previous work, I discuss how Native women activists provide alternative models for resistance that are not separate from community restoration (A. Smith 2005b).

In addition, as Robin Kelley notes, it is a mistake to separate identity and/or cultural politics from their material effects (1997, 110). In the case of Native peoples, cultural politics has a profound effect on global economic and political relations because Native cultural practices are generally land based. It is not a coincidence that Native evangelicals such as Ross Maracle still maintain that Indian nations "have their right to self-government. Whatever power the United States or Canadian governments may exercise over Indian nations is received from the particular tribe or nation—not the other way around" (Smith and Maracle 1989, 36). On an episode of his television show that aired on July 2, 2006, on the God's Learning Channel network, Negiel Bigpond asserted that Native nations are "independent sovereign nations . . . just like China." The following week on the same show, he asserted, "You better get used to it; Native peoples have the authority over this land." His cohost, Jay Swallow, also argued that the ills of this land can be attributed to broken treaties. When the United States broke its treaties with Native peoples, the land was defiled, and hence the name of God was defiled. The Web site for his Two Rivers Native American Training Center features Bigpond's work in support of tribal sovereignty. Tom Bee's Red Sea Ministries Web site asserts that "Native Americans are God's chosen people on this continent; we are the landlords appointed by God" (redseaministries.org). Jeff King similarly charges whites with a biblical mandate to uphold treaty rights. He disputes evangelical white Christian claims that America is the "New Israel" and suggests that the proper understanding of American can be found in 2 Samuel, where God deserted Saul because he broke his "treaty" with the Gibeonites. Unlike the purveyors of Christian gospel, who argue that God will abandon the United States if it does not continue to uphold biblical principles, King implies that God *has already* abandoned the United States as a result of its genocidal policies toward Indian people. If Christianity is necessary for salvation, it would seem to justify the "missionary conquest" of the United States (Tinker 1993). Ironically, however, King's essay suggests the opposite.

> Both the public schools and society in general have described America as the promised land to the early settlers, much as Joshua and Israelites properly saw Canaan as the Promised Land. . . . However, in this picture the American Indian was labeled the "heathen," or "savage," much like the ene-

mies of Israel who inhabited the lands they were to occupy based on the promises of God.

Thus, within this erroneous view the taking of the land from these people was justified, and the wrongdoings that were committed were excused. All was interpreted in the light of Manifest Destiny—God designed the land for the pioneers, who were destined to unsettle "savage" Indians from the land. (1995, 82)

Woodley explicitly describes the United States as a country based on the genocide of Native peoples and asks, "On what cost, O God, has this country been born?" (2001, 24). Similarly, Native evangelicals condemn Christians for their complicity in boarding and residential school abuses rather than praising these schools for bringing Native peoples the Gospel (Etienne 2000; T. LeBlanc 2000a; Ward 2000). *Faith Today* criticizes the Canadian government for insufficiently addressing the legacies of colonialism (Harvey 1997).

Craig Smith argues that Jesus was not white but was more similar to an American Indian because, like Indians, he belonged to a colonized tribal group: "We live with the same mixture of traditional culture, values, traditions, languages and customs, but we also pay taxes, not to Caesar, but to Uncle Sam. We don't send it to Rome. We send it to Washington D.C." (1997, 15). Thus, he suggests, Jesus would not be on the side of the United States; rather, Jesus represents those who have been colonized by it. Smith then critiques the reconciliation model developed through race reconciliation efforts as an assault against tribal sovereignty. He notes that these models require Native peoples to stand as representatives of their nations and accept apologies for genocide from whites. This model, he notes, is problematic because it does not respect the right of Indian nations to determine who shall represent them (56). Richard Twiss critiques conquest in a joke: "An older Native man once asked a group of people if they knew why America is called a free country. 'Because they never paid us for it,' the man replied" (2000a). Randy Woodley asserts that race reconciliation with Native peoples must go "beyond 'Getting Along,' and include restitution in the form of monetary payment, services and the return of lands" (2001, 176–77). The Fifth World Christian Gathering on Indigenous People (held August 7–14, 2005) discussed the importance of hunting and fishing rights (Dixon 2006). While Tom Claus claimed he would "rather have Jesus than all the land in the U.S.," this statement does not necessarily mean that he does not support Indian land rights. In all probability, Claus has no intention of giving up either Jesus or his land. In fact, in another article he specifically calls on evangelicals to lobby their representatives and "express . . . [their] opposition to those bills which would call for the abrogation of Indian treaties, water, hunting and fishing rights" (1979, 26). At the Promise Keepers Clergy conference of 1996, Claus was part of a "No More Broken Promises" walk. In explaining the meaning of this walk, he stated that there was "One who did not break his promises. That was Jesus" ("No More Broken Treaties" 1996, 8–9). This statement suggests that, from his perspective, following Jesus is inseparable from respecting Indian land claims. While Claus claims that the march was not a protest, this statement is an implicit critique of white Christian claims to truth or religious superiority: only Jesus, not Christian missionaries, has kept promises.

Even Daniel Kikawa, who suggests that white missionaries liberated Native Hawai'ians to reestablish their original relationship with the Christian God, draws the line at the overthrow of the Hawai'ian kingdom. The missionaries involved in this travesty, he argues, were not true Christians. He says of Queen Lili'uokalani, "In the end, the one who was called a pagan and a sorceress by the so-called 'Christians' proved to be the True Christian" (1994, 192). He condemns the present-day distribution of wealth in which nearly all land is owned by colonialists while Native Hawai'ians are disproportionately landless and homeless.

While performance of reconciliation can seem to offer a simple solution to the problems of genocide and colonization, some of these performances offer striking critiques of both past and present-day colonial practices. A leaflet entitled "Memorial Prayer for Reconciliation," developed by Healing for the Native Ministry, says in part:

> For the policy of genocide and for the ongoing unjust policies of the United States government, we ask your forgiveness. . . .
>
> For the destruction of the Native family structure through the demoralization of Native American men, for placing your children in foster homes and boarding schools, and for the subservient positions forced on your women, we ask for your forgiveness.
>
> For over three-hundred broken treaties, for the myth of "Manifest Destiny," and for the notion that Native people stood in the way of progress, we ask your forgiveness.
>
> For the sins of the church, for withholding the true gospel, for misrepresenting Jesus Christ, and for using religion in an attempt to "civilize the Natives," we ask your forgiveness.

The clearest identification of evangelical Christianity with Indian nationalism can be found in the words of Art Begay of Warriors for Christ. At the Culture, Christ and the Kingdom conference held in 1999, he explicitly stated that he did not identify as a U.S. citizen: "I don't push an 'American agenda' when I missionize to Indians. People think to be Christian you have to be American." But for Indians, he argued, being Christian means supporting the rights of Native peoples. The value placed on sovereignty and self-determination is evident even in the works of the writers who seem to be most accommodating to white Christian culture; even if they do not see themselves in an antagonistic relationship with white society, they are clear that they do not want to be part of racially integrated churches either. "Yes," he continued, "all races can worship together, but if we don't understand each other as far as language or culture goes, we would probably be better off in a church of our own" (Indian Life Ministries 1999, 105). This thinking runs counter to the assumptions of those involved in racial reconciliation that racial integration is an unmitigated good for people of color (DeYoung et al. 2003). In addition, while contemporary political struggles are not highlighted in the publications of these ministries, they are still featured regularly in *Indian Life*. Interestingly, *Indian Life* also began regularly featuring articles on the problems of prison, including articles by Colson (2001e), Prober (1999), Hamilton (2001), LePretre (1999), Cienski (2001), and unidentified contributors ("Daniel" 2001 and "Prisoners Showcase 2001" 2001). Some articles explicitly called for an end to racism against Native peoples within the criminal justice system (Yapi 2000; Yates 2001). Forgiveness and reconciliation is not offered unconditionally. While King discusses the importance of forgiveness, he argues that "wrongs still need to be righted" (King 1995, 95). In a similar vein, Craig Smith states, "We must teach that reconciliation is not the end, but the beginning. As previously said, one of my greatest fears is that once reconciliation has occurred, what happens to the two parties involved? Does the offender go off, absolved, and get on with his life, while the offended is lying on the roadside, beaten, naked and left for dead? . . . Scripture is clear in its admonition to offenders who repent. Prove your repentance by your deeds!" (1997, 58).

Mavis Etienne goes beyond using evangelical rhetoric to support Native sovereignty to directly engaging in sovereignty struggles. *Indian Life* prominently featured a story on Etienne, who was a negotiator during the 1990 Oka crisis, trying to bring a peaceful settlement between developers and the Mohawks, "who did not want their land bulldozed to expand a golf course" (Etienne 2004, 8). The article takes a sympathetic stance toward the Mohawk uprising and notes that it is Etienne's evangelical faith that propels her to engage in the struggle. She wrote, "I wasn't afraid because I knew they [those opposing the Mohawks] were in the wrong, and I knew God was with me" (8). *Faith Today* tells the story of evangelical Chief Billy Diamond, who led the successful battle of the James Bay Cree against Hydro-Quebec's plan to flood their territory with a dam (Dorsch 1991). States Diamond, "The New Testament Church was never intended to be a passive church. It was never intended for the church to accept the status quo. The New Testament Church that turned the world upside down. It was supposed to be a militant church" (Diamond 1991, 28). *Indian Life* also featured the evangelical national chief of the Assembly of First Nations, Matthew Coon Come, who opposed the Canadian government's attempt to stop the Mi'kmaq from using lobster traps in Burnt Church, New Brunswick. Stated Coon Come, "I see terrible, violent, oppressive and disrespectful behavior toward our people. . . . This is about Canada's persistent policy of dispossession of our land and resources, this is about a repressive government that has finally shown its true face to the world" (Kruzenga, Moal, and Fieguth 2000, 5). *Media Development* went so far as to critique the "capitalist ideology based on the importance of commercial and territorial expansion and monetary gain," which is constitutive of colonial relationships between indigenous peoples and Western nations (Bondy 1998). And Terry LeBlanc ties Native nationalism to an implicit critique of capitalism.

> The gap between rich and poor still exists In fact, it is widening at an increasing rate—despite the assurances of the World Bank and the G7 that there is overall improvement in the human condition worldwide. Sadly, those of us in the indigenous community seem to be buying it hook, line, and sinker! MBA's [masters in business administration] are being churned out in Indian country faster than the social work and legal degrees. . . . The battle against assimilation is being conceded on a selective front. We are buying into an economic world-view so foreign that it didn't even register as a remote possibility to our ancestors. . . . When, under the rubric of development, we disguise unchecked greed for bigger and better and more of Western free enterprise and big business we do a grave disservice to our fellow human beings. (T. LeBlanc 2000b)

These performances sometimes do lead to material benefits for Native peoples, as the story of the Wiyot tribe related at the beginning of this chapter demonstrates. This example is not isolated, however. For instance, Jean Steffenson founded the Native American Resource Network, which stages ceremonies in which white pastors apologize for stealing Native peoples' land. She is now looking to follow up these reconciliations with policy advocacy to address injustices perpetrated against Native peoples (J. Moore 2004). Particularly in Canada, race reconciliation efforts have encouraged at least some evangelical churches to stake stands in support of Native sovereignty. For instance, the Evangelical Fellowship of Canada put together a response to the 1996 "Report of the Royal Commission on Aboriginal Peoples," which denounced "broken treaties, abuse at residential schools, and poor public policy entrenched in the Indian Act" (Ward 2000, 37). The article in *Faith Today* that covered this report provided a list of key treaty rights and land rights cases currently pending in Canada. The article further argued that court proceedings may be necessary to bring healing from the effects of residential schools in particular, *even if* they result in church bankruptcy. This article was not without its problems; it argued that residential schools had contributed to the "reactionary movement back to native traditional religions and the reluctance of Natives to embrace Christianity" (38). However, it does condemn white Christians who say, "We didn't run residential schools or sign treaties, so they're not our responsibility," but then hypocritically take credit for any good work done one hundred years ago (37). The article further charges evangelicals to utilize international forums to look at how Canada is violating Native peoples' right "to self-government or political self determination" because it has deprived aboriginals of their "access to land and resources" (38).

Even when the politics of Native evangelicals are toned down, they are not nonexistent. They still address issues of racism and colonialism (Evans 2000; Jacobs 2000b; J. Moore 2004; Newman 2004). Their claims to land-based nationalisms run counter to the political goals of Christian Right organizations. Indian land rights also tend to run directly counter to the interests of evangelical missions. *Alliance Witness* explicitly states that it is the goal of mission work to stop the Mapuche Indians, who are subjected to genocide in Chile, from organizing for land rights and continuing to engage in their cultural practices, which *Alliance Witness* refers to as "animism" (Ottoson 1992, 19). This fight against Indian sovereignty also provides a subtext for a *World Christian* article titled "Jesus Walks among the Navajo." In this article, Tracy Stewart notes how "Joe" got saved, now has his life together, and works for a "coal mining operation on the reservation" (1985, 40). Of course, what is not mentioned is the role of coal mining-companies, particularly Peabody Coal, in forcing the relocation of the Navajo from their land in Big Mountain. *Rutherford* complains that "in revisionist history, Christopher Columbus is no longer a great explorer and father to the New World; instead, he is the white man's imperialist ancestor who stole America from the Indians" (McThenia 1995, 8–9). *Christianity Today*'s editor, David Neff, argues that, while Christians may have stolen Indian land, this theft "does not require . . . [the] restoration of long-lost lands. (Every system of justice knows of a statute of limitations)" (1991, 29). The evangelical revisionist historian John Eidsmoe is not even willing to admit that Christians stole Indian land. He argues that since Native people did not privatize land, and since their communities were not "established by God," Europeans had a right to seize the land (1992, 133). He recirculates what Gustav Jahoda argues has been a continuing rationale for Native genocide: because Native people do not sufficiently transform the land, they have no right to occupy it (1999, 20). One letter to the editor of *Christianity Today* opined that the manner in which the Cherokee were forcibly relocated during the Trail of Tears should serve as a model for how the United States should conduct the war in Iraq. Supposedly, during the Trail of Tears, "every possible kindness . . . [was] shown by the troops" (Readers Write 2004b, 12–14). Besides, according to a book review in *Books and Culture*, Andrew Jackson was not so bad because he adopted an Indian boy and loved him (Startup 2002).

In the context of contemporary sovereignty and Native rights struggles, Native people have met with widely varied opposition. For instance, Concerned Women for America was involved in opposing Indian casinos, apparently not because it objected to casinos per se but because it opposed tribal rather than state control over them (Field 1996). In fact, a number of evangelical organizations have mobilized against Indian gaming without respect for the issues of sovereignty involved, often utilizing the rhetoric that gaming tribes are not really "Indian" (Kennedy 2004; Wood 2000).[14] Many other organizations have challenged or dismissed Native rights. The Institute of Religion and Democracy belittled a call by

[14] In response to an antigaming article published by *Christianity Today*, one reader asserted, "These anti-Indian interests are simply waiting like vultures for unrestricted access to Indian real estate and mineral deposits. If Christian activists are not careful, they may unintentionally find themselves on the same side with these darker political interests. Tribes are merely trying to stay ahead of the game by building some type of economic security and hopefully, self-sufficiently." Those who oppose gaming should "encourage their own county or city governments to engage them in local economic and community projects" (Readers Write 2004c, 15).

the Indigenous People's Program of the World Council of Churches for "indigenous sovereignty . . . self-determination . . . and religious rights . . . [because] nobody mentioned Jesus Christ" (Williamson 1998–99). The American Center for Law and Justice, which is supposedly dedicated to "defending and advancing religious liberty," notes that religious liberty does not apply to protecting Indian sacred sites since it is "of immediate interest to only a few Americans" (Seculow n.d.).[15] In an effort to eliminate or weaken the Indian Child Welfare Act (ICWA), the Christian Coalition distributed action alerts to its local chapters calling for its members to lobby their representatives. *World* further complains that the ICWA leaves Indian children "at the mercy of Indian tribes" (while non-Indian foster children are apparently not at the mercy of the state) (Vincent 2006a). In fact, the Christian Alliance for Indian Child Welfare was organized specifically to eradicate the ICWA. In other cases, opponents simply ignore Native involvement in an issue. Focus on the Family supports Indian mascots for sports teams, arguing that they are "a tribute to fighting spirit" and only white liberals, not Native peoples, oppose them ("White Liberals on the Warpath" 2005). And *World* published an article supporting oil drilling in the Arctic Wildlife Refuge with no mention of the opposition of the Gwi'ichin and other indigenous peoples (Bergin 2005a).

Demonstrating extraordinary disregard for Native groups, prominent leaders of the Christian Right, such as Pat Robertson, have been active in supporting Latin American regimes that commit genocide against indigenous people. The evangelical former president of Guatemala, Rios Mott, received much financial support from Robertson, which went to support Mott's Gospel Outreach campaign to annihilate indigenous people. Stated one Gospel Outreach pastor, "The Army doesn't massacre the Indians. It massacres demons, and the Indians are demon possessed; they are communists" (Diamond 1995, 238). *Charisma* asserts that the oppression of indigenous peoples in Guatemala can be traced not to U.S. policy but to "demonic" powers that "have held Guatemala in bondage" (Winger 1998,

---

[15] *Christianity Today* did run a rare opinion piece that criticized the U.S. Supreme Court decision in *Lyng v. Northwest Indian Cemetery Protection Association*, 485 U.S. 439 (1988), which essentially obliterated religious protection for Native peoples. Stephen Carter asserted, "If your way of being religious is recognizably like the way in which the larger culture views religion, you can have a robust religious freedom. If, however, your way of practicing your religion is very different and especially very threatening to the way in which the larger culture practices religion, you will have a much harder time" (2000, 60).

71). But Christian revival liberates them from oppression. "Before the revival," the article claims, "farmers worked just enough to support their drinking habits; today they are investing in topsoil and fertilizers, and some are paying cash for Mercedes trucks and emblazoning them with names such as *Regalito de Dios* ('Little Gift from God')" (72). As Robertson, who dismisses the importance of Native cultural survival, states:

> These tribes are . . . in an arrested state of social development. They are not less valuable as human beings because of that, but they offer scant wisdom or learning or philosophical vision that can be instructive to a society that can feed the entire population of the earth in a single harvest and send spacecraft to the moon. . . . Except for our crimes, our wars and our frantic pace of life, what we have is superior to the ways of primitive peoples. . . . Which life do you think people would prefer: freedom in an enlightened Christian civilization or the suffering of subsistence living and superstition in a jungle? You choose. (1993, 153)

Echoing a similar sentiment was a joke published in *New Man* magazine: "After 43 years of working in the Amazon jungle, the Right Reverend Thornton Standish retires to pen a book titled *Traumatic Lessons from the Mission Field: I Wish Someone Would Have Told Me That 'Indigenous People' Is Just a Fancy Term for 'Naked People'*" (Meurer 2004). Meanwhile, *World* argued that David Stoll's 2001 book, *Rigoberta Menchu and the Story of All Poor Guatemalans*—which contested the veracity of *I, Rigoberto Menchu* (the Nobel Prize winner's autobiography)—also demonstrates that the U.S-financed Guatemalan war against indigenous people never actually happened (Veith 1999a). *Christianity Today* contends that indigenous peoples in Chiapas are persecuting Christians in the area because purportedly Christians do not respect indigenous culture. This complaint is false, the magazine contends, but "it is hard to help indigenous leaders see that drinking and drugs are not really a part of their true cultural values" (Alford 2005, 22).

Given the genocidal implications of missionizing, Native evangelicals utilize what Jace Weaver terms "communitist" strategies, similar to those used by William Apess and other Indian Christians, of turning the principles of evangelical faith against evangelicals in order to support Native communities (Weaver 1997, 100). When one considers how virulently anti-indigenous many evangelical and Christian Right organizations are, the importance of these Native evangelical "communitist" strategies becomes clear. As William McLoughlin has noted, the adoption of Christianity does not necessarily connote allegiance to the United States. He argues that the many members of the Cherokee Nation converted to Christianity as a means of advancing the goal of Cherokee nationalism, not as a means of assimilating into "America" (McLoughlin 1995, 335).

Craig Calhoun faults those who analyze identity politics for assuming that "everyone is equally endowed with identity, equally entitled to their own identity, and equally entitled to respect for it" (1994b, 24). It is important to consider the power imbalances between white evangelicals and Native peoples when assessing the role of Native peoples within evangelical circles. White people often do not credit people of color within evangelicalism as agents of strategy and resistance.[16] But when I conversed with people of color involved with Promise Keepers I found that their racial politics were much more radical than what is usually articulated in Promise Keepers venues. They saw their involvement in Promise Keepers as strategic: they were prepared to tone down their politics in exchange for having a broader impact on the politics of race in evangelical communities than they might otherwise have. Some people of color find an organization like Promise Keepers ultimately helpful, despite its failings, if it can convince Ku Klux Klan members to stop terrorizing people of color (something left-wing organizations do not seem to have had much success doing). And in fact I did talk to some former hard-core racists who had changed their more vicious practices (such as throwing rocks at Native spearfishers during the previously described struggle in northern Wisconsin) because of their involvement in Promise Keepers.

NATIVE RELIGIOUS AND POLITICAL IDENTITY

Critics of the Christian Right want to ascribe all sorts of evil motives to the promoters of race reconciliation. People of color involved in these movements are generally described as dupes. Some see race reconciliation efforts as an insidious gambit intended to assemble a multiracial corps of men that will later be mobilized to support secular right-wing causes (Conason, Ross, and Cokorinos 1996). Others think that it is a plot to build a constituency that will "enter the political arena as part of the religious right" ("Promise Keepers Ministry Sweeps across Country" 1995). Both groups fear that a rightward shift among religious people of color would make it impossible for Democrats to win elections ("In Theory" 1995).

[16] As bell hooks says, white people seldom credit black people with "a critical 'ethnographic' gaze" (1997, 167).

The assumption behind these analyses is that subjects are unified and consistent in their perceived interests, and power is enacted over them unilaterally: whatever agenda the leaders of Christian Right organizations promote their automaton followers will thoughtlessly pursue. These critics do not believe that a white evangelical could simultaneously support right-wing policies and be concerned about racism. They do not consider that people of color might redeploy race reconciliation discourse for their own ends. And they do not seem to grasp that, whatever the motives of those who promote race reconciliation, the effects of race reconciliation are not totally under the Christian Right leadership's control. Contestations over the meaning of race reconciliation will have unexpected and unintended effects on the body of evangelicalism specifically and socio-religio-political discourse in general. This chapter only hints at the multiple and conflicting relationships between people of color and the Christian Right and the resulting contestations over religious meetings and political action. Importantly, the analysis suggests that people interested in progressive politics should rethink who they consider their potential allies to be. This chapter also sheds light on the continuing theological debates regarding the relationship between Native peoples and Christianity. Some have argued that Christianity (even in the form of liberation theology) is at odds with Native liberatory struggles (Deloria 1999; Warrior 1991). Others have tried to synthesize the two (Baldridge 1989; Charleston 1996; Tinker 1998; Treat 1996; Weaver 1996a). And, as this chapter has shown, some have argued that Native religions are the problem and true liberation comes from Christianity. Perhaps these debates can be reframed.

As Dorinne Kondo notes, assimilation is always unfinished business: "Even when colonized peoples imitate the colonizer, the mimesis is never complete, for the specter of the 'not quite, not white' haunts the colonizer, a dis-ease that always contains an implicit threat to the colonizer's hegemony" (1997, 10). Homi Bhabha and Edward Said also argue that part of the colonization process involves the partial assimilation of the colonized in order to establish colonial rule (Bhabha 1997; Said 1994). The colonized must seem to partially resemble the colonists in order to establish the ideology that the colonizers' way of life is the only way to exist. If the colonized group seems completely different from the colonists, the colonized implicitly challenge the supremacy of colonial rule. However, members of the colonized group can never be completely assimilated; otherwise, they would be the equals of the colonizers and there would be no reason to colonize them. Within this tension, groups that attempt to replicate the dominant culture (in this case Native evangelicals) never fully do so. Further, the very act of mimesis challenges the hegemonic claims of the colonizers. And on other hand, oppositional practices are never free of reinscribing that which they contest. Thus, rather than simply choosing one side in these debates concerning religious identity, it might be useful to think about (1) what areas of resistance are possible in each site *and* (2) how all of these options for resistance continue to reinscribe colonial paradigms. This chapter has explored resistances within Native evangelicalism, but later I will trouble the notion that an anti-Christian, Native traditionalism is necessarily a stance of pure resistance as well.

CONCLUSION

Social and political theorists have often failed to ascribe political agency to oppressed communities. Such communities are often described as suffering from "false consciousness" and waiting to be awakened by a movement's vanguard into political action. As Piven and Cloward contend, "Ordinarily, in short, the lower classes accept their lot, and the acceptance can be taken for granted; it need not be bargained by their rulers" (1979, 6–7).

James Scott troubles this analysis, arguing that oppressed peoples constantly resist structures of oppression, but their resistance is strategically disguised to go generally unnoticed by those in authority. In what Scott terms "public transcripts"—that which is publicly known to community outsiders—it appears as though oppressed groups support the status quo because they wish to avoid repression. However, the hidden transcripts of the oppressed found in songs, rumors, performances, art works, and so on reveal that they do resist in ways that help them escape accountability to power elites. These forms of "everyday" resistance are not substitutes for real political struggle, according to Scott; rather, they form the groundwork from which organized political struggle can arise (1990). In questioning the notion that oppressed communities do not simply acquiesce to oppression, however, Scott goes to the other extreme and contests Gramsci's notion that dominating classes exercise forms of ideological domination over dominated classes (1985, 317). He argues that the question to be asked is not why there are so few revolutions but why there are any rebellions at all given that dominated classes lack the power and resources to effect revolutionary change (1990, 79).

Several problems emerge from Scott's analysis. The question of why there are so few revolutions becomes apparent when we consider the numbers of people who are ultimately controlled and oppressed by capitalism. Even if 1 percent of the population owns 90 percent of the wealth, the wealth would be insignificant if the other 99 percent of the population rebelled. Thus, the question Scott dismisses *is* important. Why do oppressed communities not make common cause with each other to oppose ruling elites?

The answer to the question lies to some extent in Scott's erroneous conflation of "hegemony" with "false consciousness." As Stuart Hall notes, however, the Right's ability to exercise hegemonic control depends on its ability to appeal to at least some of the real needs felt by the populace. In particular, he points out that the antistatist rhetoric of the Right in framing its dismantling of the welfare state coincides with the frustrations of the poor in trying to obtain services from a bureaucratic, inefficient, and demeaning state system. People do not have unified interests, so it is not possible to argue that, in supporting the Right instead of each others' struggles, the people are necessarily acting against their interests to some degree (Hall 1988, 49–50).

In addition, Scott's analysis depends on a unified, noncontradictory understanding of self and community. That is, people either resist or they acquiesce. However, as Dorinne Kondo notes, "Opposition can be both contestatory and complicit, and yet still constitute a subversion that matters" (1997, 11). Her work acknowledges that it is important to look for new sites of resistance, ever mindful that none of these sites is without its contradictions.

This trend toward identifying resistance everywhere within cultural studies and postcolonial theory runs the danger of ultimately trivializing the importance of developing mass-based movements for social change. If resistance is everywhere, then ultimately resistance is nowhere. As Scott argues, "the hidden transcript is a condition of practical resistance rather than a substitute for it" (1990, 191). It is perhaps helpful to adopt Cornel West's model of differentiating "thin" opposition from "thick" opposition. That is, while it is important to see resistance in everyday cultures (thin opposition), ultimately mass political mobilization (thick opposition) is necessary to make radical social changes (West and hooks 1991, 39). These types of resistance, of course, are not completely separate. We must identify hidden forms of resistance because "infrapolitics is the building block for the more elaborate institutionalized political action that could not exist without it" (Scott 1990, 201). But we must also strategically organize these hidden forms of resistance into effective forms of political action (Kelley 1996).

Thus, in light of the problems with Native evangelical politics, it is arguable that these points of resistance are insignificant in light of the harm they do in reinscribing Christian imperialism. As Philip Deloria notes, celebrating these resistances uncritically fails to consider how "when Indian people [refigure] their world, they [do] so within the constraints of American [and Christian] rules, regulations, expectations, and power" (2004, 114). And, as I discuss in the following chapters, does this site of possible resistance exist on the backs of Native women?

My point is not to say that these resistances in both evangelical prison organizing and race reconciliation movements are in and of themselves revolutionary but rather that it is incumbent on Native and non-Native peoples with more transformatory politics to consider how these resistances can be strategically mobilized for progressive purposes. It is clear from the writings and speeches of Native Charismatics that they are not uninformed by more radical analysis. Craig Smith quotes Vine Deloria extensively, usually affirming his analysis. *Indian Life* published an excerpt of his book, *Spirit and Reason* (Deloria 2000). Art Begay even speaks approvingly of AIM politics and other activist struggles for sovereignty. Certainly, the initiative to harmonize Native culture with Christianity is a reaction to critiques by non-Christian Natives that Indian Christians have sold out to white supremacy. In addition, the impact of U.S. and Christian imperialism is so extensive in Native communities that it is virtually impossible to create sites of pure resistance untainted by colonialism. Thus, it is worth considering what other kinds of alliances and relationships could be built across religious and denominational divisions to further Native sovereignty in the future. The work done by Native evangelicals through race reconciliation demonstrates that, despite the problems with this movement, the Christian Right is an unstable formation that offers possibilities for progressive rearticulations.

My Ethnographic "Mistake"

As mentioned in the preface, my ethnographic study of Native evangelicals was conducted primarily through non-participant observation in conferences and events, as well as through study of public document and periodical literature. In part this approach was determined by my status as an evangelical Christian who often cannot disclose my political views to avoid excommunication. The limitations of this approach became clear, however, when three individuals described in this chapter—Richard Twiss, Randy Woodley, and Terry LeBlanc—read an earlier version of this work in the *American Behavioral Scientist* (A. Smith 2006). It was then that I became more fully aware of what Gayatri Spivak would describe as my ethnographic "mistake" (Spivak 1999). First, I learned that the divide between academia and "community" is not as insurmountable as what both academics and activists might often think. Second, while my intent in this chapter was to focus on the progressive sectors within Native evangelicalism, I found that these sectors were even more progressive than I had assumed. Borrowing from James Scott, it is clear that when we only look at the public transcripts of Native evangelical discourse in which leaders are forced to make strategic interventions within landscapes not of their own choosing, we may miss what may be very politically radical, but can be found only in private transcripts. Thus, my ethnographic mistake actually confirms my original argument even more strongly: those interested in forging progressive political with new allies cannot assume beforehand who their allies might be. Stereotypes and assumptions can keep us—and I include myself in this category—from pursuing relationships with those who might actually share more similar political visions with us than we might have guessed.

3

"Without Apology"

Native American and Evangelical Feminisms

I can only conclude that [these] traditionalists do not realize they are involved in an inconsistent selectivity so extreme that it amounts to dishonest
scholarship. The other possibility is that they realize well enough but are using the Bible to rationalize a position they cling to for political and personal
reasons.—VIRGINIA MOLLENKOTT on evangelical feminism

I think one of the reasons why Indian women don't call themselves feminists is
because they don't want to make enemies of men, but I just say, go forth
and offend without inhibition. That's generally why I see women hold back,
who don't want to be seen as strident. I don't want to be seen as a man-hater,
but I think if we had enough man-haters, we might actually have the men
change for once. I guess I'm just not into kowtowing that way. I think that
fundamentally puts the argument in the field of the dominant, in this case,
of men. I think men, in this particular case, are very, very good at avoiding
responsibility and avoiding accountability and avoiding justice. And not calling yourself a feminist, that's one way they do that. Well, feminism, that's
for white women. Oh feminists, they're not Indian. They're counterrevolu-
tionary. They're all man-haters. They're all ball-busters. They've gotten out of
order. No, first of all that presumes that Native women weren't active in shaping our identity before white women came along. And that abusive male behavior is somehow traditional, and it's absolutely not. So I reject that. That's
a claim against sovereignty. I think that's a claim against Native peoples. I
think it's an utter act of racism and white supremacy. . . . And I do think it's
important that we say we're feminists without apology.
—JULIE STAR on Native feminism

In the first epigraph, we see Virginia Mollenkott rhetorically reversing the charge frequently made by evangelical supporters of gender hierarchy that feminism is not biblical. Rather, she contends, it is gender hierarchicalists who are biblically dishonest. Julie Star's analysis of feminism in the next epigraph speaks to the policing of coalitions within Native communities as they impact Native women. While evangelical feminists contend with conservative evangelical thought, which holds that feminism is "unbiblical," Native "feminists" contend with Native scholars and activists who argue that addressing issues of sexism in Native communities is unnecessary.

As was discussed in the preface, both evangelical and Native feminisms destabilize notions of political communities being either singularly conservative (in this case evangelicals) or progressive (in this case Native communities). However, because both communities often portray themselves or are portrayed in totalizing ways, both evangelical and Native feminisms have often been erased in the discourses within and about these communities. Because of this erasure, I must first spend some time demonstrating that these feminisms in fact exist. The first section of this chapter explains the emergence of these feminisms within the context of the sexisms and other forms of oppression they have sought to address within their specific communities. This analysis is also important if we are to consider the flip side of coalition building—that Native and evangelical identities are *already* coalitional identities that often advance political interests of some members of a community at the expense of others.

The second section of this chapter focuses particularly on violence as a galvanizing force for feminist interventions within evangelical and Native communities. Antiviolence organizing is also an important site for investigating not only the successes of feminist organizing but also the failures of Native and evangelical feminists to coalesce. In particular, I investigate how antiviolence organizing often coincides with both state-driven mandates and within colonial and white supremacist logics that hinder cross-racial feminist organizing projects.

In the third section of this chapter, I explore the specific interventions and strategies used by Native and evangelical feminists to challenge prevailing gender relations within their communities. While the previous chapters speak to the potential of rearticulating Christian Right politics into more progressive politics, at the same time a common thread within both prison organizing and race reconciliation is the gender heteronormativity that has the impact of co-opting indigenous and other social justice struggles. Consequently, it might be helpful to look at the feminist interventions being made within both evangelical and Native communities to see how they might inform a politics of rearticulation. In particular, how does feminist politics reshape what we consider alliance politics to be? How does feminist politics inform an understanding of coalition work as both an internal and external process, as well as of how these internal and external processes interface? And in communities where feminism is seen as either nonexistent (evangelicalism) or unnecessary (Native communities), what strategies do feminists utilize to transform their communities and to what effect? I conclude that, while race reconciliation and prison organizing within evangelical communities seem to open these communities up for coalition building with nonevangelical partners, feminist organizing within evangelical communities seems to have the opposite effect. While we see race reconciliation programs providing a site for coalitions between Native and evangelical communities, particularly among men, the strategies employed by evangelical feminists hinder the development of relationships between Native and evangelical women.

SEXISM AND THE EMERGENCE OF NATIVE AND EVANGELICAL FEMINISM

Analyses of the Christian Right often portray evangelical communities as singularly reactionary when it comes to gender politics. As mentioned previously, the assumption behind this analysis is that any "biblically" driven approach to gender relations is necessarily static and conservative. Consequently, until recently the existence of evangelical feminism has been largely unknown to those outside evangelicalism. Similarly, Native feminism has also been portrayed as an oxymoron. Why do Native women need feminism when, so the logic goes, patriarchy did not exist in Native communities prior to colonization? Even within Native American studies, scholars and activists have argued that Native women do not need feminism.

If both communities are portrayed so monolithically (either monolithically conservative or progressive), it obviously is more difficult to imagine coalition politics with either of them. Such a simplistic gender analysis also makes it difficult for us to see that Native and evangelical identities are already coalitional identities that can shift and change through political struggle. This chapter explores how, contrary to popular belief, Native and evangelical feminisms *do* exist by tracing their contemporary developments within the context of their critiques of sexism within their communities. In doing so, I hope to lay the groundwork for exploring in the following sections what interventions these feminisms make, as well as the implications of these interventions for both internal and external coalition politics.

"Native Women Aren't Feminists" and other Myths and Mantras

Native women are not feminists, so the commonly told story goes. For instance, one of the most prominent writings on Native American women and feminism is Annette Jaimes Guerrero's and Theresa Halsey's "American Indian Women: At the Center of Indigenous Resistance in North America." In this article, they argue that Native women activists, except those who are "assimilated," do not consider themselves feminists. Feminism, according to Native women, is an imperial project that assumes the givenness of the U.S. colonial stranglehold on indigenous nations. Thus, to support sovereignty Native women activists must reject feminist politics.

> Those who have most openly identified themselves [as feminists] have tended to be among the more assimilated of Indian women activists, generally accepting of the colonialist ideology that indigenous nations are now legitimate sub-parts of the U.S. geopolitical corpus rather than separate nations, that Indian people are now a minority with the overall population rather than the citizenry of their own distinct nations. Such Indian women activists are therefore usually more devoted to "civil rights" than to liberation per se. . . . Native American women who are more genuinely sovereign-tist in their outlook have proven themselves far more dubious about the potentials offered by feminist politics and alliances. (Jaimes and Halsey 1992, 330–31)

According to Annette Jaimes and Theresa Halsey, the message from Native women is univocal—concerns for gender justice must be subordinate to struggles for indigenous sovereignty and self-determination, as typified by these quotes from one of the founders of Women of All Red Nations (WARN), Lorelei DeCora Means.

> We are *American Indian* women, in that order. We are oppressed, first and foremost, as American Indians, as peoples colonized by the United States of America, *not* as women. As Indians, we can never forget that. Our survival, the survival of every one of us—man, woman and child—*as Indians* de-

pends on it. Decolonization is the agenda, the whole agenda, and until it is accomplished, it is the *only* agenda that counts for American Indians. . . .

You start to get the idea maybe all this feminism business is just another extension of the same old racist, colonialist mentality. (Jaimes and Halsey 1992, 314, 332)

The critique and rejection of the label of feminism made by Jaimes and Halsey is important and shared by many Native women activists. However, it fails to tell the whole story, as many Native women in WARN do and did call themselves feminists.[1] Consider, for instance, this quote from Madonna Thunder Hawk, who cofounded WARN with Lorelei Means.

Feminism means to me, putting a word on the women's world. It has to be done because of the modern day. . . . I don't think Indian people have a problem with terms like feminism because we have had to deal with paternalism for *so* long, it's part of our intergenerational thinking. So feminism is a good word. I like it. . . .

I'm not the average Indian activist woman, because I refuse to limit my world. I don't like that. . . . How could we limit ourselves? "I don't like that term; it's a white term." Pssshhh. Why limit yourself? But that's me.

My point is not to set Thunder Hawk in opposition to Means: both talk of the centrality of land and decolonization in Native women's struggles. While Thunder Hawk supports many of the positions typically regarded as feminist, such as abortion rights, she contends that Native struggles for land and survival continue to take precedence over these other issues. Rather, my argument is that Native women activists' theories about feminism, the struggle against sexism within both Native communities and the society at large, and the importance of working in coalition with non-Native women are complex and varied. They are not monolithic and cannot simply be reduced to the dichotomy of feminist versus nonfeminist. Furthermore, there is not necessarily a relationship between the extent to which Native women call themselves feminists, the extent to which they work in coalition with non-Native feminists or value those coalitions, whether they are urban or reservation-based, and the extent to which they are "genuinely sovereigntist."

More important, this mantra often serves as a policing tool around

[1] For another critique of Jaimes and Halsey, see Devon Mihesuah's *Indigenous American Women* (2003). James herself shifted her position in her essay "Civil Rights versus Sovereignty" in *Feminist Genealogies, Colonial Legacies, and Democratic Futures*, ed. M. Jacqui Alexander and Chandra Talpade Mohanty, 101–24.

coalition politics. That is, Native women who center sexism in their organizing run the risk of being named as "white" whether or not they call themselves feminists. As I discuss later in the chapter, Native women face similar policing mechanisms, as do evangelical feminists who run the risk of being named as unbiblical. The very simplified manner in which Native women's activism is theorized prevents Native women from articulating political projects that both address sexism *and* promote indigenous sovereignty. In addition, this framework does not show the complex way in which Native women organizers position themselves with respect to other coalition partners. Assessing the strategies Native women use to address patriarchy and colonialism simultaneously enables us to articulate a pro-lineal genealogy of Native feminism, a history of the future of what Native feminism *could be* that it is not necessarily bound by current articulations of "feminism." That is, just as chapters 1 and 2 highlighted the instability of "conservative" political configurations and demonstrated the possibilities of rearticulating these configurations into more progressive formations, we must also critically assess "progressive" or "radical" political configurations. In what ways might they sometimes be furthering reactionary rather than progressive political ends? At which points do they also need to be rearticulated? To begin to address some of these questions, I will focus on Native women's analysis as it pertains specifically to coalition politics. In later works, I hope to develop indigenous feminist theory in greater depth.

This chapter is an intellectual ethnography that highlights the analysis produced by Native women activists. In taking this theory seriously, I reference it, not only in this chapter but throughout the book, on a par with the writings of those situated in academia. I am informed by Kamala Visweswaran's attempts to disperse academic authority by acknowledging the authority of the "natives" through practices that call even her own representations into question. As she argues, "To accept "native" authority *is* to give up the game" (1994, 32). (As discussed in the previous chapters, I did not sufficiently question my authority in my representation of Native evangelicals.)

To ascertain some of the theoretical productions in Native women's activist circles, I have relied on books, articles, manifestos, and speeches by Native women activists, primarily in Women of All Red Nations and the Indigenous Women's Network. I have attempted not to rely primarily on books published by women that are easily accessible but on more difficult to access materials that have been distributed throughout Native communities. The reason is that so few books have been published featuring Native women's analysis that non-Natives tend to excessively rely on them as representative of Native women's activism in general. In addition, relying on written work is wholly insufficient to uncover Native women's theories about activism. Unlike the Christian Right, which has such an extensive network of written informational sources, Native activism has often relied on word of mouth. Consequently, I have also interviewed sixteen Native women activists to discuss their theories about activism; the relationship between feminism and anticolonial struggles; the relationship between spirituality, religion, and political practice; and their theories on coalition building. The goal of these interviews is not to tell their "life stories," a genre Elizabeth Cook-Lynn notes that publishers seem to be obsessed with in publishing Native works (1998a, 120). Because of space constraints, however, this book focuses primarily on Native women activists' theories about feminism, nationalism, and coalition building. The rest of the material from these interviews may be found in another work (A. Smith 2002).

By utilizing a broader range of materials, I hope to show the diversity, the complexity, and even the contradictions within these theoretical productions. My hope was to present these women's voices not as narratives but as primary texts for the development of Native "feminist" theory. Obviously, because I am presenting these theories, my particular perspective influences the manner in which they are presented. Nevertheless, I wanted to resist the temptation to streamline these theories neatly into my own as this strategy would simply replicate the problem I am trying to address—the tendency to position one Native women's theory as representative of all Native women. My thought was that a more open-ended approach will point to the complexity, contradictions, and fullness of Native women's theorizing.[2] Because of space constraints, I was not able to sufficiently represent the diversity of thought within Native women's organizing that I would have liked. However, an alternative representation of this material with a more extended archive of Native feminist theory can be found in the earlier version of this work (A. Smith 2002).

Borrowing from Stuart Hall, I use the words *feminism* and *sovereignty* with the understanding that these are concepts "under erasure." That is, these are terms that have been destabilized and are under contention in Native communities but still have significance, positively and negatively, for Native women's activism. I make no claim that the theories generated

[2] See Joy James's similar analysis of the representation of black feminist theory (1999). The earlier version of this work includes interviewees' responses to my representational practice (A. Smith 2002).

from this discussion are representative of Native women's theoretical insights as a whole or that all of the Native women cited claim the term *feminist* for themselves. In fact, many interviewees might vociferously reject the term. However, their theories are still instructive for Native feminists who are looking to articulate indigenous feminisms (which is also a heterogeneous discourse). My goal is to uncover some of the analysis taking place among Native women organizers that can be instructive to those thinking about sovereignty, feminist, and coalition politics. To develop what could be some theoretical foundations for Native feminisms, however, I must first demonstrate that Native feminisms exist.

Native Feminist Strategies and Articulations

Because Native women are generally told that Native feminism is an oxymoron (Grande 2004; Jaimes and Halsey 1992; Monture-Angus 1995; Monture-Angus 1999), the mantras around "Native women aren't feminists" can prevent us from having a fuller discussion about the strategic issues of terminology. That is, the term *feminist* is not as important as certain questions: (1) what conversations do particular terms enable us to have, (2) which interventions do they allow us to make in particular contexts, and (3) which conversations and interventions do they impede? Thus, behind Native women's use and/or disavowal of feminist politics are interventions into how sovereignty and feminist politics are articulated.

First, not all Native women activists disassociate themselves from the term *feminist*.[3] Furthermore, for many women who do call themselves

[3] For reasons of space, I am focusing on Native women who do call themselves feminists since they have received relatively little attention. However, many Native women disassociate themselves from this term for a variety of reasons. Below are some examples.
Yvonne Dennis: I don't believe I'm a feminist; I believe I'm a nationalist, because if we could get our nationalism back, then we wouldn't have a problem with feminism. I think we have a lot of answers in our doctrine and traditions. We've lost our balance of power between men and women. I don't have issues with . . . I don't want what the National Organization of Women wants. I don't want that. I want balance. I don't see men as the enemy. I just see that we're out of kilter. We have to bring back the harmony and the balance. All of life, we have male and female. Even in building construction, you have a female part and a male part to make the building fit together. So I believe in the balance.
Sammy Toineeta: On my reservation, women always had a voice. We could get up and speak anytime; we could take on any role we wanted. It's just that the western people never believed it. White women never believed it. . . . They don't have that;

feminists the appropriation of the term becomes a strategy through which many Native women activists refuse the policing of their gender politics. Hence, some women assert not only that they are feminists but that they call themselves "feminists without apology."

> Thomas: I think it's important for Native women to say, "Yeah, I'm a feminist." Because you know what? I think it causes kind of a tension that has a potential for growth, not only for the person that will say it, even though you vacillate sometimes, but for the person who has to hear it. Like when some dumb guy is going to go, "Hey, you're one of them feminists or something?" "God damn right, and what are you going to say about it?"

> Ross: Yes, that [Native women not calling themselves feminists] does bother me. And I'm not sure why. What I think off the top of my head is 1972, working so hard to bridge the gap at these different conferences that were being held in the state of Montana between white women feminists who I knew and Native women who were feminists and who never were identified and recognized for their leadership and having the Indian women just hate being called a feminist and me saying, but we are, we are one too. It's an empowering term. I guess it goes back to my history and my struggle and at the same time white women never fully accepting them. But it still

---

they never had that voice. Whereas we at least within our own community have the voice. So I think even though those other people didn't know we had a voice, didn't believe we had a voice, we had an outlet, and they didn't. So they felt they had to have this outlet, so they developed this feminist movement.

Rebecca VanVlack: I don't think feminism has a good connotation to it necessarily. Because I think in a lot of ways feminism is for white women. Women's power and women's strength I don't think has ever been totally denied or gone away with Native women. I think we've allowed it to slip out of our hands, and when you have so much else to do, but I figure it's a matter of taking it back rather than gaining it in the first place, like it is for Europeans.

Heather Milton: I find that a lot of feminists are really anti-men. And I'm not anti-men. With indigenous people, I have to tell them I'm uncomfortable with you talking like that or doing something that is really derogatory toward men because I think they have value too. I seem that way sometimes because I'll get mad as all hell for getting treated like crap sometimes, but when it comes down to it I don't really feel that way.

Ingrid Washinawatok: Indigenous women have responsibilities that are distinct from those of men. When men and women follow the original instructions, there is complementary balance. We do not want to be men, nor do we want to fight men. We want to fight sexism. However, the dominant-culture feminist movement seeks "equality" between the sexes. This ignores the distinct sexual differences and the essence of the feminine is lost (1995a, 26).

bothers me. But I understand, right, because I do it too. But it still does bother me.

Rencontre: Feminism is defending our status as keepers of our nations.[4]

Lee Maracle critiques her previous disassociation from the "women's movement" and "feminism" as a reflection of her own "enslavement."

Until the March of 1982, feminism, indeed womanhood itself, was meaningless to me. Racist ideology had defined womanhood for the Native woman as nonexistent; therefore, neither the woman question nor the European rebel's response held any meaning for me . . .

I responded, like so many other women, as a person without sexuality. Native women did not even like the words *women's liberation*, and even now it burns my back. . . . I woke up. I AM WOMAN! (Maracle 1988, 19)

Their reasons for and the manner in which they adopt the term *feminist*, as well as how they define feminism, is as varied as for the women who do not choose to call themselves feminists. Thomas, for instance, describes her feminism as an "everyday, practical feminism."

I think a lot of Native women have to be feminists. . . . Because they're trying to kick your ass. They're taking numbers! That's what my father told me. They're taking a number and standing in line to kick your ass, kick you dead in your ass, so don't bother to do it to yourself. Why bother? When you're raised from when your real little that this is the way it is, I haven't found anything that tells me different, and I think that's why the old man raised me to think. I was real little and everything, but he raised me to think I could box somebody, and stand up for myself, and be a surveyor when nobody else was, and have a good time! Not be all crushed by it. It's like, you're trying to piss on my parade? What I'm going to do is I'm going to like kick your ass out of the way and keep on parading because if I have to work I'm not going

---

[4] See also:

Star: I'm a feminist because I think anything else is unintelligent (laughs). And I just can't go with turning my brain into Jell-O for someone else's fantasy fulfillment.

Ross: I know. There was a workshop I did on Indian feminism, and I even called it that. I talked about the F-word, . . . and most of the Native women were from Fort Belknap, Blackfeet, and Rocky Boys, and they were so excited to hear an Indian woman talk and name all the things they felt that it was very well received by them. And yet that night, as I was eating dinner with several women who were my friends and were in my audience, one of them, their husband came in, dragged her into the bathroom and tried to beat the shit out of her.

to have it be a grim, horrid experience every day. I'll make it real horrid experience for your first! I think that's an everyday, practical feminism.

Other activists use the term on a more strategic, contingent basis. Their notion of "strategic feminism" suggests an alternative possibility for articulating one's relationship to feminism. Rather than understanding "feminist" as an identity one either does or does not have, one can articulate "feminism" as a complex set of tools for political practice that can be selectively employed.

> Pamela Kingfisher: I will identify in certain political arenas, but I always say what I just said—Native women do not work for our rights; we work to fulfill our responsibilities, and it's a different way.
>
> Rencountre: Yeah, right now, during this period I am in, I do [consider myself a feminist]. But I think when I reach another certain age I probably won't be because I'm hoping males will have the respect back so I won't have to be.
>
> Ross: Well, you know I vary that from situation to situation. Because when I'm back home, I'll say I'm a feminist just to rile the guys so they know where I still stand. So there's nothing tricky about who I am and what I'm doing. And when I'm out here in a white women's studies department, I won't call myself [one] because I don't want to align myself with their politics.

Ross's quote, in conversation with the following quotation from Toni Sheehy, points to the false binary between feminism and nonfeminism among Native women. While Ross uses the term selectively, Sheehy reports that she supports feminism but does not call herself a feminist. Her reluctance to adopt the term *feminist*, comes not so much from a disagreement with feminist politics as from the lack of a term for *feminist* in her indigenous language: As she expresses it, "It's not the term that fits within my culture. I'm an Indian woman, first and foremost. I'm a strong Indian woman, very directed, and I believe in feminism as I understand society, and that I would be a part of that. . . . The word doesn't equate with any Indian word that I would know. That's what I mean, there isn't a word."

Similarly, Patricia Monture-Angus, while not adopting the term *feminist* for herself, does not completely reject the term. She says that because the suffrage movement in the 1800s was based on the suffragettes' exposure to positions of women in the Haudensosaunee: "To fully reject feminism means to reject part of my own Mohawk history and the influence of my grandmothers. It is important for both Aboriginal women and feminists to reclaim our histories and to note that our histories are, in fact, shared. It is equally important to see how parts of this shared history have been erased" (1995, 231).

Thus, within Native women's organizing we can see similar interventions being made into what is termed "feminist" politics by those who do and do not call themselves feminists. First, whether or not they call themselves feminists, Native women activists affirm the importance of Native women organizing as women. A common sentiment is reflected in Toineeta's statement about why Native women's organizing is important: "I think it goes back to the joke they always make: the men show up and the women do the work."

In addition, Native women cast open for debate the way sexism is defined. Many Native women argue that women and men have distinct, though equally valuable, roles to play, particularly in ceremonies. Some women presume that they cannot call themselves feminists, for instance, because they think women should not be on the drum or engage in particular ceremonial roles. This assumption speaks to the importance of further discussions in feminist circles about how and why practices become deemed as sexist. According to Tonya Gonnella Frichner,

> If you look at our traditional ways of life, men and women were not separated per se in the Euro-American model, but they were separated in terms of responsibilities. Men had their responsibilities, and women had their responsibilities. We went down the river of life side by side with parallel responsibilities.
>
> In contemporary times, I often hear people say it is sexist that women cannot be chiefs. But it really is not sexist if you understand our history. Non-Native peoples often apply a white model of sexism to Native peoples and then think what we do is sexist. But if you look at how things work within our community, you understand. Just like the flora and fauna of the world, we have responsibilities that don't cross over, so do women and men have separate responsibilities that do not cross over.
>
> For the Haudenosaunee, women have responsibilities that non-Indians would agree are incredibly powerful. Women were very directly involved in the choosing and selection of our spokesperson, the man that sits in council and brings our voices to the council fire. The suffragette movement in the U.S. was inspired by our constitution, the Great Law of Peace. Women have a lot of responsibility in government, in ways of life, in leadership, and even the power of recall of leaders who fail to fulfill their

responsibilities. This idea of separation is just a different way of looking at things. Men and women have different responsibilities based on our original instructions, and who am I to question that? It works, it worked, and I respect that. . . .

No, I don't consider myself a feminist. I think because if I did I would think it is okay to change our laws and allow women to be chiefs. But I understand why the laws are the way they are, and we should respect them.

This viewpoint seems to echo the evangelical complementarian argument about gender roles (to be discussed later in this chapter) that women and men have distinct roles, even though both are valued equally by God. Yet there are some important distinctions. Native women activists do not call for male headship. In fact, during the United Nations Third Permanent Forum on Indigenous Issues, when the Indigenous Women's Caucus was developing its statement to the forum, it contemplated using the language of "complementary" gender roles and then chose to reject this terminology so as to avoid association with the Christian Right. In addition, Toineeta and Alfonso suggest that these distinct roles do not necessarily have to be tied to specific male or female bodies.

> Toineeta: What you need to do is go back to the community, a community where no role or no job was lesser. Every job had equal importance in keeping that community moving. . . .
> Me: If there was a situation in which all roles were equally valued, are there some roles women should be doing as compared to men, and if so, what?
> Toineeta: No, but I've never felt that way. I think it's the role that should be equally valued; it doesn't matter who does it. Culturally, we had the *winkte*, the gay man, the man with two spirits, but they had certain roles. They were a lot of times brought out with the contraries into battle and were just as brave. They weren't stereotyped in a certain way, they just had a different role, and that role was very valuable to the tribe. So we have to spend a little more time focusing on the roles, and I think if the roles become more equal, then the person who does that specific thing is more equal.

Toineeta suggests an alternative possibility for theorizing about gender difference and oppression. She is suggesting that liberal feminism has often identified the primary problem with the distinction in gender roles. If we center Native women's histories in a feminist analysis, we might instead identify the problem as one of devaluing certain roles rather than gender role distinctions. However, there is some tension between supporting a gender complementarianism politics (which presumes two genders) when Native societies were not necessarily structured on gender binary systems prior to colonization (Jacobs, Thomas, and Lang 1999). As Michelene Pesantubbee's groundbreaking work on Choctaw gender relations argues, gender complementarianism should be understood as "multiple" rather than dichotomous (2005, 6). Perhaps we must speak of gender polymentarianism instead.

In addition, another common distinction made between white and Native women's struggles is that white women struggle for power they never had in society, whereas Native women are fighting to regain power they did have and in fact have never completely lost. Rebecca VanVlack observes, "Women's power and women's strength I don't think has ever been totally denied or gone away with Native women. I think we've allowed it to slip out of our hands, and when you have so much else to do, but I figure it's a matter of taking it back rather than gaining it in the first place, like it is for Europeans."

Implicitly, this analysis calls into question the progressive assumptions behind liberal feminism—that the status of women is steadily improving from its previous degraded status. This progressive notion of liberal feminist history often coincides with primitivist notions of indigeneity. As an example, a 1985 Virginia Slims ad reflected a similar notion that white patriarchy saves Native women from oppression. On the left side of the ad was a totem pole with cartoonish figures of Indian women. Their names were Princess Wash and Scrub; Little Running Water Fetcher; Keeper of the Teepee; Princess; Breakfast, Lunch, and Dinner Preparer; Woman Who Gathers Firewood; Princess Buffalo Robe Sewer; Little Woman Who Weaves All Day; and Woman Who Plucks Feathers for Chief's Headdress. The caption atop the totem pole read: "Virginia Slims remembers one of many societies where the women stood head and shoulders above the men." On the right side of the ad, there was a model in makeup, a tight skirt, nylons, and high heels, with the familiar caption "You've come a long way, baby." The message is that Native women, oppressed in their tribal societies, need to be liberated into patriarchal standards of beauty where their true freedom lies. In this Virginia Slims ad, feminism is tied to colonial conquest and (white) women's liberation is founded on the destruction of supposedly patriarchal Native societies. By arguing that Native societies were not patriarchal prior to colonization, Native women are challenging the assumption that brown women need to be saved from brown men (Spivak 1994).

Many activists do echo Jaimes and Halsey's critique as well as critiques developed by many women of color—that white feminism strives for gender equality within a capitalist, colonial context without questioning the economic and political system itself. Winona LaDuke (an Anishnabe) for instance, argued in her keynote speech at the United Nations' Beijing Conference on Women that attempting to be "equal" with men under the current capitalist and imperialist world order will do nothing to liberate most women: "It is not, frankly, that women of the dominant society in so called first world countries should have equal pay, and equal status, if that pay and status continues to be based on a consumption model which is not only unsustainable, but causes constant violation of the human rights of women and nations elsewhere in the world" (1995b).

A coalition of indigenous women and women's organizations from around the world issued a statement critiquing the Beijing platform on women on similar grounds.

> The "Beijing Draft Platform for Action," unfortunately, is not critical at all of the "New World Order." . . . Its recommended "strategic objectives" and actions focus on ensuring women's equal access and full participation in decision-making, equal status, equal pay, and integrating and mainstreaming gender perspectives and analysis. These objectives are hollow and meaningless if the inequality between nations, races, classes, and genders, are not challenged at the same time. Equal pay and equal status in the so-called First World is made possible because of the perpetuation of a development model which is not only non-sustainable but causes the increasing violation of the human rights of women, Indigenous peoples, and nations elsewhere. The Platform's overemphasis of gender discrimination and gender quality depoliticizes the issues confronting Indigenous women. ("Beijing Declaration on Indigenous Women" n.d., 26–28)

Thus, one central intervention made by Native women is recentering colonialism within gender analysis. Almost across the board, Native women activists trace the degradation of Native women's status, not from a universal phenomenon of "patriarchy" but from the processes of colonization that resulted in the imposition of European patriarchal relationships on Native communities. According to Janet McCloud, "Many Anglo women try, I expect in all sincerity, to tell us that our most pressing problem is male supremacy. To this, I have to say with all due respect, bullshit. Our problems are what they've been for the past several hundred years: white supremacism and colonialism. And that's a supremacism and a colonialism of which white feminists are still very much a part" (Jaimes and Halsey 1992, 332). Even women who consider themselves feminists do not necessarily prioritize issues that have been stereotypically defined as "feminist" in light of the pressing land rights struggles they face. As Thunder Hawk, who calls herself a feminist, states, "I'm pro-choice, I'm all for [it], in this modern day, but . . . again looking from the Indian standpoint in Indian society, to me, to argue about just equal pay and all that kind of thing, to me that struggle's like frosting on a cake. When you get done with the survival stuff, then we can tackle that." For feminism to resonate with Native women, it must be reconceptualized such that land rights issues, self-determination, and sovereignty are conceptualized as feminist issues. And, as I have argued elsewhere, it must address the United States as a colonial entity rather than a bastion of freedom (A. Smith 2005b).[5]

This reappropriation of the term *feminist*, however, does not necessarily connote a desire to coalesce with white feminists. In fact, while Native "feminists" may be accused of selling out to white feminists, in fact, their reappropriation of the term may signal just the opposite. Many Native women argue that rejecting the term *feminist* for its connotations of whiteness allows white women to determine the meaning of the word rather than allowing Native women to define it. Such a move allows white women to define both feminism and the way gender politics should and could be addressed rather than more directly challenging the politics they carry on in the name of feminism. This sentiment was expressed by several activists.

> Thomas: They [white women] think they define feminism. This kills me! There's a whole bunch of people who think they do. And it just kills me . . . Maybe there isn't a global feminism. The word has a meaning, and I think that the meaning that it has for me, is different than the meaning it has for other people.
>
> Rivera: [On Native women rejecting the term *feminist*] I think that's giving that concept to someone else, which I think is ridiculous. It's something that there has to be more discussion about what that means. I always considered, they took that from us in a way. That's the way I've seen it. So I can't see it as a bad thing because I think the origins are from people who had empowered women a long time ago.
>
> Star: [On the notion that feminism is "white"] To me that kind of gives white women power in saying they can define a movement, they can define an order of relationships based on their particularity. I don't grant them that. I don't grant that they own that term. I don't grant that feminism

5 See also (Kazanjian 2003).

looks like them, acts like them, thinks like them, or should be ordered
by them.

Lee Maracle writes that it is important for all women, including Native
women, to develop a more global perspective on the women's movement
—that white women from North America are only one small part of this
movement.

> A good number of non-white women have addressed the women's move-
> ment and decried the fact that we are outside the women's movement. I
> have never felt outside of that movement. . . . I have never felt that the wom-
> en's movement was centered or defined by women here in North America.
> That the white women of North America are racist and that they define the
> movement in accordance with their own narrow perspective should not
> surprise us. . . . We are part of a global movement of women in the world,
> struggling for emancipation. The world will define the movement. We are
> part of the women who will define it. . . . I represent the future of the women
> in North America, just as any other woman does. That white women only
> want to hear from me as a Native and not as a voice in the women's move-
> ment is their loss. (1988, 180–82)

Interestingly, the African National Congress Women's Section made a
similar analysis of feminism that challenges any essentialist understanding
of the term: "There is nothing wrong with feminism," it claims. "It is as
progressive or reactionary as nationalism. Nationalism can be reactionary
or progressive. We have not got rid of the term nationalism. And with
feminism it is the same" (McClintock 1995, 384). Such moves resonate
with the manner in which other women of color have laid claim to the
term *feminist*, such as Barbara Smith's definition of the term: "Feminism is
the political theory and practice that struggles to free all women: women
of color, working-class women, poor women, disabled women, lesbians,
old women—as well white, economically privileged, heterosexual women.
Anything less than this vision of total freedom is not feminism, but merely
female self-aggrandizement" (1982, 49).

These theoretical insights fundamentally challenge how feminism has
been both theorized and historicized in scholarly and activist circles. For
instance, the feminist movement is generally periodized into the so-called
first, second, and third waves of feminism. The first wave is characterized by the suffragette movement; the second wave is characterized by
the formation of the National Organization for Women, abortion rights
politics, and the fight for the Equal Rights Amendment. Suddenly, dur-

ing the third wave of feminism, women of color make an appearance to transform feminism into a multicultural movement (Heywood and Drake 1997; Kaschak 2001; Kesselman, McNair, and Schneidwind 1999; Nicholson 1997). This periodization necessarily centers the histories of white middle-class women to which women of color attach themselves. So it is not a surprise that many women of color and Native women resist identifying with this movement. However, if we *recentered* Native women in an account of feminist history, we might begin with 1492, when Native women collectively resisted colonization. In this new history, the importance of the anticolonial struggle would be central in our articulation of feminism.[6] We might understand that there are multiple feminist histories emerging from multiple communities of color, which intersect at points and diverge in others. Such a reperiodization would not minimize the contributions made by white feminists but would decenter them from our historicizing and analysis.

The value I see of such a project was evident to me when I taught a class entitled "Native American Feminism." What was interesting was how, by giving the class that name rather than "Native American Women," non-Native women in the class were directly challenged to rearticulate the assumptions behind their own feminist politics in a way that disassociating Native women from feminism would not have done. As with all English terms, including *feminism* (as well as *sovereignty* and *nationalism*, which will be discussed later), we have the task of what Patricia Monture-Angus describes as taking a language that does not work for us and giving it new life (1995, 35) or what Joy Harjo and Gloria Bird describe as "reinventing the enemy's language" (1997). Such a task of "infiltrating feminism," as Sammy Toineeta describes it, is not at odds with Native women activists also developing alternative terminology that might successfully mobilize Native communities to address issues of sexism more directly. The partial refusal to coalesce with white feminism derives not so much from a fear of being deemed "white" by association as from a strategic intervention that challenges not only the practices of Native men but the practices of white women (a much different strategy than that adopted by conservative evangelical feminists, as will be discussed in the next section). In addition, the

[6] Such an attempt is developed in Serna Berer Gluck's "Whose Feminism, Whose History?" which attempts to draw out multiple feminist histories. Yet she sometimes recapitulates white hegemonic articulations of feminist history when she states that in the early 1980s "Indian women had planted themselves firmly in the women's movement" as if the organizing they had been doing for centuries was not the "women's movement" itself (Gluck 1998, 43).

mantra "Native women aren't feminists" silences a broader discussion on rhetorical strategy. That is, rather than arguing over terminology, we could discuss our strategies behind the terms we choose. In addition, our rhetorical strategies may change over time. For instance, based on my own organizing history, I was more sympathetic to a disavowal of the term feminist during the "sisterhood is global" period of the 1980s when white women seemed to assume an alliance and solidarity with indigenous women and women of color. This disavowal was a strategy intended to call this assumption into question. Now, however, I see this assumption as having been sufficiently called into question, such that it might make sense to intervene in feminist politics again. That is, so many colonial policies are being conducted under the banner of feminism (such as supporting the war on terror in order to "liberate" Arab women from repressive regimes) that it seems necessary to wrest the term from this colonial discourse and claim it for anticolonial, anti-white-supremacist projects. Of course, other Native women could make compelling arguments as to why we should adopt a different rhetorical strategy. But the important discussion becomes less about which term is best than about which rhetorical strategies we should adopt in particular contexts.

Evangelical Feminism

While Native feminisms destabilize notions of Native communities as singularly progressive, evangelical feminisms destabilize notions of evangelicalism as singularly conservative. While histories of the Christian Right often characterize feminism as fundamentally based on antifeminist politics (Alexander and Mohanty 1997; Domigues 1994), in fact, feminism is also constitutive of evangelicalism. I will contextualize my discussion of evangelicalism with a brief history of the evangelical feminist movement. However, since several versions of this history have recently been published, I will not describe this history at length (see, e.g., Cochran 2005; Gallagher 2003; Horner 2002; and Ingersoll 2005).[7]

---

[7] As in chapters 1 and 2, this analysis is informed by extensive surveys of Christian periodical literature and participant observation in Christian Right and conservative evangelical events. However, it is supplemented with material from thirty informal interviews I conducted among gender complementarians and egalitarians (those who support gender hierarchy and equality, respectively) involved in various degrees within the Promise Keepers movement. These interviews were conducted as part of an educational project of the National Council of Churches during the summer of

At the same time that the Christian Right was mobilizing against the political gains of liberal feminism, including campaigning to reverse *Roe v. Wade* and stop the passage of the Equal Rights Amendment, sectors within conservative evangelicalism were inspired by these struggles to call for reform within evangelicalism itself. A starting point of contemporary evangelical feminism was the founding of the Evangelical Women's Caucus (EWC, now EWCI), which was formed in 1973 from the women's caucus of Evangelicals for Social Action (Hearn 1993, 219). Some of the most prominent founding members of EWCI were Virginia Ramey Mollenkott, the author of *Women, Men, and the Bible* (1977), and Letha Scanzoni and Nancy Hardesty, the authors of *All We're Meant to Be* (1974). Another evangelical feminist organization, Christians for Biblical Equality (CBE), was formed in 1985 as a splinter group from EWCI. Prominent CBE figures include Patricia Gundry, the author of *Woman Be Free!* (1977), her husband Stanley Gundry, Catherine Kroeger, and Alvera Mickelsen.

The early works of evangelical feminists tended to be concerned with the exegesis of "problem passages," that is, passages in which the biblical authors seemed to argue for the subordination of women to men. Because evangelicals view the Bible as authoritative for Christian living, evangelical feminists did not have the option of following Rosemary Radford Ruether's advice regarding patriarchal texts: "We no longer need to apologize for them or try to interpret them as words of truth, but we cast out their oppressive message as expressions of evil and justifications of evil" (1985, 137). Instead, they had to account for the problem passages within an evangelical tradition, usually by arguing that these passages said something other than what traditional evangelicals claimed. Rather than argue that the Bible poses a problem for women, they argued that, properly understood, the Bible liberates women. As Mollenkott states, "It is precisely my study of the Bible that has radicalized me" (1980, 26).

Virginia Mollenkott and Patricia Gundry characterize two important strands of evangelical feminist biblical exegesis during this period. Gundry presumes biblical inerrancy (the Bible contains no errors of any kind), while Mollenkott presumes neither inerrancy nor infallibility (the Bible

1997 (names and identifying features have been changed). The interviewees were selected based on availability and convenience. While I make no claims that the ideas expressed in these interviews are representative of evangelicals in general, they do provide further insight into the dynamics of race and gender within Christian Right discourse.

teaches no errors regarding Christian doctrines of faith or practice). Gundry's inerrantist position requires that she account for even the most difficult passages with a feminist reading and argue that Paul in particular, properly understood, supports gender equality in the church and home (Gundry 1977). She also attributes all Pauline books to Paul and does not argue that any passages are interpolations.

Mollenkott, by contrast, does not hew to either an inerrantist or infallibilist interpretation of Scripture, although she does maintain that the Bible is authoritative for Christian living (1977a, 100; 1977c, 105). She does try to insulate Paul against charges of sexism to a certain extent (1976, 21; 1977b, 75–76). Unlike Gundry, however, Mollenkott does not believe Paul consistently preaches women's equality. She writes, "Although there are some feminists who think that all of Paul's words and attitudes can be explained in a completely harmonious egalitarian fashion once we achieve a full understanding of the cultural conditions and the Greek usage involved, to date I have not found their interpretations convincing" (1977c, 95). Nevertheless, even these passages are divinely inspired insofar as they are instructive for Christians in considering how to balance biblical imperatives with societal norms.

These differences prove to be critical because of the central importance to mainstream evangelicals, in their response to evangelical feminism, of feminist stances on biblical inerrancy. During the time of these writings, evangelicals were locked in a "Battle of the Bible" (Price 1986). Evangelicals argued over whether or not the Bible was inerrant, infallible, or neither.[8] Inerrantist evangelicals also argued over whether or not noninerrantist evangelicals could properly call themselves evangelical.[9] These debates in inerrancy contributed to a reconfiguring of fundamentalism and neo-evangelicalism. As is outlined in greater detail in appendix 1, militant fundamentalists broke away from moderate fundamentalists, such as Jerry Falwell, who were beginning to cooperate with nonfundamentalists to further right-wing political goals (they interpreted this coop-

[8] On inerrancy, see Harold Lindsell's *Battle of the Bible*, which was one of the most influential books espousing this point of view. Lindsell argues that the Bible "does not contain error of any kind, including scientific and historical facts" (1976a, 18). See also the "Chicago Statement on Biblical Hermeneutics" in Radmacher and Preus 1984, 881–904). On infallibility, see Bloesch 1978, 65; Fuller 1973, 68; and Hubbard 1970, 58. On the view that the Bible is neither inerrant nor infallible, see Beegle 1973, 278–80.

[9] See, for example, Hanger 1984, 19–22.

eration as violating the fundamentalist principle of separation from non-believers).[10] Meanwhile, neo-evangelicals (who shared fundamentalists' beliefs in the five fundamentals of faith but separated from them around the time of World War II because they did not want to separate from the larger society) were beginning to split into conservative, mainstream, and radical groups, largely based on approaches to biblical inerrancy.[11]

This debate over inerrancy tended to overshadow discussions of any other issues, particularly issues of women's equality. Robert Johnston argued that discussions among evangelicals, such as those in the Evangelical Theological Society, had become "one-topic convocations" on biblical inerrancy (1979, 46).[12] Margaret L. Bendroth similarly notes, "This theological stalemate [over biblical inerrancy], escalating into a full-fledged battle for the Bible, has obscured the larger issue of women's role within evangelical Protestantism" (1984, 134). Consequently, mainstream evangelicals critiqued early evangelical feminist writings almost solely on grounds of biblical inerrancy and even ignored other controversial views espoused by evangelical feminists, such as Mollenkott's universalism (Mollenkott 1980, 104),[13] which contradicts one of the five fundamentals. There was a clear sense among mainstream evangelicals that on the matter of the biblical interpretation all would be won or lost.

Thus, responses to evangelical feminism varied depending on the critic's commitment to biblical inerrancy. Some thought of evangelical feminists themselves as a priori noninerrantists, regardless of how they approached the Bible, and therefore not evangelical. Militant fundamentalists did not acknowledge the existence of Christian feminism since feminism itself was regarded as heresy. This sentiment is conveyed in Stewart Custer's review of Mollenkott's *Speech, Silence, Action!* published in *Biblical View-*

[10] See Nash 1987, 67.

[11] The five fundamentals of faith include biblical inerrancy, the deity of Christ, substitutionary atonement, bodily resurrection, and the second coming of Christ. The lack of attention to Mollenkott's universalism is surprising considering that even evangelicals, who generally have a more liberal view of biblical interpretation and/or women's equality, still reject antiuniversalist approaches. See, for example, Conn 1984, 104; Davis 1977, 17; Johnston 1979, 3; and Quebedeaux 1974, 45.

[12] Works expressing similar viewpoints include Ammerman 1991; Lightner 1978, 46; Noll 1984, 11–19; and Osborne 1985, 82.

[13] Universalism is the belief that all peoples will attain eternal salvation. In fact, prominent mega-church pastor, Carlton Pearson of the Higher Dimensions Family Church in Tulsa Oklahoma lost 90 percent of his 5000 person congregation when he started preaching universalism. He lost an election bid for mayor in 2002, and ended up losing his church in 2006 (Sherman 2006; Tiansay 2002b).

point, a Bob Jones University journal (and Mollenkott's alma mater), in which he wrote, "Virginia Ramey Mollenkott has written one of the most self-centered books to come out of the press in recent years. . . . One wonders whether the subtitle of the books should be the 'cycle of unbelief' rather than 'the cycle of faith.' The reading of such a book reminds one that the 'public and final repudiation of what one formerly professed' is still a proper definition of apostasy" (Custer 1981, 67). In the eyes of militant fundamentalists, evangelical feminism was a theology "utterly devoid of Bible truth but Satan-inspired" that would lead Christians to believe in a "soft and effeminate Christianity—exotic, but cowardly" (Dollar 1973, 103).

Among the conservative evangelical and moderate fundamentalist periodicals, discussions of evangelical feminism were virtually nil. My survey of *Moody Monthly* (published by the Moody Bible Institute) from 1973 to 1985 uncovered virtually no articles published by evangelical feminists nor reviews of their works. As Gundry noted, this absence was not accidental, for "Traditionalists have always pretended feminists weren't there" (Williams 1980, 17). One exception was an article by Gundry in which she very cautiously argued that perhaps evangelicals should reconsider the claims of feminism in light of biblical teachings (1975). That was the extent of Moody's tolerance of feminism. Four years later Gundry's husband Stanley, who was a professor at the Moody Bible Institute, was fired from his job a few months after Patricia gave a press interview describing her feminist journey. Afterward Ms. Gundry was banned from the institute, its radio station, and all of its publications (Stentzel 1979). The official reasons for firing Stanley Gundry were (1) that the couple's views on feminism were being represented as the views of the institute and were "bringing financial loss" to it"; (2) that Stanley Gundry was in serious violation of the school's "historic position" regarding the role of women; and (3) that the teaching of Scripture is "so perfectly clear on the feminist issue" that Gundry was guilty of serious doctrinal error (Stentzel 1979).

In general the more conservative evangelical and moderate fundamentalists were reluctant to discuss even the most conservative evangelical feminists. At most, they made passing references to the travesty feminism had wrought on society and Christianity, for example:

> Women's libbers as a group are not bad people, their only crimes being those harmless ones of blasphemy, baby murder, prostitution, homosexuality, marriage breaking, hate mongering, and free sex—certainly forgiv-

able if we consider the terrible repression they have been subjected to in the past. (Boop 1975, 54)

No, let's not take a second look at the feminist movement or Equal Rights Amendment or whatever you want to call it. Let's take a second look at the Word of God. (Gorcoff 1975, 56)

Nevertheless, it does appear that feminism had some impact on them. A few readers of *Moody Monthly*, for example, did express some sympathy toward feminism. Some examples include:

I found the book *[All We're Meant to Be]* to be an excellent and much needed Christian work in these days of re-evaluation of male-female relationships. (Wilson 1975)

We should certainly take another look before we write off the women's movement as entirely secular and irrelevant to the biblical Christian. There are many of us "out here" who are wrestling with issues concerning our own personhood. (Mahler 1975, 55)

It would also seem that feminism induced many traditionalists to at least pay lip service to the idea that women should have equal pay for equal work, should have equal employment and educational opportunities, and are equal to men before God (even though they must remain subordinate to men while they are on earth) (Hart 1983; Neff 1980, 36; Senter 1973; Williams 1982, 175). A conservative evangelical, A. Duane Litfin, wrote, "Much of what they [evangelical feminists] have written is valid, even praiseworthy" (1979, 270–71). Even Jerry Falwell, not known for his progressive views regarding women, asked, "How much thought have we given to what has caused the rise of feminism? Could it be that we failed to objectively consider some legitimate inequities that need balancing? . . . Too many Fundamentalist Christians have wrong mental attitudes toward women" (1983, 1).[14]

If there were only glimmerings of a discussion on feminism in the conservative evangelical and moderate fundamentalist community, the mainstream evangelical community seemed to be more actively involved in discussing feminist issues as represented by such neo-evangelical periodicals as *His, Eternity* (both defunct), and *Christianity Today*. In these periodicals, feminism was discussed as a controversial subject, not heresy.

[14] By contrast, *World* suggested in 1999 that men and not women were facing gender discrimination in the educational system, concluding that "feminists are the real sexists" (Veith 1999c, 26).

A typical article on feminism was "Women: Second Class Citizens?" which appeared in *Eternity*. Nancy Hardesty wrote the article, and several people wrote reactions to it—some favorable, some not—in inserts within the article. The editors prefaced the article by describing the controversy inherent in feminist issues, saying that Christians "need to come to God's work with an open mind, leaving prejudices behind as much as possible" (Hardesty 1971, 14). Such periodicals often featured articles on feminism in which several viewpoints were represented in order to create a "balanced view."[15] This approach indicates that, although mainstream evangelicals were not wholeheartedly accepting feminism, they were willing to converse with feminists. This willingness to converse, however, depended on a feminist's take on inerrancy.

For instance, Harold Lindsell, whose *Battle of the Bible* sounded the call for biblical inerrancy as a litmus test for evangelicalism, rejected any evangelical feminist's claims to be considered evangelical if she rejected inerrancy. As he stated, "I do not for one moment concede . . . [that] anyone can claim the evangelical badge once he has abandoned inerrancy" (1976a, 18). He argued that someone like Mollenkott could not be called evangelical because "the way Mollenkott interprets the Bible means she cannot hold to an infallible Scripture. . . . What is the issue for the evangelical is the fact that some of the most ardent advocates of egalitarianism in marriage over against hierarchy reach their conclusions by directly and deliberately denying that the Bible is the infallible rule of faith and practice. Once they do this, they have ceased to be evangelical; Scripture no longer is normative" (Lindsell 1976b, 45–46).[16] (Note that in this paragraph Lindsell conflates infallibility with inerrancy.)

Whether or not Lindsell thought it is possible to argue for an inerrant evangelical feminist approach to the Bible is unclear. Some writers argued that they could not (Bubna and Bubna 1980; Edwards 1986; Laribee 1976; Zoscher 1976). But many were also willing to concede that evangelical feminists can properly call themselves evangelical. Litfin referred to "the feminists who call themselves evangelical—and the writer does not question their use of the term" (1979, 259). Part of the reason for this concession may have been the unwillingness of some evangelicals to make inerrancy the litmus test for evangelicalism. Carl Henry has stated that the

---

[15] Other articles that have appeared in such a format include Carlson and Barnhouse 1975; "Coming a Long Way" 1973; "How to Create a Woman" 1973; "Jesus and Women" 1973; Jewett and Elliot 1975; and Suffer and Knight 1981.

[16] See also House 1979, 53.

"distaste for the use of inerrancy as a polemical weapon in the absence of reasoned supports, must not be ignored. Neither can the increasing fragmentation of evangelical cohesion over the issue of inerrancy.... The duty of the evangelical enterprise requires something higher than invalidating every contribution of evangelicals who halt short of that commitment" (1984, 25).[17]

Other writers approved of writings that explicitly advocated inerrancy, such as Gundry's, but rejected those that did not, such as Mollenkott's. For instance, Harvie Conne critiqued Mollenkott's approach to the Bible, saying, "I struggle with how far one can move to the left of the evangelical continuum on biblical authority before moving off it altogether" (1984, 108). However, he speaks approvingly of Gundry's inerrantist approach to feminism, observing that she could "speak to evangelicals in a way not possible for . . . Mollenkott" (108; see also Rausch 1976, 22; and Siddons 1978, 40). Finally, there are many evangelical writers that spoke approvingly of evangelical feminists who did not subscribe to inerrancy. Many writers positively reviewed Mollenkott's work (Nelson 1981; Newman 1976; Vander Broek 1984). Shirley Nelson, for instance, in reviewing *Speech, Silence, Action!* wrote, "It is a healing book, not in the sense of soothing balm, but with the discomfort that healing often entails: stretching, moving unused muscles, seeing with a light that burns" (1981, 44).

Similarly, Paul Jewett's *Man as Male and Female* (1975) argued that Paul was a product of his patriarchal culture and hence did not always reflect God's will in his teachings (Jewett 1975). When he was brought up on charges at Fuller Seminary for teaching partial fallibility, the seminary found that the book was not a negation of the "Fuller Statement of Faith," which declares the Bible to be infallible (Johnston 1979, 35).

But in all cases commentators consistently ignored evangelical feminists' social and political concerns and commented only on their exegesis. For instance, Mollenkott wrote "The Women's Movement Challenges the Church and Three Responses" (1974). Her article was not designed to discuss biblical interpretations of women's role in society but to discuss the contemporary struggles of women with which the church had to come to terms. Mary Stewart Van Leeuwen, Robert Saucy, and Charles Ryrie basically wrote similar responses: Mollenkott's article was of limited value to evangelicals because it did not "discuss these questions from a Biblical Perspective" (Mollenkott 1974, 321). Another example was Walter M. Dunnet's review of *All We're Meant to Be* in *Moody Monthly.* Although he

[17] See also Hanger 1984.

concedes that "much of the cultural and sociological data in the book point up inequities in society," he proceeds to dismiss this book because he disagrees with its biblical interpretations (1975, 74). Feminists recognized that this preoccupation with inerrancy often masked an implicit reactionary political agenda, as Mollenkott's quotation at the beginning of this chapter indicates. However, evangelical feminism during this period created little space in which to discuss this political agenda because it was trapped into concentrating its efforts almost solely on providing alternative exegeses.

Nevertheless, it would not be accurate to argue that evangelical feminism had no impact on the evangelical community. The first Evangelical Women's Caucus in 1975 was filled to capacity (360 people attended and others had to be turned away), and *All We're Meant to Be* was so influential that it was named *Eternity*'s book of the year for 1975 (Buckley 1980, 33). As mentioned previously, even those traditionalists who were completely hostile to evangelical feminism acknowledged its impact on the evangelical community in statements such as:

> The feminist movement continues, inexorably, to make inroads into evangelical circles. (Litfin 1979, 258)

> There are few of us, however, who have not heard the Lord's Prayer begin, "Our Father/Mother, who is in heaven," or have not noticed a "Timeless One" in place of "Father" in pastoral prayers. (Edwards 1986, 30)

> The role relationship of women and men is one of the most discussed topics of our day, in evangelical circles as well as elsewhere. (Knight 1976, 13)

Mainstream evangelical responses to evangelical feminism began to change rather dramatically around the mid-1980s. At least three factors seemed to play a role in this shift: (1) the split in the Evangelical Women's Caucus and the formation of Christians for Biblical Equality, (2) the changing debate around biblical inerrancy in mainstream (and even conservative) evangelicalism, and (3) the rising consciousness of sexual, domestic, and clergy abuse in evangelical communities (this factor is addressed later in this chapter).

The Slippery Slope to Lesbianism

The first factor important in the development of evangelical feminism was the schism in the evangelical women's caucus and the formation of CBE as a result of EWC passing a resolution in support of gay and lesbian civil rights (Spring 1986). Heterosexual marriage, CBE holds, is "the pattern God designed for us" ("Christians for Biblical Equality Statement of Faith" 1994). Patricia Gundry represents this viewpoint when she states, "I refuse to link gay rights to women's rights" (1988, 15).[18] As a result, the feminists represented by CBE became much more acceptable for inclusion in the mainstream evangelical discourse than had been EWCI. They became the "good" evangelical feminists, unlike the hopelessly "bad" "lesbian" evangelical feminists. While gender hierarchicalists may not have agreed with CBE members' point of view, they were now taking greater pains to show them respect and take their arguments more seriously. For instance, the gender hierarchicalists John Piper and Wayne Grudem said of evangelical feminists (only those associated with CBE qualify as such), "We consider these authors to be brothers and sisters in Christ, and we have endeavored to respond to them in sincerity and love" (1991, xiii).[19]

The remaining members of EWCI (Mollenkott, Hardesty, and Scanzoni) are now seen as having "crossed over to liberalism . . . from the boundaries of evangelical Christian doctrine" (Kassian 1992, 216–17), and their writings are no longer included in mainstream evangelical journals and other periodicals. In 1991, EWCI changed its name to the Ecumenical/Evangelical Women's Caucus (EEWC) in order to reflect the fact that evangelicalism was no longer the community of accountability for many of its members (Kassian 1992). In addition, several of its key members, such as Virginia Mollenkott and Nancy Hardesty, have come out as lesbians. This shift was reflected in the advertising for its 2004 conference. It featured non-evangelical speakers such as Riffat Hassan, Rosemary Radford Ruether, and Phyllis Trible. Its statement of faith also reflects these changes: "EEWC welcomes members of any gender, race, ethnicity, color, creed, marital status, sexual orientation, religious affiliation, age, political party, parental status, economic class, or disability. . . . We believe that the gospel is good news for all persons. We also recognize that faith is expressed through a

[18] Gundry argues that she does not want to be associated with gay rights because when her husband was fired from the Moody Bible Institute as a result of her work, her critics were denouncing her as a lesbian. She (as well as members of the CBE) has been able to accrue more respectability in evangelical circles by openly denouncing evangelical lesbians (though Gundry does maintain in this article that she is not against gay rights, simply not interested enough to become informed as to what the Bible has to say on the issue).

[19] Note that Mollenkott and the current members of EWCI are not included in the list of acceptable evangelical feminists.

rich diversity of traditions and forms of spirituality."[20] Mollenkott's own theology has radically shifted and is now more under the purview of radical Christian theology as well as much less Christian-centric.[21]

Biblical feminists in CBE now find themselves more consistently included in the mainstream evangelical discourse. In fact, they became sufficiently powerful that the Council of Biblical Manhood and Womanhood (CBMW) was founded in 1987 specifically to counter CBE. The fact that Piper and Grudem of CBMW took the time to compile a book more than five hundred pages in length to respond in excruciating exegetical detail (and also using psychological, sociological, and legal analysis) in order to denounce evangelical feminism (i.e., those feminists represented by CBE), including a specific position paper in response to CBE's statement of purpose (previous denunciations of evangelical feminists were usually no longer than a page), indicates how seriously CBMW takes the work of CBE.[22] It is also a sign of CBE's influence that CBMW does not describe itself as supporting gender *hierarchy* but rather gender *complementarianism* (the belief that men and women have gender-complementary roles and men's role is to serve as heads of households and/or hold the office of pastor).[23] Thus, even gender hierarchicalists feel sufficiently compelled to soften their positions with euphemisms. Members of CBE, by contrast, have become known as gender *egalitarians*. Later in the chapter, I discuss the complementarian versus egalitarian debate in greater detail.

While CBE has gained considerable influence, the EWCI feminists function as a left-hand boundary to its religious critiques. If CBE says anything

[20] Evangelical/Ecumenical Women's Caucus Web site, www.eewc.org.

[21] For an analysis of Mollenkott's shifting theology, see Cochran 2005.

[22] Other changes in the attitude of traditionalists toward biblical feminists are reflected in these works. See *Recovering Biblical Manhood and Womanhood* (Piper and Grundem 1991). See also Packer 1986; and Pinnock 1986.

[23] Some complementarians, particularly Charismatic Christians, may support women as pastors but still support male headship in marriage. Women feature prominently in the development of Pentecostal and Charismatic Christianity. See Hyatt 2000, 121. In 1998, *Charisma* published a reader response to the question "Should women be ordained?" All but two of the nine who wrote responses said women should be ordained. *Charisma* further noted that Charismatic and Pentecostal churches were ordaining increasing numbers of women (Sound Off 1998). Other *Charisma* editorials call for support of the increased prominence of women leaders in Charismatic churches (Jackson 2006; Strang 1997). In another set of letters to the editor, all those printed supported women in the ministry (Letters 1999b). It also ran an op-ed piece, which stated that men must "become 'man enough' (and humble enough!) to admit that it's not the Bible but our male pride and cultural bias that prevent us from releasing women into ministry" (Grady 2000c).

too radical, complementarians charge that it is heading down the slippery slope toward the lesbian apostasy of EWCI. As Nancy Kassian argues, "It appears that many evangelical believers who adopted a conservative feminist position regarding the role of women at one point gravitated towards a more radical one as time wore on. EWC began by being evangelical, but is now far from it. Given this trend, it is entirely possible that the most recent evangelical and feminist leaders and CBE may be destined to follow suit" (Kassian 1992, 216).

The Politics of Inerrancy

Establishing correct meanings entails lots of hard, interpretive work. When disagreements arise, it is tempting to retreat from the hard work under the banner of tolerance and sensitivity. Instead, we should underscore in a loving, sensitive manner that only one of several conflicting interpretations can be correct. . . . [Otherwise] we find few contextual safeguards in this land of "what-it-means-to-me" and probably very little of God's voice.
—WALT RUSSEL

It follows then that persons within *different* discursive systems will not be able to hear the other's reasons *as* reasons, but only as errors or even delusions.—STANLEY FISH

The second factor critical to the evolution of evangelical feminism is the changing debate over biblical inerrancy. It appears as though evangelicals are increasingly describing themselves an inerrantists. This trend may be an indication of the strength of biblical conservatives. In order to even be heard, evangelicals must take up the banner of inerrancy. But at the same time evangelicals disagree on what inerrancy means. As Norman Geisler notes, "The de jure battle of inerrancy has calmed among mainline American evangelicals. Most have reaffirmed faith that the Bible is God's inerrant Word. However, the waters are still troubled in the area of what constitutes a de facto denial of inerrancy. There is a tendency to affirm inerrancy with the theological right hand, and then to deny it with the hermeneutical left hand" (Geisler 1987, 27).

Most evangelicals (though not all) argue that the Bible is inerrant only in the nonextant original manuscripts.[24] Most further qualify inerrancy in

[24] The doctrinal basis of the Evangelical Theological Society is "The Bible alone, and the Bible in its entirety, is the Word of God written and is therefore inerrant in

other regards. For instance, the "Chicago Statement on Biblical Inerrancy" of 1978 qualifies inerrancy such that it applies only to original autographs regardless of their lack of modern technical precision, irregularities of grammar and spelling, observational descriptions of nature, reporting of falsehoods, use of hyperbole and round numbers, topical arrangements, variant selection of materials in parallel accounts, and use of free citations (Humphreys 1987, 325).[25] In addition, some evangelicals shift the locus of inerrancy of the text to the author, arguing that the Bible is inerrant in the sense that God (through humans) has written exactly what he wants to.[26] Thus, if there seems to be an error of fact it is because God was not interested in relaying specific scientific details. Consequently, evangelical feminists seem to have more leeway in their selection of exegetical methods. For instance, it might be acceptable to argue that a passage is an interpolation, provided one argues that the interpolation was also divinely inspired.[27] At the same time, the "acceptable approaches" toward biblical exegesis depend on one's relationship to power within the mainstream evangelical discourse. For instance, D. A. Carson (a male complementarian) approaches the Bible in a more liberal fashion than the females Scanzoni and Hardesty do, yet Scanzoni and Hardesty are much more likely to be accused of heresy.[28]

---

the autographs." Even George Dollar, a militant fundamentalist, argues that only the autographs are inerrant (and that the King James Version translation is the only reliable one) (1973, 264). Fisher Humphreys (a nonmilitant fundamentalist) is an exception, arguing that all responsible translations are inerrant (1987, 329).

[25] For further description of the varieties of inerrancy, see Young 1987, 404–406.

[26] Hodges 1994, 26; Johnston 1992; Noll 1993, 233; Silva 1988, 69. Clark Pinnock describes himself as an inerrantist while still maintaining that (1) the divine authority of some of Paul's teaching are questionable, (2) the early chapters of Genesis are saga, (3) the Book of Jonah is didactic fiction, and (4) Ephesians and the Pastorals are not Pauline. He also defends the source theory of the Old Testament among other, more controversial statements as described in Yarbrough 1991. Of course some scholars, including Yarbrough, are disturbed by this expansion of the definition of *inerrancy.*

[27] Those conservative evangelicals who argue that exegeting certain passages as interpolations, even to support women's ordination, is potentially still within the purview of evangelical scholarship include Carson (1991, 144), Padgett (1987, 41), and Schreiner (1991, 485 ff.). Of course, many evangelical scholars reject this approach, and others argue that it does not matter if they are interpolations. Since they are still part of the canon, they must be exegeted as such (similar to what Mollenkott argues). Cf. Wall 1988, 273.

[28] Carson, for instance, argues that John 7:53–8:11 is an interpolation—and apparently not a divinely inspired one (1991, 144). No one seems to argue that he is not evangelical because of this interpretation, and he is included in an anthology (*Re-*

The extent to which support for biblical inerrancy simply becomes a code for supporting gender hierarchy is particularly apparent in Julie Ingersoll's study of the fundamentalist takeover of the Southern Baptist Convention (SBC). Feeling that the bureaucracy of the convention was dominated by theological moderates, fundamentalists began to meet and form alternate institutions in the 1970s. They started their own journal, the *Southern Baptist Journal*, and organized the Mid-America Baptist Seminary, Criswell Bible College, and Luther Rice Seminary. The International Council on Inerrancy was founded in 1977 by W. A. Criswell. Leaders of this fundamentalist movement within the SBC included Adrian Rogers, Criswell, Jerry Vines, Fred Wolfe, Charles Stanley, and Robert Tenery. Their churches gave minimal amounts to the SBC Cooperative Program,[29] and they continued to be peripherally involved with the SBC as the loyal opposition. The situation changed in 1979 when Paul Pressler, now a federal appeals court judge in Houston, and Paige Patterson, currently the president of Southeastern Baptist Seminary, announced a ten-year plan to take over the convention. They would elect fundamentalist presidents who would use their powers to appoint fundamentalists to agency and seminary boards until the denomination was transformed (Ammerman 1991; Rosenberg 1984, 191). In 1979, they began the takeover; by 1990, it was complete (Mohler 1998). While the issue was originally framed in terms of adherence to biblical inerrancy, as the fundamentalists took over the boards of seminaries and agencies they changed the orthodoxy requirements for maintaining positions within SBC institutions (Maxwell 1995). In particular, Ingersoll notes, Albert Mohler Jr., who was appointed by the fundamentalists to oversee the SBC's most prominent seminary, the Southern Seminary in Kentucky, the four stances candidates have to articulate to be eligible for a position at the seminary do not include inerrancy. Rather, the orthodoxy requirements are conservative positions on the issues of abortion, homosexuality, women's ordination, and the uniqueness of the Gospel. Ingersoll concludes that "the inerrancy of the Bible is no longer the central test of orthodoxy at South-

---

covering Biblical Manhood and Womanhood) that denounces the weak biblicism of evangelical feminists. Meanwhile, in the third edition of *All We're Meant to Be* (1993), Scanzoni and Hardesty continue to maintain their infalliblist biblical hermeneutic, which does not contradict even conservative standards of inerrancy, and yet they are considered apostates.

[29] Member churches donate funds to the Cooperative Program (the general fund), which are then disbursed to agencies and seminaries within the SBC.

ern; it has been replaced by opposition to women's ordination and gay rights" (2005, 59).[30]

This dynamic establishes the extent to which what is at stake is not how inerrant the reading of the Bible is but who becomes established as an inerrant reader. As Katherine Boone writes, "No matter how much one may claim to take the Bible as one's authority, one is judged by one's fidelity to the fundamentalist interpretative model. That allegiance established, it seems that one may apply biblical texts to life circumstances and situations with considerable freedom" (Boone 1989, 89).

As I have argued elsewhere, those who are established as inerrant readers have the ability to argue for "biblical" positions on a wide variety of political and social issues (from abortion to the flat tax) that have no reference in the Bible (A. Smith 1999a). Evangelicals hold what Martin Marty describes as "the iconic regard for the Bible as an object in the national shrine, whether read or not, whether observed or not: it is seen as being basic to national and religious communities' existence" (1987, 164). Interestingly, this analysis of inerrancy emerges from within evangelicalism itself.[31] According to the evangelical feminist Van Leeuwen, "If you come from a tradition that says the Bible is clear and self-interpreting, you can never admit that the lens through which you look at Scripture might change from time to time, even though Scripture doesn't change. People want to forget that their great-great-grandparents used the Bible to endorse slavery and misogyny, because to acknowledge that might suggest that the Bible is not as clear and self-interpreting as they thought it was" (Frame 1999, 103).

But the politics of who can be an inerrantist is not unchanging either. The gendered nature of inerrancy took an interesting turn in the *Today's New International Version* (TNIV) Bible controversy.[32] Zondervan and the

[30] The fundamentalist takeover did have some impact on the fundamentalists as well, as Patterson was fired from his position at Criswell Bible College for devoting too much time to denominational activities but was later reinstated.

[31] Interestingly, the Christian Right activist Thomas Atwood has made a similar analysis of Christian Right uses of the Bible. He writes, "In recent years some well-meaning Evangelical Right organizations have applied biblical 'scores' to candidates' positions on such issues as the INF [Intermediate-Range Nuclear Forces] Treaty, South Africa Sanctions, tax reform, and Contra aid. . . . Well intentioned though they are, one has to question whether some of these uses of Scripture aren't violations of the commandment against taking the name of the Lord in vain" (1990, 47).

[32] For another description and analysis of the TNIV controversy, see Cochran 2005. Another slight controversy arose with the publication of the Good as New

International Bible Society (IBS) were ready to publish a gender-neutral version of the New International Version (NIV) of the Bible in cases in which the Greek or Hebrew words are themselves gender neutral (New International Version Inclusive Language Edition). Zondervan and IBS had formed the Committee on Bible Translation (a fifteen-member group) to oversee the translation. Many complementarians, such as Wayne Grudem, *World* magazine, Pat Robertson, Jack Hayford, and James Dobson, organized to squash the translation. *World* helped spark the controversy by running an article that accused this new version of being a "stealth bible" designed to further an unbiblical feminist agenda (Olasky 1997) and has since continued to publish articles criticizing the project.[33] This article inspired Focus on the Family to host a meeting in 1997 among twelve Christian leaders and representatives from the International Bible Society and Zondervan and developed the "Colorado Springs Guidelines" for translations. The tactic taken by the opponents was that those who supported the translation were "feminist" and "politically correct," and therefore, by definition, not inerrantists (Grudem 2002; Lister 2001; Makkai 2001). Members of the committee included Timothy Bayly, John Piper and Wayne Grudem from CBMW, *World*'s publisher Joel Belz, and Focus on the Family's Charles Jarvis. The guidelines they devised include: retaining masculine references to God (although the new NIV would have retained masculine references to God); using "man" as a designation for the human race; refraining from making changes from singular to plural to avoid gender-specific language; and not changing "brothers" to "brothers and sisters," "son" to "children," "father" to "parent," or "fathers" to "ancestors" (LeBlanc and Rabey 1997).

Zondervan and IBS agreed to permanently drop plans for a "gender-neutral" NIV. Then, in February 1999, the Forum on Bible Agencies began planning a conference on gender language and *World* became involved in trying to stop it. It was rescheduled once with a broader theme, "Accuracy

---

translation Bible, which advertises itself as "women, gay and sinner friendly." This version leaves out the pastoral epistles and Revelations and includes gnostic texts. The prominent evangelical Tony Campolo of the Emergent Movement says of this version, "It spoke to me with a powerful relevancy that challenged me to re-think all the things that I have been taught." But when *World* accused him of endorsing this Bible, Campolo stated that he did not endorse it because "our traditional Bible needs no radical revision to be the friendliest book in the world for every single one of us" (Veith 2005a).

[33] Bayly and Olasky 1998; "Dobson's Choice" 2002; "NIV's Twisted Sister" 2002; S. Olasky 1999a, 1999b, 1999c, and 1999d; Poythress 1998. Some of its readers have criticized *World*'s one-side coverage of the issue (World Mailbag 1998).

in Translation." The Council on Biblical Manhood and Womanhood accused this conference of simply being a strategy to counter the Colorado Springs guidelines. The Summer Institute of Linguistics, the translation arm of Wycliffe Bible Translators, then withdrew its sponsorship. Eventually, the conference was canceled (Plowman and Olasky 1998a). Later Zondervan and IBS decided to revive the project and published a different gender-inclusive version of the Bible, the TNIV, in 2005 (Morgan 2002b; Winn 2002). The rationale for publishing the TNIV after promising there would be no revision of the NIV along issues of gender was that the TNIV would be a completely new translation. The Committee on Biblical Translation rejected the Colorado Guidelines in the development of the TNIV. The Southern Baptist Convention and Focus on the Family are boycotting this version, but one prominent egalitarian megachurch, Willow Creek Church, has pledged to promote it (Begin 2005; S. Olasky 2002; Plowman and Olasky 1998b; Reed 2002). Larry Walker, who was a CBT member, was forced to retire from the Mid-America Baptist Theological Seminary because he would not dissociate himself from the CBT (LeBlanc and Rabey 1997). One significant shift in this translation was the elimination of a statement that would have been in the preface to the effect that the purpose of the new version was "to mute the patriarchalism of the culture of the biblical writers through gender-inclusive language when this could be done without compromising the message of the Spirit" (Morgan 2002a, 19).

Ironically, the charge that one side was translating based on politics rather than inerrancy was used *against* the translation opponents, particularly as many complementarians became supportive of the TNIV. Even many gender complementarian scholars were concerned that it was now antifeminist politics that was derailing a more accurate biblical translation (Blomberg 2002; Poythress and Strauss 2002; Tiansay 2002a; Winn 2002). In fact, a rationale for the attack on the TNIV Bible was that a more accurate translation would be "awkward" (Grudem 1997). Even complementarians who did not necessarily support the TNIV began to complain about the tactics of the Colorado Springs contingency. Stated a formal Moral Majoritarian, the fundamentalist pastor Ed Dobson:

> The people I know who are evangelical and egalitarian have come to that conclusion through their study of the Scripture and not their desire to conform to the winds of cultural change. While I disagree with them, I do not suspect their commitment to the Bible. What troubled me most was that anyone who was egalitarian or who was interested in updating the English language of the NIV to include both genders was accused of opening

the evangelical tent to a humanist, radical feminist, liberal agenda. Such accusations are nothing less than evangelicalism's own form of political correctness. (Maudlin 1997a)

The pro-TNIV camp also accused the anti-TNIV camp of placing obstacles in the way of spreading the Gospel message with such criticisms as, "Gender-specific translations would be counterproductive on secular college campuses. Translations for the general public should not erect unnecessary barriers to the gospel" (Grudem and Osborne 1997, 39). The Evangelical Press Association (EPA) then censured *World* for its coverage of the TNIV, saying it did not adhere to the EPA code of ethics by relying on "inflammatory language" and "slanted, first-person editorializing" (Grady 1997a). *World* had thought the EPA would rule in its favor and withdrew from it when it did not ("A Perilous Venture" 2006; Grady 1997a; D. LeBlanc 1997). Later the EPA concluded that there were "major errors" in the handling of the case and set aside the independent ethics inquiry (Moore 1997). It was dismissed in late 1997 (M. Olasky 1999a).

Other publications presented a more balanced view of this issue. *Charisma* presented the debate from a neutral perspective (Blomberg 2002; Grudem 2002). It published an anti-TNIV advertisement in its July 2002 issue, although it did not itself take a stand.[34] *Christianity Today* also ran a number of TNIV debates in which it attempted to present both sides of the conflict (Grudem and Osborne 1997; Poythress and Strauss 2002). While it did not take a particular stand on the TNIV itself, it seemed to clearly take a stand against the tactics of the Colorado Springs contingent, refusing to print an anti-TNIV advertisement (Poythress and Strauss 2002) calling the tactics "bullying" (Christianity Today 2002b, 27; Zoba 1999). In another *Christianity Today* article, John Stackhouse also complained, "Does this issue warrant blasting a Bible with a shotgun and mailing it back to the publisher? Enough to sanction threats to a Bible society if it doesn't cease production of the offending version? Enough to justify the dismissal of a seminary professor involved in the translation

[34] This advertisement, titled "100 Christian Leaders Agree: The TNIV Bible is Not Trustworthy," claims that the TNIV is not trustworthy but interestingly refused to call it a feminist version. It can be found on www.no-tniv.com. Signers of the ad included P. Bunny Wilson, Bruce Wilkinson, Donald Wildmon, Charles Swindoll, R. C. Sproul, Pat Roberson, Sandy Rios of Concerned Women for America, Adrian Rogers, Paige Patterson, Janet Parshall, J. I. Packer, R. Albert Mohler, Josh McDowell, Bill McCartney, James Kennedy, Mary Kassian, W. Wayne House, Jack Hayford, Wayne Grudem, Steve Farrar, Jerry Falwell, James Dobson, Nancy Leigh DeMoss, Charles Colson, Joel Belz, and Tim Bayly.

project a year before his retirement? Enough to keep a new translation out of the hands of people who would welcome it both for their own reading and for sharing the gospel with friends who might be very sensitive to gender questions?" He calls this debate "Bible rage" and suggests that the issue is not about inerrancy but a "social and political agenda" (1999a, 84).

D. A. Carson, who, as mentioned previously, was featured in the Council on Biblical Manhood and Womanhood's anthology and had served on its board of reference, wrote a book strongly critiquing *World*'s coverage of the debate, particularly Susan Olasky's article, as well as the role CBMW played in it. He suggests that many people opposing the TNIV do so not based on any real knowledge about biblical scholarship but simply to support what they see as a complementarian cause (1998). Similar critiques are made in a book on the inclusive Bible by Mark Strauss, a fellow complementarian (1998). He contends that the CBT is clearly not a feminist conspiracy since many complementarians are part of it. He then turns the question of who is really motivated by a political agenda rather than a simple desire to achieve greater biblical accuracy: "One must indeed ask who has the stronger social agenda: the CBT, many of whom are complementarians and whose goal is to produce the clearest and more accurate translation of Scripture, or the CBMW, whose whole purpose is to promote complementarianism in the church" (30). The biblical scholar John Kohlenberger even claimed that this controversy propelled him from the complementarian to the egalitarian side of the fence. He contended that if complementarians were so quick to dispense with biblical accuracy to support their complementarian politics how could he trust their biblical exegesis on any other issue?[35] Thus, it was the anti-TNIV group (generally associated with complementarians) that was becoming marked as unbiblical and politically motivated. Ironically, biblical inerrancy became a tool that could help dismantle the patriarchal house.

Using the work of Trinh T. Minh-ha, Ruth Frankenburg analyzes how those in marginalized cultures are considered nameable and "bounded" in relation to the dominants, which are considered normative and universal. In other words, for instance, only people of color are perceived to have a culture. White people are perceived as having normative experiences; they are not "cultured," or "raced" (1993, 193). Cathy Cohen further describes, in her study of black responses to AIDS, how groups that define themselves in opposition to the dominant public police the boundaries of what

[35] Christians for Biblical Equality biannual conferences, Texas, 2001, and Minneapolis, 1997.

can be represented as part of that group. "Through the process of public policing, which communicates the judgements, evaluations, and condemnations of recognized leaders," she writes, "the full membership of certain segments . . . is contested and challenged" (1999, 74). Similarly, mainstream evangelicals define themselves as normative evangelicals who objectively state biblical "truth." Evangelical feminists, by contrast, are guided by "special (and secular) interests—regardless of the exegetical tools they use."[36] In order to compete in this sort of discourse, biblical feminists in general do not opt for the strategy of Elisabeth Schussler Fiorenza, a feminist biblical scholar, who labels her hermeneutic as an explicitly feminist one: "A Feminist critical interpretation of the Bible cannot take as its point of departure the normative authority of the biblical archetype, but must begin with women's experience in their struggle for liberation" (Fiorenza 1984, 13). Rather, they argue that they are merely exegeting "the truth" in the Bible; it is the complementarians who are misguided (Stackhouse 1999b). In contrast to Fiorenza's "hermeneutics of suspicion" approach to the Bible, Catherine Kroeger (CBE's cofounder) and Mary Evans outline an evangelical feminist hermeneutical strategy in their *IVP Women's Bible Commentary*.

> Much contemporary feminist criticism has viewed the Bible as hostile to women because it has been used for unjust oppression in contemporary societies. Some feminists have understandably viewed the Bible as inimical to the concerns of women and have employed what has been called a "hermeneutic of suspicion." . . .
>
> In contrast to such efforts, this commentary is written by women of faith who believe that all Scripture is inspired by God and given for the benefit of all humanity. The contributors have examined the difficult texts from a "hermeneutic of faith." . . . It argues for the full inspiration of the Bible and the full equality of women. (2002, xiv–xv)

As the profeminist Stanley Gundry states, Many biblical feminists have come to their position from traditionalism because they felt compelled to do so by Scripture itself. . . . The ideal, it seems to me, is that we be aware of

---

[36] As Robert Letham states, "It is incontestable that the agenda [of evangelical feminism] has been set by the wider feminist movement, inside and outside the church. The nature of that agenda is increasingly plain. The direction of that wider movement, its own internal logic, is taking it away from any semblance of biblical Christianity" (1990, 77). For similar viewpoints, see Achtemier 1993, 17; Felix n.d.; Kassian 1992, 206; and Kersten 1994.

and freed from our subjective personal and cultural biases and predisposi-tions so that we can be subjectively changed by God's Word" (1986).[37]

Similarly, Rebecca Laird contends that women's calls for women's ordi-nation "came not from a demand for more social freedom but from their reading of Scripture" (2000, 107).[38] This disavowal of feminist politics is especially apparent in the TNIV controversy. Of course, as mentioned previously, many of those who support the TNIV are gender complemen-tarians. In response, even those who are evangelical feminists disclaim any feminist reasons for supporting the TNIV; the only interest is in providing a more "accurate" translation of the Bible. As Mimi Haddad, the president of Christians for Biblical Equality, argued, this translation is driven not by feminists but by "distinguished scholars" (Tiansay 2002a, 83). According to Mark Strauss, "The TNIV does not slant the Bible toward a feminist agenda. All members of the TNIV translation committee are evangelical scholars and some are complementarians. . . . Their goal was not to pro-duce a politically correct version, but to render God's Word accurately into contemporary English" (Poythress and Strauss 2002, 42).[39] Evangeli-cal feminists vie to be "unbounded" and included in the universal evan-gelical discourse.

The contemporary emergency of Native and evangelical feminisms be-lie the notion that Native or evangelical communities are singularly reac-tionary or progressive. These feminisms also demonstrate the multiple interests and standpoints within these communities, pointing to the pos-sibilities that these interests can shift and change through struggle. How-ever, as I will discuss below, the ways in which feminist politics become

[37] See also Alexander and Alexander 1975; Bilezikian 1987, 421; Peters 1977; and Williams 1980.

[38] Wendy Zoba similarly distances herself from feminism in an article critiquing the increasing restrictions on evangelical women in missionary positions. "By limit-ing half of the evangelical force that have legitimate spiritual gifts," she writes, "we're not hurting the cause of women so much as the cause of Christ," quoting Jim Plueddemann, the general director of Serving In Mission (Zoba 2000b, 45).

[39] Ted Haggard of the New Life Church declared, "As someone who believes men and women have equal value but contrasting roles that complement one other, and someone [who] believes that God is 100 percent masculine, I was pleased with the TNIV. The gender issues are appropriately addressed in my view. The TNIV does not read like a Christian feminist translation at all—not even close" (Tiansay 2002a, 84). See also Craig Bromberg of the Denver Seminary (2002) and Ronald Youngblood, chairman of the board of the International Bible Society, who claims, "There's not a feminist bone in our bodies . . . no ideological or feminist bias" (Winn 2002, 29).

articulated can also hinder the development of internal and external coalition politics. These difficulties become especially clear in the following discussion of Native and evangelical antiviolence organizing.

VIOLENCE

A key factor in the development of both evangelical and Native feminist organizing is the rising consciousness around sexual and domestic violence. Given these commonalities, one might presume that violence would be a likely starting place to develop coalitions between Native and evangelical feminists. While the possibility exists for future coalition politics, we can also see that, ironically, evangelical feminist articulation of antiviolence politics, while paving the way for greater coalitions with nonfeminist evangelicals, actually hinders the development of coalitions with non-evangelicals.

Within evangelical communities, this consciousness began to develop in the 1980s. Opened in 1977 and waxing in influence throughout the 1980s, the Center for the Prevention of Sexual and Domestic Violence, headed by Rev. Marie Fortune, was formed to deal with issues of abuse in religious communities. Fortune's *Sexual Violence: The Unmentionable Sin* (1983) and *Is Nothing Sacred?* (1989) helped raise awareness of issues of abuse in evangelical communities. Since then, evangelicals have sent publishers a flood of books and articles dealing with abuse.[40] Many of these writings argued that, not only does membership in evangelical homes and communities *not* protect one from abuse, but in fact it makes abuse *more likely*.[41] Furthermore, studies conducted by evangelicals themselves found

[40] See, for example, Brewer 1991; Feldmeth and Finley 1990; Giles 1993; Hannah 1998; Jordan-Lake 1992; McManus 1994; Midgett 1993; "Sexual Abuse" 1999; Uttley 1999; and Wright 1999. It is interesting that in these articles Marie Fortune, who is not an evangelical, is held in universal esteem. See also Alsdurf and Alsdurf 1989a; Cagney 1997; Christianity Today 2002a; Cutrer 2001, 2002b; Daigle 2001; Farhart 2003; Hutchinson 2002a; Jewell 2006; Kennedy 1994, 2002a; Liparulo 2005; Lowe 2000; MacHarg 2004; Mailbag 2002; Moeller 1993; "More Wounds of Rape" 1992; Newman 2005; Patterson 1992; "Private Sins of Public Ministry" 1988; Tarro 1992; "The Secret Crime" 1988; Veenker 1999; Veith 2005c; Vincent 2004; Willoughby 1999; and Wilson 1988. The *Washington Times* (the newspaper associated with the Moonies but frequently displayed at Christian Right events) published a special section entitled "The War against Women" (n.d.) calling for an end to gender violence. Christians for Biblical Equality held a conference in April 1994 in Chicago on this very topic, Women, Abuse, and the Bible. The National Coalition of Christians against Abuse was also formed to address abuse within churches.

[41] In a survey conducted by James and Phyllis Alsdurf, two-thirds of the Christian

churches completely wanting in their ability to deal with these crises. The evangelical scholar James Alsdurf, for instance, in a 1980s study of 5,700 Protestant pastors, found the following.

—Twenty-six percent normally tell battered women to submit to their husbands "and to trust that God would honor her action by either stopping the abuse or giving her the strength to endure it."

—Twenty-five percent said a lack of submissiveness in the wife is what triggers abuse, and a majority said that it is better for women to tolerate abuse than to separate from their husbands.

—Seventy-one percent would never advise a battered wife to separate from her husband because of abuse.

—Ninety-two percent would never counsel divorce for abuse. (Grady 2001, 41).

The World Evangelical Fellowship set up an international task force on violence against women when an African woman stood up at a general assembly and asked, "When will this organization address violence against women? There are men in this very room who abuse their wives" (Kroeger and Nason-Clark 2001, 8). She received a standing ovation. This task force has published several publications and prayer journals for abused women (McVicker 2001). In 2001, it also passed a statement calling for a spotlight on domestic abuse, for churches to denounce abuse from the pulpit, for the promotion of healing and safety for survivors, and for admonishment of the perpetrators of violence (Stephen 2001). Janice Shaw Crouse of Concerned Women for America stated that the response to feminists who say the church promotes violence against women is "We must face an unwelcome truth." That is, the church needs to more fully address violence against women committed within the church. According to Crouse,

---

women they surveyed believed it was their Christian responsibility to submit to their husbands' violence (1989b, 84). Carolyn Heggen notes that the second-best predictor of whether sexual abuse will occur in a home (next to drug or alcohol addiction) is whether or not parents belong to a conservative religious community (Heggen 1993, 73). See also Christianity Today 1999b, 51; Gil 1988; Jacobs 1984; and Kane, Cheston, and Greer 1993, 228.

This understanding was challenged in W. Bradford Wilcox's *Soft Patriarchs, New Men: How Christianity Shapes Fathers and Husbands* (2004). He contends that evangelicals *who attend church regularly* actually have the lowest rate of domestic violence. It is only "nominal" evangelicals (who do not attend regularly but describe themselves as evangelical) who have the highest divorce and domestic violence rates compared to peoples of other faith backgrounds (D. LeBlanc 2004).

"The church is the bride of Christ. This bride is not meant to be battered—neither are any of her members!" (2005). *World* ran an article strongly denouncing the epidemic of sexual abuse committed by evangelical pastors (Vincent 2002a). It even launched a mini campaign call for the ouster of Haman Cross from Campus Crusade for Christ after he was accused of sexual abuse and Campus Crusade declined to discipline him (this campaign was successful) (Vincent 2002b).

As evangelicals began speaking out on gender violence, they often tempered their stances on gender subordination (Peake 2001).[42] *Charisma* ran an article on Alberto Mottessi, who has been described as the Latin American Billy Graham. He has preached to over twenty million people, condemning domestic violence (particularly violence committed by pastors), challenging gender subordination, and calling for women to join the ministry. He prays "for women who suffer from the effects of machismo" (Tiansay 2003, 42). Another *Charisma* story featured George Boomer, a traveling pastor who previously served time in prison. This article notes that his father abused his mother and he, too, was an authoritarian leader in the home—"using Scripture to support his oppression" (Harmon 2002, 50). However, once, when he tried to hit his wife, she knocked him unconscious with a cast-iron frying pan. According to his wife, "That was one thing my mother did: She didn't allow my father to hit her. . . . Marriage is not a dictatorship. . . . Instead . . . [it] is built with understanding and respect for the other partner within the house" (50).

The reality of abuse in evangelical communities called into question the value of male headship advocated by complementarian evangelicals and forced many to temper their positions (Baly 1975; Beane 1998a; Bender 1971; Henry 1975; Neff 1980; "Women's Role in Church and Family" 1985). They had traditionally argued, without any explanation or evidence, that because the Bible clearly mandates female subordination patriarchy must be beneficial to women. The reality of abuse belied this argument. As James and Phyllis Alsdurf argue, "The Christian community, for the most part, espouses a distribution of power that puts the man in charge and sees the woman as needing his control. For battered women, the assigning of ultimate authority to men opens the door for husbands to wield power that is characterized by coercive force and unreasonable demands" (1989b, 95).

The empirical data published in evangelical venues seemed to support

[42] Concerned Women for America distributed a pamphlet, "Violence against Women Bearing One Another's Burdens" (written by Janice Crouse), that criticized calls for wifely submission in the face of domestic violence (n.d.).

the position of evangelical feminists rather than that of complementarians. The epidemic of abuse unmasked the politics of their exegesis: the defense of male privilege at the expense of women. Consequently, complementarian responses to biblical feminism, which still dismiss feminism as unbiblical, have had to spend much more time defending the social value of patriarchy and arguing that it does not *necessarily* lead to abuse.[43] For example, the complementarians John Piper and Wayne Grudem state, "Commending Biblical truth involves more than saying, 'Do it because the Bible says so.' . . . Not only must there be thorough exegesis, there must also be a portrayal of the vision that satisfies the heart as well as the head. . . . We must show that something is not only right but also good. It is not only valid but also valuable, not only accurate but also admirable" (1991, 33).

This, in turn, has given biblical feminists a platform on which to discuss issues of women's status other than through direct biblical exegesis.[44] Ironically, then, it was probably not so much the theological arguments of evangelical feminists as the material conditions of women's lives that strengthened the legitimacy of evangelical feminism among mainstream evangelicals. This is not to argue that evangelical feminist hermeneutics was completely unimportant. As Susan Thistlethwaite argues, it is the reality of abuse (rather than biblical studies) that causes abused evangelical women to question presuppositions of divinely sanctioned male domination and propels them into a crisis of faith. However, learning how to appropriate the Bible in a more liberatory fashion can be indispensable to healing. She states, "Women can learn to imagine themselves in the text . . . that does affirm women (such as women's discipleship) and on the basis of their own experience, which shows that they have been the ones to hear the Word of God and do it. This type of imagining challenges traditional interpretation . . . and moves interpretation to a new level of en-

[43] Even when complementarians defend patriarchy, they have been forced to concede that there is widespread abuse in its application. See Bowman 1994, 62; "Child Sexual Abuse" 1990; Kassian 1992, 207, 214–15; Kellogg and Hunter 1993; and Piper and Grudem 1991, xiii, 469–72. *New Man* ran an article declaring that male authority does not necessarily lead to violence and abuse (Hunter 2005).

[44] For instance, Mary Stewart Van Leeuwen published *Gender and Grace* (1991), which discusses women's equality from a more social psychological point of view rather than a more exegetical point of view, and it was awarded the Critics Choice Award by *Christianity Today* ("Critics Choice Awards" 1991; Van Leeuwen 1991). Ironically, she is the same person who earlier dismissed an article by Mollenkott for being unbiblical, though Mollenkott argued essentially the same things that Van Leeuwen does in her book.

gagement with the contemporary life of the church" (1985, 104). As a result, evangelical feminism has found a broader audience in the evangelical community. For instance, the World Evangelical Fellowship's International Task Force on Violence against Women states that it has not taken a position on complementarianism versus egalitarianism. However, a prominent CBE spokesperson, Catherine Kroeger, has produced much of the material coming from this task force, so its work has a very strong egalitarian slant.[45]

It is undoubtedly significant that issues of gender violence have also been central to many Native women organizing from a "feminist" position. A common argument made about why Native women do not need feminism is that Native communities were egalitarian prior to colonization (Grande 2004; Jaimes and Halsey 1992; Monture-Angus 1995). As J. Kehaulani Kaunui argues, if we are to follow this to its logical conclusion, we would also have to argue that indigenous nations do not need decolonization today because they were not colonized prior to colonization.[46] Just as violence in Christian homes is evidence that the Bible does not necessarily protect evangelical women, violence in Native homes is evidence that precolonial gender roles in Native communities does not necessarily protect Native women today (Mihesuah 2003; A. Smith 2005b).

Regardless of the origins of sexism in Native communities, it operates with full force today and requires strategies that directly address it. Before Native peoples fight for the future of their nations, they must ask themselves who is included in the nation. It is often the case that gender justice is articulated as being separate from issues of survival for indigenous peoples. Such an understanding presupposes that we could actually decolonize without addressing sexism, which ignores the fact that it was precisely through gender violence that we lost our lands in the first place (A. Smith 1999b).[47] Beatrice Medicine's poem "Border Town" (Medi-

[45] The Women's Commission of the World Evangelical Fellowship has also published books with a strong egalitarian slant, including *Gender or Giftedness* (M. Smith 2000).

[46] Speech delivered at the symposium "Native Feminisms without Apology," University of Illinois, Champaign-Urbana, April 28–29, 2006.

[47] See Ingrid Washinawatok (1995a), who writes, "Indigenous cultures are the only remaining matrilineal societies left in the world. Male dominated western governments used colonization to destroy matrilineal societies to achieve the goal of stealing land and resources. The 1820 Civilization Act enabled the United States to remove women from their traditional roles in self-governance and spiritual positions" (27). See also LaDuke 1995a, 5; and Senogles n.d., 30.

cine 1996) illustrates the relationship between colonization and gender violence.

> Protecting two teen-aged white
> males for fifteen years
> for beating and raping a whimpering, terrified Lakota girl.
> Then, shooting her in the head
> with a "twenty-two."
>
> Silencing in the Border Town and
> protecting their own.
> Where Lakota women are called
> "easy,"
> "welfare mothers,"
> "bottle whores" and
> treated like bitch dogs.
>
> Listening "What's the big deal?"
> "They shoot each other and if they
> don't, they get drunk and freeze to
> death" states a White male merchant . . .
> A conspiracy of silence for fifteen
> years in the Border Town
> Discovering the body of the brutalized
> Lakota teen-ager nine months after her
> disappearance hidden in a bay of the
> lake formed by damming a river and
> damning a people to live in Border
> Towns where we are viewed as
> "worthless and easy women" or worth
> five "twenty-two" bullets, blaming the victim—"She was looking for
> sex."

This tendency to separate the health and well-being of women from the health and well-being of our nations is critiqued in Winona LaDuke's call not to "cheapen sovereignty." She discusses attempts by men in her community to use the rhetoric of sovereignty to avoid paying child support. She contends that " 'Sovereignty' has become a politicized term used for some of the most demeaning purposes" (1996b). Her words speak to the importance of recentering. That is, rather than articulating gender justice as oppositional to sovereignty, the question becomes "What does sovereignty look like if we recenter Native women in the analysis? An intersectional analysis of nationhood is evoked when Mililani Trask challenges who we perceive to be the builders of the "nation."

> To this very day, we are the only group of Native Americans that live and die as wards of the state. . . . And so we told this story and it was a story that has a bitter history. And when we spoke openly about it in the circle, we wept, we wept openly. . . . Everyone in the circle was quiet, and then in the corner, this crotchety voice started speaking and this woman was saying, "What are you crying about? You've been crying for a hundred years! . . . You're crying because you don't have a nation? What are you waiting for? You're waiting for Washington to make your nation? You cannot trust them. You should stop crying. You should make your nation." . . . And we looked at each other and said, "We better stop crying, we better make our nation. We're matrilineal, we've been waiting for the men to do it. We've been waiting for Washington to wake up to our prayers and get justice. They're colonizers; they're liars; they're not going to do it. It's our job, we have to do it." (2001, 5)

What this analysis suggests is that rather than adopting the strategy of fighting for sovereignty first and then improving Native women's status, as Jaimes and Halsey suggest, we must understand that attacks on Native women's status are themselves attacks on Native sovereignty. By leaving these patriarchal gender systems in place, we are unable to decolonize and fully assert our sovereignty. Consequently, Native women have begun organizing what one could term "feminist sovereignty projects." One such attempt to tie indigenous sovereignty to the well-being of Native women is evident in the materials produced by the Sacred Circle, a national American Indian resource center for domestic and sexual violence based in South Dakota. Its brochure, "Sovereign Women Strengthen Sovereign Nations," reads:

TRIBAL SOVEREIGNTY:
All Tribal Nations Have an
Inherent Right to:
1) A land base: possession and control is unquestioned and honored by other nations. To exist without fear, but with freedom.

2) Self-governance: the ability and authority to make decisions regarding all matters concerning

NATIVE WOMEN'S SOVEREIGNTY
All Native Women Have an
Inherent Right to:
1) Their body and path in life: the possession and control is unquestioned and honored by others. To exist without fear, but with freedom.

2) Self governance: the ability and authority to make decisions regarding all matters concerning them-

the Tribe without the approval or agreement of others. This includes the ways and methods of decision-making in social, political and other areas of life.

3) An economic base and resources: the control, use and development of resources, businesses or industries the Tribe chooses. This includes resources that support the Tribal life way, including the practice of spiritual ways.

4) A distinct language and historical and cultural identity: Each tribe defines and describes its history, including the impact of colonization and racism, tribal culture, worldview and traditions.

Colonization and violence against Native people means that power and control over Native people's life way and land have been stolen. As Native people, we have the right and responsibility to advocate for ourselves and our relatives in supporting our right to power and control over our tribal life way and land—tribal sovereignty.

selves, without others' approval or agreement. This includes the ways and methods of decision-making in social, political and other areas of life.

3) An economic base and resources: the control, use and development of resources, businesses or industries that Native women choose. This includes resources that support individual Native women's chosen life ways, including the practice of spiritual ways.

4) A distinct identity, history and culture: Each Native women defines and describes her history, including the impact of colonization, racism and sexism, tribal women's culture, worldview and traditions.

Violence against women, and victimization in general, means that power and control over an individual's life and body have been stolen. As relatives of women who have been victimized, it is our right and responsibility to be advocates supporting every woman's right to power and control over her body and life— personal sovereignty

This brochure suggests that sovereignty for Native women occurs within the context of sovereignty for Native nations. It also suggests that sovereignty for Native nations cannot occur without respect for the autonomy of Native women. And, as I have discussed elsewhere, the Boarding School Healing Project, founded in 2002, seeks to build a movement to demand reparations for U.S. boarding school abuses (A. Smith 2005b).[48] The strategy of this project is not to seek remedies on the individual level but to demand a collective remedy by developing links with other reparations struggles that fundamentally challenge the colonial and capitalist status quo.

[48] For more information, see www.boardingschoolhealingproject.org.

The strategy of this project is to organize around boarding schools as a way to address gender violence in Native communities. This project attempts to organize against interpersonal gender violence *and* state violence simultaneously by framing gender violence as a continuing effect of human rights violations perpetrated by the state. This organization theorizes that it is through boarding schools that gender violence in our communities was largely introduced. The continuing effects of boarding school abuses continue today because these abuses have not been acknowledged by the larger society. As a result, silence continues within Native communities, preventing Native peoples from seeking support and healing as a result of intergenerational trauma. Because boarding school policies are not as acknowledged as human rights violations, Native peoples individualize the trauma they have suffered, contributing to their shame and self-blame. If both boarding school policies and the continuing effects from these policies were recognized as human rights violations, it might alleviate the shame and provide an opportunity for communities to heal and further their decolonization struggles.

It should be mentioned that while the issue of violence has been critical in the development of a "feminist" consciousness within evangelical and Native communities, antiviolence organizing does not necessarily correlate with progressive politics. Within evangelical circles, gender complementarians assert that violence is not particularly prevalent in evangelical homes. In response to the University of Colorado scandal, in which women said they were raped by male athletes, *World* asserted that sexual abuse is a result of liberals promoting homosexuality and pornography: "Wrong as the right wing is in some of its selfish attitudes toward women, we conservatives haven't done one-tenth what you liberals have done to enslave women" (J. Belz 2004a, 6). And at the 1997 National Association of Evangelicals conference the representative of the Council on Biblical Manhood and Womanhood informed me that most domestic violence is caused by lesbians!

In addition, violence is often deployed in the service of civilizing and missionizing projects within evangelicalism to enable white evangelical women to "save brown women from brown men" (Spivak 1994). While this trend is explored in another work (A. Smith forthcoming), a prescient example of this deployment was an article on the Ecumenical Coalition on Women and Society (ECWS), which is sponsored by the Institute of Religion and Democracy (an organization that tries to counter what it considers to be liberalizing trends within mainline denominations). The ECWS is focused on organizing against secular feminist politics and more liberal feminist theologies. It does, however, bring together egalitarians and complementarians. *Christianity Today* reported that a strategy it developed to alleviate divisiveness across complementarian-egalitarian lines was to focus its work on addressing violence against women in the Third World. Women in this group might not agree that women in the United States are oppressed by gender hierarchies, but they can all agree that women in the Third World are. According to Kay Rader of the Salvation Army, "Western women have more education, power, and influence compared to women in the developing world" (Gardner 1999). The women's sector of the World Evangelical Fellowship adopted a similar strategy of shying away from controversial issues such as women's ordination and wifely submission in order to focus on violence against Third World women such as "slavery, poverty-driven prostitution, female genital mutilation, and the dowry system" (Gardner 1999). This strategy is reflected in the increasing involvement of evangelical women in the movement to "liberate" women and children involved in the sex trade (Carnes 1999; Christianity Today 2006; Lawson 2005; Noll 2000; Zoba 2003), which is "ten times larger than the trans-Atlantic slave trade at its peak" (Lawson 2004).[49] Thus, in one rhetorical swoop, white evangelical women can minimize their accountability for the privileges they have accrued as the genealogical beneficiaries of the trans-Atlantic slave trade in the United States while running off to save brown women from slavery in other countries. As Kamala Kempadoo notes, this antitrafficking movement fails to address how states tie antitrafficking laws to repressive anti-immigration laws that control the labor of Third World women who are not trafficked. Furthermore, the 2000 Victims of Trafficking and Violence Protection Act selectively uses sanctions against countries deemed in opposition to U.S. interests (Israel and South Korea were reclassified from potential targets for sanctions while Cuba and North Korea were not) (Kemadoo 2005).

As Julie Ingersoll notes, the one area of influence white women are almost always allowed even within the most fundamentalist circles is "preaching to the 'unsaved' in foreign lands" (2005, 130). In fact, this notion of saving "brown women" is explicitly delineated in a *Christianity Today* article in which a Christian persecution advocate argues that the paradigmatic Christian is "a poor and brown third-world female" (Horowitz 2005). As pamphlets distributed by Project Hannah, a woman-

---

[49] See this same civilizing logic about saving women from gender oppression in India and the Congo in Olasky 2004; and Phiri 2006.

focused mission project, state, "We can rescue their [oppressed Third World women's] souls from continuing to live in hell, not just here, but for all eternity!"[50] Furthermore, Project Hannah asserts that indigenous women in Chiapas, Mexico, need rescuing by making the dubious claim that "from pre-Hispanic times, the cultures that have developed in Latin America have been patriarchal, and this has been the pattern until the present time" (apparently European cultures are not).[51] Thus, at least currently, evangelical feminism seems to be less a site for potential coalitions with Native women than a site that reinscribes colonial relationships with indigenous women, Third World women, and women of color.

Meanwhile, women of color and Native women are beginning to address the cooptation of the antiviolence movement by the state (INCITE! 2006; A. Smith 2005b; Sokoloff 2005).[52] For many years, activists in the rape and domestic violence movements have promoted strengthening the criminal justice system as the primary means of reducing sexual and domestic violence. Particularly since the passage of the Violence against Women Act in 1994, antiviolence centers have received a considerable amount of funding from the state to the point where most agencies are dependent on the state for their continued existence. Consequently, their strategies tend to be state friendly: hire more police, give longer sentences to rapists, pass mandatory arrests laws, and so on. There is a contradiction, however, in relying on the state to solve the problems it is responsible for creating. The antiviolence movement has always contested the notion of home as a safe place because most of the violence women suffer happens at home. Furthermore, the notion that violence occurs "out there," inflicted by the stranger in the dark alley, prevents us from recognizing that the home is, in fact, the place of greatest danger for women. However, the strategies the domestic violence movement employs to address violence are premised on the danger coming from "out there" rather than at home. That is, reliance on the criminal justice system to address gender violence would make sense if the threat was a few crazed men who we can lock up. But the prison system is not equipped to address a violent culture in which an overwhelming number of people batter their partners unless

---

[50] Hannah, Legacy of Hope brochure. Project Hannah is program of Trans World Radio. See www.twr.org.

[51] Women in Mexico brochure, Project Hannah.

[52] Much of the work being done by women of color to organize around violence without going through the state is occurring through the organization INCITE! Women of Color against Violence (www.incite-national.org).

we are prepared to imprison hundreds of millions of people. Furthermore, state violence—in the form of the criminal justice system—cannot provide true safety for women, particularly Native women and women of color, as it is directly implicated in the violence women face. Even Pat Nolan notes the contradiction of expecting an institution based on violence to solve the problem of interpersonal violence: "With over 600,000 prisoners being released each year, the level of violence inmates experienced inside prison will play a large part in determining the type of neighbors they will be after their release" (2005b).

Unfortunately, the remedies that have been pursued by the mainstream antiviolence movement have often strengthened rather than undercut state violence. While the antisexual and antidomestic violence movements have been vital in breaking the silence around violence against women and in providing critically needed services to survivors of sexual and domestic violence, these movements have also become increasingly professionalized in providing services, and consequently there is often reluctance to address sexual and domestic violence within the larger context of institutionalized violence. In addition, those who go to prison for domestic violence are disproportionately people of color. Julie Ostrowski reports that of the men who go to domestic violence courts in New York, only 12 percent are white. Half are unemployed, and the average income of those who are employed is $12,655 (2004). But the issue is not primarily that antiviolence advocates are supporting the prison industrial complex by sending batterers and rapists to jail since many anti-violence advocates simply say, "If someone is guilty of violence, should they not be in jail regardless of their racial background?" The co-optation of the antiviolence movement by the criminal justice system has far-reaching effects besides aiding the immediate victims of domestic violence. The Right has been very successful in using antiviolence rhetoric to mobilize support for a repressive anticrime agenda that includes three-strikes legislation and antidrug bills. These anticrime measures mean that abused women are more likely to find themselves in prison if they are coerced by partners to engage in illegal activity, as even Pat Nolan notes (2006a). When men of color are disproportionately incarcerated because of these laws, which were passed in part through the co-optation of antiviolence rhetoric, the entire community, particularly women, who are often the community caretakers, is negatively impacted. For instance, the Violence against Women Act was attached to a repressive anticrime bill that was then heralded by antiviolence advocates as feminist legislation. Ironically, this critique of the antiviolence movement is implicit in Charles Colson's op-ed piece "Why Women Love Big Government." He suggests that women are more likely to support state solutions to social problems because of their vulnerability to violence and oppression (Colson and Pearcey 1996). He does not suggest that we should support expanded social or economic programs, nor does he propose any clear recommendations. If we follow Colson's argument to its logical conclusion, it would be safe to say that it is unhelpful for Native communities to tell women *not* to seek help from the state if the community declines to do anything to end violence. At the same time, those of us in the antiviolence movement may ask ourselves why we think "big government" or the state is going to solve the problem of violence. Perhaps the mainstream antiviolence movement could learn from the critical stance toward the state adopted by evangelical prison organizers, who could themselves learn from feminist groups how to challenge the gender-normative assumptions behind their organizing.

As Angela Davis notes, violence is a powerful ideological conductor capable of shaping coalition politics in a number of ways (2000). On one hand, it is clear that the antiviolence movement was critical in shaping both Native and evangelical feminist politics. On the other hand, this movement can also be divisive within feminist politics by positioning Third World communities and communities of color as particularly prone to violence. If antiviolence politics is to further rather than disable coalition politics between different communities of women, it is clear that antiviolence analysis and organizing must address the intersections between gender violence and state violence (INCITE! 2006).

NATIVE AND EVANGELICAL FEMINIST INTERVENTIONS: IMPLICATIONS FOR COALITION POLITICS

Having explored the contemporary emergence of Native and evangelical feminisms, this section explores the specific intervention these feminisms seek to make both within their communities and in the world at large. Of course, as Native and evangelical feminisms are not monolithic, I explore the complexities and varieties within these discourses. "Mainstream feminism" is itself not monolithic, but in this section I am pointing more to how mainstream feminism is created, imaged, and positioned within Native and evangelical feminisms rather than analyzing its complexities on its own terms.

Despite appearances to the contrary, Native and evangelical feminisms are having and can have transformative impacts on evangelical and Native organizing. The fact that these transformations do occur speaks to the possibilities of further political rearticulations along more progressive lines in both communities. These feminisms also challenge theoretical and organizing paradigms in what both Natives and evangelicals perceive to be mainstream feminism. Additionally, as I will explore in chapter 5, Native feminism fundamentally challenges how we understand the concepts of sovereignty and nationhood. However, while feminist articulations within Native and evangelical communities speak to the promise of new politics of coalitions, they can also foreclose coalition politics. When we looked at the unlikely alliances created through evangelical prison organizing and race reconciliation, a limitation to these alliances is that they are founded on a patriarchal, heteronormative framework. It would seem, therefore, that evangelical feminist interventions might provide a helpful corrective to these failings. However, the development of evangelical feminist thought seems to tell another story, as I will explore later in the chapter. In fact, evangelical feminism often forecloses alliances with nonevangelicals, particularly women of color, rather than providing openings for new coalitions.

Prolineal Genealogies of Native Feminisms

The implicit assumption behind the way Native women's organizing is policed (through the equation of feminism with whiteness) is that Native women who organize around the basis of gender have betrayed Native men by working in coalition with non-Native women. Yet, in looking at the analysis produced and the politics enacted by Native women activists, whether or not they define themselves as feminist, it is apparent that their engagement with feminism constitutes a strategic redeployment of the concepts of both feminism *and* Native sovereignty.

Sovereignty and Tradition As Julie Star's quotation at the beginning of this chapter suggests, Native women who call themselves feminists are often accused of divisiveness.[53] They have essentially forsaken their coali-

[53] For instance, see Patricia Monture-Angus's analysis of the Native Women's Association of Canada (1999, 143–52).

tion with Native men to work in coalition with white women. With few exceptions (Mihesuah 2003), narratives of Native women's organizations minimize sexism within Native communities as a reason for their formation. Yet Janet McCloud recounts how sexism in the Native rights movement contributed to the founding of the Indigenous Women's Network.

> I was down in Boulder, Colorado and Winona LaDuke and Nilak Butler were there and some others. They were telling me about the different kinds of sexism they were meeting up with in the movement with the men, who were really bad, and a lot of these women were really the backbone of everything, doing a lot of the kind of work that the movement needed. I thought they were getting discouraged and getting ready to pull out and I thought, "wow, we can't lose these women because they have a lot to offer." So, we talked about organizing a women's conference to discuss all the different problems. . . . Marsha Gomez and others decided to formally organize. I agreed to stay with them as a kind of a buffer because the men were saying the "Indignant Women's Organization" and blah, blah, blah. They felt kind of threatened by the women organizing. (McCloud n.d., 50; see also Gomez n.d.-b, 49)

Whether or not Native women call themselves feminists, all those that I interviewed universally agreed that sexism is a problem within both Native activism in particular and Native communities in general, and most were vociferous in their complaints. Talking about sexism within Native communities to a larger audience is problematic given the tendency of the larger society to stereotype Native communities as more sexist than white society. However, the extent to which Native women activists identify sexism as a major hindrance in their organizing efforts suggests that these issues need to be more publicly discussed. Perhaps, rather than denying that sexism exists in Native communities, Native peoples could position themselves as models for other communities on how to address these issues openly in order to inspire other communities to do so as well.[54] However, this discussion must take place within an analysis of colonialism and its effects on gender relations in Native communities. For instance, Luana Ross speaks to how sexism hindered the development of the Amer-

---

[54] While interviewees universally recognized sexism, not all saw it as problematic as those quoted here. Both Madonna Thunder Hawk and Lakota Harden stated that, while sexism is rampant in the American Indian Movement, they did not always experience it in their circles.

ican Indian Movement by preventing women from working to their fullest potential.[55] According to Luana Ross:

Anyway, there was such a big cry to get all of the Indians involved [in the American Indian Movement] and reclaim who you are and blah, blah, blah, and they treated women so horribly that they just made it damned hard. Why was I the secretary? We were always cooking dinners; they were out with white girls or getting young Indian girls pregnant. So there was a lot of sexism in the movement. . . . I think the major way that I remember has to do with leadership of the organization always being male—spokespeople always being male. The women are always seen as the drudges, and, as well, the number of young women that those guys got pregnant, and I mean just used and abused is staggering to the point of where I'd say by the mid-1970s the American Indian Movement was no longer welcome on reservations on Montana. And a lot of it had to do with the treatment of young girls.

[55] Other interviewees felt that sexism had been a major obstacle in their work:
Me: Have you experienced problems with sexism in your organizing?
Heather Milton: Oh, definitely! In a big way! Oh, oh, God! Really bad! Like, well it's not bad; it's good. I don't know. It was interesting. It reached a point in the group back in the day, where us women were really wanting to explore what the role of women was, and looking at it in a ceremonial way, or whatever. We've seen older women, and they had been really strong and were taking back their role in the community, and we thought, we had to do that too. It's our right as young women that we have a role in the community. Then we fought with our men. They were young men, but we still fought with them. And there was a time where there was this big split. Where we wouldn't work with each other; it was horrible.
Loretta Rivera: [Sexism] is most irritating; most irritating because some of it still goes on here, where I see a lot of men who are put in the forefront and there are women behind the scenes who are brilliant women who do all the writing, who get the money, but they won't stand out there, and it irritates me so because it's such a poor message to young women that you would still do that. . . . I think whenever there's been situations when people have wanted to put someone in a political position, they don't even want to talk about supporting a woman. They're pretty quick to vote for a man, and it's the Indian women who are pretty quick to vote for a man. So it makes it really a hard thing. I can't believe I can still go to a meeting and they'll spend three-quarters of their time talking about how to get men at the meeting.
Mona Rencountre: Their way of thinking is paternal. "Well, no matter what you think, it's always going to be this way. So if you think that way, why don't you just get off the reservation?" The thing that irks me the most is they don't even know. "How was I disrespectful to you?" After firing me from my job, one of my bosses said that [was] because I told him he was very disrespectful to women. That's what he said. "How was I disrespectful?" He didn't even know.

As Pamela Alfonso indicates, this sexism has a bigger impact than simply excluding women. Often a feminist analysis changes the way one organizes around the issue generally. Alfonso's approach to organizing challenges the professionalization of movements, which gives those with elite standing more say in determining the direction of a political strategy. She suggests that a gender analysis of Native organizing might also challenge its investment in professionalization. According to Alfonso:

Oh, I'm constantly challenged. A recent example. We were at a meeting. There were two Indian women and six Indian men. There was one Indian man who was an educated attorney, and the other Indian men were just community folks. Various characters. . . . As we were sitting there, this very smart Indian man was making recommendations, but to me, as an activist, we always have a menu of choices, and if you want to be in right relation to the community you lay out the choices and you let the people choose. This guy was dictating a plan of action and was saying everything else was fruitless. Well, I'm sorry, I don't give that thinking away to anybody. Tell me what you're thinking; tell me what the other options are; we can make our own decision. And some of the decisions we make may be based more on courage than on intellectual ability to win. After that meeting, and we were going back and forth, and there was this little spat going on because I was doing that to him. I was saying, wait a second, so you don't think we'll win, but that's not what I'm asking. I'm asking, who makes the decision, who does this and that . . . ? And he was just being a real *ass*. Basically, condescendingly talking to me. I may not have a law degree, but I understand enough about law, and, I'm sorry, the truth is you have a masters' degree, you don't have any more education than anyone else; you just happen to know the law. And the law is only one tool when you're talking about social change. To me, the law, we're not good at it. If you give me a bow and an arrow or a rifle, and I suck at a rifle, I'm most likely not going to choose that weapon. So if you're telling us the legal tools, that's all you're telling us. You're not telling us about the bow and arrow, about the knife, about the sneak-up, about strategy, nothing. So, anyway, this little dodgeball was going on at the meeting. At the end of the meeting, the men, I think were upset with me for asking all those questions and being disrespectful to him. So what they did at the end, they said they needed someone to write something, and I said there's a laptop computer. Let's take it out and write it right here. He said, I'm a professional speechwriter, and they said, why don't you do that? The men did that to the other men. The other woman jumped in. She was feeling the same disconnect that these men were, disregarding our experience and our concerns and supporting this man who is Indian but who is not a part of the community, and he only had one tool to offer us. I felt very disrespected. . . . They think I'm an aggressive, impolite woman. I don't apologize for being a warrior. I've chosen to be a fighter. I'm not an at-home momma. That's not the role I've chosen. I'm not a docile, second-support spouse. I choose to be at the forefront at this kind of work. I don't apologize for the skills I have. I'm sorry I'm a woman and that bothers you.

And, as Lisa Thomas notes, sexism is not an issue that, contrary to Jaimes's and Halsey's assertions, Native women have put on the back-burner. In fact, as Lisa Thomas's story indicates, Native women have often confronted this issue strongly, even through physical confrontations. According to her:

Guys think they've got the big one, man. Like when——had to go over there, and she went to these Indians because they thought they were a bunch of swinging dicks and stuff, and she just let them have it. She just read them out. What else can you do? That's pretty brave. She was nice; she could have laid one of them out. Like you know——, well, of course this was more extreme because I laid him out! He's way bigger than me. He's probably five foot eleven. I'm five feet tall. When he was younger, and I was younger, I don't even know what he said to me, it was something really awful. I didn't say nothing because he was bigger than me, I just laid him out. Otherwise you could get hurt. So I kicked him right in his little nut, and he fell down on the floor—"I'm going to kill you! You bitch!" But then he said, "You're the man!" If you be equal on a gut and juice level, on the street, they don't think of you as a woman anymore, and therefore they can be your friend and they don't hate you. But then they go telling stuff like "You're the man!" And then what I said back to him was, "I've got it swinging!"

Of course, as both Sammy Toineeta and Thunder Hawk note, sexism within Native activism needs to be seen within the context of sexism in the larger society. They point to the importance of further developing the intersectional analysis proffered by the critical race theorist Kimberle Crenshaw, which emphasizes the intersections of racism and sexism in the lives of women of color. The "intersection," however, that this analysis does not emphasize is the intersection of sexism in the dominant society with sexism in Native communities or other communities of color. Historically, one of the ways in which patriarchal relationships became inscribed in previously nonpatriarchal Native societies was through European colonists' refusal to engage in economic-political negotiations with

Native women designated by their nations for that role (Perdue 1999; Pesantubbee 2005; Shoemaker 1995). Indigenous nations as a result began to devalue Native women's leadership themselves. In the contemporary context, as Thunder Hawk notes, this practice continues, as the media of the dominant society has consistently refused to recognize the leadership of women in the American Indian Movement, which further contributes to sexism within the movement. She sees sexism in the larger society as a bigger issue to Native women than sexism on the part of Native men. However, she notes that women have sometimes been able to use that sexism to their advantage by engaging in activism that falls under the radar of the forces of government repression. By using this strategy, Native activists were able to continue more radical work under the auspices of Women of All Red Nations. Thunder Hawk says,

> A lot of the "male leadership" [in AIM] ended up in jail or on the run. But when you're dealing with tribal people who still have the inner workings of a tribalistic society then that's how you operate. So what do you do? You learn right away that women could just about do anything under the eyes of the feds and the press because you were invisible. . . . We decided then that we have to get organized and we have to do it as women. . . . And the women's, feminist movement was taking off real good, and we were hearing about it. So we said, okay, give ourselves a name [Women of All Red Nations] and let's get organized.

In my own experience working with Women of All Red Nations in Chicago, it was the case that we were one of the most politically active Native organizations at that time. We organized countless rallies and demonstrations, which often garnered good media attention. However, never once was WARN credited with organizing these events. One time a man from AIM in Kentucky came to Chicago to support our event, and the media dubbed it as an AIM-organized event even though there was no AIM chapter at that time in Chicago. As another example, during that same time, Roxy Grignon, a Menominee activist, spearheaded a campaign to close an open Indian burial mound in Dickson, Illinois. Through her tireless efforts, she and the group she cofounded, To Enable Our Ancestors to Reach the Spirit World (TEARS), were successful. However, at a press conference that announced the closing of the burial mound, two men from AIM chapters in other states attended and were credited with its closing. Grignon received no press mention at all. Thus, in all these instances the prominence of Native men was not necessarily their doing or even their desire but the result of the media's refusal to acknowledge American Indian women's leadership.

Another factor identified by Sammy Toineeta explaining the lack of women's public prominence in AIM was the types of activism AIM typically engaged in. Toineeta makes this argument in her distinction between activism (which she sees as male dominated) and organizing (which she sees as female dominated). She argues that activist work designed to bring media attention to an issue is often male dominated. Because AIM often engaged in this kind of work, men tended to receive more attention. Whereas organizing work, usually dominated by women, involves the slow process of building community support and is not something that has the same public visibility.

> Activists and organizers are very different. A lot of people equate them. . . . Activists kind of hit and run. You're there; you try to help solve a problem, and then you move onto the next one. Organizers look at it and say, we can develop a program around this. We can organize and get the town together and get them to work on a citizen's monitoring board. Long-term things. And you work with them; you keep working with them. When we first started becoming more active, I think the men saw themselves really in the role of an activist, and the women were in the role of the organizers. I don't know if that's still true today because we're not doing the same kind of activist work. We're doing more organizing work. Now, if we went back to a situation where we were going to go for the headlines, I might still see that exist.

Toineeta concludes that Native activism today is more female dominated than it was in the 1970s precisely because it is dominated by organizing rather than activism. It is certainly the case, for instance, that during the United Nations (UN) Conference against Racism the indigenous caucus at the preparatory meetings, as well as at the UN meeting itself, was dominated by women (which is not to say sexism was absent during these meetings).

Sherry Wilson similarly notes that often the work women do, such as cooking, goes undervalued—not just by Native men but by the larger society as well. Both Wilson and Toineeta's insights are important correctives to many of the current theories developed about Native activism by scholars. In these accounts, the activism women were involved in goes unrecorded in order to highlight the more dramatic roles often dominated by men. For instance, in their germinal and noteworthy account of the rise of the American Indian Movement, Paul Chaat Smith and Robert Warrior write, "In the years that followed [the occupation of Wounded Knee in 1973], the Indian movement built on its experiences and matured in some respects, but it rarely demonstrated the kind of bold, imaginative strokes of genius that, for a brief season at the end of the 1960s, were poised to change everything" (1996, 278).

This statement, perhaps unwittingly, conveys the idea that the critical work done by Native women after the 1960s, such as the founding of WARN and the Indigenous Women's Network, their success in making sterilization abuse a public issue, their work in making environmental racism a commonly understood concept, and their success in organizing a global indigenous movement that has had a significant impact in the UN process, is not "bold" and "imaginative" because this work has not been centered around headline-grabbing, dramatic demonstrations and occupations. Similarly, Troy Johnson discusses in *The Occupation of Alcatraz Island* how the media focused on one or two spokespeople, invariably men, as the leaders of the occupation, thus marginalizing the contributions of others who took an equal part in this effort. Yet his account tends to replicate the same error, focusing on the dramatic actions that were often led by men and downplaying the work done by women. For instance, the work women did in setting up a school on the island earns less than a page in his account (1996, 87). Elizabeth Castle argues that because "traditional historians rarely consider 'unofficial' political power significant, and feminist revisionists often measured such informal power against white patriarchal standards and then declared it second best," the role of Native women in organizing is marginalized within scholarly discourses (2000, 166).

At the same time, however, it would be a mistake to argue that Native women just cooked and cleaned and supported the men. As demonstrated by a documentary film about the death of a prominent AIM activist, Annie Mae Aquash, *The Spirit of Annie Mae*, women were also at AIM protests on the front lines with guns, just as men were (Martin 2002). Toineeta and Trask argue that, while Native women's labor is often welcomed within Native activist circles, it is often devalued in the arenas of land struggle and sovereignty. By devaluing women's work as only relevant to the family, Native activists have failed to see how women's work also fundamentally shapes the project of nation building. States Trask:

> The commonly held perception is that "women's issues" relate only to the family, children, nutrition and health. And in recent times, their issues relat-

ing to employment, pay equity and gender bias have been included under the umbrella. This is due largely to the recognition of women laborers. However, there continues to be great reluctance to the local, regional, national and international levels to accept self-determination and nation-building as primary issues of concern to women–especially women of color . . .

As a result of this tragedy of assimilation and imperialism, the traditional role of indigenous women in the political arena has diminished–casting them aside or relegating them to subservient and marginal positions in today's world. It is this oppression that should be viewed as a primary political threat to the survival of all indigenous peoples. Its eradication should be a central goal and the paramount objective of indigenous women who are committed to this survival of their cultures, communities and nations. . . . Nation building is everyone's work. (1995, 14–15)[56]

Jennifer Denetdale further argues that, while Native women are part of the nationalist project, where they are involved as "cultural symbols and signifiers of the nation in many masculinist discourses," they are simultaneously marginalized as producers of theory about Indian nations and nationalisms (2006). Consequently, argues Patricia Monture-Angus, the absence of women in indigenous nation building contributes to nation-building projects that are top down rather than community based (1999).

The work of Angela Davis points out that the focus on political demonstrations and occupations has serious consequences not only for women but for social justice organizing as a whole. She notes that something similar happened in the Black Power movement. The increasing focus on flashy demonstrations not only marginalized women, who were often the ones doing the organizing, but it undermined the movement as a whole. While activism has its place in a movement, it is through the tedious and slow processes of organizing that a movement attracts new members and builds power. She states, "Revolution . . . [is] no fashionable club with newly minted jargon, or new kind of social life—made thrilling risk and confrontation, made glamorous by costume. . . . Serious revolutionary work consists of persistent and methodical efforts through a collective of other revolutionaries to organize the masses for action" (1988, 162).

Addressing the marginalization of Native women in political organizing

---

[56] See also Sheila Tousey: "One of the things I worry about is the role of Indian women in society today. It's got to change. You don't see a lot of Indian woman leaders within the tribal government. Indian society has developed to become very sexist and sometimes I wonder whether that is why I have a hard time being able to find work there" (n.d., 35).

within both Native communities and the larger society means more than simply the exclusion of women's voices. As discussed in the preface, when we *recenter* Native organizing from the perspective of Native women we also change the kinds of organizing and activisms we value and promote.

Given that sexism is widely held to be a problem for Native women, within both Native communities and the dominant society, does their activism entail a rejection of sovereignty? To the contrary, Native women's "feminism" enables them to redefine sovereignty, tradition, and Native organizing rather than rejecting them. For instance, as the Mending the Sacred Hoop Project in Duluth, Minnesota, notes, Native women involved in the antiviolence movement often have to struggle against those in the community who argue that domestic violence is "traditional." The debate then becomes a question of what is "traditional" and how Native women position themselves in relation to "tradition." On one hand, some activists, such as Tonya Gonnella Frichner, are firm in their belief that Native traditions have clear principles that provide direction in organizing gender relationships to which Native peoples should adhere since they are based on the natural world: "Our original instructions are never outdated. The Great Law of Peace doesn't go out of fashion, doesn't become outdated. Whether it's now or 500 years ago, those original instructions still apply. The rules of the natural world still apply. If you let something go in your hand, it's going to drop to the floor. That's the law of gravity; that's the natural law."

Some Native women describe feminism as ultimately "traditional." As Julie Star states:

> Well I would say our traditional ways are feminist, properly understood. I do see feminism as ordering right relations and I think that's what our traditions are all about, is being in balance with one another. Being in balance with all creation, be it the environment, be it nation-to-nation, and I think feminism is that, but it does so from the particular vantage point that women are able to provide. . . .
>
> So people talk about going back to the traditional ways. My question is, what traditional way are you really talking about because the traditional way is much more feminist than anything that's been articulated yet. Generally what it means is some perverted tradition which is a Hollywood male creation, which has nothing to do with our walking in balance or living as a true sovereign nation.

The rhetoric of the antidomestic and antisexual violence movement in Indian country is largely framed around the notion that "violence against women is not an Indian tradition." An example can be seen in the analysis of Anishnabe traditional practices regarding domestic violence:

> Wife battering, as we have seen, was neither accepted nor tolerated among the Anishinabe people until after the freedom to live Ojibwe was subdued. Wife battering emerged simultaneously with the disintegration of Ojibwe ways of life and the beginning use of alcohol. The behavior of the Ojibwe people under the influence of alcohol is often totally contrary to Anishinabe values. It is especially contrary to the self discipline previously necessary to the development of Ojibwe character. . . .
>
> Today we have lost a lot of the traditions, values, ways of life, laws, language, teachings of the Elders, respect, humility as Anishinabe people because of the European mentality we have accepted. For the Anishinabe people to survive as a Nation, together we must turn back the pages of time. We must face reality, do an evaluation of ourselves as a people—why we were created to live in harmony with one another as Anishinabe people and to live in harmony with the Creator's creation. (Anishinabe Values/Social Law Regarding Wife Battering n.d., 49)[57]

While this perspective is widespread, it is not universal. Linda Epperly (Muscogee) contends that, while many Native nations were not marked by gender oppression, some did sanction gender violence and other forms of gender oppression. She says that, while she previously subscribed to the popularly held viewpoint that domestic violence did not exist in Indian tribes prior to colonization, after conducting further historical research she concluded that it is not possible to make such universal claims about tribal practices. She argues that to do so is to put Indian peoples into a savage-innocent dichotomy in which Native peoples are either completely barbaric or perfect.[58]

Her arguments point to another issue addressed by Lakota Harden and Loretta Rivera, that accessing what Native nations did prior to colonization is not always easy. Epperly, for instance, relies on missionary accounts of tribal practices, which obviously were written with Eurocentric biases and after Native nations had been subjected to colonization.

Second, what is remembered as "traditional" is also political. Jennifer Denetdale critically interrogates the gendered politics of remembering "tradition" in her germinal analysis of the office of Miss Navajo Nation.

[57] See similar viewpoints in Asetoyer 1995; and Mousseau and Artichoker n.d.

[58] Linda Epperly, talk presented at the Oklahoma Native American Coalition against Domestic Violence conference, Tulsa, Oklahoma, December 10, 2002.

She notes that this office is strictly monitored by the Navajo nation to ensure that Miss Navajo models "'traditional' Navajo women's purity, mothering and nurturing qualities, and morality [which] are evoked by the Navajo Nation to extol Navajo honor and are claimed on behalf of the modernizing project of nationalism." She notes that "when Miss Navajo Nation does not conform to the dictates of ideal Navajo womanhood, she is subjected to harsh criticism intended to reinforce cultural boundaries. Her body literally becomes a site of surveillance that symbolically conveys notions about racial purity, morality, and chastity." Meanwhile male leaders, who may be guilty of everything from domestic violence to embezzlement, are rarely brought before any tribal committees. She argues that the ideals that Navajo women are supposed to represent are not simply traditional Navajo values but also unacknowledged European Victorian ideals of womanhood. She asserts, "Navajo leaders, who are primarily men, reproduce Navajo nationalist ideology to re-inscribe gender roles based on Western concepts even as they claim that they operate under traditional Navajo philosophy" (2006, 18–19).

Harden argues as well that Native peoples' memories of traditions are not untainted by the experiences of Christian boarding schools and other historic traumas, which impact what we remember about our histories. She states:

> In trying to piece together our history and our stories and our legends, it seems that much of what we remember has actually been tainted and changed by colonization. We do not actually remember what happened before colonization because we were not there. So we have to ask ourselves, how much of what we think is tradition was really originally ours; and how much of it is Christian-influenced? Knowing how powerful Native women are now, how could we have ever accepted anything less then? How could we have let ourselves be ignored or degraded? I'm not saying that I know, because I don't. But those questions have brought me to wonder how much of the tradition is really ours, and how much does that even matter?
>
> I remember at our school, all us were preparing a sweat lodge in our backyard. Our backyard was huge, the plains. And I remember one of the boys saying, "Women can never carry the pipe." "Women never used to do this or that." (Now I realize that all comes from Christianity.) And I remember feeling very devastated because I was very young then. I was trying to learn these traditions. I was quite the drama queen and going to the trailer and my aunt was making bread or something. "Auntie, this is what they're saying!" She said, "Well you know, tradition, we talk about being traditional.

What we're doing now is different. When we talk about trying to follow the traditions of say our ancestors from 100 years ago, it's probably different from 300 years ago. If when the horses came, what would have happened had we said, 'Oh we don't ride the four-legged, they are our brother. We respect them; we don't ride them?' Where would we be? Hey man, we found those horses and we became the best horse riders there ever were, and we were having good winters. So tradition is keeping those principles, the original principles about honoring life all around you. Walk in beauty is another interpretation. Respecting everything around you. Leave the place better than you found it. Those were the kind of traditions that we followed. But they change as we go along."

   And in a few minutes [after talking to my Auntie], then I went back to the room. Now, being a pipe carrier means that you don't drink alcohol, you don't smoke marijuana, you don't take drugs, you don't fight with people, and you don't abuse anyone. And I was really trying to follow that because that's what my uncle taught me. So I went to the middle of the room, and I said to the guys in the room, "I want everybody here who is following the tradition, who has given up the things I just named to stand here in the circle with me." And no one did. I said that until this circle is filled with men, when it's filled with men, I'll do something else like learn to cook. But until then, there has to be someone standing here doing this, and if you're not going to do it, I will. And no one ever said anything to me or anything about women not doing these things ever, at least from that group.

Loretta Rivera also points to the selective remembering of tradition in Native communities and further suggests that the questioning of tradition is itself a traditional practice: "So when I find a young person who wants to question the rhetoric, question the traditions, I just love it, because that's the kind of teenager I was. I always tell people, in the village two hundred years ago I would be doing the same thing, questioning the stuff. That we were a range of people then, and we're a range of people now." And, even as she affirms tradition, Tony Sheehy also speaks to the gendered politics of remembering tradition.

I subscribe to all the feminist things [but] . . . I describe myself more as a traditionalist. I truly believe when we were created that we had some god-given roles as human beings, and in those roles we weren't subservient to anyone. We weren't taught to walk two steps behind anyone. . . . In understanding who I am and valuing who I am as a traditional woman, I know that I have a right to be a leader. I have a right to be in all of these places. I have a right to speak. I also know by tradition that sometimes I have to question tradition as to whose tradition was that. Is this our traditional way from my tribe or from the community that I live in? Or was it something that the colonists or in the colonization process we adapted and now claim it to be our tradition? So I challenge that. That's where it gets into—maybe I'm bringing in feminist views to traditionalism.

Rosalva Castillo calls for a more flexible relationship between Native women's activism and tradition that is based not just on reclaiming traditional gender relationships but on reinventing them in light of the contemporary context.

> More than rejecting their "traditional" practices, many Indigenous women have insisted on reinventing it under new terms and within this transformation process. . . . Zapatista women demand for the right to participate in the revolutionary struggle to the extent that their will and capacity allows them, to work and receive fair wages, to decide on the number of children they can have and take care of; to have posts of responsibility and to be allowed to participate in the running of the community, to the right to health and education; to the right to marry the partner of their choice and to not be forced into an arranged marriage; to not be the victims of any kind of violence and finally, to the right to positions of leadership within the revolutionary forces. (N.d., 4–5)

Lee Maracle goes so far as to ask: is "tradition" an Indian tradition? At the 2005 Native Women and Feminism conference (Edmonton, Alberta), some participants argued that feminism is not traditional. Maracle's reply was "Who defines what is traditional?" She said that her tribe had a system of slavery prior to colonization, but then it abolished the system. So what is traditional in her tribe, she asked, slavery or the abolition of slavery? Maracle then argued that prior to colonization tribes always adapted to changing circumstances. So is our current relationship to tradition actually traditional? Or is it the product of colonialism in which any change can seem threatening?

On the other hand, it should be observed that those who argue that traditional practices do contain clear, accessible guidelines for how to order gender relations note that these principles manifest themselves differently today than they did in precontact times. Frichner describes how following these principles would translate in her context of UN advocacy: "I think what it would be would be when we do our work, we are treated as equals and we're treated in a good way instead of dismissed on some levels because we're women. Nowadays, it seems like the Euro-American model is playing itself out in the way Native women are treated."

The articulations of Native women organizers speak to more than the exclusion of Native women within either feminist or Native sovereignty struggles. They challenge the very terms on which these struggles articulate themselves.

Is Biblical Feminism Either? Complementarianism versus Egalitarianism
While evangelicals and their critics often portray themselves as untainted by feminist politics, the instability of gender politics within evangelicalism is demonstrated by the clear impact biblical feminism has had on this discourse. This impact can be missed, however, amid the increased effort to tie evangelical orthodoxy to support of gender hierarchicalism. For instance, the Southern Baptist Convention amended its Baptist Faith and Message in 1998 to include a statement on male headship: "A wife is to submit herself graciously to the servant leadership of her husband even as the church willingly submits to the headship of Christ. She, being in the image of God as is her husband thus equal to him, has the God-given responsibility to respect their husband and to serve as his helper in managing the household and nurturing the next generation" (Land 1999, 2).

In 2000, it was amended to say "the office of pastor is limited to men as qualified by Scripture." In May 2002, the SBC fired 13 missionaries who did not affirm these revisions. Twenty more resigned for the same reason. Ten others took early retirement. Seventy-seven missionaries altogether have declined to work under this message, but 99 percent of the 5,500 overseas SBC missionaries have affirmed it, publicly at least ("Baptists Fire Missionaries" 2003). Many signed but did so "in order not to destroy their ministries" rather than because they actually affirmed the statement (Cutrer 2002c). The Baptist General Convention of Texas, which opposes the current SBC leadership, began forming an alternative global organization and an emergency fund in 2002 to help missionaries who had left as a result of these revisions (Cutrer 2002a). It received $1.4 million in contributions within the first eleven months (Walker 2003). *Christianity Today* also criticized the message, arguing that is was unnecessarily restrictive and alienating (Christianity Today 2000b). The response of Paige Patterson, a former SBC president, to the egalitarian critiques of the message was "The problem is they have to argue with God, not with us" (37).

As discussed earlier, the Council of Biblical Manhood and Womanhood was formed in 1987 to oppose Christians for Biblical Equality. It was central in the efforts to squash the TNIV translation. It has also conducted campaigns against evangelical churches that support gender equality such as the famous Willow Creek Church in Barrington, Illinois, which is not only one of the largest evangelical churches in the country but has taken a stance affirming women's leadership in all positions of the church (Winner 2000a).

It is possible that this backlash does not signal the triumph of gender hierarchicalists. In fact, it may testify to the success of the evangelical feminist movement in changing gender roles within evangelicalism. Pierre Bourdieu's description of doxa may be helpful in this analysis. Bourdieu separates fields of knowledge between doxa and opinion. *Doxa* is defined as "undisputed, unquestioned understandings of the world," that which seems natural. The dominating class secures domination by making the processes of domination seem natural—within the field of doxa. Through crisis, Bourdieu argues, the field of doxa can enter the field of opinion— fields of knowledge that are understood as contestable. Once this process of change occurs, agents of reaction can attempt to institute "orthodoxy," which is the attempt to turn the field of opinion back to the field of doxa. But it is never entirely able to do so (Bourdieu 1998, 169). Thus, we can interpret this backlash as a reassertion of orthodoxy based on gender hierarchy, but the extent to which orthodoxy needs to be reasserted is indicative of how much it has eroded. What we may be seeing among conservative evangelicals is an increasing mandate to verbally assent to the demands of gender hierarchy while de facto living lives based on the at least partially economically determined need for gender equality. As James Scott puts it, "Only when contradictions are publicly declared do they have to be publicly accounted for" (1990, 51). Husbands can let their wives be in charge as long as there is "no public challenge to their authority" and they are still given "credit for running things" (52).[59] Evangelicals publicly subscribe to gender hierarchy while increasingly living their lives based on egalitarian principles. Thus, I will demonstrate how these growing cries of orthodoxy are concurrent with pronounced but generally

[59] Similarly, Brenda Brasher contends that this gender flexibility is what allows gender insubordination to remain in place. She writes, "To the extent that male pastors are pressed by female congregants to address particular issues rather than redistribute authority in a nonsexist manner pastors are able to maintain an image of being responsive to women's concerns, thereby destabilizing women's impetus toward change and retaining congregational authority as a prerogative of males" (1998, 90).

unacknowledged shifts in the gender politics of evangelical communities. As a result, evangelicalism is marked by contestations between gender complementarians (those who support gender hierarchy in the church and/or the home) and egalitarians (those who support gender equality in the church, home, and society).[60] Even in groups that seem to support complementarianism, important shifts in gender politics are apparent.

As mentioned previously, CBMW's mission is to root out egalitarianism. While its organizing efforts have certainly done much to undermine the work of egalitarians in evangelical communities, the fact that gender hierarchicalists found CBE sufficiently threatening to form a countergroup is significant. In addition, even within its literature we find unacknowledged shifts in terms of gender hierarchy. First, the fact that gender hierarchicalists feel the need to call themselves complementarians instead of hierarchicalists indicates that they feel the need to distance themselves from male supremacy. In fact, one flyer they promoted ranks their position between "the effeminate left" and the "male dominant right." This signals another interesting shift in that CBMW seems to want to distance itself not only from male dominance but from the political Right as well.[61] In addition, in 1997 the Campus Crusade for Christ, which has affiliated itself with CBMW and supported SBC's statement on male headship, announced a revision of its "Four Spiritual Laws," which now feature inclusive language. Meanwhile, Concerned Women for America, while organized for the express purpose of countering feminism, increasingly adopts (and co-opts) its history, principles, and issues. In an article in *Family Voice*, Concerned Women for America calls for mobilization against the global trafficking in women and even contends that feminists support trafficking! Clearly these developments did not occur in a vacuum but are the result of feminist struggles within neo-evangelicalism that have shifted the terms of the debate about gender roles.

---

[60] *Christianity Today* lists the complementarian versus egalitarian seminaries. Fuller, North Park, the Palmer Theological Seminary, Ashland, and the Church of God School of Theology are egalitarian and not likely to hire complementarian faculty. Westminster, the Dallas Theological Seminary, Covenant, and the six seminaries of the Southern Baptist Convention require complementarian allegiances. Trinity, Gordon-Cromwell, Denver, and Regent College have faculty with varying perspectives on this issue (George 2005).

[61] Interestingly, in the flyer's chart, which graphs the varying positions taken by the "effeminate left," the "male dominant right," and the complementarian center, conservative "get tough on crime" approaches to criminal justice are categorized with the male dominant right whereas restorative justice models are categorized with the complementarian center, where CBMW situates itself.

Contestations in evangelical politics have become particularly pronounced with the rise of the Promise Keepers movement. Promise Keepers has perhaps been most severely criticized for its gender politics, particularly by liberal feminist organizations such as the National Organization for Women (NOW) and the Fund for a Feminist Majority. Eleanor Smeal, a former NOW president and current president of the Fund for a Feminist Majority, declared, "Don't be fooled by their [Promise Keepers'] outward appearances; the Promise Keepers are preaching that men are ordained to lead—women to submit or follow. We have been there, done that. These out-moded attitudes have led time and time again to low pay, low status, and the abuse of women" (Smeal 1997). When critics of Promise Keepers want to highlight its sexism, they invariably quote Tony Evans, who advises men to "sit down with your [wives] and say something like this: 'Honey, I've made a terrible mistake. I've given you my role. I gave up leading the family, and I forced you to take my place. Now I must reclaim that role.' . . . I'm not suggesting that you *ask* for your role back, I'm urging you to *take it back.* . . . There can be no compromise here. If you're going to lead, you must lead . . . Treat the lady gently and lovingly. But *lead!*" (Conason, Ross, and Cokorinos 1996, 14).[62]

These cries of gender oppression often do not coincide with the reality experienced by the female partners of Promise Keepers. I talked to several women on staff at Promise Keepers who said that the organization has a reputation for being one of the most women-friendly evangelical organizations. Even evangelical women who were critical of Promise Keepers conceded its reputation for being a good place for an evangelical woman to work. Staff members did report a glass ceiling in terms of how far women could advance (although one believed that Promise Keepers would hire women as vice presidents even though it had not yet done so) (Horner 2002). But it has provided comprehensive sexual harassment training for all the staff, and women report being treated and paid well. The women partners of Promise Keepers widely report positive changes in their marriages.[63] Even egalitarian women have many positive things to say about

[62] After Promise Keepers received much criticism for this statement, its rhetoric around gender relations softened considerably. In a very clever rhetorical tactic, Promise Keepers appointed Tony Evans as a speaker at the Stand in the Gap rally, where he reframed this quote so that it would not sound like it supported male supremacy. He explained that what "male leadership" actually entails is treating one's wife as an equal and recognizing that leadership is mutual, not a matter of oppressing or abusing one's wife.

[63] One notable exception was a woman I talked to who is active in the domestic

Promise Keepers. Says one CBE member, "My husband has attended [Promise Keepers events], people from my church attend, and I have seen wonderful, wonderful things happen in the lives of men who attend.... Do I think they have the whole message on egalitarianism? I do not. Do I think they espouse the views that I support about women in the church? I do not. But for the good they do, I don't want to discredit them completely."

Doug Smith, another proponent of egalitarianism, contends that "The driving force behind Promise Keepers is women. Every woman I have talked to says that when their man comes back from Promise Keepers, that he is a better husband and a better father as a result. Women are praying for Promise Keepers." *U.S. News and World Report* followed ninety men from Promise Keepers and interviewed their families. It found that these men were treating their wives more equally as a result of Promise Keepers (Shapiro 1995). During the 1996 Promise Keepers rallies, Mc-Cartney advised husbands to sit with their wives and together rate their marriages on a scale of one to ten. Then compare the scores. "Your wife's score will be lower, and your wife is right," he predicted. The message men receive from this advice is that it is women who are the ultimate authority in evaluating the health of a relationship. Elijah Muchina told me that he learned he can be oblivious to the pain his partner may be in and he must actively listen to ensure that he is treating her respectfully. Articles in *New Man* (which was a Promise Keepers publication before it went independent) and Promise Keepers publications generally advise men on how to treat their wives respectfully and meet their needs rather than asserting their authority over them (McGuire 2000). Thus, the messages of gender hierarchy in Promise Keepers rhetoric are often subverted by messages of gender egalitarianism, and consequently liberal feminist critiques of Promise Keepers often do not resonate with evangelical women.

Promise Keepers's gender politics is much more complex than is articulated by its critics because it is a coalition of complementarians and egalitarians. Contrary to popular opinion, Promise Keepers has not taken a stand on the issue of complementarianism versus egalitarianism (Frame 1999; Van Leeuwen 1997). Probably most of the leaders, such as McCartney, are complementarians, and they often do not distinguish their posi-

---

violence field. She reported that a friend of hers runs a Christian batterer's program, and 70 percent of the participants are men who do not think being a Promise Keeper is inconsistent with being a batterer. At that time, Promise Keepers had refused to make statements against battering or sexual abuse. Since that time, many evangelical women have complained, and Promise Keepers finally made a fairly strong statement against sexual and domestic violence at Stand in the Gap.

tions from those of Promise Keepers (Frame 1999).[64] However, a significant number of men who have served in leadership positions are egalitarians. A prominent egalitarian among the Promise Keepers ranks is Bill Hybels (a former board member and spiritual adviser to President Clinton) who heads the very influential Willow Creek Church. In my research, I found that most Promise Keepers (including the staff) are not in consensus about (1) what Promise Keepers' position is on gender issues, (2) where it stands on egalitarianism versus complementarianism, or (3) what defines complementarianism or egalitarianism. However, I have noticed that, even while complementarians may vociferously defend their positions, what is considered complementarian sounds increasingly more egalitarian than it did a decade ago. Here is one exchange I had with a Promise Keepers (PK) staff member.

Me: Is Promise Keepers complementarian or egalitarian?

PK: Definitely complementarian?

Me: What exactly is complementarianism?

PK: That means men must exercise servant leadership in the home.

Me: So that means men have the final say in a marriage if there is an impasse in the decision-making process?

PK: No, they must work things out together. He can't just decide for them both.

Me: Does it mean that women and men have different roles? Perhaps women should be concerned more with the family and the husband with work?

PK: No, they both have the same roles. Women should have the same job opportunities as men.

Me: But men are to be servant leaders? What about women?

PK: They're supposed to be servant leaders, too.

Me: So what exactly is the problem with egalitarianism?

PK: Hmmm. Well, I'm not exactly sure what egalitarianism is. Maybe I should find out.[65]

Promise Keepers staffer Charles King's definition of male headship seemed to center primarily around the importance of men being spiri-

[64] McCartney, Charles Colson, Joseph Stowell, and Tony Evans (all prominent Promise Keepers speakers) took out a full-page advertisement affirming the SBC's 1998 amendment to its Faith and Message, which affirmed male headship (Land 1999, 3).

[65] Ingersoll and Gallagher found similar trends in their research on evangelical women (Gallagher 2003; Ingersoll 2005).

tually active in the home. He asserted in an interview that "wherever a dad is actively involved as a believer in the home, there is a 75 percent chance that the children will be believers. Where the dad is no longer home and the mother is charged with the responsibility of being the spiritual head of the household, there is only a 15 percent chance that the children will be believers." This leadership does not seem to translate into decision-making authority, however.

> Me: Hypothetically speaking, let's say you have a great job. But your wife gets this great, once-in-a-lifetime job offer in another state. Who decides what to do?
>
> King: Decision is made through prayer. Ask God for the answer because it can go both ways. If I was a technician and my wife was an anchor lady who got an offer at CNN [Cable News Network], then it might make sense to follow the wife around. Jan has followed me around because my job dictated such moves. But, if the shoe were on the other foot, then absolutely, I would follow her. Don't leave God out of the decision. See what God says, and God might very well say follow your wife. God must run the show; it gets messed up when I try to take control.[66]

For many complementarians, male headship does translate into decision-making authority. Nevertheless, even in these situations, complementarians stress the importance of mutuality in decision making and equality in the workplace. They also stress that gender roles, while helpful, should not be overly restrictive. In an interview, Robert Tyler stated:

> Tyler: The man should take initiative to sacrifice for the family. For me headship means that the husband leads in loving service. There is mutual submission in different roles. So much in popular culture is about who controls power. But the Gospel is he who will serve. There is some differentiation of roles, and there's difference in initiative. I think even secular writers are picking up this theme: "Men are from Mars; Women are from Venus." I think one thing that happened is that there was a real outcry about abuse and neglect and subjugation of women and their devaluation. I think that cry has been heard. And now the church is starting to say, but women and men are not identical; they are different, and there's things we can learn from that.

[66] Of course, it is also true that many Promise Keepers staffers have become skilled at sidestepping discussions on gender hierarchy in order to diffuse critiques by liberal feminists, but, even so, the fact that Promise Keepers would feel the need to be accountable to liberal feminism is significant.

Me: Egalitarians will say that male headship itself will naturally promote the conditions for abuse. That is, if a woman see a man as the authority, she won't be able to challenge his hitting her. So, how do you correct these kind of dynamics when someone is seen as in charge?

Tyler: In a family, I would hope that the loving initiative by a father would not make demands for respect but would command respect. Any situation where a man is being abusive is clearly wrong and should not be tolerated. In Malachi, it says God hates divorce, but God hates more a man's violence toward his wife. If I hear about that, I would say that the woman should be removed until violence stops. There should be some intervention.

Similar themes are echoed in my interview with Clark Clements.

Me: What is male headship then?

Clements: Headship has to do with responsibility. My wife is equal to me before God, an equal image bearer, and has equal access to God and the Spirit, but we have different roles. The roles aren't rigid, but there are general propensities that we are responsible for. Probably most men cut the yard, and women cook, but women can certainly cut the yard. But if I am the head of cutting the yard, it doesn't mean I have to do it, but if it doesn't get done, I will stand accountable for it.

Me: What are you the head of?

Clements: My wife, my children, and my home.

Me: On a hypothetical level, let's say you have a great job in one state and your wife gets a great job in another state. Who makes the decision?

Clements: Like any loving couple, we have to work it out. If that's a great opportunity, I want to make sacrifices for that. I think I do have the final veto power, but I don't really go there. . . . And in eleven years there have been very few decisions that have come to me making the decision.

This blurring of lines can also be found in the National Fatherhood Initiative promoted at the Promise Keeper events of 2004. Its goal is to "improve the lives of children by encouraging all fathers to be responsible, committed and involved in their children's lives." Yet none of the basic principles it espouses focuses on male headship; in fact, the principles stress respecting and supporting one's wife and children.[67] Interestingly,

---

[67] The principles are: (1) respect your children's mother, (2) spend time with your children, (3) earn the right to be heard, (4) discipline with love, (5) be a role model, (6) be a teacher, (7) eat together as a family, (8) read to your children, (9) show affection, and (10) realize that a father's job is never done. ("Ten Ways to Be a Better

in its newsletter, the benefit that daughters gain from having good fathers is that "she is more willing to attempt challenging tasks which, in turn, usually result in better jobs, higher incomes, and financial self-reliance" (Degraffenred 2004, 9). There are no benefits listed that speak to daughters becoming better wives and mothers or leading more domestic lives. Larry Jackson, a speaker at the 2004 rally defined *servant leadership* in such a way that it almost seems to grant the authority to the wife. "You can't say you're the king unless you're a servant first," he said. So, if you are the head of the household and the dishes are not washed, you need to wash them. You should only focus on what you should give rather than what you receive, and your wife "may not give anything because you haven't given her anything." *Christianity Today* similarly opined that complementarian and egalitarian marriages often look surprisingly alike (Horner 2002). In his study of Promise Keepers literature, Sean Everton concludes that Promise Keepers "employ the language of male headship in largely symbolic terms while at the same time embracing a day-to-day egalitarianism" (2001, 60).

Similarly, at the 2005 Promise Keepers conference in Lansing, Michigan, and the 2004 conference in Seattle, several speakers argued that male "headship" (though they did not use that term explicitly) only means that the man must serve his wife and does not entitle him to boss his wife around. Dan Seaborn, of Winning at Home, said at the 2005 Lansing event that the men in the audience had pain they needed to heal from, but they had also caused pain to other people. He declared that his mother was a victim of domestic violence by his father, and that he now represented to the men the child that is hurting because of what they were doing to their wives. This speaker said nothing to the men about asserting power in marriage; rather, he admonished them to think about how they can prioritize the needs of their wives and children.

The issues of domestic and sexual violence within evangelical communities have also contributed significantly to a blurring between complementarian and egalitarian lines. An example is a Steven Tracy article on male headship on violence. While he says he is a complementarian, he contends that we must critically interrogate what biblical headship is. He notes that a man in his congregation justified his sexual abuse of children,

---

Dad," National Fatherhood Initiative brochure. Gaithersburg, Md., n.d.) Its other brochures, including "Creating a Father-Friendly Workplace" and "12 Ways to Balance Work and Family," stress that fathers should adopt flex-time work schedules and limit their career aspirations in order to spend more time with their families.

saying, "I guess I did it because I was the head of the family, and it was my right to do whatever I wanted to my wife and kids" (Tracy 2003, 50). However, proffers Tracy, we must distinguish male headship from male domination. While the man is the head of the woman as the Father is the head of the Son, it is also true that "the work of the Father and the Son is the collaboration of intimate equals. In this reading of biblical headship, submission is not a matter of mere duty, but a delightful response from a woman who is loved, partnered with, and trusted as an equal" (52). He further challenges the idea that men should wield all the authority in the church and the home: "Feminists have long argued that male headship necessarily denotes inequality. Christian men who insist on maintaining a monopoly on all domestic and ecclesiastical authority validates this misconception" (54). Godly women have the authority to proclaim the Gospel, prophesy, run a household, manage commercial enterprises, hold men accountable, and serve as colaborers in ministry. In the end, Tracy concludes, "Male headship means protection, not domination" (54).

J. Lee Grady's article on domestic violence in *New Man* argues that evangelical teachings on male headship have "unknowingly, created an environment that encourages abuse" (2001, 40). However, in his effort to redefine headship in a manner that does not encourage abuse, he adopts the hermeneutical strategies of evangelical feminists, even explicitly citing the prominent CBE scholar Catherine Kroeger. For instance, he contends (borrowing from Kroeger) that the charge for women to "submit" (*hupatosso*) was really a declaration that women would be "identified with" their husbands and no longer kept under the control of their fathers. He also suggests that the description of men as the "head" (*kephale*) of their wives should be translated as "source" rather than "head" (44), a hermeneutical strategy commonly adopted by evangelical feminists.[68]

Jane Hansen attacks feminists for "declaring war" against men but ultimately calls for an end to "gender wars," which stop women from fulfilling their potential in the church (1997, 58). David Neff similarly notes in his review of the edited collection *Does Christianity Teach Male Headship? The Equal Regard Marriage and its Critics* (2004), that many are redefining headship as a codeword for responsibility. In fact, he contends that the basic problem is that men do not want to fulfill their familial roles, so the

[68] In fact, Grady was the keynote speaker at CBE's annual conference in 2003, so he may have shifted his position to the egalitarian perspective. Another *Christianity Today* article espouses female submission in marriage but contends that submission correlates with male sacrifice not male headship (summer 2005).

concept of headship is more about not being a deadbeat father than about asserting authority in the home. In fact, one contributor suggests that the concept of headship is really a strategy to get men excited about fulfilling their responsibilities. That is, they will not be excited about being fathers and husbands unless they get to claim headship and hence feel indispensable (Neff 2004). A prominent charismatic pastor, Jack Hayford, also announced his split with CBMW's position because, he contends, male headship is part of a temporary social order rather than God's intended plan for gender relations. "Let me put it plainly, he writes. "There is no way that male authority over women can be properly deduced from the Bible as being God's original intent" (Hayford 2003).

Thus, while liberal feminist organizations have expressed concern that Promise Keepers is against all the gains made by liberal feminism, it has actually been supportive of many of them. In fact, most of the Promise Keepers I talked to saw the organization as a *positive* response to feminism rather than a reaction against it. Says King:

> When I saw that article in the paper written by the head of NOW and realized they were very upset about Stand in the Gap, I thought, this is just a six-hour prayer gathering. What possible threat could that be to the women of America? First of all, we know that many women have been abused over the years by male power and dominance, and there has been a real need for women to get together and to stand up and say we're not going to take it anymore. It's the male abuse of power that has caused that to happen. So I don't have any quarrel with NOW. But when I saw Patricia Ireland saying she was really angry and hurt, I prayed for her, wondering why is she angry with men who want to walk closer to Jesus, honor our families, and honor our wives? Maybe, she's concerned Promise Keepers will go too far and try to keep women barefoot and pregnant, down and out. But that's not possible; the women of America are way beyond that. So what I talk about is servant leadership. When a man and woman get married, they first serve Jesus and then they serve each other. As they serve each other, I don't see any domination. I don't see men doing the things NOW wants to be concerned about. So they are hurt, angry, and distrustful. So our response is just watch us over time and see what we do. You need to remain critics. You need to remain vigilant. That's fine.

In fact, in a 1997 issue of *New Man*, the cover article on feminism concluded that "Christians need feminism. . . . Why do women receive 70 percent of what men receive for comparable work? Why does a woman's mental health and life expectancy go down when she marries while a man's mental health and life expectancy go up? Why are the faces of those living in poverty overwhelmingly female? Is this what God desires?" (Maudlin 1997b, 34). Promise Keepers also produced a video in which it declared that eradicating sexism is at the top of its agenda. In fact, I learned at the 1997 Minneapolis conference that the Promise Keepers founder, Bill McCartney, invited CBE to oversee one of its rallies to ensure that nothing sexist was evident. Of course, I do not mean to argue that Promise Keepers is a profeminist organization or that sexist and patriarchal ideologies are not intertwined in its practice. Rather, the relationship between feminism and Promise Keepers is a much more complicated one than is generally articulated by its critics.

Despite evangelical rhetoric about the importance of women staying at home, remaining married despite the quality of the marriage, and not supporting abortions, it seems that evangelicals are actually little different from their secular counterparts in these areas (Gallagher 2003, 175).[69] According to the Barna Research Group, divorce rates are actually higher among evangelicals than among other sectors of the population, including atheists. Ninety percent of born-again Christians who divorce do so *after* becoming a Christian ("Till Death Do Us Part?" 2000). According to *Christianity Today*, more than half of born-again Christians do not think divorce is a sin even when adultery is not involved (MacHarg 2004). A prominent Southern Baptist pastor, Charles Stanley, promised to resign from his pastorate in the First Baptist Church of Atlanta if he were to divorce. But when his marriage ended the church's administrative pastor told the congregation that Stanley would continue as the senior pastor, and the congregation stood and applauded (Christianity Today 2000a).[70] The majority of evangelical women are employed outside of the home (Ammerman 1993, 136; Miller 1997, 196–97). In fact, *Charisma* ran an article calling on Christians to stop harassing women who work outside the home, declaring, "Working mothers are not the source of all society's ills" (Minter 1997, 69). In one study of parishioners in the new Charismatic churches (the Vineyard, Hope, and Calvary Churches), 75 percent disagreed with the idea that women should "take care of the home and leave running the country to men" (208). Evangelicals complain that abor-

---

[69] In recognition of this fact, Focus on the Family organized the Council on Biblical Sexual Ethics to issue a statement to counter sexual immorality within Christian churches specifically (Council on Biblical Sexual Ethics 2001).

[70] Another well publicized conversation about divorce arose over the marriage breakup of a popular contemporary Christian artist, Amy Grant (Veith 1999d; Zoba 2000a). For more coverage on divorce in evangelical communities, see Veith 1999b.

tion rates are high within Christian colleges ("Abortion" 1989). According to some studies, conservative evangelical women are not so solidly anti-choice as one might guess (Brasher 1998, 160–61). A writer for *Christianity Today*, Lauren Winner, notes in her book *Real Sex* that three surveys of single Christians conducted in the 1990s found that two-thirds were not virgins. In 1992, a *Christianity Today* survey of one thousand readers found that 40 percent had had premarital sex, 14 percent had had an affair, and 75 percent of those who had affairs did so when they were Christians. In 2003, North Kentucky University found that 60 percent of students who signed sexual abstinence commitment cards broke their pledges. Of the 39 percent who kept them, 55 percent had had oral sex and did not consider it to be sex. Winner reported that many evangelical college students she talked to did not consider anal intercourse to be sex (2005). Thus, it would appear that to a large degree evangelicals have adapted to the demands of the secular world much more than they have transformed it. However, as Julie Ingersoll contends, feminist strands have always been part of what has never been a monolithic and static fundamentalist movement, so all apparent "deviations" from stereotypical gender repressive practices cannot be dismissed as mere "accommodation to the larger culture" as if fundamentalism is itself completely separate from the larger culture (2005, 146).

In addition, more women are coming into prominence as evangelical pastors or spiritual leaders. Women pastors are often prominently featured in charismatic venues such as *Charisma* (Johnson 2002). *Charisma* also has run articles supporting women's ordination (Grady 2000a). Beth Moore, Kay Arthur, and Anne Graham Lotz are popular Bible teachers, although they are not without their detractors. For instance, Lotz describes how some men turn their backs on her when she speaks because they feel it is unscriptural for a woman to speak from a pulpit if men are in the audience. Nonetheless, her popularity has grown to the point where half of the people in her audiences are men. Of course, part of her acceptability undoubtedly rests on the fact that, in addition to being Billy Graham's daughter, she espouses conservative gender views such as male headship and the exclusion of women from senior pastor positions (she is unsure whether or not women should be ordained) (Eha 2002).

An even more marked shift in the Christian Right position vis-à-vis feminism is Ralph Reed's retelling of the "women's movement." In *After the Revolution,* he argues that the women's movement of the nineteenth century was actually a Christian movement and thus implies that the Christian Right rather than the contemporary feminist movement is the true inheritor of this so-called first wave of the women's movement (1990, 141–55). Concerned Women for America (CWA) makes a similar argument in "Sisterhood or Liberalism." Contemporary feminists, CWA argues, "choose to ignore history that clearly reveals that the original suffragists were largely pro-life and pro-family" (Concerned Women For America 1997). A writer for *Christianity Today* recently opined: "I am a feminist because of Christ, the world's most avant-garde emancipator. When he praised Mary for choosing to learn from him over kitchen work (which we will always have with us), he was more radical than Gloria Steinem" (Tennant 2006). The fact that these sectors choose to align themselves with some parts of feminist history indicates that there has been a shift in gender politics within the Christian Right.

While most neo-evangelicals are not embracing an explicitly feminist perspective, despite the efforts of evangelical feminism, it is important not to underestimate the impact of evangelical feminism on neo-evangelical communities. In many instances, neo-evangelicals have unconsciously adopted feminist principles while rejecting the label of feminist for themselves. As Margaret Bendroth acknowledges, "even the most antifeminist polemics in recent evangelical literature accept feminist norms of self-realization and personal autonomy. Modern evangelicals, it would seem, are not nearly as conservative as they, and others, would like to think they are" (1993, 120).

Internal Coalitions at the Expense of External Coalitions

While Christians for Biblical Equality seems more successful than was the Evangelical Women's Caucus in developing internal coalitions within mainstream evangelicalism, it has done so at the expense of building external coalitions with feminists and other social justice activists outside evangelicalism. This disavowal of coalition building with nonevangelical feminists can be traced to the CBE split with the EWCI over the resolution to support the civil rights of gays and lesbians. Interestingly, despite this split, most of the CBE members I interviewed supported gay civil rights. The issue at stake, they claimed, was that they could not afford to be in an organization that made a public statement about the issue. Said one member, "I personally believe homosexual relationships are contrary to biblical morality. Having said that, though, I think the church has not been a community of redemption. Further, I believe there should not be discrimination against homosexuals in terms of public policy. I would oppose the amendment in Colorado [which would not include gays and lesbians in antidiscrimination policies]." Another member recounts the split between the two groups.

Me: Can you talk about CBE's break with EWC? I understand it was over homosexuality?

CBE member: Not really. I would say it was over power plays. The thing of it was that all of us coexisted very nicely. We knew there were lesbians. What happened was that at the 1984 conference there were various resolutions. The board decided that the resolutions were very confrontational, and we decided to stop doing them. At the Fresno conference, people put up three resolutions and subvert[ed] this properly made decision. The first two everyone supported (the first was on people of color, which we all supported), but we wanted them to stop the resolution process, which the board had already decided to do. The second one was in favor of battered women, and the third was the one on homosexuality. With the third one, I said, "Look, if we pass this one, we are forcing the conservative women out. We are all here together, but when we give special recognition to one group, the poor timid woman who comes from a conservative church—that church will never let her come if they hear we have passed the resolution. Can't we just continue to be here together?" I tried to point out it was an exclusionary tactic. Women were crying, running from the room. There were people in the corridors crying. The vote was taken in an unfortunate way. Lots of people were brought in right before the vote, and no one was checking their credentials. The Boston chapter went to Denny's and cried until 2:00 a.m. the first night. Women would say, "I either have to leave EWC or leave my job; I can't do both." And it was clear that many women had just been forced out, and they had been discriminated against. If there wasn't room for them, there was not room for me."[71]

Me: So is there any space now for dialogue between evangelical lesbians and biblical feminists who don't support homosexuality?

CBE: I think dialogue is important. We need sister organizations. One that will appeal to the more conservative women, and another that will be more open. That was the original idea of EWC, but the heavy-fisted

[71] It is interesting how this individual reverses the charge of discrimination from one leveled by gays and lesbians against evangelicals to one she is leveling at gays and lesbians for being "anti-evangelical." This strategy is becoming increasingly popular in evangelical discourse, where evangelicals attempt to assume the mantle of an "oppressed minority." (A. Smith forthcoming)

women started maneuvering. One woman was the dean of ——, and she had to get out *real* fast to keep her job. It was not that they were a nasty bunch of women, but they had taken away a place for conservative women. With feminists, you have very strong-minded women, but sometimes we don't work well together.

Ironically, CBE, in order to maintain its evangelical credentials, maintains a more actively antigay and antilesbian stance than do other evangelical organizations, making it part of its statement of faith. Another avenue of discussion between straight and lesbian evangelical feminists was *Daughters of Sarah*, an evangelical feminist publication that featured debates and discussions on issues of feminism and lesbianism. It folded in 1996. In 1978, Scanzoni and Mollenkott's *Is the Homosexual My Neighbor?* came out, which provided an evangelical defense of homosexuality. Now we see virtually no debate at all on this issue.[72] The most significant thing that seems to have happened recently is the dialogue and collaboration between Mel White (the former ghostwriter for Pat Robertson and others) and Jerry Falwell in 1999. As this was another unlikely alliance, Falwell reports that he felt it was important to collaborate and dialogue with White (with whom he maintained his friendship even after White came out) against the growing violence in American society.

> I believe homosexuality is wrong. . . . But we never fought over it. . . . I believe the Bible teaches that. But with the violence of the last decade, particularly over the last two years—at Wedgewood Baptist and Columbine, where Christians were targeted, and the attacks against gays, like Billy Jack Gaither and Matthew Shephard—something has to change. Mel and I were

[72] This may change with the increased visibility of the National Gay Pentecostal Alliance, Soul Force, Potter's House Fellowship in Tampa, and the University Fellowship of Metropolitan Community Churches and other Gay Christian groups (Dean 2006; DeVore 2000; Grady 2004b; Letters 2000; Shepson 2001, 2002). Soul Force, an evangelical gay activist group formed by Mel White (a former ghostwriter for Jerry Falwell, Pat Robertson, and Billy Graham), organized a speaking tour of Christian colleges in 1996 to call on them to change their policies against homosexuality (Van Loon 2006). Gay alumni from Oral Roberts University in Tulsa, staged a "coming out" during the homecoming celebration in 2002. And *World* reported that Fuller Seminary, while maintaining an official position that homosexuality is sinful, is increasingly providing venues in which those who oppose this position can voice their views (J. Belz 2006b). However, unlike the topic of evangelical feminism, these groups receive only negative coverage in the evangelical periodical literature. For another example of the consistent affirmation of homosexuality as sinful among evangelical egalitarians, see Willow Creek's position both supporting gender equality and opposing homosexuality (Winner 2000a).

talking about the violence on both sides. We're never going to agree on the rightness or the wrongness of the gay lifestyle. But we certainly can agree on an antiviolence theme (Gilbreath 2000, 114).

This collaboration was sharply criticized by James Dobson, who insisted that no food be served at this dialogue because Christians are not supposed to break bread with unrepentant Christians (Religious News Service 1999). In general, this event was an exception rather than the rule.

This split between EWCI and CBE signaled a reconfiguration in evangelical feminist politics. Whereas the Evangelical Women's Caucus saw itself as being in coalition with secular and liberal Christian feminists over issues such as abortion rights, the Equal Rights Amendment, and so on, women involved with Christians for Biblical Equality began to define themselves in opposition to secular feminist politics, opposing abortion rights and homosexuality, organizing against the Beijing conference on women, and decrying the influence of "Goddess religion" (Groothius 2001; Spencer 1995; Stackhouse 1999b). For instance, some representatives of CBE have been involved in the previously mentioned Ecumenical Coalition on Women and Society. Says Janice Shaw Crause, the director of the coalition:

> We're not out there saying that feminism itself is inherently bad; that is not our position. But the religious radical feminists go so far as to say that there are five genders, or that gender is fluid, or that you really ought to experiment with all the various types of gender. The bottom line is, our churches are being destroyed by radical feminist ideology, which is a combination of heresy and paganism, and that is what we're trying to combat. . . . Both groups (CBMW and CBE) are within our parameters, and they war with each other. But we're all up against radical feminists who say that Jesus was not divine . . . so it's foolish to start arguing about the things that we disagree on. (Bauer 1999, 66–67)

Signaling her desire to distance biblical feminism from other nonevangelical feminists, Rebecca Merrill Groothius writes, "There is a prevalent fear among evangelicals that if we affirm any idea deemed 'feminist' we will be stepping out onto a slippery slope that will have us all sliding swiftly into paganism, witchcraft, goddess worship, abortion-rights and gay-rights agendas, and, of course, the destruction of civilization. In reality, however, anyone who affirms gender equality on the basis of *biblical* teaching must be as thoroughly opposed to such trappings of contemporary feminism as any antifeminist might be" (Groothius 1999).

The reaction of CBE to the split with EWCI seemed to be that in order to maintain legitimacy within evangelicalism, it had to police its own boundaries even more strictly than other evangelical groups do. Unlike Native women's feminist articulations, this evangelical feminist strategy seems more intent on avoiding guilt by association (in this case, association with secular or liberal Christian feminists, particularly lesbian feminists). By closing itself off from other coalition partners, this more conservative evangelical feminist movement became less of a potential space for political rearticulations into more progressive politics.[73] In doing so, however, CBE did position itself to exponentially expand its influence on mainstream evangelicalism. It should be mentioned, however, that Mary Stewart Van Leeuwen of CBE does challenge some of this "guilt by association" politics, arguing, "I call myself a feminist. I decided I would not give up a perfectly good word because some have misused it. Otherwise, I couldn't call myself a Christian either" (Frame 1999, 102).

While CBE has had a tremendous influence on evangelical communities, its influence its based precisely on its unwillingness to challenge the evangelical community on other issues. As Pamela Cochran notes, CBE assiduously adheres to all other social, political, and theological boundaries of Christian Right politics in order to advance its gender-egalitarian agenda (Cochran 2005, 185). Timothy George, the executive editor of *Christianity Today,* affirms this trend, calling on complementarians and egalitarians to stand together against "radical feminism" and arguing that, in the end, there is more that unites than divides complementarians and egalitarians (George 2005, 53). Consequently, he sees himself as unaligned with either side of the debate. In answering the question posed at the beginning of the chapter—whether or not evangelical feminism can provide strategic interventions to advance the work of race reconciliation and prison organizing beyond a heteronormative frame—the answer would appear to be no, at least in its current configuration. Whereas these other movements have provided opportunities for coalition building between evangelicals and nonevangelicals, the more conservative evangelical feminist movement has eschewed these coalitions, particularly those with secular feminists, in order to legitimize itself within the evangelical commu-

[73] When I talked to people involved in CBE, many really did see women's ordination and the issue of male headship as single issues detached from a broader social justice agenda. In fact, many members were supporters of the Christian Coalition, the Institute for Religion and Democracy, and other explicitly right-wing Christian organizations.

nity. The split between EWCI and CBE might be instructive in considering strategies for coalition building in the future. It would seem that prior to the passage of the gay civil rights resolution in Fresno, EWCI *did* provide a critical space for a rearticulation of gender politics that could influence other sectors of evangelical organizing because it brought together progressive, social-justice-minded, evangelical feminists with those who were more conservative and had more credibility with mainstream evangelicals. The EWCI provided a space for dialogue and conversation that had the potential to extend more progressively political ideas to a broader evangelical audience. After the resolution passed, however, the space for this conversation was gone. Ironically, the strategy of pushing this resolution forward may have had the unintended impact of making evangelical feminism more conservative. Perhaps the lesson to be learned in developing coalitions with unlikely allies is that the most important strategy might not be to convince potential allies to explicitly support the same political agenda but to provide spaces and venues for continuing conversations and relationships that can change political consciousness over time.

The lessons emerging from evangelical feminisms also point to the question of what organizing models we can develop for creating unlikely alliances that do not depend on heteronormativity. Chapter 5 explores such models as they are employed by Native women organizers.

4

Unlikely Allies

Rethinking Coalition Politics

This book has focused on Native and Christian Right organizing as sites to assess the possibilities and limitations of developing unlikely alliances and coalitions. However, as this work is an intellectual ethnography, it is also important to look at how Native women and Christian Right activists have themselves theorized about unlikely alliances. This chapter explores this theorization to explore the ethics and strategies of forming coalition politics across political divides. When Native women and Christian Right activists have engaged in unlikely alliances, what is their rationale for doing so? What ethics guide their alliance building? What do they perceive to be the political benefits and risks of engaging in such alliances? How do these alliances shift the way they see their own constituency as itself a politics of alliance? In addition, I explore how a discussion of coalitions with unlikely partners forces us to reconsider how we form coalitions with "likely" ones. That is, just as we must not presume that we cannot work with unlikely allies, we must not presume that we should always work with people who are perceived to be our likely allies.

Following this discussion, I put the Native and Christian Right organizing into conversation with others in order to develop a prolineal genealogy of reproductive justice coalition politics. I look at Native women's conceptualizations of reproductive justice as a possible basis of redefining alliance politics across "pro-life" and "pro-choice" divides. That is, if we follow a politics of reframing and rearticulation, how might the alliance politics shift on an issue that seems intractably divided?

Cowboys and Indians Coalitions

As was discussed in the introduction to this volume, Native peoples have had much success in carving what Madonna Thunder Hawk terms "cowboys and Indians" coalitions. There are other successful examples to report. Thunder Hawk notes that because South Dakota is a Republican state and Native peoples are a small percentage of the population Native peoples have had to create unlikely alliances to further their issues: "The main thing I see about the importance of coalitions is because, in Indian country, our lack of political and economic power. It's as simple as that. If you want to do something, you've got to have coalitions going. . . . But for local politics in the state of South Dakota, [it] is a staunch Republican, basically anti-Indian state. So how do we deal with that kind of stuff?"

Thunder Hawk notes that white farmers in South Dakota often face issues similar to those of Native peoples—protecting their lands from large corporations. So Native peoples can create alliances with them by arguing that treaty rights can protect their lands as well.

> You don't bring up treaty rights or anything else, except to the extent where a lot of times [white] people find out also that they exhausted all their avenues to the state government, the federal government, and they turn to treaties. They think this was ratified by Congress and this is our last resort. It's in their self-interest. They're about to lose either their water, their rights are going to get violated, or else they're going to eminent domain; boy, it really focuses down. Well, we just say, you people are the modern day Indians. They want your water, they take it. They want your land, they take it. Although they don't understand it, and some of them really don't want to know, and maybe they'll just be for that issue alone, but still you have them see this.

This approach, she notes, helped Native peoples ally themselves with at least some white, small landowners who opposed a planned resort owned by the actor Kevin Costner and his brother Dan. White landowners, Thunder Hawk observes,

> don't like development, and they don't like Indians; they don't like anybody. They're just self-centered, just I, me, my. But they found that they could be gone overnight. [What] Dunbar, Inc. [the Costner brothers' company], was trying to do was get these easements for this railroad. But not only that; they

were going to need a million gallons of water a day for the eighteen-hole golf course they're planning, so there's all kinds of water rights issues. And that's basically what it was, land and water rights. And they started finding out, that little landowners are unorganized. Twenty acres here, forty acres there, three acres here, they looked around them and who's going to support them? Who's organized? Is Deadwood Chamber of Commerce going to care? Hell no! They want Dunbar in there. So they were looking around, and all the sudden who was standing there with the documentation? The only firm foundation for land and water rights was the 1860 treaty with the Great Sioux Nation. They jumped in line right away [to support us]. Of course, not all of them, but a lot of them just sold out. They were just in it for the money; they didn't care that their ancestors came over on a wagon train or whatever. They just want the money. But there are some that are still land-based people, and those are the only ones you want to work with anyway.

Alex Ewen describes how creating unlikely alliances was central to the indigenous victory against Hydro Quebec's proposed dam in James Bay, which would have detrimentally impacted the environment of the Cree peoples living in the area. The activists found that within the New York company that was funding the project, Consolidated Edison, there was a small department tasked with developing energy-efficient projects. Instead of assuming this company was a monolith, the activists carved out an alliance with this small department, which, in turn, leaked information about the company to the activists (this was similar to the strategy NACE adopted with the workers of Kerr McGee described in the introduction). Con Edison eventually backed off from the project, saying that instead it was going to focus on policies of energy efficiency to address energy problems in the state of New York. According to Ewen:

> Who are our friends? . . . As things get worse and worse, there are more and more people on our side in a way because fewer and fewer people benefit from this process. So we should actually have better and more and more allies. . . . We got friends, and we should look to them wherever we can find them. We don't have to necessarily assume that they will only be found among people of color. We should not assume things. . . . To what extent do you really want to make friends with people you really don't like but maybe we'll make friends now and later on settle our differences later, after the victory? (Ewen 1996)

These examples, as well as those mentioned at the beginning of the book, demonstrate the extent to which Native peoples have been able to create unlikely alliances to further their struggles for justice. What seems to be a key element in the success of these coalitions is that the organizing issue is framed as one of universal concern rather than of concern just to Native peoples. The ability of Native groups to do this framing confirms Robin Kelley's argument that identity politics, rather than necessarily leading to a politics of isolation, "may just free us all" (Kelley 1997, 124). In addition, even if these coalition partners did not support Native rights at the outset, sometimes (though not always) their work with Native groups increased their support for Native rights. In progressive circles, often the common assumption behind coalition work is that groups need to develop strong relationships before they can work together. In these coalition efforts, the process is reversed—groups work together first, and in that process they perhaps develop strong relationships. To quote Judy Vaughn, the former director of the National Assembly of Religious Women, "You don't think your way into a different way of acting; you act your way into a different way of thinking." Sherry Wilson similarly notes, "That's where most coalitions grew from. You can work with them on the things you agree with and hope that in getting to know people better both sides can mellow out and agree on more and more. By that I mean, of course, that they should come to our viewpoint and not influence us very much (laughs). You take that for granted."

In addition, these groups allowed their unlikely coalition partners to participate in a manner that let the partners feel comfortable. Often a reluctance to expand one's set of coalition partners in progressive circles is the reluctance to be publicly associated with certain groups. However, as these examples attest, working in coalitions can take different forms. Some of these coalitions operate behind the scenes yet still yield favorable results. Pamela Alfonso discusses how Native coalition efforts in Chicago often require coalition partners to maintain a low profile in certain situations, such as when a partner needs to secure state funding while the coalition is challenging a state policy. Alfonso notes, "When we did the march on the mascot down at City Hall, the [executive director] of the [Indian agency], he was very clear: we're in dialogue with the state over this contract and trying to get arts money. I can't be on the front line with this. . . . We need to respect that. I'm just glad he said it. But he didn't stop us from doing it. In fact, he showed up, and his picture ended up on the first page of the paper! . . . So there's a lot of fear, but you also have to respect the autonomy."

While Native women's organizing receives little attention within social movement theory because their small numbers seem insignificant, it is precisely their small numbers that have forced them to develop creative coalitions that can be instructive to all social justice activists. The success of their coalition depends in part on their understanding of the strategic role indigenous peoples play, in global social justice movements regardless of their numbers. While mainstream progressives may feel they have the luxury to organize in isolation or in simple opposition to conservatives, Native peoples know they do not have this option. Yet, at the same time that they are carving these unlikely alliances, they have the challenge of maintaining alliances within their own communities, as well as negotiating effectively even within progressive coalitions. Before assessing the politics of these coalitions, I wish to explore Pamela Alfonso's analysis of how Native women's organizing highlights the fact that Native identity is itself a form of coalition politics.

Native Identity as an Unlikely Alliance

As discussed in chapter 3, Native women's organizing around sexism within Native communities highlights the coalition politics inherent within Native identity itself. Thus, a corollary to the assumption that it is not possible to carve out coalitions with unlikely partners is that it is simple to carve out alliances with those who are like "us." This work demonstrates that a stable Native identity cannot be assumed—that Native peoples must seek coalitions across various divides, including gender divides, to achieve political coherence, and that these coalitions can be as difficult to create as the ones we form with unlikely allies.

As Alfonso notes, this internal coalition politics within Native communities requires the building of alliances across tribal lines, geography, issue-orientations, and so on. While many divisions exist under the rubric of "Native organizing," one of the most difficult barriers to overcome seems to be the divisions between reservation and urban-based Native communities and activists. Renya Ramirez's pathbreaking work on urban Indian communities calls into question the way the urban-reservation dichotomy has been conceptualized in the scholarship about Native communities. She contends that urban and reservation Indians tend to be conceptualized as completely distinct, with reservation Indians depicted as the "real" Natives and urban Indians depicted as hopelessly assimilated and alienated from their cultures. She argues, by contrast, that Indian people frequently travel between reservations and urban areas and hence these communities are not completely distinct. Urban areas, she argues, often function as hubs through which communications between different reservation communities are facilitated. Unfortunately, Native peoples are imaged as people who cannot travel, and so their journeys to urban areas are always understood as one-way trips toward cultural alienation (Ramirez 2007).

Ramirez's work is important in breaking down static conceptions of urban versus reservation Indian communities. In fact, most of my interviewees lead the lives of traveling back and forth between reservations and urban Indian communities that she describes. At the same time, however, it is important to note that almost everyone I interviewed, no matter how much they traveled, had clear conceptions of their identities as urban or reservation Indians. The divisions between urban and reservation activism and community life were very clear in their minds, and these divisions were not easily surmountable.

Some activists, particularly those who are reservation based, describe urban Indians as more culturally "assimilated" while reservation communities are more spiritually intact. Because of the perception that reservation communities are more culturally and spiritually intact, reservation-based activists complain that urban Indians approach reservation communities in a romanticized fashion.

> Harden: People come to the reservation from wherever with romanticism and stars in their eyes. A good example is this guy who I knew in California. Tall, good looking, urban Indian. And he started Sun Dancing in South Dakota, and I started seeing him because I come back every year and Sun Dance. And finally I came back one year, and I said, "You're sold on this place." And he said, "I live here, right in Pine Ridge." And he was so proud, and he was so, "I ain't never going back." Just totally dug in. Now, it's like three years later, and I talked to the woman he was dug in with. She started telling me the whole story, and it was the romanticized "I'm going to live on the rez, and I'm going to have me a full-blooded-rez, she-can-make-fry-bread woman." Then he started to see all the warts, and the history of living on your land base and not moving, and what that meant. And the kind of abuse and violence you have to live with generation after generation here. And, now he's gone, and he's not EVER coming back. So the fantasy wore off, and that's a lot of the problem. People see us, and they see Indians who look like Red Cloud and Sitting Bull, and who have names like Red Cloud and Sitting Bull, and speak the language. This fantasy comes into their head. And I've heard people say, "I would give anything to live on the reservation." And I just want to punch

them square in the face, "You have no clue of what you're talking about!" There is so much more to living on the reservation that you just don't understand.

Ross: What I first noticed when I left the reservation was that urban Indians almost have a comical sense of their tradition. It was too sad. It was too tragic for me to be around. It made me feel bad for them. And so that didn't feel good. Like their drum groups were really bad and nobody could dance. It was all pan-Indian. And so it seemed like an eclectic, sad attempt at trying to be Indian. Gee, that just sounds awful! Okay, now reservation Indians can play that same game, but you really can't in a small community. They play other games. So there's always some weird game going on. But the urban experience, that has been the turnoff. Now what has bothered me about reservation activism is it's a handful of men, half of them assholes, the other half bastards. And we're supposed to follow them? So that's been a real turnoff to me.

Meanwhile, some urban-based activists critique what they see as romanticism about the cultural integrity of reservation communities and argue that often urban Indians pay more attention to issues of cultural preservation than do reservation Indians. According to Alfonso:

I had to go up there [to Menominee] to meet with the head of the enterprise that runs the lumber mill, and I wanted him to come to Chicago and do a presentation. I kept sending him messages, and he kept going, who the hell is this Pam Alfonso? So anyway, I said I'll go up and meet him. I understand he doesn't know who I am. When I went up there, he spent a half an hour just laying into me. He said, "I hate city Indians. They come back here, and they think blah, blah, blah. And I hate the city; you have no culture, blah, blah blah." [So I said] "I just traveled five hours to get here because I understood you needed to meet me face to face. But are you done?" So I moved my chair closer, and I said, "I want to tell you something. I'm a foster child. I grew up in Milwaukee and Chicago, it's true. But if you're going to talk about some romantic notion of the Menominee tribe and how culturally sound they are, how traditional they are, then why the hell did you lose me and thousands of other kids? My mom had nowhere to turn. I'm in Chicago because I had no choice. But don't you double victimize me when I come home. Because whether you like it or not, I'm an enrolled Menominee member. So you can either reach your hand out and educate me, and I'll reach back, or you can suffer with my ignorance because no one invited me here. You know what the other thing is, I've been up here for three funerals, and you know who did it traditionally? The Menominees from Chicago came up here and kept the sacred fire going. The Menominees living here didn't even know what to do. Or they didn't care. They were in the corner of the parking lot drinking. So don't you talk to me about some fantasy. I'm a good mother; I'm a good sister; I'm a good leader in the community. You know in Chicago we're spread out all over the place, but we still find each other and we care about each other and watch our backs. You guys are within three minutes of each other, and you're not meeting on a regular basis. So don't you talk to me about that. So are we going to find a way to relate because, whether you like it or not, we're related. Or are we done?" He laughed. He said, "Okay, I'll work with you. I'll be down there." Now he's like my best buddy.

While these differences in cultural and spiritual expression can create much tension between urban- and reservation-based activists, Sammy Toineeta describes how these differences manifested themselves in the birth of the American Indian Movement in a manner that was beneficial to both urban- and reservation-based communities. She describes how, while her tribe has always maintained its spiritual and cultural traditions on her reservation in Rosebud, South Dakota, it was a "breath of fresh air" when urban Indians from AIM arrived publicly displaying their Indian identity. She says that her reservation community was able to provide an opportunity for urban activists to learn traditional spiritual and cultural traditions. Meanwhile, the urban activists' public display of their indigenous identity reinstilled pride among reservation members about their identities as Native peoples.[1]

Another source of tension that relates to differences in cultural/spiritual expression is the complaint by some activists that urban Indians are overly pan-Indian in their cultural and spiritual practice. Ross asserts:

Well, I think pan-Indian politics are great. But I think it's the pan-Indian culture, and I don't know the Penobscot guy with the Lakota regalia, or it would be a costume in that case, on at the powwow, that bothers me, because it's that kind of appropriation that white people do that bug us. So why shouldn't it bug us when Indians do it? And then using that costume to play the big Indian. Then that really bothers me. If it's a sincere attempt, and I have seen those, and people adopted into other cultures, then that's different. But it's the appropriation thing that really bothers as it's used to benefit themselves.

[1] See also Robert Warrior's and Paul Chaat Smith's account of the American Indian Movement in Warrior and Smith 1996.

And according to Kimberly TallBear:

> Espousing a global Indigenous identity says much less about tradition, than about the common politics of colonialism. If we try to link environmental, spiritual, and other traditions of Indigenous Peoples globally (rather than discussing such connections at the level of parallel colonial experiences), there are opportunities for the neglect and erosion of tribal cultures and the loss of tribal histories. Cultural practices are in particular danger if viewed as contradictory to the emerging definition of a morally superior Indigenous environmental consciousness that is at the core of the global Indigenous identity. In organizing internationally we must be careful not to violate our political and cultural integrity as peoples with distinct beliefs, histories, and cultural practices. If we racialise ourselves in to one monolithic Indigenous race, we diminish understanding of the diversity among us and we present risks (in addition to those the coloniser thrusts upon us) to the specific knowledge and histories that we carry. We may also undermine the cause of tribal-specific political rights. (TallBear 2001, 170)

Wilson suggests, by contrast, that the pan-Indian orientation that marks many urban Indian communities can have the positive effect of leading to greater political solidarity with other tribal communities, as well as other oppressed communities.

> The issues [in urban communities] were often not tribal specific. It was like, Indians are being oppressed by the police. . . . Well, that's a big thing. I think there's a lot more opportunity for coalition work when you live in the city. People didn't seem to dwell on the difference in tribes or that kind of thing. And it didn't matter to the police what tribe you were, so the resistance to that was not so much based on a tribal thing. I think people on reservations tend to be kind of isolated and don't have as much access to interaction on a daily basis with others, with other people of color, for instance. It always shocks me the racism Indians have against other people of color.
>
> And I remember doing the [gaming] compact thing too. It [was] just sort of weird because they came and said the other tribes had gotten together on this or one tribe was suggesting that we all have a memorandum of understanding to negotiate the compacts together as a group. Well, our legislature, no, we don't want to do that—we're Ho-Chunks. How weird! How very weird! Then their reason was, well, because they thought the Ojibwes were trying to move [in] on some of our market. We'll get a compact and then worry about this, you know! I thought that was really short-sighted. And so what happened was, of course, we negotiated ours on our own, and now

we're paying a whole lot more to the state than the other tribes are. And this was because we were so damned smart! I just thought this was very weird. I'm not used to rez life really; I still have culture shock, apparently.

Another critical issue that marks urban- versus reservation-based activism is the lack of resources on reservations, which makes it difficult for reservation people to work on issues that do not seem directly tied to their basic survival. Because tribal lands are disproportionately targeted for resource extraction or toxic waste dumping, activists note that reservation communities do mobilize around environmental issues. But because of the different living conditions urban- and reservation-based Indians face, different strategies are required to organize them. As Thunder Hawk describes it:

It's very elementary community organizing that has to go on because of the mind-set of our people and because it's survival. That's how everybody thinks from that point of view. If we were to going to try to stop a Columbus Day parade here, it wouldn't happen. Everybody would say, "What?" First of all, where we would have it and how would we get there? There's a lot of driving back and forth to work, but it's people that work in Eagle Butte, and they have nothing else on their agenda. So people are hiring people to take them to town. If you're in that category, then you're not going to be involved in nothing because you can't get there. So I think it's real important for urban Indians to keep one foot at home on the rez. Even if they were born off that and raised out there, that's their connection, and they need to keep one foot.

Even today, I have to tell the average person, I say, "Okay, here's what you do [to organize in reservation communities]. This is what I do. I call up my council." "Oh, they won't do anything." Well, you know what? A lot of times they don't do anything because they don't have a clue what's going on. They don't automatically know this stuff. You have to tell them. So call them up and tell them. Tell them here's what I need, this is what I need for you to do. And they'll do it. Or at least try. And if they ignore you, then call me. That's what I do. I'm not all that powerful, but they know I'm not afraid to speak up. But I nail them in the council chambers where there's twenty other people standing and listening. Then I say, "So and so said she called you and you didn't call back. What happened? You know she's got——." Everyone looks, gee, what kind of rep are you? So it's real basic organizing that goes on. But at the same time, let people know, a handful of people know—key people—and it could happen. It could happen at one meeting because if you get credibility, and I worked on mine, and people trust you, they'll go for it.

So it's not so much a situation of convincing people that they need to do it; it's to let them know what's going on. And they'll say, "Let's go for it!"

Activists, both urban and reservation based, generally comment that urban Indians often have greater access to resources and skills that can be of tremendous benefit to reservation communities. However, Wilson and Yvonne Dennis contend that urban Indians often go back to their reservations to organize their communities and are not always tuned into the specific dynamics that affect reservation life. Consequently, the communities they hope to organize perceive these would-be organizers as patronizing and often treat them with suspicion and distrust. Alfonso similarly describes how her attempts to work with reservation members on her tribe's gaming commission were viewed with distrust before she was able to build solid working relationships with them. When she first began working on this commission, they wouldn't reimburse her for her expenses even though she, unlike the other members, had to drive for five hours to attend the meetings. However, she did not complain, and eventually the other participants recognized the contribution she was making to the commission and began reimbursing her for her expenses.

Another common source of tension is disagreements about the allocation of tribal resources. Related to this tension is the fact that many tribes have a high percentage of members in urban areas, enough to affect the outcome of tribal elections and so determine how resources are allocated. Alfonso notes,

> Our tribe has 8,000 members. Only 2,300 live on the reservation. And those 2,300 get to use the free clinic, get to use the youth centers. And so our 25-million-dollar budget is mostly used by 2,300 people when the rest of us don't get that. For instance, we had a settlement in a lawsuit against the BIA [Bureau of Indian Affairs]. Twenty-five years it took us to get that, and when we were going to get it, it was going to be a huge amount of money. They had testimonies all over—what should we do with the money? Put it in an endowment? Give it in a per cap? Put it in the program budget? What should we do? Well, you can imagine, the urbans were like, "If you put it in the health clinic, it don't do shit for me. I want a per cap. I'm going to buy a house; I'm going to pay off my bills. You put it in the program budgets for the tribe, add on to the college all you want, but I don't go all the way up there to go to college. You're not teaching my third grader the language, so if you put it in a language program, it ain't going to help me." So there are tensions like that.

The interviewees seem to universally regard developing coalitions between reservation- and urban-based Native communities as one of the most difficult tasks they face, yet such coalitions are critically needed to support the sovereignty of Native nations. While they do not see many successful coalitions, a number were able to point to some successes that might suggest ways to develop more in the future. Loretta Rivera and Julie Star suggested that organizing around issues of concern to Native youth and children is a promising area to explore.

> Rivera: I do see [coalitions] working when it comes to working with you. Reservation-based adults may think they know better than urban Indians. But when you get the youth together, the youth think the opposite. They think the city kids are more with it, have more confidence, know more of the world than they do. In a weird way, it sort of balances itself out when they come together.

> Star: [One area where urban-reservation coalitions work] is under Indian Child Welfare. You have a significant number of people, Indian people going to urban areas, and that's a lot of time where the kids get lost. You have the tribal court system trying to follow those children and work within the state and the city court system to make sure those children stay within tribal communities and tribal families. That's one of the few places that I think you see a genuine sense of common purpose. If you lose the child, whether they're on the reservation or [in] the urban areas, it doesn't matter, you've lost the child.

Alfonso describes how she was able to build a successful coalition between the urban-based Menominees of Chicago and the Menominee tribe in Wisconsin. The key to this success was the Menominee Community Center of Chicago, which was organized independently and developed alliances without initially asking for resources from the tribe.

> It became a question personally for me because I was doing all this stuff for the Indian community. I guess I was challenged a couple of times of how Indian I am because I do have an education, and I am an urban Indian, and I do like to wear little dresses and skirts. I was like, you've got a point. To be the kind of leader I would like to be, to be the human being I would like to be, I do have to pay attention to tradition. And so I'm not going to go out like you would go to the church and learn the language, but I'm going to pay attention, and spend time with elders and people who are culturally knowledgeable and just kind of hang out.

So I got together with other Menominees in Chicago, and a number of us said, "Why do we only gather for funerals?" We'd always be there at funerals, mostly. There was a Menominee woman who passed away. All of a sudden there's a roomful of hundreds of Menominees. Why do we always do that? I'd like to know more. You knew my dad; I never knew my dad. I'd like to know more about my dad. Who are your kids? I didn't know those two kids were yours. So we formed this Menominee social club. And our only goal was kinship and support. No tribal recognition, no nothing. That happened about three years. We had little fund-raisers to raise bereavement funds if someone needed food for a gathering. We met, and we did some things socially, chatted, mostly gossiped, and talked about our families and our kids got to know each other.

And then we said, "Let's invite the [Menominee tribal] legislators down and tell them—they're sending us campaign literature—they should come down and meet us if they want our vote because we do vote [in Menominee tribal elections]." They looked at the numbers and said, "460 Menominees in Illinois, 280 voting members. If people are getting elected on 300 votes, I'm going to Chicago and talk to these people." They came down, and we had 60 to 125 people in the Indian Center hall. Dinner, microphones, "Like you guys are really organized. You should apply for community status." They were just redoing the organization chart for the tribe, and they have all these little community areas off the reservation, and the legislators wanted our votes for tribal chairman, and he added Chicago. So now we're on the organization chart. You pull it out, and it says all these things, and Chicago.

Next thing you know, there is the relationship building. Now, all of a sudden, you [anyone from the Menominee tribe in Wisconsin] want anything in Chicago—you're coming down because you're going to a conference and you want to talk about a housing program that's for off-reservation, they know who to call and contact.

In turn, Harden describes how she was able to build alliances with urban-based activists.

When I first got there at Berkeley, I was like God, these people aren't Indian. I was really bummed out.

But then . . . I went to a play with a friend of mine from the women of color conference that was in the Bay Area at the same time I was, and she got me a ticket, and we went to see the Dance Brigade, and they were a women's dance group, and they were multicultural. It was a magical play, the *Revolutionary Nutcracker Sweety*. There was a scene in the underwater world where they talked about a beautiful race, and the men came to hunt them and steal their colors. Then they all started hiding colors. They looked like jellyfish with these beautiful streamers of color, and they would spin around, kind of like a cervical cap on up. And the ones who were hunted and the colors were stolen, they were just plain. They were mistrustful of each other. But she goes, every now and then, they would find each other, and they would leave together, sharing each other's colors. Then later on in the song, when there's other things going on, the same two come back on and they both have colors.

It was such a beautiful story, and it made me realize that we were all affected by the genocide. It was like a bomb exploded, and we were all shot shrapnel. Some fell over here with the language, the land, and the ceremonies, but no education, no clean water, no good food. And then some flew over here with the best education, the best this, the best that, but no language, no land base. And that's what I realized then and became very generous with teaching and sharing what I knew and encouraging people and saying "welcome home" to people I thought before, I'd say they're not Indians. I would say, "Welcome home, I'm glad you found us. I'm glad you made it back." I would counsel people on it and say, "Your ancestors, your great-grandmother, and my great-grandmother are standing together right now and saying they found each other."

Similarly, Mona Recountre, while arguing that urban Indians are more assimilated, says that they still have a place back "home."

The urban [Indian] is more assimilated, which is good, because they always go home. It's a connectedness which you [urban Indians] have with your people, with our land, where our ancestors were, that we always go home. I always used to hear my aunties say, "I'm never going back to the reservation" because of all the hurts they experienced. "I'm never going back to that reservation." And then, when they turn about forty, they come back. They fight to get their own home, and they do everything to get a house on the reservation. And then I always say, "I thought you said you were never coming back here. What made you come back?" And they say, "I don't know; I don't even want to be here and here I am."

The analysis emerging from Native women's organizing that highlights Native identity as politics resonates with poststructuralist discourse that fragments notions of self, identity, and community, problematizing the uncritical manner in which Native peoples may represent both themselves and their communities in a singular and static fashion. Poststructuralism's contribution is useful because a failure to analyze the complexities of oppressed communities—both the ways in which they resist and at the same time are complicit in structures of oppression—limits our ability to organize effectively. We cannot mobilize communities if we are oblivious to their complexities. This analysis also troubles the notion that working with "likely" allies is necessarily less difficult than working with unlikely ones.

Some, of course, view poststructuralism not as an opportunity but as a threat. Nancy Hartsock asks why it is that just as communities of color have begun to claim themselves as subjects of intellectual discourse, poststructuralist thought has called into question the value of subjectivity (1990, 163–64). In addition, many poststructuralist theorists have adopted a kind of vulgar constructionism, essentially arguing that because axes of identity (race, class, etc.) are socially constructed they do not "really" exist (Clough 1994; Gilroy 2001; Vizenor 1994). However, as Kimberle Crenshaw states, "To say that a category such as race or gender is socially constructed is not to say that category has no significance in our world" (1996, 375). She and Anne McClintock note that social constructionism is helpful in showing how naturalized categories exclude and exercise power against excluded groups. Yet these categories are still performative and help shape those who are defined by them (McClintock 1995, 8). In other words, as long as many members of society define an individual as "Indian," this category will shape his or her subjectivity, even if the person is not comfortable with that identity. To borrow from Linda Nicholson's analysis of gender, the fact that the term *Native* lacks a single meaning does not mean that it has no meaning at all (1995, 16).

Unfortunately, this vulgar constructionist argument is often used to contend that non-Native people can engage in Native scholarship just as well as Native people can, and thus there is no particular reason to privilege Native voices. Native peoples struggling to give voice to the concerns of their communities are now essentially told by members of relatively more privileged communities, "You do not need to speak out any more; we are just as qualified as you to speak about your realities." However, one's position within the social fabric *does* affect one's insights into social oppression; from a practical standpoint, it is clear that those who live with the dynamics of oppression are likely to know more about it than those who do not. That this "epistemic privilege" comes from social position rather than biology does not make it less real (Warrior 2005). Crenshaw notes that "a strong case can be made that the most critical resistance strategy for disempowered groups is to occupy and defend a politics of social location rather than to vacate it and destroy it" (1996, 375). What the work of Native women's organizing suggests, then, is not that identity politics has no value but that it is possible to organize around a nonessentialist form of identity politics. This discussion is further developed in chapter 5.

Why Coalitions with Native Women Matter

Related to the question of building coalitions is another: we know that building coalitions with particular groups is possible, but is it important? Because Native peoples represent less than 1 percent of the U.S. population, most scholars fail to see Native activism's broader significance. Resource mobilization theory, for instance, which concerns itself with social movements' impact on electoral politics, is unlikely to concern itself with a constituency that does not constitute a significant voting bloc. Because of its narrow understanding of politics, resource mobilization theory underestimates the political impact of Native activism (McAdam 1995; Zald 1987).[2]

In addition, Native activism is generally subsumed under the larger category of "identity politics" (McAdam 1995; Wiley 1994). Some sectors of the Left blame people of color, and, by extension, Native communities, for fracturing the Left through identity politics. People of color are viewed as hopelessly mired in identity struggles with little ability to critique and organize against oppressive economic and political structures. James O'Connor typifies this position in his critique of the environmental justice movement, which he claims privileges "culture" over class and consequently "suppresses the class politics of ecological socialism . . . in favor of a cultural nationalism or separatism of some kind. By so doing, the 'petty bourgeois' element within multiculturalism tends to surface" (1998, 286). Todd Gitlin similarly complains that racial identity politics is detrimental to "real" movements for social change because it supposedly splinters oppositional forces. In addition, the argument often goes, identity politics ignores capitalist domination and is concerned primarily with issues of cultural representation. As Gitlin states, "For many reasons, then, the proliferation of identity politics leads to a turning inward, a grim and hermetic bravado which takes the ideological form of paranoid, jargon-clotted, postmodernist groupthink, cult celebrations of victimization, and stylized marginality" (Gitlin 1994, 156; see also Boggs 2000, 185). National identity impedes rather than promotes exchange within the public

---

[2] For an examination of Native political activism from the perspective of resource mobilization theory, see Cornell 1988.

sphere(s), and consequently movements based on identity are unable to mobilize around "universalist" concerns (Bauman 1999; Boggs 2000, 185; Calhoun 1994a; Epstein 1995; Larana, Johnston, and Gusfield 1994; Scheff 1994; Turner 1995; Wiley 1994). These writers lament that with the rise of identity politics "there has been no universal ideology . . . that could rise above the local often spontaneous and dispersed modes of thought and action" (Boggs 2000, 207). It is problematic to assume that identity-based groups or "nations" are incapable of speaking to the "universal" through their particularity. In fact, no one is capable of articulating the universal outside the particularity of a social context. In the "modernist" framework, however, the white middle class becomes the site of universality, while other groups are viewed as ensconced in particularity. The fact that the liberal democratic public sphere is not seen as an expression of identity politics—that is, a politics based on a white, property-owning, male identity—is evidence of this point. As Robin Kelley notes, "A careful examination of the movements dismissed as particularistic shows that they are often 'radical Humanist' at their core and potentially emancipatory for all of us. We need to seriously re-think some of these movements, shifting our perspective from the margins to the center. We must look beyond wedge issues or 'minority issues' and begin to pay attention to what these movements are advocating, imagining, building. After all, the analysis, theories and visions . . . may just free us all" (1997, 124).[3]

A related problem is that even theorists who take identity seriously tend to separate issues of identity from issues of political economy. New social movement theory in particular, because it sees Native activism only in terms of cultural preservation, often trivializes Native movements. However, the so-called particularities that define these "identity movements" generally have universalist implications, as is certainly the case with Native peoples' land-based identity claims. The majority of energy resources in this country are located on or near Indian land (Churchill and LaDuke 1992; LaDuke 1993). Fighting to protect Native cultural identity necessarily involves fighting for control over land bases and energy resources that the U.S. government and corporate interests want (Eichstaedt 1994; Grinde and Johansen 1995; LaDuke 1999; Weaver 1996b). These struggles interfere with multinational capitalism's ability to conduct business as

[3] Shane Phelan argues, "Identity politics is not fragmenting or divisive; it is the failure to acknowledge and respond to the inequalities and injustices that mark some identities that is divisive" (1995, 343).

usual (J. Smith 1996). This connection was made clear in Scott Matheson's Senate testimony on behalf of mining interests in opposition to proposed legislation to protect Native sacred sites: "Much of the country's natural resources are located on federal land. For example, federal lands contain 85% of the nation's crude oil, 40% of the natural gas, 40% of the uranium, 85% of the coal reserves (60% in the West), and 70% of the standing soft wood timber. . . . It is obvious that [the Native American Free Exercise of Religion Act] by creating a Native American veto over federal land use decisions, will . . . severely interfere with the orderly use and development of the country's natural resources."[4]

This relationship between identity and political economy calls into question the assumption of new social movement theorists that new social movements "ignore the political system and generally display disinterest towards the idea of seizing power" (Melucci 1996, 102). What Mindy Spatt notes in the case of lesbian organizing can be applied to Native organizing: lesbians have unacknowledged roles in other struggles. Their so-called identity-based politics is based on more than affirmation of identity; it is tied to larger struggles of political and economic justice (1995).

An example in Native communities is that of the California Basket-weavers, who continue the basketry tradition because each basket "has its own spirit or soul. The materials are taken from the earth and trans-formed into another life. Because of its soul, a basket must never be put in a dark or out of the way place. They must be free to dance around the world each night, and to grow old. . . . Similarly, Brush Dances, and other ceremonies held during the year, involve these baskets and [are] an inte-gral part of the tradition; and as increasing numbers of Native people return to and strengthen these traditions, the baskets too have increased in number" (Bill n.d., 43).

This activism might be dismissed by non-Native progressives as simply "cultural" with no implications for challenging capitalism. However, in order to gather materials for these baskets, the basket weavers have come into direct conflict with corporations such as the Simpson Timber Com-pany, which sprays herbicides on the lands from which they gather the materials to make the baskets. Native peoples similarly cannot preserve

[4] Religious Freedom Act Amendments, Hearings on S. 1124 before the Senate Select Committee on Indian Affairs, 101st Cong., 1st sess. 136 (1989), prepared statement of Scott M. Matheson for the American Mining Congress, Timber Asso-ciations of California, Rocky Mountain Oil and Gas Association, Western States Public Lands Coalition, et al.

their culture without calling for a fundamental restructuring of the global economy.

The critique of O'Connor and others that Native activism is centered around "cultural separatism" with no analysis of the global economy simply cannot be justified in light of the sheer number of writings by Native activists that situate their work within the context of globalization.[5]

Mililani Trask directly challenges the stereotype white progressives often have about Native activism as simply about "culture" without analysis about the economy.

We cannot stand by the stream and say our chants and beat the drum and pray that the river people will survive. . . . Natural resource management is a tool, a skill, and a weapon that the women warriors of today need to attire themselves with if they are going to be prepared for battle. Prayers are the foundation, but the scientific knowledge, the legal capacity, the ability to

[5] See Renee Senogles, who writes, "The glue that holds the whole system of oppression together is the multi-national corporations' stranglehold on the economy of the Western Hemisphere" (n.d., 29). Carrie Dann, a prominent Shoshone activist, proclaimed that she was a "communist" at the 2005 U.S. Human Rights Network conference held in Atlanta (November 12, 2005). She argued that Native societies prior to capitalism were communist in that Native peoples shared what they had, held everything in common, and did not honor private ownership of land. See also the statement of the Mining and Indigenous Peoples Consultation: "We therefore condemn in the strongest terms the transnational mining companies, armed with international and national organizations, and multi-lateral agreements, with the complicity of the states and their national laws, their denial of our existence, their land-grabbing, their continued destruction of our land and territories and our air and our environment, their exploitation of our resources, and the continuing decimation of our peoples" (1998, 46). Ingrid Washinawatok writes, "As long as profit is the main motivator, justice is not going to be served. So the strategy has to be [developed] around that" (1999a, 15). The Indigenous Women's Network, the Indigenous Environmental Network, and Seventh Generation Fund were part of the World Trade Organization protests in Seattle because "the majority of the world's valuable resources exist on Indigenous lands. . . . Economic globalization policies endanger Indigenous cultures, communities and traditional subsistence lifestyles by clear-cutting forest, destroying fisheries, displacing population and undermining Indigenous Peoples power over their land and natural resources" (Settee n.d., 45).

See also Asetoyer 1996; Beaucage 1998; Beijing Declaration on Indigenous Women n.d.; Bell-Jones 2001; Cook n.d.; Davids n.d.; Echohawk 1999; Gomez n.d.-a; Harawira 1998; Highway n.d.; Indigenous People's Statement from Seattle 2001; Indigenous Women's Network 1995, n.d.; LaDuke 1996a, 1998, n.d.; Martinez n.d.; Mining and Indigenous Peoples Consultation 1998; Settee 1998, 1999, n.d.; Sullivan 1998; Tailman Chavez n.d.; Taliman n.d.; Tbishkokeshigook 1998; "The Case of the U'Wa vs. Oxy" 1999; Venne 1998; White n.d.; and Yazzie n.d.

plan, develop programs, and the understanding of strategic planning are the weapons we need to acquire. We can not go out and fight America with a spear and a prayer, we need to do more. (n.d., 26)

In contrast to this critique that Native peoples do not concern themselves with capitalism, all the Native women activists I interviewed for this project agreed that the struggle for indigenous sovereignty must be an anti-capitalist struggle—that capitalism inherently contradicted their political vision of sovereignty. And many argued that the bottom line in analyzing the oppression of Native peoples is economics. States Sammy Toineeta, "Racism, I think, is an economic problem. It started economically, and it continues. . . . All the isms are economically driven, but racism more so."[6]

Where Native peoples are placed within the current global political economy has significant ramifications not only for Native peoples but for all peoples interested in social justice. Native women's analyses of the importance of indigenous struggles demonstrate why coalitions with Native people really do matter and that it is possible to develop a nonessentialist identity politics based on a materialist framework. This analysis also intervenes in recent works that try to identify one class of people, usually white, working-class people, as the most important one to organize (Frank 2005; Gitlin 1994). In addition, it calls on us to consider the strategic importance of the way groups that are typically marginalized within social movements, such as peoples with disabilities, interact with social justice struggles beyond a politics of inclusion.

The Difficulties of Coalition Building

Despite the remarkably successful coalitions that Native activist groups have been able to build, it is important not to romanticize these efforts. Native women activists still face tremendous challenges in building coalitions between Native and non-Native organizations. Often, they contend, Native communities do not value coalitions. Others point to the difficulties created when organizations attempt to combine activism with social service delivery. This trend speaks to the larger impact of the non-

[6] Despite the problematic critique that Native activism does not concern itself with class or the economy, it should be noted that a common critique made by Native women activists themselves is that, while they recognize the evils of capitalism, they have not necessarily developed a sophisticated understanding of the economy sufficient to fully articulate an alternative economic vision.

profit system on social movements as a whole, which allows organizations to fund themselves through foundation support without having to build a base of community support for their work. A systemic critique of the nonprofit system is beyond the scope of this project, but it is addressed in the anthology, *The Revolution Will Not Be Funded: Beyond the Non-profit Industrial Complex* (INCITE! 2007). According to Alfonso:

> There's a lot of Indian organizations operating as fiefdoms with no accountability, and social services are administered but their organizations are not based on participation. . . . All they do, and the accountability factor they have, is to provide services. Their accountability basically is to pay them. Where's the accountability to the community? . . . If you could go through every one of the Indian organizations and analyze where they are at and what's their motivation and self-interest, and try to find what their accountability to the community is, I would tell you that it is seriously lacking. The only way that Indian people deal with that is [by] not coming. We shun them. We don't attack them. We don't take them down. That's a very white thing. White people might go after them, but we don't. We just go, "Yeech, they're like that." And it takes a long time for them to die because as long as the funder is happy they're providing a service, they stay alive. . . .
>
> I think they [social service providers] shouldn't be at the forefront representing our issues. Governor's office—Do not call [the Indian social service provider] and ask them to represent the political interests of the Indian community. What are they going to worry about? The contract they got on the table. Are they going to worry about that you haven't hired anyone in your policy team to represent Indian issues? They're not going to fight you for that. Are they willing to take a rock and throw it in the window if they don't get what they want? No, because they have a contract on the table. So I think that if you look at the parameters of service coming out of the Indian community . . . you'll see a lot of social service—a lot of service in general. No politics. Politics is an afterthought, and it's a scary one.

An issue that strikes Native communities particularly hard is their lack of numbers. This problem often contributes to Native activists creating powerful coalitions, often with groups other progressives would never choose. At the same time, Native activists find themselves overextended, often being asked to join innumerable coalitions.[7] In addition, because

---

[7] For example, I was once asked to give a presentation on indigenous perspectives on brain surgery since I was apparently the only Native person the organizers could find.

Native activists tend to join coalitions in smaller numbers than other communities, they are often not able to wield the same political power as others in these coalitions. Many activists complain that the racial prejudices about other communities of color have been so internalized in Native communities that it is difficult to work in coalition with others.

> Sheehy: One of the things I think, somewhere along the line, we as communities of color have been segregated. . . . We see ourselves very different from other communities of color rather than seeing our sameness. We will align with mainstream, with white people before we will align ourselves with black groups or Asian groups. It has nothing to do with the fact that we understand—we have so much in common in treatment and thought process and issues. . . . But most of us would not align ourselves because we've been taught to mistrust other communities of color. And for us we have to unlearn that. We're more like them than we are like white people. I used to say, look at all of these tribes [and who holds powerful positions within each tribe]. In there, you're going to find some white person that's in a very powerful position. Why? Why today are they in that position? Somewhere that we might not want to deal with maybe in our unconscious, we have to remember we've been taught white is right.

> Thomas: And in the Big Mountain thing here in Chicago, well now, we wanted to bring somebody from Big Mountain to speak and raise awareness and all that kind of thing, and the people were older than me, so I'd do tasks. . . . So, here comes one of the older people, and they were going to go with Greenpeace and this and that, and I really didn't feel particularly great about that because I know there's good folks in it and all that, but for my life, those people are more foreign than some other people. The foreignness, I guess. But Greenpeace wasn't really interested in raising awareness, so I'm thinking to myself, why spend five more minutes dicking around over here? But then they want something; they want people coming from the Southwest to come and bless their peace garden. And I thought that was outrageous. It was outrageous because you don't make old people stand out freezing their asses off at the end of November so that you can feel gratified, and then the reason they're here, there's no attention to that, no commitment to that. So I thought that was scandalous bad manners, really. And I think the time frame we had to move on everything was not real long. And all the time we spent dicking around so that we could find out that they weren't happening. So me and this other woman said we should go to Operation Push because they've got radio and all that stuff. Now they weren't foreign to me because I've

lived all over the city of Chicago, and I'm from Chicago and I lived like on Ninety-third Street for some time, and all that, and I guess with me they had a good reputation. I felt they were worthy of approach and easier to approach than some other things where you didn't know what it was, and it really wasn't connected to you in any way. So we go down there, and they were really nice and really forthcoming and didn't ask for nothing. And they had people who it was their job to know about media, and they had equipment for making the right size of tape to send to the television and this, that, and the other. And then there was this big fallout because peoples' feelings were hurt or something, I don't know, because their thing [with Greenpeace] didn't work out.

Of course, just as Native peoples have internalized prejudices about other communities, non-Natives have problematic attitudes toward Native peoples. As Yvonne Dennis notes, Native peoples tend to become romanticized icons in progressive movements. Native women are commonly invited to give the opening prayer at conferences, for instance, without being asked to speak on any substantive issues. In her view, "Well, what I've found is that when you're working with leftists, it's rare that you'll find someone who's evolved enough to treat you like a real person instead of a romantic icon. And I'd do an experiment with coming out with the most bizarre shit, and no one would call me on it because they didn't want to offend me. But that's not what it is to work in a coalition." Sharon Venne complains that non-Native supposed allies pay lip service to supporting Native sovereignty struggles but continue to exercise paternalistic control over Native peoples within the context of coalitions through hoarding information, disrespecting the ability of indigenous peoples to make their own decisions, and so on (1998, 24).

A particular hindrance in forming coalitions is the inability of non-Natives to understand Native peoples' unique legal status in this country and how their political vision of sovereignty differs from the civil rights perspective that informs many progressive movements in this country. An example of how ignorance about indigenous peoples' sovereignty struggles can negatively impact the ability to carve out coalitions is the organizing work around the United Nations World Conference against Racism in 2001. A source of particular tension was the demand of some African-descendant organizations for land reparations within the Americas. At the nongovernmental organization (NGO) preparatory meeting in Quito, Ecuador, both Roma and African-descendant groups called for "self-determination over their ancestral landbases in the Americas." Of course, indigenous peoples took issue with this demand as it implicitly denied indigenous title to these same land bases. Wilson describes the similar tensions that have existed between Native activist organizations and the Republic of New Afrika, which calls for land titles in the United States to be transferred to New Afrikans. Her comments were provoked by her reaction to a representative of the Republic of New Afrika who stood up at a preparatory meeting for the conference that took place in Atlanta on November 2000, and said: "Welcome to the Republic of New Afrika." Wilson recalls, "She got up and said 'Welcome to the Republic of New Afrika.' I don't think any other people of color would object to reparations who were victims of slavery. I certainly would support that. I just don't think it's going to be somebody else's land though. That's like participating in the oppression of another person."

Wilson's frustration echoes the work of many peoples involved in the politics of people of color who come to this coalition space expecting alliances and often find that activists from other communities of color are no more sympathetic to or knowledgeable about their struggles than are white activists. In my activist history, I have noticed a change, consequently, in the rhetoric about organizing by women of color. In the 1980s, during my involvement in various organizing projects, we would emphasize the idea of creating "safe spaces" in which women of color could work together. We soon found that the only time we got along was when we were organizing against white people. Once they were out of the room, we had vitriolic fights with each other. In the past few years, however, I have seen that the rhetoric of organizing by women of color as a safe space has shifted to the notion that such spaces are the most dangerous place to do organizing. Now, in these organizing spaces, we do not assume that we like each other or will be allies—rather, we have to actually carve out these alliances and coalitions. This shift coincides with a rethinking of identity politics from a nonessentialist perspective. Rather than assuming that there is something inherent to women who might fall under the category of "women of color" that would result in organizing becoming a safe space, "women of color" is reconfigured as a contested, shifting, and unstable political category that requires alliances to be built rather than assumed.

Limits of Coalitions

While exploring the possibilities of coalitions, I found in my interviews that an important corollary to creating coalitions with groups with which one would not necessarily expect to find common ground is sometimes choosing NOT to work with certain groups, even groups in which one WOULD expect to find common ground. I learned that any discussion of building coalitions must address the limits of coalitions.

Julie Star, for instance, brings up ethical issues in terms of forming coalitions. She makes the distinction between working with groups that are organized specifically to oppose Native peoples (such as the Ku Klux Klan) and working with groups that are not explicitly anti-Indian but may have a large number of anti-Indian activists. For instance, she argues that the sportfishers (referred to in the introduction) are organized because they are interested in protecting fish, even though many of the members may be anti-Indian as well. But their interest in protecting fish serves as a potential window for alliance building.

> The Klan, they organize based on racism. In order to work with them, you would have to accept that. Sportsfishers don't organize because they're racist. They organize because they're sportsfishers. In fact I've had quite a lot of luck working with those communities because they're actually very, very into Native stuff because they share so many similar values about being very, very respectful about how do you harvest resources, knowing the environment very, very well. Being very observant about changes in the environment and being concerned about those changes. And they know Native peoples know that. . . . But I would say that some people organize foundationally against you. But I don't think there's a lot. . . .
>
> Now I may work with that same individual who's a part of the Klan and part of Farmer's Aid, but I wouldn't work with him or her as [a] Klan member, so that's what I'm trying to say [though I would work with him or her in Farmer's Aid].

Star also analyzes coalition politics on the Left. For instance, while she supports abortion rights, she would not necessarily ally herself with groups that are population control organizations as she sees them as fundamentally organized to oppress people of color. But she might conceivably work with a group that is organized only around abortion rights, even though it might have some population control advocates.

> Star: When you look at that, I would say this. . . . I would say population control groups, they are organized against vast numbers of people of color and women. Unless they can actually put into their platform that we're about sustainable development in a positive way rather than just

about controlling people's of color fertility, then I would have serious concerns about that. Now that doesn't mean I might not try and change their minds, but would I work with them?

Me: Like on the issue of abortion? . . .

Star: Right on abortion, there's certain things that when people are fundamentally organized around an issue of injustice of the annihilation of another, I think you've got to draw some lines.

In addition, it is important to consider under what circumstances it is appropriate to not work in coalition with other progressive organizations. For instance, Pamela Kingfisher describes how an important element in the success of NACE was not just its ability to work with a broad sector of peoples in Oklahoma but its refusal to work with Greenpeace: "We wouldn't work with Greenpeace. And that was a big issue. . . . What we didn't like about Greenpeace was they would show up, bring their big bus in full of activists from all over the place. Fly their big banners, get all the media, cause a bunch of trouble, and leave town. And that is not our way because then we're stuck with that aftermath and the fallout and people pointing the fingers at us for bringing in the troublemakers. Plus, they stole our thunder. Then we didn't get in the newspaper, Greenpeace did, or whatever. So we never brought them in."

Many progressives argue that such splits result in a "fracturing of the Left" and are a result of "narcissism of small differences" (Boggs 2000; Epstein 1995; Gitlin 1994). These critiques are important. However, Native activists pose some important theoretical challenges to these analyses of fragmentation. Their analysis suggests that it is also important to ask whether such splits necessarily translate into permanent rifts. Is it possible that sometimes such splits become strategies for Native groups to call on other organizations to account for racism in a manner that could create space for more meaningful coalitions in the future? Do we all have to be in the same room or the same organization to support each other's work? That is, on one hand, sometimes organizations engage in a politics of purity in which they refuse to work with anyone or any organization that does not have politics identical to theirs. The politics of purity thus enables them to work with practically nobody. On the other hand, some groups are so uncritical of the coalitions they engage in that they are never able to set the terms of the coalitions. This approach can be particularly problematic for women of color, who often find issues of racism and/or sexism constantly marginalized in either male-dominated racial justice coalitions or white-dominated gender justice coalitions. Because these activists think that whatever complaining women of color may do they will eventually join the coalition, those who hold hegemonic control within the coalitions have no incentive to change their politics. Sometimes it can be strategic for women of color to refuse to join a coalition on a *temporary* basis in the hope that they can force accountability for an intersectional race-gender politics in these coalitions in the long term. I explore this thought later in this chapter.

Coalition Building in the Christian Right

One might ask, what is the benefit for the Right in joining such movements. Interestingly, one often hears within evangelical discourse more interest in rethinking coalitions than one does in the Left. This sentiment was reflected in an op-ed piece by Richard Cizik of the National Association of Evangelicals in response to the publication of *Blinded by Might*, by Ed Dobson and Cal Thomas, which challenged evangelical involvement in conventional party politics. Cizik did not agree that evangelicals should or will withdraw from politics but argued that the nature of this political involvement is changing. Evangelical influence is not tied to the success of a "religious Right," and evangelical involvement is becoming less single issue and more bipartisan. "Evangelical coalition-building is breaking new ground on a variety of issues," he writes. "Fears of guilt by association no longer dissuade evangelicals from finding common ground with erstwhile opponents to seek a larger end" (2000, 82). Consequently, he contends, evangelicals are *less* tied to the Republican Party. According to Cizik, thirty percent of evangelical voters said they were strong Republicans in 1990; in 2000 that number was twenty-five percent. Cizik's ethical recommendations for developing coalitions with nonevangelicals is that evangelicals must differentiate civil goals, which "are never to be confused with the religious goals that Christ set out for a kingdom of righteousness, holiness, and conformity to the Savior" (83). Of course, the problem is how to differentiate between civil and religious goals. Is same-sex marriage a civil or a religious issue?

Ted Haggard, the former president of the National Association of Evangelicals, also believes that "evangelical does not mean any particular political ideology" (T. Stafford 2005, 42) and actually lauded the Supreme Court decision in *Lawrence v. Texas* for "ordering the government out of the private lives of homosexuals" (45).[8] *Faith Today* (the Canadian counterpart of *Christianity Today*) contended that there is no religious Right in Canada for evangelicals exhibit the same voting patterns as the rest of the population (Stackhouse 2005). And in one study Richard Dixon and his colleagues found that even in the United States being a born-again Christian is not a predictor of sociopolitical conservatism (Dixon, Lowery, and Jones 1992). The Institute for Religion and Democracy complained that the 2001 World Evangelical Fellowship was espousing "leftist" positions such as calling for international debt cancellation—although it conceded that these positions did not abandon "biblical orthodoxy" (Knippers 2001). *Christianity Today* held a forum on homosexuality and public policy in which some of the participants advocated domestic partnerships because it was important for Christians to advocate policies that are cognizant of the fact that "we live in a large, pluralistic culture with people of many different religious and nonreligious persuasions" (Christianity Today 1999b, 50). And, in a complete political turnaround, John Whitehead, the founder of the anti-gay, Christian Reconstructionist Rutherford Institute, now supports gay civil rights, opposes the Colorado Amendment, and contends that the Christian Right is suffering from homophobia (Olsen 1998, 40). His firm now takes on broad civil rights cases, including supporting Native Americans on issues of religious freedom. And *Christianity Today* ran an article by Alice Evans, who describes how she realized that she could be a liberal feminist while belonging to a conservative evangelical church (1999). In an article on pro-life politics, *World* seems to implicitly critique the National Right to Life Committee for only endorsing Republicans, including Republicans who are moderate on the issue of abortion over Democrats who are solidly pro-life. It contends that pro-life politics must go beyond partisan politics (Jones 1998).

According to *Christianity Today*, the ethics of coalitions sometimes require evangelicals to work with "enemies" to further long-term goals. One editorial took issue with Christians who challenge U.S. support for regimes that "persecute Christians" to maintain the war on terror. "If politics is the art of compromise, international relations is the art of getting along with thugs," it opined. "Our prophetic calling—to seek real liberty for the oppressed—is sometimes best advanced by dealing with un-

[8] Ted Haggard was later outed for soliciting a male prostitute and removed from his position at his church and NAE. The current NAE president is Leith Anderson.

savory oppressive states" (Christianity Today 2001, 30). In this respect, *Christianity Today* shares Alex Ewen's recommendation that we work with all possible allies today in the hope of transforming them in the future.

These might not be the kind of alliances progressives would find beneficial. Nonetheless, even in the hardcore Republican *World* magazine we see increasing coverage of the topic of coalition building with groups that are more progressive. As mentioned previously, Justice Fellowship prides itself on working in coalition with diverse constituencies, and it worked with Satanists to support the Religious Land Use and Institutionalized Persons Act. In addition, Jerry Falwell filed a lawsuit challenging a Virginia law that prohibits churches from incorporating. The American Civil Liberties Union (ACLU) of Virginia filed a friend of the court brief agreeing with Falwell, and the district court judge ruled in April 2002 in favor of him (Taylor 2002). A number of unlikely coalitions between conservative groups (such as Christian homeschooling, pro-gun, and Christian Right organizations) developed coalitions with civil liberties groups to resist implementation of the Patriot Act in diverse local communities in a move consistent with the Right's suspicion of the state (Hentoff 2003; Jasper 2003; Lilienthal 2001; Miller and Stern 2003; Left Coaster 2003). *Christianity Today* published an article on what it termed "odd couple" politics between the Christian Right and some sectors of the feminist movement on the issue of trafficking in women (Carnes 2000). The *New York Times* similarly noted an "odd coalition" of Christian Right and liberal groups lobbying the Bush administration on the issues of Sudan, AIDS, and trafficking (Bumiller 2003). *Christianity Today* ran an editorial challenging the notion that evangelicals can be split neatly into right- and left-wing categories and called for increased dialogue along political and theological divides (Stackhouse 1998). *New Man* featured the liberal celebrities Bono and Brad Pitt as men of the year in 2005 for their work on debt relief and HIV and commended Pat Robertson for working with political liberals on the issue of HIV through Project ONE (Mansfield 2005). It also published pieces calling for coalition building with disability groups (in response to the famous Terri Schiavo case) and environmental groups to oppose cloning (as issue that many indigenous peoples are also organizing against, particularly through the Indigenous Peoples' Council on Biopiracy).[9] In the article on disability rights, *World* called on Christians to work with Not Dead Yet on the issue of euthanasia in response to the

[9] See www.ipcb.org for more information.

Schiavo case.[10] Interestingly, in calling for this coalition, the *World* article ended up reframing the issue around Schiavo because Not Dead Yet does not see itself as a pro-life group, which the article admits. Rather, the article framed Schiavo, not as a person who needed to be saved but as a person with a disability deserving of full protection under the law. Quoting Not Dead Yet, the article reads, "It's the ultimate form of discrimination to offer people with disabilities help to die without having offered real options to live" (Aikman 2005). This article further notes that Not Dead Yet was able to convince ACLU members not to support right to die legislation because it would deprive people with disabilities full protection under the law and prioritize health care for those who seem to be more physically "fit." Says *World*, "Christians should support Not Dead Yet and other disability groups. Even though the organization does not identify as Christian . . . it is a powerful ally in the fights we Christians are engaged in to prevent the values of barbarism from prevailing in our society" (Aikman 2005).[11]

On even the Far Right, Eleanor Burkett documents the attempts by militia groups in Missouri to work *with* the National Association for the Advancement of Colored People (NAACP), NOW, and the ACLU to protest a picnic held by the Ku Klux Klan. Said Kay Sheil, the head organizer of the protest, "Obviously racism is a political issue in the United States. They have the right to have a racist picnic, but we have a responsibility to protest it" (Burkett 1998, 84). Ironically, none of the liberal "antiracist" groups protested the picnic; only the militia groups did.

World has recently recommended coalescing the Green Party and other environmental groups over the issue of cloning. According to *World*, the Greens oppose cloning because it violates the laws of nature. So if Christians work with the Greens over cloning as a violation of nature, perhaps evangelicals will be able to convince the Greens that homosexuality and

[10] Incidentally, Charles Colson wrote an op-ed piece basically ridiculing claims made by disability groups, particularly the deaf community (2002a). An article that supports disability rights is *World's* review of the film *Murderball* (Veith 2005b). *Christianity Today* also took up the issue of disability in relationship to both the Schiavo case and disability critiques of the movie *Million Dollar Baby*. (Christianity Today 2005a).

[11] There is no clear consensus among evangelicals about what should have happened with Terri Schiavo. Members of the Christian Medical Association are divided as to whether or not we should maintain people in a persistent vegetative state, but they all agree that if you take a feeding tube out of a patient you must offer food and fluids by mouth. Their rationale is if you offer it and they don't take it then the disease has killed them; otherwise you have killed them (O'Connor 2005, 48)

abortion are also violations of nature. Given that coalition building involves a process of give-and-take, Christians should be prepared to support some environmental causes they might have previously eschewed.

> If we can take over some of their arguments, which seem uniquely persuasive to people today, and get them to fight on our side, we may have to give them some concessions and support them on some issues in return. For example, they are concerned about endangered species. And while this can be easy for us conservatives to mock, Christians, having a high view of creation, might pause. . . . We believe that God created the snail darter, which means that God willed that there be snail darters. On what theological grounds can we justify driving the snail darter or any other species to extinction? Success in the political arena often depends on strategic and tactical alliances. Evangelicals have worked with feminists to fight pornography and with the ACLU to fight religious discrimination. So Christians can, in some things, be green. (Veith 2004b)

Given that *World* usually publishes articles hostile to the environmental movement and has previously asserted that there is no such thing as an endangered species (Beisner 1993), and also given the fact that the Southern Baptist Convention opposed the Endangered Species Act (Beisner 1998; Bergin 2006a; Frame 1996; Thomas 1999b), this is a significant change in the Christian Right's rhetoric around environmentalism.[12] At one point, *World* contended that pro-environment policies would mean that "the American way of life as we've known it since the end of World War II will come to an end" (Thomas 1999b). But recently *World* has been tempering its approach, arguing that environmentalism should be a "conservative" cause (Veith 2006b). It also noted that evangelicals are increasingly supporting environmental causes, which might cause the Republican Party to shift its position on the issues of global warming (Stammer 2004). In fact, the National Association of Evangelicals (NAE) partnered with the Evangelical Environmental Network (EEN) to write a statement on "creation care." According to the EEN, "You can't just assume that because these liberal environmentalists have identified something as a problem, that it's not a real problem. Don't do guilt by association" (Bergin

---

[12] It should be mentioned that there is a significant evangelical environmental movement, including such groups as Restoring Eden, the Evangelical Environmental Network, Christians for Environmental Stewardship, the Christian Environmental Project, and the Christian Society of the Green Cross (Frame 1996; Richardson 2005).

2005c, 22). However, NAE stopped short of developing an official position on global warming in light of differing opinions on the issue (Bergin 2006b).[13] Instead, over eighty evangelical leaders signed on to a statement calling on government leaders to address global warming, including representatives from the National Association of Evangelicals, *Christianity Today*, and Vineyard Churches and the charismatic leader Jack Hayford (Noble 2006). The NAE took an approach to the environment similar to the one CBE took on issues of gender relations: in order to maintain a credible position on environmentalism within evangelical circles, it eschewed coalitions with environmentalists. Ted Haggard, the former president of NAE, claimed that he did not return phone calls from environmentalists because "We are not their allies" (Bergin 2005c, 23). The NAE's goal, rather, is "evangelicals talking to evangelicals" (Bergin 2005c, 23). NAE sought to avoid environmentalists for fear of losing credibility with its evangelical constituency. Its strategy is similar to that of evangelical feminists who eschewed coalitions with secular feminists to maintain credibility with mainstream evangelicalism. Interestingly, the growing support for environmentalism among evangelicals was further complicated when Ted Haggard, who had shown support for this issue, was ousted from NAE for homosexual activity. James Dobson and other evangelical leaders then called on NAE to fire NAE Vice-President Richard Cizik for supporting environmentalism. However, the Board refused to respond to the call or reprimand Cizik, and reaffirmed its position that environmental protection is an important issue (Cooperman 2007).

Theorization of unlikely alliances within both Native and evangelical circles demonstrates the complexities of rearticulation. Organizers must address the tensions of developing coalitions *within* communities at the same time that they develop external alliances. Unlikely alliances also bring with them the dangers of co-optation and the possibility of failure. Despite these dangers, it is clear that mass movements for social change cannot develop without them. The next section explores a possi-

[13] Those who hold opposing stands on global warming include Charles Colson, James Dobson, and E. Calvin Beisner of the Knox Theological Seminary. Nor did *World* express support for the statement (Bergin 2006a). On October 1999, twenty-five evangelical leaders released the Cornwall Declaration on Environmental Stewardship to counter the National Religious Partnership on the Environment and put more emphasis on the importance of free market capitalism ("A Different View of the Environment" 2000).

ble model for rearticulating political alliances to further social justice struggles in the future.

DEVELOPING NEW ALLIANCE POLITICS: BEYOND PRO-CHOICE AND PRO-LIFE REPRODUCTIVE RIGHTS ORGANIZING

As this book is a prolineal genealogy of alliance politics, I will now shift my focus from what is currently happening to what *could be* happening in rearticulating new coalitions. Having looked at theories about the coalition building being produced within Native women's organizing and Christian Right circles, I will put these theories in conversation with each other through the topic of reproductive justice. That is, can the Native American concepts of recentering and rearticulation provide a possible way to reformulate a political issue that now seems intractably divided along pro-life versus pro-choice lines? If we examine the rearticulations of the issue by Native women, it may be possible to reframe it in a manner that can shift the way abortion politics are configured. If reproductive justice is recentered through the experiences and perspectives of Native women, how might the issue look different for all peoples? Such a methodological approach might be instructive for the ways we can frame similarly divisive issues.

Once I was taking an informal survey of Native women about their position on abortion—were they "pro-life" or "pro-choice"? I quickly found that their responses did not neatly fit these categories.

Example 1
Me: Are you pro-choice or pro-life?
Respondent 1: Oh, I am definitely pro-life.
Me: So you think abortion should be illegal?
Respondent 1: No, definitely not. People should be able to have an abortion if they want.
Me: Do you think, then, that there should not be federal funding for abortion services?
Respondent 1: No, there should be funding available so that anyone can afford to have one.
Example 2
Me: Would you say you are pro-choice or pro-life?
Respondent 2: Well, I would say that I am pro-choice, but the most important thing to me is promoting life in Native communities.

Example 3

Respondent 3: I would say the fetus is a life, but sometimes that life must be ended.

These responses make it difficult to place these women neatly into pro-life or pro-choice camps. Is respondent 1 pro-life because she says she is pro-life? Or is she pro-choice because she supports the decriminalization of and public funding for abortion? Is respondent 2 pro-choice because she says she is pro-choice or is she pro-life because she says she wants to promote life? And what do we make of respondent 3, whose theoretical formulation challenges the logics of both the pro-choice and pro-life paradigms? The reproductive framework these Native women are implicitly articulating is that, unlike pro-life and pro-choice advocates, who make their overall political goal either the criminalization or decriminalization of abortion, Native women fight for life and self-determination in their communities, for which the criminalization of abortion may or may not be a strategy. In previous works, I have focused more specifically on Native women and reproductive justice (2001). Here I am working with these Native women's articulations about abortion to serve as a starting point for reconceptualizing what seem to be entrenched binaries within reproductive justice issues, which seem to prevent peoples from politically coalescing across the "pro-choice versus pro-life" divide. Recentering Native women in the analysis affords us the opportunity to critically interrogate the framing devices of the pro-choice and pro-life movements and to ask who profits from the manner in which this issue has been framed along these dualistic lines. In fact, by centering Native women in the analysis, it becomes apparent that, while the pro-choice and pro-life camps on the abortion debate are often articulated as polar opposites, they both depend on similar operating assumptions that do not necessarily support either life or real choice for Native women. Consequently, it can be difficult to ascertain which "side" best represents the interests of Native women. Are their interests served by pro-choice organizations, which have supported access to abortion and contraceptive services but did not support remedial action for the abuses suffered when Native women were being routinely sterilized without their consent during the 1970s? Such groups have also promoted the distribution of contraceptives with dubious safety records in Native communities, often before they are approved by the Federal Drug Administration. Or are the interests of Native women best served by pro-life organizations, which have organized against sterilization abuses, population control policies that negatively impact Native women, and potentially dangerous contraceptives. But at the same time these groups support racially discriminatory legislation such as the Hyde Amendment, which, besides discriminating against poor women by denying federal funding for abortion services, racially discriminates against American Indian women, who largely receive their health care through Indian Health Services, a federal agency.

In addition to the sources covered in chapter 3, this section is informed by my fifteen years as an activist in the reproductive justice movement through such organizations as the Illinois chapter of the National Abortion and Reproductive Rights Action League (NARAL), the Chicago Abortion Fund, Women of All Red Nations, INCITE! Women of Color against Violence, and the Committee on Women, Population, and the Environment.

Pro-life Politics and the Prison Industrial Complex

The pro-life position maintains that the fetus is a life so abortion should be criminalized. Consequently, the pro-life stance situates its position around moral claims regarding the sanctity of life. In a published debate on pro-life versus pro-choice positions on the issue of abortion, Gray Crum (a former vice president of South Carolina Citizens for Life) argues that the pro-life position is "ethically pure" (Crum and McCormack 1992, 54). Because of the moral weight he grants to the protection of the life of the fetus, Crum contends that abortion must be criminalized. Any immoral actions that impact others should be considered a "serious crime under the law" (28). The pro-choice position counters this argument by asserting that the fetus is not a life, and hence policy must be directed toward protecting a woman's ability to control her own body. To quote the sociologist Thelma McCormack's response to Crum, "Life truly begins in the . . . hospital room, not in the womb" (121). Gloria Feldt, the president of Planned Parenthood, similarly asserts that if the fetus is established as a life the principles of *Roe v. Wade* must necessarily be discarded (2004, 90).

But the statement in example 3 in the interviews quote above suggests another critical intervention in the pro-life argument. That is, the critical flaw in the pro-life position is NOT the claim that the fetus is a life but the conclusion it draws from this assertion—that because the fetus is a life abortion should be criminalized. In this regard, reproductive rights activists and scholars on both sides of the fence could benefit from an analysis of prison organizing (including evangelical prison organizing) if we were to take the logics of that movement to their logical conclusion. To further this development, I will briefly restate the critiques of the prison system developed by a multitude of antiprison scholars and activists.

The movement that opposes the prison industrial complex has highlighted the complete failure of the prison system to address social problems. As was discussed in chapter 1, not only do prisons fail to solve social problems such as "crime," but they are more likely to increase rather than decrease crime rates (Currie 1998; Donziger 1996; S. Walker 1998). Most people in prison are there for drug- or poverty-related crimes. Prisons do not provide treatment for drug addiction, and it is often easy to access drugs in prison. For people in prison because of poverty-related crimes, a prison record ensures that it will be much more difficult for them to secure employment once they are released. Study after study indicates that prisons do not have an impact on decreasing crime rates (Box and Hale 1982; Colvin 1986; Jankovic 1977; S. Walker 1998, 139). In addition, as documented by prison activist groups such as the Prison Activist Resource Center, government monies are siphoned away from education and social services into prisons, thus destabilizing communities of color and increasing their vulnerability to incarceration.[14]

The failure of prisons is well known to policymakers. In fact, at the 1999 Justice Fellowship Forum, several policymakers noted that elected officials across the political spectrum know that prisons do not work, but they support prisons to help win elections. Consequently, it is likely that the purpose of prisons has never been to stop crime. Rather, as a variety of scholars and activists have argued, the purpose has been in large part to control the population of communities of color. As Michael Mancini and Angela Davis point out, the racial background of the prison population prior to the Civil War was white. After the Civil War, the Thirteenth Amendment was passed, which prohibits slavery—except for prisoners. The slavery system was essentially replaced by the convict leasing system, which was often even more brutal than the slavery system. Under slavery, slave owners at least had a financial incentive to keep slaves alive. In the convict leasing system, no such incentive existed; if a prisoner died, she or he could simply be replaced with another prisoner (Davis 2003; Mancini 1991). The regime of the prison was originally designed to "reform" the prisoner by creating conditions for penitence (hence the term *penitentiary*) (Ignatieff 1978). After the Civil War, the prison system adopted

[14] See the Prison Activist Resource Center's Web site, www.prisonactivist.org.

regimes of punishment similar to those found in the slavery system, which coincided with the reenslavement of black communities under the convict leasing system (Davis 2003). Davis argues that "racisms . . . congeal and combine in prisons" and exist to maintain the capitalist and white supremacist underpinnings of American society (26). The continuing racism of the prison system is evidenced by who is in prison. In 1994, for instance, one out of every three African American men between the ages of twenty and twenty-nine was under some form of criminal justice supervision (Mauer 1999). Two-thirds of men of color in California between the ages of eighteen and thirty have been arrested (Donziger 1996, 102–4). Six of every ten juveniles in federal custody are American Indian. Two-thirds of the women in prison are women of color.[15]

Davis further argues that it is critical to disarticulate the equation between crime and punishment because their primary purpose is not to solve the problem of crime or social problems.

> "Punishment" does not follow from "crime" in the neat and logical sequence offered by discourses that insist on the justice of imprisonment, but rather punishment—primarily through imprisonment (and sometimes death)—is linked to the agendas of politicians, the profit drive of corporations, and media representations of crime. Imprisonment is associated with the racialization of those most likely to be punished. . . . If we . . . strive to disarticulate crime and punishment . . . then our focus must not rest only on the prison system as an isolated institution but must also be directed at all the social relations that support the permanence of the prison. (2003, 112)

Prisons are not only ineffective institutions for addressing social concerns, but they drain resources from institutions that could be more effective. They also mark certain peoples, particularly people of color, as inherently "criminal" and undeserving of civil and political rights, thus increasing their vulnerability to poverty and further criminalization.

Davis's principle of disarticulation is critical in reassessing the pro-life position. That is, whether or not one perceives abortion to be a crime, it does not follow that punishment in the form of prisons is a necessary response. Criminalization individualizes solutions to problems that are the result of larger economic, social, and political conditions. Consequently, it is inherently incapable of solving social problems or addressing crime. Alternative social formations and institutions that can address

[15] These statistics are collected by the Prison Activist Resource Center (www.prisonactivist.org).

these large-scale political and economic conditions are the appropriate place to address social issues such as reproductive justice. As Davis argues, "Prison needs to be abolished as the dominant mode of addressing social problems that are better solved by other institutions and other means. The call for prison abolition urges us to imagine and strive for a very different social landscape" (Rodriguez 2000a, 215).

Thus, even if we hold that a top social priority is to reduce the number of abortions, there is no evidence to suggest that involving the criminal justice system will accomplish that goal given that it has not been effective in reducing crime rates or addressing social problems generally. In addition, increased criminalization disproportionately impacts people of color. An interrogation of the assumptions behind the pro-life movement (as well as the pro-choice response to it) suggests that what distinguishes the pro-life position is not so much its explicit commitment to life (since criminalization promotes death rather than life, particularly in communities of color and poor communities) as its implicit commitment to criminal justice interventions in reproductive justice issues.

An assessment of recent debates within the movements that oppose domestic and sexual assault further illustrates this argument. As I and others have argued, the antiviolence movement, as it became increasingly funded by the state, began to rely on criminal justice interventions (A. Smith 2005c; White 2004). Domestic violence and sexual assault agencies formed their strategies around the notion that sexual and domestic violence is a crime. The response of activists was to push for increased criminalization of sexual and domestic violence through mandatory arrest policies, no-drop prosecution policies, longer sentences, and so on. Sadly, this approach did not reduce violence rates and often increased women's victimization. For instance, under mandatory arrest laws, the police often arrest the women who are being battered. The *New York Times* recently reported that under strengthened anti-domestic-violence legislation battered women kill their abusive partners less frequently but batterers do *not* kill their partners less frequently (Butterfield 2000). Ironically, the laws passed to protect battered women are actually protecting their batterers!

Similarly, the pro-life position implicitly supports the prison industrial complex by unquestioningly supporting a criminal justice approach that legitimizes rather than challenges the prison system. As Davis argues, it is not sufficient to challenge the criminal justice system; we must build alternatives to it (Davis 2003). Just as the women of color antiviolence movement is currently developing strategies to end violence (INCITE! 2006; A. Smith 2005c; Sokoloff 2005; White 2004), a consistent pro-life position would require activists to develop responses to abortion that do not rely on the prison industrial complex.

As was discussed in chapter 1, this critique of the prison system is prevalent even within conservative evangelical circles. Yet, despite his sustained critique of the failure of the prison system, Charles Colson and his compatriots never critique the wisdom of criminalization as the appropriate response to abortion. If they are clear on the inability of prisons to solve most social problems, is it such a huge leap to ask why prisons are expected to solve the problem of abortion? Given that this critique of criminalization is not inaccessible to large sectors of the pro-life movement, there should be opportunities to make anticriminalization interventions into pro-life discourse. Already we see the sentiment within this discourse that "the mother of the aborted child [is] a person who needs compassion, not incarceration" (M. Olasky 2000).

Thus, the major flaw in the pro-life position is not so much its claim that the fetus is a life as its assumption that because the fetus is a life abortion should be criminalized. A commitment to the criminalization of social issues necessarily contributes to the growth of the prison system because it reinforces the notion that prisons are appropriate institutions for addressing social problems rather than causes of the problems themselves. Given the disproportionate impact of criminalization on communities of color, support for criminalization as public policy also implicitly supports racism.

In addition, those committed to pro-choice positions will be more effective and politically consistent if they contest the pro-life position from an antiprison perspective. For instance, poor women and women of color are finding their pregnancies increasingly criminalized. As Dorothy Roberts and others have noted, women of color are more likely to be criminalized for drug use, as a result of greater rates of poverty in communities of color, and are more likely to be in contact with government agencies where their drug use can be detected. While white pregnant women are slightly *more* likely than black women to engage in substance abuse, public health facilities and private doctors are more likely to report black women to criminal justice authorities (Maher 1990; Roberts 1997, 175). Meanwhile, pregnant women who would like treatment for their addiction can seldom get it because treatment centers do not meet the needs of pregnant women. One study found that two-thirds of drug treatment centers do not treat pregnant women (Roberts 1997, 189). Furthermore, the criminalization approach is more likely to prevent pregnant women who are substance abusers from seeking prenatal or other forms of health care for fear of being reported to the authorities (190). Dorothy Roberts critiques communities of color for often supporting the criminalization of women of color who have addictions and failing to understand this criminalization as another strategy of white supremacy, which blames women for the effects of poverty and racism. Lisa Maher and Rickie Solinger note that a simple "choice" perspective is not effective in addressing this problem because certain women become marked as women who make "bad choices" and hence deserve imprisonment (Maher 1990; Solinger 2001, 148).

Similarly, Elizabeth Cook-Lynn argues in "The Big Pipe Case" that at the same time Native peoples were rallying around Leonard Peltier, no one stood beside Marie Big Pipe when she was incarcerated on a felony charge of "assault with intent to commit serious bodily harm" because she breast-fed her child while under the influence of alcohol. She was denied services to treat her substance abuse problem and access to abortion services when she became pregnant. Not only did her community fail to support her, but it supported her incarceration. In doing so, Cook-Lynn argues, the community supported the encroachment of federal jurisdiction on tribal lands for an issue that would normally have been under tribal juris-diction (1998b, 110–25). Cook-Lynn recounts how this demonization of Native women was assisted by the publication of Michael Dorris's *The Broken Cord*, which narrates his adoption of a Native child who suffered from fetal alcohol syndrome (Dorris 1989). While this book has sensitized many communities to the realities of fetal alcohol syndrome, it also por-trays the mother of the child unsympathetically and advocates repressive legislative solutions targeted against women substance abusers. Thus, within Native communities the growing demonization of Native women substance abusers has prompted tribes to collude with the federal govern-ment in whittling away their own sovereignty.

Unfortunately, as both Roberts and Cook-Lynn argue, even commu-nities of color, including those that identify as both pro-life *and* pro-choice, have supported the criminalization of women of color who have addiction issues. The reason they support this strategy is because they focus on what they perceive to be the moral culpability of women of color for not protecting the lives of their children. If we adopt an antiprison perspective, however, it becomes clear that even on the terms of moral culpability (which I am not defending),[16] it does not follow that the crimi-

[16] As Roberts and Maher note, addiction is itself a result of social and political conditions such as racism and poverty, which the U.S. government does not take steps to alleviate and then blames the women who are victimized by these condi-tions. Furthermore, it provides no resources to help pregnant women end their

nal justice approach is the appropriate way to address this social concern. In fact, criminal justice responses to unwanted pregnancies and/or pregnant women who have addiction issues demonstrate an inherent contradiction in the pro-life position. Many pro-life organizations have been ardent opponents of population control programs and policies, advocating against the promotion of dangerous contraceptives or the promotion of sterilization in Third World countries.[17] They have also critiqued population control policies from an antiracist perspective. According to one observer, "One other factor undergirding the eugenics-population control matrix is racism. As minorities have become more vocal . . . the racist element of the population control movement remains. . . . For example, there is evidence that the opening of state-supported birth control clinics is closely related to the concentrations of poor black people in various states. . . . At this juncture, population control . . . and racism become one and the same—planned death for those unfortunate souls unable to resist" (Whitehead 1995). Yet their position depends on the prison industrial complex, which is an institution of population control for communities of color in the United States.

Meanwhile, many pro-choice organizations, such as Planned Parenthood, have supported providing financial incentives for poor women and criminalized women to be sterilized or take long-acting hormonal contraceptives (Saletan 2003).[18] As I will discuss later, part of this political inconsistency is inherent in the articulation of the pro-choice position.

---

addictions; it simply penalizes them for continuing a pregnancy. Thus, assigning moral culpability primarily to pregnant women with addiction problems is a dubious prospect.

[17] M. Belz 1998a, 1998b, 1999a, 1999c, 1999d, 1999e; N. Belz 1998; Chacko 1995; "Economic Development in Bangladesh" 2000; "Ending the Myth of Overpopulation" 1999; Freedman 1999; Harris 1995; Morrison 2000a, 2000b; "Norplant Linked to Strokes" 1995; "Peru's Forced Sterilization Campaign" 1999; PRI Staff 2000; Stanciu and Mohammed 1995; "The New Law of the Land" 1999; Public Forum 2000; Trunk 2000. The Christian agency World Vision was accused by *World* of supporting population control policies, so there is obviously no single evangelical perspective on this issue either (Belz 1999b).

[18] Additionally, several reproductive rights advocates at the historic Sister Song conference on women of color and reproductive justice, held in Atlanta in November 2003, noted that local Planned Parenthood agencies were offering financial incentives for women who were addicted to accept long-acting contraceptives or were distributing literature from Children Requiring a Caring Kommunity (CRACK). This policy was not uniform among Planned Parenthood chapters, however, and many condemned this practice.

But another reason is that many in the pro-choice camp have not questioned criminalization as the appropriate response for addressing reproductive health concerns. They may differ as to which acts should be criminalized, but they do not necessarily question the criminalization regime itself.

Pro-choice and Capitalism

By contrast, the pro-choice position claims a position that offers more "choices" for women making decisions about their reproductive lives. A variety of scholars and activists have critiqued the choice paradigm because it rests on essentially individualist, consumerist notions of "free" choice that do not take into consideration all the social, economic, and political conditions that frame the so-called choices that women are forced to make (Patchesky 1990; J. Smith 1999; Solinger 2001). Solinger further contends that in the 1960s and 1970s abortion rights advocates initially used the term *rights* rather than *choice*, rights understood as those benefits owed to all those who are human regardless of access to special resources. By contrast, argues Solinger, the concept of choice is connected to the possession of resources, creating a hierarchy among women based on who is capable of making legitimate choices (2001, 6). Consequently, since under a capitalist system those with resources are granted more choices, it is not inconsistent to withdraw reproductive rights choices from poor women through legislation such as the Hyde Amendment (which restricts federal funding for abortion) or family caps for Temporary Assistance for Needy Families recipients.[19] Her argument can be demonstrated in the writings of Planned Parenthood itself. In 1960, it commissioned a study, which concluded that poor and working-class families lack the rationality to do family planning and that this lack of rationality is "embodied in the particular personalities, world views, and ways of life" of the poor themselves (Rainwater 1960, 5, 167). As Solinger states, "'Choice' also became a symbol of middle-class women's arrival

[19] For further analysis of how welfare reform marks poor women and women of color as those who make bad choices and hence should have these choices restricted through marriage promotion, family caps (or cuts in payments if recipients have additional children), and incentives to use long-acting hormonal contraceptives, see Mink 1999.

as independent consumers. Middle-class women could afford to choose. They had earned the right to choose motherhood, if they liked. According to many Americans, however, when choice was associated with poor women, it became a symbol of illegitimacy. Poor women had not earned the right to choose" (199–200).

What her analysis suggests is that, ironically, while the pro-choice camp contends that the pro-life position diminishes the rights of women in favor of "fetal" rights, the pro-choice position does not ascribe inherent rights to women either. Rather, women are ascribed reproductive choices if they can afford them or are deemed legitimate choice makers.

William Saletan's history of the evolution of the pro-choice paradigm illustrates the extent to which it is a conservative one. He contends that pro-choice strategists, generally affiliated with NARAL, intentionally chose to reject a rights-based framework in favor of one that focused on the protection of privacy from "big government." That is, government should not have the right to intervene in the decision to have children. This approach appealed to those with libertarian sensibilities who otherwise might have no sympathy for feminist causes. The impact of this strategy was that it enabled the pro-choice side to keep *Roe v. Wade* intact, though only in the most narrow of senses. This strategy undermined any attempt to achieve a broader pro-choice agenda because the strategy behind this approach could be used against a broader agenda. For instance, the argument that government should not be involved in reproductive rights decisions could be used by pro-life advocates to oppose federal funding for abortions on the argument that government has no business providing funding for abortion services (Saletan 2003). Consequently, Saletan argues, "Liberals have not won the struggle for abortion rights. Conservatives have" (1998, 114).

This narrow approach has contributed to some pro-choice organizations, such as Planned Parenthood and NARAL, developing strategies that marginalize Native women and other women of color. Both supported the Freedom of Choice Act in the early 1990s, which retained the Hyde Amendment (Saletan 2003). As mentioned previously, the Hyde Amendment, besides discriminating against poor women by denying federal funding for abortion services, discriminates against American Indian women, who largely receive health care through the federally funded Indian Health Services. One of NARAL's petitions stated, "The Freedom of Choice Act (FOCA) will secure the original vision of *Roe v. Wade*, giving *all* women reproductive freedom and securing that right for future generations [emphasis mine]."[20] This rhetoric leaves the impression that poor and indigenous women do not qualify as "women."[21]

Building on this analysis, I would argue that, while there is certainly a sustained internal critique of the choice paradigm, particularly among women of color's reproductive rights groups, this paradigm continues to govern many of the policies of mainstream groups in a manner that continues the marginalization of indigenous women, women of color, poor women, and women with disabilities.

One example is the extent to which pro-choice advocates narrow their advocacy around legislation that affects the choice of whether or not to have an abortion without addressing all the conditions that gave rise to a woman having to make this decision in the first place. Consequently, politicians, such as former president Bill Clinton, will be heralded as pro-choice as long as they do not support legislative restrictions on abortion, regardless of their stance on issues that may equally impact the reproductive choices women make. Clinton's approval of federal welfare reform, which placed poor women in the position of possibly being forced to have an abortion because of cuts in social services, while often critiqued, is not critiqued as an antichoice position. On the Planned Parenthood and NARAL Web sites (www.plannedparenthood.org and www.naral.org), there is generally no mention of welfare policies in their pro-choice legislation alerts.

The consequence of the choice paradigm is that its advocates often take positions that are oppressive to women from politically marginalized communities. For instance, this paradigm often makes it difficult to develop nuanced positions on the use of abortion when the fetus is determined to have abnormalities. Focusing solely on the woman's choice to have or not have this child does not address the larger context of a society that sees children with disabilities as having lives not worth living and provides inadequate resources to women who may otherwise want to have them. As Martha Saxton notes, "Our society profoundly limits the 'choice' to love and care for a baby with a disability" (1998). If our response to disability is to simply facilitate the process by which women can abort

[20] The petition can be found on the Web at http://www.wanaral.org/so1take action/200307101.html.

[21] During this period, I served on the board of the Illinois chapter of NARAL, which was constituted primarily of women of color. Illinois NARAL broke with national NARAL in opposing FOCA. Despite many arguments with NARAL's president, Kate Michelman, she refused to consider the perspectives of women of color on this issue.

fetuses that may have disabilities, we never actually focus on changing economic policies that making raising children with disabilities difficult. Rashmi Luthra notes, by contrast, that reproductive advocates from other countries, such as India, who do not operate under the choice paradigm, are often able to make more complicated political positions on issues such as this one (1993).

Another example is the difficulty pro-choice groups have in maintaining a critical perspective on dangerous or potentially dangerous contraceptives, arguing that women should have a choice of contraceptives. Many scholars and activists have documented the dubious safety record of Norplant and Depo-Provera, two long-acting hormonal contraceptives (Krust and Assetoyer 1993; Masterson and Gutherie 1986; Roberts 1997; A. Smith 2001). In fact, lawsuits against Norplant have forced an end to its distribution (although it is still on the shelves and can still be given to women). In 1978, the Food and Drug Administration (FDA) denied approval to Depo-Provera as a contraceptive on the grounds that (1) dog studies confirmed an elevated rate of breast cancer, (2) there appeared to be an increased risk of birth defects in human fetuses exposed to the drug, and (3) there was no pressing need shown for use of the drug as a contraceptive (Masterson and Gutherie 1986). In 1987, the FDA changed its regulations and began to require cancer testing in rats and mice instead of dogs and monkeys; Depo-Provera did not cause cancer in these animals, though major concerns regarding its safety persist (Feminist Women's Health Centers 1997). Also problematic is the manner in which such drugs are promoted in communities of color, often without informed consent (Krust and Assetoyer 1993; Masterson and Gutherie 1986; A. Smith 2001).[22] Yet none of the mainstream pro-choice organizations has ever seriously taken on the issue of informed consent as part of its agenda.[23] Indeed, Gloria

[22] I was a coorganizer of a reproductive rights conference in Chicago in 1992. There, hotline workers from Chicago Planned Parenthood reported that they were told to tell women seeking contraception that Norplant had no side effects. In 2000, women enrolled in a class I was teaching at the University of California, Santa Cruz, informed the class that when they asked Planned Parenthood workers about the side effects of Depo-Provera, the workers said they were not allowed to reveal the side effects because they were supposed to promote Depo-Provera. Similar problems in other Planned Parenthood offices were reported at the Sister Song conference. Again, these problems around informed consent are not necessarily a national Planned Parenthood policy or uniform across all Planned Parenthood agencies.

[23] In 1994, when NARAL changed its name to the National Abortion and Reproductive Rights Action League, it held a strategy session for its state chapters that I attended. Michelman and her associates claimed that this name change was reflec-

Feldt, the president of Planned Parenthood, equates opposition to Norplant and Depo-Provera with opposition to choice in her book *The War on Choice* (Feldt 2004, 34, 37). In fact, Planned Parenthood and NARAL opposed restrictions on sterilization abuse, despite the thousands of women of color who were being sterilized without their consent, because such policies would interfere with women's "right to choose" (Nelson 2003, 144; Patchesky 1990, 8). Particularly disturbing has been some of the support given by these organizations to the Center for Research on Population and Security, headed by Stephen Mumford and Elton Kessel, which distributes globally a form of sterilization, Quinacrine, that has no proven safety record, is highly vulnerable to abuse, and is being promoted by this center from an explicitly anti-immigrant perspective.[24]

Despite the threat to reproductive justice that this group represents, the Fund for Feminist Majority featured it at their 1996 Feminist Expo because, I was informed by the organizers, it promoted choice for women. In 1999, Planned Parenthood almost agreed to sponsor a Quinacrine trial in the United States, but outside pressure forced it to change its position.[25] A

---

tive of NARAL's interest in expanding its agenda to new communities and informed consent around contraceptives would be included in this expanded agenda. I asked how much of NARAL's budget was going to be allocated to this new agenda. The reply: none. The organization would issue a report on these new issues, but it was going to work only on NARAL's traditional issues.

[24] Quinacrine is used to treat malaria. It is inserted into the uterus, where it dissolves, causing the fallopian tubes to scar and rendering the woman irreversibly sterile. Family Health International conducted four in vitro studies and found Quinacrine to be mutagenic in three of them. It, as well as the World Health Organization, recommended against further trials for female sterilization, and no regulatory body supports Quinacrine. However, North Carolina's Center for Research on Population and Security has circumvented these recommendations through private funding from such organizations as the Turner Foundation and the Leland Fykes organization (which funds pro-choice *and* anti-immigrant groups). The center has been distributing Quinacrine for free to researchers and government health agencies. There have been field trials in eleven countries, and more than seventy thousand women have been sterilized. In Vietnam, one hundred female rubber plant workers were given routine pelvic exams during which the doctor inserted Quinacrine without their consent. So far, the side effects linked to Quinacrine include ectopic pregnancy, puncturing of the uterus during insertion, pelvic inflammatory disease, and severe abdominal pains. Other possible concerns include heart and liver damage and exacerbation of preexisting viral conditions. In one of the trials in Vietnam, a large number of cases of women who had experienced side effects were excluded from the data ("Controversy over Sterilization Pellet" 1994; Norsigian 1996).

[25] Committee on Women, Population, and the Environment, internal correspondence, 1999.

prevalent ideology within the mainstream pro-choice movement is that women should have the choice to use whatever contraception they want. Such positions do not consider that (1) a choice among dangerous contraceptives is not much of a choice; (2) the pharmaceutical companies and medical industry have millions of dollars to spend to promote certain contraceptives; and (3) the social, political, and economic conditions women may find themselves in are such that using dangerous contraceptives may be the best of several bad options. Interestingly, a similar critique of choice was made in *Christianity Today,* which links the choice framework to consumerism (in this case, contraceptive consumerism): "Transpose the political notions of liberty into a commercial framework and you get choice, with the maximization of choice as a supreme value" (Christianity Today 2005b).

One reason that such groups have not taken a position on informed consent on potentially dangerous contraceptives is because of their investment in population control. As Betsy Hartmann has argued, while contraceptives are often articulated as an issue of choice for white women in the First World, they are articulated as an instrument of population control for women of color and women in the Third World (1995). The historical origins of Planned Parenthood are inextricably tied to the eugenics movement. Its founder, Margaret Sanger, increasingly collaborated with eugenics organizations during her career and framed the need for birth control in terms of the need to reduce the number of those in the "lower classes" (Roberts 1997, 73). In a study commissioned in 1960, Planned Parenthood concluded that poor people "have too many children" (Rainwater 1960, 2), yet something must be done to stop this trend in order to "disarm the population bomb" (178). Today Planned Parenthood is particularly implicated in this movement as can be seen clearly by the groups they list as their allies on their Web site (www.planned parenthood.org): Population Action International, the Population Institute, Zero Population Growth, and the Population Council. A central campaign of Planned Parenthood is to restore U.S. funding to the United Nations Population Fund (UNFPA). In addition, it asserts its commitment to addressing "rapid population growth" on this same Web site. I will not rehearse the problematic analysis critiqued elsewhere behind this population paradigm, which essentially blames Third World women for poverty, war, environmental damage, and social unrest without looking at the root causes of all these phenomena (including population growth): colonialism, corporate policies, militarism, and economic disparities between poor and rich countries (Bandarage 1997; Hartmann 1995; Silliman and King 1999). However, as Hartmann documents, the UNFPA has long been involved in coercive contraceptive policies throughout the world. The Population Council produced Norplant and assisted in its trials in Bangladesh and other countries, which were conducted without the informed consent of the participants (Hartmann 1995). In fact, trial administrators often refused to remove Norplant when requested to do so (Cadbury 1995). All of these population organizations intersect to promote generally long-acting hormonal contraceptives of dubious safety around the world (Hartmann 1995). Of course, Planned Parenthood does provide valuable family planning resources to women around the world as well, but it does so through a population framework that inevitably shifts the focus from family planning as a right in and of itself to family planning as an instrument of population control. While population control advocates, such as Planned Parenthood, are increasingly sophisticated in their rhetoric and often talk about ensuring social, political, and economic opportunity, the "population" focus of this model still results in its advocates focusing their work on reducing population rather than providing social, political, and economic opportunity.

Another unfortunate consequence of uncritically adopting the choice paradigm is the tendency of reproductive rights advocates to make simplistic analyses of who our political friends and enemies are in the area of reproductive rights. That is, all those who call themselves pro-choice are all our political allies while all those who call themselves pro-life are our political enemies. As an example of this rhetoric is Gloria Feldt's description of anyone who is pro-life as a "right-wing extremist" (2004, 5). As I have argued throughout this book, this simplistic analysis of who is politically progressive or conservative does not do justice to the complex political positions people inhabit. As a result, we often engage uncritically in coalitions with groups that, as the antiviolence activist Beth Richie states, "do not pay us back" (2000). Meanwhile, we often lose opportunities to work with people with whom we may have sharp disagreements but who may, with different political framings and organizing strategies, shift their positions.

To illustrate, Planned Parenthood is often championed as an organization that supports women's right to choose with which women of color should ally. Yet, as discussed previously, its roots are in the eugenics movement and today it is heavily invested in the population establishment. It continues to support population control policies in the Third

World, it almost supported the development of Quinacrine in the United States, and it opposed strengthening sterilization regulations that would have protected women of color.

Meanwhile, the North Baton Rouge Women's Help Center in Louisiana is a crisis pregnancy center that articulates its pro-life position from an antiracist perspective. It argues that Planned Parenthood has advocated population control, particularly in communities of color. It critiques the Black Church Initiative of the Religious Coalition for Reproductive Choice for contending that charges of racism against Sanger are "scare tactics" (Blunt 2003, 22). It also attempts to provide its services from a holistic perspective by providing educational and vocational training, high school equivalency classes, literacy programs, primary health care and pregnancy services, and child placement services. Its position: "We cannot encourage women to have babies and then continue their dependency on the system. We can't leave them without the resources to care for their children and then say, 'Praise the Lord, we saved a baby'" (Blunt 2003, 23).

It would seem that, while both groups support some positions that are beneficial to Native women and other women of color, they also support positions that are detrimental. So, if we are truly committed to reproductive justice, why should we presume that we must work with Planned Parenthood and reject the Women's Help Center? Why would we not position ourselves as independent of both of these approaches and work to shift their positions to a stance that is truly liberatory for all women?

Beyond Pro-Life versus Pro-Choice

Many reproductive advocates have attempted to expand the definitions of *pro-life* and *pro-choice* depending on which side of this divide they favor, but they are essentially trying to expand concepts that are inherently designed to exclude the experiences of most women, including poor women, women of color, indigenous women, and women with disabilities. First, if we critically assess the assumptions behind both positions, it is clear that these camps are more similar than they are different. As I have argued, they both assume a criminal justice regime for adjudicating reproductive issues (although they may differ as to which women should be subjected to this regime). Neither position endows women with inherent rights to their bodies. The pro-life position pits fetal rights against women's rights, whereas the pro-choice position argues that women should have the freedom to make choices, rather than having inherent rights over their bodies regardless of their class standing. They both support positions that reinforce racial and gender hierarchies that marginalize indigenous women and women of color. The pro-life position supports a criminalization approach that depends on a racist political system that will necessarily impact poor women and women of color, who are less likely to have alternative strategies for addressing unwanted pregnancies. Meanwhile, the pro-choice position often supports population control policies and the development of dangerous contraceptives that are generally targeted in communities of color. And both positions fail to question the system of capitalism; they focus solely on the decision of whether or not a woman should have an abortion without addressing the economic, political, and social conditions that put her in this position in the first place.

So perhaps there is room to develop a framework that does not rest on a pro-choice versus pro-life framework. Such a strategy would enable us to fight for reproductive justice as part of a larger social justice strategy. It would also free us to think more creatively about who we could work with in coalition while allowing us to hold those who claim to be our allies more accountable for the positions they take.

To be successful in this venture, however, it is not sufficient to simply articulate an independent reproductive justice agenda; we would also have to develop a nationally coordinated reproductive justice movement. While there are many reproductive organizations for women of color, relatively few focus on bringing new women of color into the movement and training them to organize on their own behalf. To the extent that these groups exist, they are not generally coordinated with national mobilization efforts. Rather, national work is generally done on an advocacy level with heads of women of color organizations advocating for policy changes but often working without a solid base to back their demands (Silliman et al. 2005). Consequently, women of color organizations are not always in a strong position to negotiate with power brokers and mainstream pro-choice organizations or to hold them accountable. As an example, many women of color groups mobilized to attend the 2004 March for Women's Lives in Washington, D.C., in order to expand the focus of the march from a narrow pro-choice abortion rights agenda to a broad-based reproductive rights agenda. While this broader agenda was reflected in the march, it was co-opted by the pro-choice paradigm in the media coverage of the march. My survey of the major newspaper coverage of the march indicates that virtually no newspaper described the march as anything other than a pro-choice, abortion rights rally.[26] To quote the New Orleans health activist Barbara Major, "When you go to power without a base, your demand becomes a request."[27] Such base-building work, which many women of color organizations are beginning to focus on, is very slow and may not show results for a long time. After all, the base-building work of the Christian Right did not become publicly visible for fifty years (Diamond 1989). But this may be a historical moment in which a refusal to take part in a coalition could be a wise move because it might afford Native and other women of color the space in which to devote their resources to developing a strong movement that would later have the power to transform the mainstream pro-choice and pro-life movements.

In rethinking alliance politics within these movements, it is important to note that, as Clyde Wilcox's study on the Christian Right and the pro-life movement demonstrates, these movements are not overlapping and the pro-life movement is much more moderate on issues such as "foreign policy, spending on social welfare, other women's issues and gender equality, [and] minority issues" (Wilcox and Gomez 1990, 386). And even within the Christian Right pro-life movement there have been some

[26] The papers surveyed that focused solely on abortion rights include: the *Baltimore Sun* (Gibson 2004); *Chicago Daily Herald* (Ryan 2004); *Chicago Sun-Times* (Sweeney 2004); *Cleveland Plain Dealer* (Diemer 2004); *Columbus Dispatch* (Riskind 2004); *Connecticut Post* ("Abortion-Rights Marchers Crowd D.C." 2004); *Dayton Daily News* (Dart 2004, Wynn 2004); *Madison Capital Times* (Segars 2004); *Marin Independent Journal* ("Marchers Say Bush Policies Harm Women" 2004); *Memphis Commercial Appeal* (Wolfe 2004); *Milwaukee Journal-Sentinel* (Madigan 2004); *Minneapolis Star Tribune* (O'Rourke 2004); *New York Newsday* (Phelps 2004); *New York Times* (Toner 2004); *North Jersey Record* (Varoqua 2004); *Richmond Times Dispatch* (T. Smith 2004); *Salt Lake City Tribune* (Stephenson 2004); *San Francisco Chronicle* (Marinucci 2004); and *Syracuse Post Standard* (Gadoua 2004). The coverage of "other" issues in a few papers was limited to "The concerns they voiced extended beyond the issues of abortion to health care access, aids prevention, birth control and civil rights" in the *Los Angeles Times* (Marinucci 2004); "Another group flashed signs calling for the government to recognize same-sex marriage" in the *Houston Chronicle* (Black 2004); "Various tents and vendors on the Mall also promoted other political causes, including welfare, the Falun Gong movement in China, homosexual 'marriage,' the socialist movement, environmentalism, and striking Utah coal miners" in the *Atlanta Journal-Constitution* (Dart and Pickel 2004); and "'This morning I was saying that I was mainly here for abortion,' said Gresh, reflecting on the march. 'But now, going through this, I realize that there are so many issues. Equal pay is a big issue. And globalization, and women's rights around the world'" in the *Pittsburgh Post-Gazette* (Belser 2004).

[27] Keynote address, National Women's Studies Association National conference, New Orleans, June 2003.

writings that make some moves in the direction of rethinking pro-choice and pro-life alliances. For instance, Democrats for Life of America (DLA) drafted the 95–10 initiative, whose aim is to reduce abortions in the United States by 95 percent in ten years. This initiative does *not* call for the criminalizaton of abortion. Rather it calls for federal funding for a toll-free number in each state that would direct women to nonprofit adoption centers to help them carry babies to term, as well as funding for pregnancy prevention, which could include condoms. It is interesting that these specific agenda items are more closely aligned with the platforms pro-choice groups claim to support (NARAL, for instance, says it supports increased contraceptive availability, does not support the criminalization of abortion, and wants to make "abortion less necessary," presumably by making other options available to women who want them).[28] Meanwhile, many Christian Right pro-life groups do not support condom distribution, do support the criminalization of abortion, and often do not support Democratic Party initiatives. Yet the initiative received no comment from NARAL or Planned Parenthood, though it did receive an endorsement and/or support from CareNet, a nationwide network of pregnancy centers, and Americans United for Life. In fact, Peter Samuelson, of Americans United for Life, said, "I do think it will help them [Democrats] at the ballot box, but I'm far more pro-life than Republican" (Bergin 2005d, 25). Even *World* presented this initiative in a positive light. At the same time, we see increasing numbers of evangelicals, particularly people of color, calling for the pro-life movement to be less single-issue oriented and to adopt a broader social justice framework. James Meeks, for instance, pastor of one of the largest black churches in Chicago and a member of Operation Push, says, "Evangelicals must be very careful not to be irrelevant. . . . Evangelicals will grab . . . one issue—like abortion—and they think that because they take a tough stand on abortion then they have addressed a societal ill. I don't hear the same outcry from any evangelical pulpit about the unequal funding for education among the haves and the have-nots" (Smietana 2004, 35). And *Christianity Today* ran an op-ed piece in which Frederica Matthews-Green suggested that the pro-life movement should back away from its current emphasis on criminalization: "Since there is no present opportunity to make abortion illegal anyway, when the topic does come up, let's avoid the temptation to let the conversation get hijacked into a polarizing discussion that offers no prac-

[28] This was the rhetoric used by national NARAL at the 1994 strategy session it held with its state affiliates.

tical application" (1998). It ran another article that tried to seek common ground between pro-life and pro-choice camps (Monroe 2004, 46). And Elinor Burkett documents a sector of Christian Right women coming out of the militia movement who broke with the traditional pro-life stance precisely on the grounds of criminalization. Criminalization invites more government interference in one's life, echoing the Christian Right's suspicion of the state described in chapter 1 (1998, 118). These trends suggest that it *could* be possible to mobilize pro-life constituencies through a platform that makes abortion less necessary through a social justice platform rather than criminalization. Such has been my experience in doing grassroots organizing around reproductive justice issues; when I framed the issue around criminalization instead of "choice versus life," I was able to work with people across the so-called pro-life to pro-choice continuum.

CONCLUSION

In assessing the practices of developing unlikely alliances, the ethics behind these practices, and the possibilities of developing alliances in the future, a number of questions arise. First, when to coalesce or not to coalesce? Second, how do groups mediate between two polarized tendencies, (1) to organize around a politics of purity in which groups coalesce with people in which they are in complete ideological agreement or (2) to coalesce with anyone under any circumstance, often resulting in co-optation of one's work that serves a political agenda that may be antithetical to one's goals? On the one hand, to develop effective movements for social change, we have to forego the "politics of purity" to develop a movement based on strategic political alliances. Many groups on the "Left" or identity-based movements have often refused to ally themselves with groups that do not share their identity or their proper political ideology. This isolationist tendency undermines the ability of progressive organizations and communities to develop a mass movement for social change (Gitlin 1994). In light of the economic power wielded by multinational capitalism, the only thing those committed to social change could potentially have on their side is numbers of people all fighting for social justice. To develop a mass movement that could change the current state of affairs, it is necessary to realize that the majority of the world's population (even white, middle-class men) do not benefit *in the long term* from the current social, economic, and political arrangements. Most people do not have control over their lives and live at the whim of decisions made by people who they cannot even identify in the corporate world (Marcuse 1972). The key to developing a mass movement is to convince people to exchange their pursuit of short-term interests (such as maintenance of their white-skinned, economic status or gender privileges) for their long-term interest in creating a world based on social equality and justice for all.

On the other hand, how do progressives develop alliances without fear of co-optation, particularly when the unlikely allies might have much more power than progressives do? Within both evangelical and Native organizing circles, the issue of political marginalization is often central to how one chooses to develop alliances. For instance, we saw that members of one strand of evangelical feminism responded to their marginalization within evangelical circles by eschewing coalitions with secular or liberal Christian feminists, which they feared might further their marginalization within evangelicalism. By contrast, one reason asserted by some Native women as to why they were willing to take on the issue of sexism within Native organizing was their perception that they "were doing all the work anyway," and hence they felt they could call Native organizing to account from a position based on power. At the same time, some Native women have refused to enter into coalitions with mainstream feminist and environmental groups when they did not feel they were in a sufficiently powerful position to shift the agenda. Ralph Reed speaks compellingly to this issue, contending that groups on both the Left and the Right often wanted to circumvent the long road to influence and power by avoiding the grassroots organizing necessary to develop an independent power base in favor of what Brooklyn-based Sista II Sista activist Paula Rojas calls "smoke and mirrors" organizing, that is, work that is based on simulating the illusion of power (such as networking with governmental and corporate leaders, organizing national events, or setting up nonprofits that have no constituency) rather than actually building power (Rojas 2007). Says Reed, "I felt, just as a matter of political strategy, that the religious conservative movement had always gotten it backwards. It always tried to leap-frog over the preliminary steps to political influence with one long bomb: trying to win the White House. But if you win the White House and you can't control anything underneath it, it can be a Pyrrhic victory, as we discovered with Reagan, and as the left is discovering with Clinton" (Martin 1996, 304).

In order to build this power, it becomes necessary to articulate a political vision from which to organize. While many groups on the Left organize *against* something, as we saw in chapter 1, the Christian Right is actually fighting for something, a world based on biblical principles (even though its members might disagree as to how these principles might manifest themselves). Certainly, if a movement has a clear vision of the world it wants to create, it would also seem less likely that it can be co-opted by another movement. One problem we have seen with the Christian Right, is that this vision, in all its manifestations, is a heteronormative vision that is not really capable of challenging social inequity since the building block of its vision is a hierarchically constituted nuclear family based on a gender binary system. Unfortunately, many national or racial liberation struggles have explicitly or implicitly adopted this same vision, contending that what will liberate communities of color is a strong, male-headed household that does not tolerate gender nonconformity. Thus, in chapter 5 I will look to alternative visions for the world that challenge this model within Native women organizers' visions of sovereignty.

5

Native Women and Sovereignty

Beyond the Nation-State

If many of the unlikely alliances have been carved out of a heterornorma-
tive politic, what is the alternative to this framework? This chapter explores alternatives articulated by Native women. It becomes clear that
Native feminisms do not just intervene in the sexism in Native organizing
or the racism and colonialism in feminist movements; they also challenge
the framework of liberation itself by recasting how we understand nation,
sovereignty, and nationalist struggle. In doing so, Native feminisms reshape the manner in which we might build movements and coalitions for
social change. As Mililani Trask argues:

> One of the political dialogues that Indigenous women tend to be excluded
> from, not only by the larger white society but many times by the patriarchs
> of our own culture, is the dialogue on self-determination, the basic debate
> on sovereignty and setting the agenda for the Nation. . . . Women need to be
> part of this dialogue. Women need to be concerned with the political status
> of themselves and their children. This means rising up and participating not
> only in political struggles and issues that confront the state and the federal
> government of the United States but it also calls us to participate in our own
> communities when we are organizing with our own government or with
> tribal governments. (n.d., 23)

In these "postcolonial" times, terms such as *sovereignty* and *nation* have
gone out of fashion within the contexts of cultural studies, postcolonial
theory, and so on. Nationalism and sovereignty, it is suggested, inevitably
lead to xenophobia, intolerance, factionalism, and violence. All sovereignty struggles, it seems, are headed down that slippery slope toward the

ethnic cleansing witnessed in Bosnia (Calhoun 1994a; Holloway 2005; Kennedy 1995; Scheff 1994; Wiley 1994). Post 9/11, Bush's evocation of sovereignty prompts theorists to reduce sovereignty to "providing legitimacy of the rule of law and offering a guarantor for the presentational claims of state power" (Butler 2004, 52). According to Judith Butler, the resurgence of sovereignty happens in a content of "suspension of law" (2004, 55) whereby the nation can, in the name of sovereignty, act against "existing legal frameworks, civil, military, and international. . . . Under this mantle of sovereignty, the state proceeds to extend its own power to imprison indefinitely a group of people without trial" (57). Of course, as the legal scholar Sora Han points out, none of these post-9/11 practices are extraconstitutional or extralegal. In fact, the U.S. Constitution confers the right of the state to maintain itself over and above the rights of its citizenry (Han 2006). Butler's analysis is predicated on what David Kazanjian refers to as the "colonizing trick"—the liberal myth that the United States was founded on democratic principles that have been eroded through post-9/11 policies rather than a state built on the pillars of capitalism, colonialism, and white supremacy (2003). Certainly, Native American studies should provide a critical intervention in this discourse because the United States could not exist without the genocide of Native peoples. Genocide is not a mistake or aberration of U.S. democracy; it is foundational to it (A. Smith 2005b). As Sandy Grande states:

> The United States is a nation defined by its original sin: the genocide of American Indians. . . . American Indian tribes are viewed as an inherent threat to the nation, poised to expose the great lies of U.S. democracy: that we are a nation of laws and not random power; that we are guided by reason and not faith; that we are governed by representation and not executive order; and finally, that we stand as a self-determined citizenry and not a kingdom of blood or aristocracy. . . . From the perspective of American Indians, "democracy" has been wielded with impunity as the first and most virulent weapon of mass destruction. (2004, 31–32)

The political imperative that seems to derive from this Butlerian analysis of sovereignty is that coalition politics would seem to be at odds with nationalist politics or a political vision based on sovereignty. Conveniently, academics who live in countries that are not being colonized, and are thus able to exercise sovereignty, suddenly decided that the nations that continue to be colonized, and from whose colonization they continue to benefit—for example, indigenous nations—should give up their claims to nationhood and sovereignty. It is important to consider the perspectives of indigenous peoples, particularly indigenous women, who have the most at stake in these debates. In particular, how do Native women shape a "nationalist" politics from a coalitional framework? Underpinning these "feminist" articulations of sovereignty is a critical interrogation of what a nation is. Who is included in a nation? And how can a political vision of nationhood and sovereignty be disarticulated from a nationalist struggle that seeks a nation-state as its goal?[1] These questions provide the basis for a prolineal genealogy of sovereignty: a history of the future of sovereignty, what sovereignty *could mean* for Native peoples.

Gender analysis also contributes to a reshaping of sovereignty politics beyond a heteronormative framework. As discussed in chapter 3, what are we to make of comments that say, let us not worry about domestic violence. Let us worry about survival issues first? When we call into question who is actually considered part of the nation, it forces us to consider how are we conceptualizing the nation in the first place.

The Mohawk scholar Taiaike Alfred contends that, while the term *sovereignty* is popular among Native scholars and activists, it is an inappropriate term to use to describe the political, spiritual, and cultural aspirations of Native peoples. He contends that sovereignty is premised on the ability to exercise power through the state by means of coercion and domination. Traditional forms of indigenous governance, by contrast, are based on different understandings of power.

> The Native concept of governance is based on . . . the "primacy of conscience." There is no central or coercive authority and decision-making is collective. Leaders rely on their persuasive abilities to achieve a consensus that respects the autonomy of individuals, each of whom is free to dissent from and remain unaffected by the collective decision. . . .
>
> A crucial feature of the indigenous concept of governance is its respect for individual autonomy. This respect precludes the notion of "sovereignty" —the idea that there can be a permanent transference of power or authority from the individual to an abstraction of the collective called "government." . . .
>
> In the indigenous tradition . . . there is no coercion, only the compelling force of conscience based on those inherited and collectively refined principles that structure the society. (1999, 25)

As long as indigenous peoples frame their struggles in terms of sovereignty, Alfred argues, they will inevitably find themselves co-opted by the

---

[1] See Audra Simpson's critical intervention in this discussion (2003).

state—reproducing forms of governance based on oppressive, Western forms. In addition, the concept of sovereignty continues to affirm the legitimacy of the state: "To frame the struggle to achieve justice in terms of indigenous 'claims' against the state is implicitly to accept the fiction of state sovereignty" (1999, 57). He generally juxtaposes *nationhood* and *nationalism* as terms preferable to *sovereignty*, arguing that sovereignty "is an exclusionary concept rooted in an adversarial and coercive Western notion of power" (59). It is "with indigenous notions of power such as these that contemporary Native nationalism seeks to replace the dividing, alienating, and exploitative notions, based on fear, that drive politics inside and outside Native communities today" (53).[2]

The work of the literary scholar Craig Womack (a Muscogee) challenges non-Native scholars who dismiss "nationalism" and "nationhood" as concepts based on political exclusion. Unlike Alfred, he affirms the importance of the term *sovereignty*. He contends that Native nationalism and sovereignty are not fixed, static concepts but are dynamic and fluid. He further contends that imagining sovereignty and nationalism outside of the narrow realm of political science enables Native peoples to imagine a flexible notion of the nation.

> Sovereignty, it seems to me, like the oral tradition, is an ongoing, dynamic process, rather than a fixed creed, and evolves according to the changing needs of the nation. This "unfixing" of the idea of nationhood is needed to avoid some of the problems that . . . postcolonial writers discuss regarding the problem of the emergent nation simply becoming a "colored" version of the old oppression. . . . The concept of nationhood itself is an intermingling of politics, imagination, and spirituality. Nationhood is affected by imagination in the way that the citizens of tribal nations perceive their cultural and political identity. Nationhood recognizes spiritual practices, since culture is part of what gives people an understanding of their uniqueness, their difference, from other nations of people. . . .
>
> Extending the discussion of sovereignty beyond the legal realm to include the literary realm opens up the oral traditions to be read contemporary by tribal nations so that definitions of sovereignty, which come from the oral

---

[2] Alfred's follow up work, *Wasase*, has come out during the publication of this book. *Wasase* brilliantly expands his theorization of indigenous nationhood within the context of global multinational capitalism and deserves close study (Alfred 2005). Emerging Dene scholar, Glen Coulthard (University of Victoria), will also soon be publishing critical interventions into how we can reconceptualize indigenous sovereignty and nationhood.

tradition, might be used as a model for building nation in a way that revises, modifies, or rejects, rather than accepts as a model the European and American nation. (1999, 60)

Influenced by Womack's work, I was equally eager to reclaim the term *nationalism*. I was struck, however, by the extent to which the term either had no meaning or had a negative connotation for most of the interviewees. When so many people were saying "I've never heard it used in Indian country in my life. I've never heard that used" (Sheehy), I began to wonder if I was guilty of Mujerista theologian Ada Maria Isasi-Diaz's charge of answering questions that those at the grass roots were not asking (1993, 63). *Sovereignty*, by contrast, seems to be the term of preference to express indigenous peoples' political vision.

For many activists, *nationalism* has negative connotations, even when describing oneself as a nationalist in relation to one's indigenous nation. As Alfonso and Toineeta contend:

Alfonso: Nationalism to me is a brainwash identity. You're part of the gang, and here's our mantra. Sovereignty is about choice. People have the right to make choices for themselves for their destiny and what's important to them in life, and their values can be acted out. If it's just nationalism . . . someone else gets to rule the culture and then we all have to learn the mantra. That's what my initial reaction is.

Toineeta: *Sovereignty* means, it takes in all the things like self-determination and all these political things, but it really means total and absolute independence for that nation so they can be self-determinate and they can live the way they want to in that area where they live. And they have the total freedom to do that.

Nationalism is something else. To me, nationalism is saying, our way is the only right way. . . . I'm a nationalist. I think that the only right way *is* our way. That other people are sadly lacking, and their life is not really fulfilled because they have a different way. And to the point that's been told to me over and over and over, that the *Sioux* way of life is the only way. I'm trying to work on that. . . .

I think a real true sovereignty is a real, true acceptance of who and what's around you. And the nationalist doesn't accept all that. . . . Like me, down deep inside I know that all people, *all* people, could learn from the Lakota way. But I'm not going to run around saying that like I used to because I don't want the whole world mad at me again. . . . Sovereignty is what you do and what you are to your own people within your own confines, but there is a realization and acceptance that there are others who are around you.

And that happened even before the Europeans came; we knew about other
Indians. We had alliances with some and fights with others. Part of that
sovereignty was that acceptance that they were there.

Similarly, Wilson distinguishes her understanding of nationalism from
an indigenous nationalism that would set one's nation apart from other
nations.

My definition [of *nationalism*], I guess, that would mean my nation. I don't
like to set my nation apart from other Native nations. You know it's different
here [in my home community]. People kind of think differently about other
Indians. I don't know, maybe I'm just doing this ostrich thing, but it seemed
to me like when I was in the city people were more like Indians are Indians,
and if you're tall, short, Ojibwe, or Cherokee, you know, it was just a description, it wasn't necessarily something you were in conflict with. I'm sure
there was that kind of thing, but not as much. Here it's kind of weird to me
because people sort of set themselves apart from other tribes, and I think
that's odd. There's this one woman who's very educated herself, and she's a
smart person. I was talking, well, it was when they massacred some of those
people in Brazil, and she was just like, "I'm not real interested in that." So
then we started talking about THAT, and she said, "That's not about Ho-
Chunks. And besides Ho-Chunks are the most oppressed people." And that
just blew me away. People are being hunted down like animals in South
America today as we speak, and you can say that? What are you thinking?!
This diminishes all of us when something like that happens. It so startled me
that any Native person could not have sympathy or want to help them in
their situation. I guess that I never thought it was a Native value to be
indifferent to some of our people. But apparently she's not thinking of them
as "our people."

While they disagree with Womack's use of the term *nationalism*, in a
sense the manner in which these activists juxtapose sovereignty positively and nationalism negatively actually confirms Womack's point that
Native activists are able to propound a national identity that is not necessarily based on exclusion and intolerance of those who are not part of the
nation.

Whereas Alfred sees sovereignty as inherently premised on Western notions of the nation-state, which in turn are based on governance through
domination and coercion, Native women's theorists seem to define sovereignty much differently, more akin to how Alfred defines nationhood.
The activists frequently asserted that sovereignty is not a European con-

cept. States Sharon Venne, "Sovereignty is not a foreign concept brought by the colonizers to Indigenous America. We are born as sovereign beings. Our struggle as sovereign peoples is to live the laws of the Creation. . . . Our Elders and leadership never sold any lands at the time of the treaty. We could never sell, surrender or cede our lands to the colonizers. These lands and territories were given to us by the Creator. The land makes us. We do not make the land. To sell or give up the lands is to give up ourselves" (1999, 27).[3]

It is not fundamentally based on rule of law but on kinship interrelatedness. As Crystal Ecohawk (a Pawnee) states, "Sovereignty is an active, living process within this knot of human, material and spiritual relationships bound together by mutual responsibilities and obligations. From that knot of relationships is born our histories, our identity, the traditional ways in which we govern ourselves, our beliefs, our relationship to the land, and how we feed, clothe, house and take care of our families, communities and Nations" (1999, 21).[4] This interconnectedness exists not only among the nation's members but in all creation—human and nonhuman. Ingrid Washinawatok writes, "Our spirituality and our responsibilities define our duties. We understand the concept of sovereignty as woven through a fabric that encompasses our spirituality and responsibility. This is a cyclical view of sovereignty, incorporating it into our traditional philosophy and view of our responsibilities. There it differs greatly from the concept of western sovereignty which is based upon absolute power. For us absolute power is in the Creator and the natural order of all living things; not only in human beings. . . . Our sovereignty is related to our connections to the earth and is inherent" (1995b, 12).[5]

This approach to sovereignty coincides with a critique of Western no-

[3] See also Womack, who writes, "Sovereignty is inherent as an intellectual idea in Native cultures, a political practice, and a theme of oral traditions; and the concept, as well as the practice, predates European contact" (1999, 51). The Indigenous Women's Network Emerging Leadership Program affirms in its statement on sovereignty, "Sovereignty is an inherent right given to us by the Creator. It is our right to be full human beings and to collectively determine our destinies. The right to self-determine was bestowed by the Creator and not the United Nations" (Sovereignty 1999).

[4] Ingrid Washinawatok (Menominee) writes, "While sovereignty is alive and invested in the reality of every living thing for Native folks, Europeans relegated sovereignty to only one realm of life and existence: authority, supremacy and dominion. In the Indigenous realm, sovereignty encompasses responsibility, reciprocity, the land, life and much more" (1999b, 23).

[5] See also Venne 1999; and White Hat 1999.

tions of property. Monture-Angus notes that indigenous nationhood is not based on control over territory or land but on a relationship with and responsibility for land.

> Although Aboriginal Peoples maintain a close relationship with the land . . . it is not about control of the land. . . . Earth is mother and she nurtures us all . . . it is the human race that is dependent on the earth and not vice versa. . . . Sovereignty, when defined as my right to be responsible . . . requires a relationship with territory (and not a relationship based on control of that territory). . . . What must be understood then is that [the] Aboriginal request to have our sovereignty respected is really a request to be responsible. I do not know of anywhere else in history where a group of people have had to fight so hard just to be responsible. (1999, 125, 36)

Thus, like Kingfisher's definition of Native feminism, sovereignty is often articulated as being fundamentally based on responsibilities more than rights. It is also articulated as an open concept that suggests that a nation cannot be completely insular but must position itself in a good way with the rest of the world. It is interesting to me, for instance, how often non-Indians presume that if Native people regained their land bases they would necessarily call for the expulsion of non-Indians from them. It is striking that a much more inclusive vision of sovereignty is articulated by Native women activists. For instance, Milton describes what can be seen as a possible vision of sovereignty (although she does not necessarily describe this vision as sovereignty): "This beautiful world where all the people came over to the states, and we were cool with them, we let them live on our land, but they understand the natural laws. Imagine how different the U.S. would be if everybody respected our natural laws and our territories. Everything would be a lot of different." Harden describes how indigenous sovereignty is based on freedom for all peoples.

> Harden: It goes back to what I said about if it doesn't work for one of us it doesn't work for any of us . . . going back to when I first learned the definition of sovereignty, when we'd say, none of us are free unless all of us are free.
>
> Me: Does that include non-Native peoples?
>
> Harden: Yes, for me it does. Because we're all in this together. We can't, we won't, turn anyone away. We've been there. That's what I learned in doing this work. I would hear stories about the Japanese internment camps or the binding of the feet . . . and I could relate to it because it happened to us. Or with the Jews, or with white people and amnesia, being totally cut

off from your root. All those stories, Africans with the violence and rape, we've been there too. So how could we ever leave anyone behind?

A subject of major contention is how these visions of sovereignty relate to the current political context. In particular, how do Native women activists position themselves and their nations vis-à-vis the U.S. government? This is one of the contradictions faced by Native nations with a particular legal status that renders them "domestic dependent nations" in the eyes of the U.S. government. This gives them some measure of self-administration but at the same time leaves them subject to the congressional plenary power to abrogate the terms of the relationships at any time. As Alfred rightly points out, understandings of sovereignty often accede to this limited notion of it, as can be seen in Susan Williams and M. Kathryn Hoover's description of sovereignty: "The relationship that the United Status bears to Indian tribes has been defined as a "trust" relationship. As trustee, the United States is obligated to act in the best interest of tribes, even to the extent of putting tribal interests before those of the United States. However, the United States also has plenary or broad powers over the relationship of the federal government to Indian tribes which includes the ultimate power to terminate the federal/tribal relationship. There is an inherent tension in these positions" (1999, 31).

Regardless of how indigenous peoples may want to envision sovereignty, we must deal with the realities of the government and its treaty relations with tribal governments.

Frichner's response to this challenge, while not disputing the importance of treaties, is to argue that indigenous nations' understanding of the law cannot be defined by the United States or Canada.

Law was not introduced to the Haudenosaunee by the Europeans. Some scholars argue that concepts of nationhood, sovereignty and treaty making were European inventions that were introduced to the Haudenosaunee. We soundly reject such notions as paternalistic. . . . We do not believe that the United States, England or Canada has ever had plenary power over us. The Haudenosaunee have never consented to be subjects of these foreign governments. The Haudenosaunee have never been defeated in war nor surrendered to England, the United States or Canada. Therefore, they cannot claim, by right of conquest, that the Haudenosaunee are subject to their law. (1999, 34–35)

Often these tensions in articulating the relationship between indigenous peoples and the United States manifest themselves in the debates in

Indian country over whether or not to consider oneself a U.S. or Canadian citizen and hence whether or not to vote. Many activists do not consider themselves U.S. citizens, as indicated by these responses to the question "Do you consider yourself a U.S. citizen?"

> Rencountre: No, I don't. But I know everyone else does. "You have to be a U.S. citizen because you live in the United States." . . . I was born a Dakota. And if I follow the Dakota ways I'll find the answers for why I'm here. But if I think I'm under the United States—I don't know the laws the God gave the United States, the sacred laws you're supposed to follow—I'll be confused and out of balance.

> Frichner: I can't judge other people who say, I'm an American citizen but I'm also a citizen of my Native nation. It's not my responsibility to judge. If that's how they feel, that's their prerogative, and I respect that.

> But where I'm from the focus is on your nationhood. If you travel on a Haudenosaunee passport, which I do, there's a lot of responsibility attached to that. You're very careful about how you act and what you say because you're accountable to the people who counted on you to act properly when they issued you that passport. So for me the experience is very personal and very strong, and for others it may not be.

Others consider themselves dual citizens, though all seem to prioritize tribal over U.S. citizenship. Sheehy argues that, however indigenous peoples define themselves, the fact that the U.S. government defines them as citizens continues to impact their lives.

> When I graduated from college recently, they said, "If you are a U.S citizen or . . . a member of another country, please identify that country if you have a flag." So I put "other"; I said "I'm a member of the Blackfeet nation, and yes, we have a flag." . . . A week and a half before graduation, my strategic management leadership class instructor called me and said, "I've been instructed to tell you that you cannot bring a Blackfeet flag to graduation." I said, "Really, why?" "Because you're not a member of the United Nations." . . . I thought about a lot of things because I realized that it doesn't matter what I consider myself, that mainstream society will dictate whether I am and how that applies to me. So it doesn't matter what I think. So I'm still first and foremost a Blackfeet woman. According to the law, I'm a U.S. citizen. But by self-identification I'm from the Blackfeet nation.

The issue of voting is similarly contentious. At a 2001 Indigenous Women's Network gathering, a lively debate ensued on the topic of whether or not Native peoples should vote in U.S. elections. Members of the Mohawk nation argued that it is a contradiction to vote in another nation's election and claim to truly be a member of your nation. The extent to which you vote is the extent to which you really do not see yourself as sovereign. They based their rationale on the Two Row Wampum Belt, as Frichner explains.

> [It] comes from some teachings that happened a very long time ago when our people actually made an agreement with the Dutch, and it was memorialized in something called the Two Row Wampum Belt. The wampum belt itself is very beautiful, and the wampum is all white and has these two dark strips running parallel through it. This belt represents the agreement, which says that you [the Dutch] will stay in your boat, and we will stay in our canoe. We will travel along the river of life in peace and friendship. But our boats will not cross over. You will keep your way of life; we will keep our way of life. Our lifeways, our laws, and our traditions will be separate, but we will live in peace. We will respect each other while going down this river of life. . . . And still today we have the understanding that we don't cross over in the river of life. We respect others, but we stay in our boat. We can't go along the river of life with one foot in a boat and one foot in a canoe. It just doesn't work that way.

VanVlack echoes this sentiment, stating, "This is our land. We never gave that up. We're still nations as defined by the UN. We can still consider ourselves nations. So as that, why would I try to be a Democrat or Republican or liberal when I have my own nation to stand for?"

Mililani Trask, by contrast, suggested at this Indigenous Women's Network gathering that voting in another election is an act of political subversion rather than acquiescence. She argued that the problem with the Two Row Wampum metaphor is that the captain of the U.S. boat is not swimming parallel to the indigenous canoes but is trying to ram our canoes. It is a matter of survival, she argues, that we take out their captain by any means necessary. But, Sheehy argues, voting in the U.S. elections, even as a matter of political subversion, can alter Native peoples' perceptions of themselves as members of sovereign nations. "Everything I check says U.S. citizen," she notes, "and after awhile you begin to believe it." These contradictions continue to manifest themselves in our politics. As Wilson confides, "You know I go and vote sometimes, and I think what did I do that for? . . . No, I guess I don't consider myself a United States citizen. But we're inside their borders, and when we have to step off our land we have to obey their laws. Maybe not the spirit of them but just because we might get caught."

In addition to these tensions, there is the contradiction that comes from having been colonized by the United States and at the same time enjoying some privileges and benefits as a result of it, especially compared to the situation in some other countries. For instance, much of the United Nations work around indigenous peoples takes place in either Geneva or New York. While indigenous peoples in the United States can travel almost anywhere, indigenous peoples in other parts of the world have a much easier time getting into Geneva than into the United States. Consequently, some activists identify as U.S. citizens in terms of the need to be accountable for the privileges they feel they accrue from living within the borders of the United States, despite the colonial relationship that exists between them and the U.S. government. That is, by virtue of living within the political geography of the United States, they see themselves as accruing benefits from U.S. policies that are maintained at the expense of the rest of the world. Claiming citizenship has less to do with allegiance to the United States than with acknowledging and claiming responsibility for these privileges. This sentiment is reflected in Harden's and Ross's accounts of why they call themselves U.S. citizens.

> Harden: Yeah, I don't support this government, but I do reap benefits from it. I think of that because I'm also responsible for what's happening in the Middle East. I'm responsible for what we're doing to Cuba, what we're doing to Colombia. I can't sit back and blame somebody else for that. We do participate in this system. Not by choice, and most Indian people will say, "I never chose this." But I'm still living here. I'm still getting the education they've given us. Yes, we don't have a choice in a lot of it; we're here. It's like white people living in the Black Hills who say, I didn't murder the Indians a hundred years ago. . . . They're still living in our Black Hills. There's something they can do. There's something we can do. If nothing else but educate people about it and make people aware of it and encourage people to have [an] unplug America day or whatever I can do to bring it to peoples' attention that we're not deaf and mute about things. So, yes, in my opinion, I benefit from this government, and I live here. When I go to other countries, I'm seen as an American.
>
> Ross: I definitely see myself as a member of the confederated Salish and Kootenai nations first, and then . . . well actually way down the line, but I always feel that since I'm out here enjoying the "benefits," like a big paycheck, that I should claim U.S. citizenship.

Wilson and Star take Native peoples to task for disclaiming their allegiance to the United States and then uncritically supporting U.S. military policies.

Wilson: In fact, people run off to join the military. That's another thing that blew me away when I moved here [Black River Falls, Wisconsin] . . . all these people who worship the United States military. Ten years ago, the United States was all involved in Central America, and most of the people they were persecuting were Native people. The question in my mind was, were all these people willing to go down there in Central America and kill other Indians on behalf of the United States? Well, they went to Asia, and they killed Asian people who were fighting for their homeland on behalf of the United States. I think that's another manifestation of extremely internalized oppression. . . . Most of the men in my family have been in the military, and I was a person who goes out and protests every war. For me, it's always been (maybe it's the AIM influence), fight for your own people! What're you thinking?! It's really hard for me to make that logical.

Star: I think there are certain realities that in some ways we do benefit from U.S. policy. And I also think unfortunately many Native nations support U.S. policy. And if you support U.S. policy, whether you're located in the United States or not, I think you're absolutely accountable for those actions. Now I think, if a Native nation opposed U.S. policy and actively worked along a different agenda, I do think one can say that you wouldn't hold Spain accountable for something the U.S. did. I don't think you would be able to hold a Native nation accountable for something the U.S. did. But I just really think that, unfortunately, most Native nations are very, very supportive of U.S. policy and criticize the U.S. when the U.S. does not give funding to tribal governments, but does not criticize the U.S. when they go bomb a Third World nation. And that to me is really inexcusable, and in that sense I think absolutely Native nations must be held accountable for that U.S. policy. And that's why I think when we talk about defining sovereignty and such, I hear this all the time where different Native nations say, we don't want to vote in U.S. elections. And I think that's not really the big issue.

The big issue is, whose army are you fighting in? I don't hear that critique of fighting in the U.S. army too often. That to me is so incongruous. You generally don't fight for the government of a foreign nation. I do see people try and vote in other peoples' elections to try and change the political outlook, but you don't fight in their things. And then critique them! You send out all your young people to go fight for the U.S. government, and then you critique the U.S. that a significant percentage of your tribal population has just died supporting.

At the same time, the value of the "privileges" Native peoples receive in the United States because they live here is questionable, as Thomas argues. For one thing, not all indigenous peoples living within the borders of the United States and Canada travel under a U.S. or Canadian passport; they travel under their own nations' passports. And, as Thomas notes, many reservations are not geographically close to services and the people living there often do not have transportation to them. Life expectancy and other social indicators are lower for Native peoples than anyone else. She asks, "Is a mortality rate for forty-seven years average a benefit? . . . If an Indian woman who has got to work for a living to put pennies on her ass and food on the table, what's she supposed to [do]? Go to jail for not paying taxes? Would that be preferable?"

What this discussion suggests is that Native women's articulations call for developing a vision of sovereignty that does not see current tribal government structures as the political endpoint while still operating within the U.S. government system with all ambiguities that entails. Keeping these two struggles in tension is central, these theories suggest, because how can we measure the efficacy of our short-term political goals if we do not have a long-term political vision to measure it against? This long-term vision takes on a spiritual dimension as it provides a vision of nationhood that is based on connectedness and relationships with the rest of the world.

SPIRITUALITY AND SOVEREIGNTY

Religion is for those who are afraid of going to hell; spirituality is for those who have been there.—DOUG TROUTEN

In this era of George W. Bush's "faith-based politics," white-dominated progressive organizations often look particularly askance at attempts to combine spirituality and politics. The Native women activists I interviewed, by contrast, see spirituality as inextricably linked to their political activism.[6] As a consequence, the concept of sovereignty is often under-

[6] How these spiritual practices manifest themselves varies widely in the lives of Native women activists. Some see themselves as Christians, others as traditionals, others as neither. And many relate to a variety of traditions, from Judaism to Santeria to tribal traditions that are not their own. In a future project, it would be beneficial to analyze in further detail the complexities of the Native American re-

stood as a spiritual as well as a political concept. Mililani Trask argues that a spiritual foundation "is an important element of our constitution which begins with our definition of sovereignty. . . . Because a Nation that is spiritually bankrupt is not going to be able to stand up to fight for its rights and to support children and future generations. So the beginning of Nationhood, the beginning of sovereignty, and working for self-determination has to do with making right your path with the Creator, practicing our ceremony and your culture" (N.d., 24).

What seems to make sovereignty a spiritual concept for many activists is that sovereignty as a political and spiritual vision is the dream of living outside the constraints of both U.S. colonialism and multinational capitalism. Because sovereignty entails a vision that is beyond what we can see now, it is not necessarily something that can be clearly articulated. In that sense, it echoes a biblical passage frequently quoted in evangelicalism (Heb. 11:1): "Faith [or in this case sovereignty] is the substance of things hoped for, the evidence of things not seen." Star notes:

> I think in some ways, we've really lost vision of what it is, not only what the possibilities are, but even of how to dream again. And I remember because Lavina White, she had this statement one time, she was speaking to the Indigenous Women's Network, and she spoke at length about her experience as an Haida woman and having grown up in the traditions and then becoming very active in Canadian politics. And she looked at everybody, and she said, you all are fighting for sovereignty and you don't even know what sovereignty truly means. You think you do. You think doing international, or the United Nations, is sovereignty, and it's so limited. And . . . [not] until you really come back to the traditions and find out who and what we've always been and who we truly are will you really know what sovereignty means. . . . Everything is just really working within the system rather than transforming what does it really mean to be indigenous sovereign. And then how do we actually implement that? And I don't think we're thinking along those lines. And until we think along those lines I don't think we'll ever achieve it.

Thus, while it is easy to dismiss Native politics as narrowly nationalistic, it is clear that these visions of sovereignty go beyond concern for one's community and address concerns for the world at large. On one hand, Native nations often have to close themselves off because of the onslaught

---

ligious identity, which are often not addressed in religious studies' anthropological focus on Native religious traditions.

of New Agers, pharmaceutical companies, and a host of others who wish to market or appropriate indigenous cultures (Whitt 1998). But it is a mistake to always equate attempts to build cultural autonomy with political isolation. Many activists, such as Toineeta, make a distinction between political alliances and cultural autonomy and in fact suggest that the best way to achieve autonomy is *through* coalition.

> This family called someone in Minneapolis saying they needed help. A nine-year-old girl was walking home from school, and the policeman stopped her. And she was real trusting, and she got into the car with him, and he raped her. And he took her home and just sort of pushed her out of the car. So when the family found out about it and they started to raise a fuss, and they went to the police and complained about it, and they were told, "Well, that's part of your culture." . . . So those little incidents have an impact on me, and that's one of the things that made me really get protective of our culture and our spiritual values and what little bit we have left. It's hearing that woman say that the cops said having your daughters raped is part of your culture. I thought, people can't continue thinking that about us if that's what they think. And even if they don't think that they're able to use that as an excuse. And they just can't keep on doing that. I got really drawn more into the cultural thing. And I thought, we have to work it at that and stop letting other people in because that's how we lose [our traditions]. . . . And I know a lot of people disagree with me, that that is how we lose them. But that was the one incident that said to me, we really have to protect our culture. We have something nobody else in this country has, and we have to keep this.
>
> When you talk about coalitions or networking . . . it always go back to our small population. Politically, we have to become stronger, and the only way we're going to be stronger is if we have more numbers. . . . The only way we can have political power and get on the political agenda is to develop these coalitions and go to these people and say, this person is really bad, and we can't get a meeting, but you can. You can go in and bring us with you and talk to him and explain to them why they shouldn't be doing this. As hard as it is, with our own deep sense of pride, we have to, at least politically. We can isolate as much as we want culturally, but politically we need to build these coalitions with everybody. .

Toineeta's words echo Bernice Johnson Reagon's delineation between "coalitions" and "home." As Reagon argues, "You don't get fed a lot in a coalition. In a coalition you have to give, and it's different from your home. You can't stay there all the time. You go to the coalition for a few hours and then you go back and take your bottle wherever it is, and then you go back and coalesce some more" (Johnson Reagon 1983, 359). Thus, the precondition for being able to do effective coalition work is having a home, however that might be defined.

National liberation politics becomes less vulnerable to being co-opted by the Right when we base it on a model of liberation that fundamentally challenges right-wing conceptions of the nation. As I have argued elsewhere, to colonize peoples whose societies were not necessarily based on social hierarchy, colonizers must first naturalize hierarchy by instituting patriarchy (A. Smith 2005b). Patriarchy, in turn, rests on a gender binary system in which only two genders exist, one dominating the other. Consequently, Charles Colson *is* correct when he maintains that the current world order depends on heteronormativity (as discussed in chapter 1). Just as the patriarchs rule the family, so do the elites of the nation-state rule their citizens. Any liberation struggle that does not challenge heteronormativity cannot substantially challenge colonialism or white supremacy. Rather, as Cathy Cohen contends, such struggles will maintain colonialism based on a politics of secondary marginalization where the most elite class will further its aspirations on the backs of those most marginalized within the community (1999). Through this process of secondary marginalization, the national or racial justice struggle takes on, either implicitly or explicitly, a nation-state model as the endpoint of its struggle —a model of governance in which the elites govern the rest through violence and domination and exclude those who are not members of "the nation" (Hardt and Negri 2000; Holloway 2005).

However, as the articulations of Native women suggest, there are other models of nationhood we can envision, nations that are not based on exclusion and not based on secondary marginalization—nations that do not have the heteronormative, patriarchal, nuclear family as their building block. Indigenous sovereignty and nationhood, rather than constituting the antithesis of coalition and alliance building, can serve as a model for how it can be done.

Conclusion

This project has attempted to utilize Native American studies methodologies of recentering, rearticulation, and intellectual ethnography in order to focus on the intellectual contributions of social movement actors to inform both scholarly and activist analysis about social change. While this project makes no claims about what Christian Right or Native activists think in general, it has revealed the complexities of political and theological discourse within these communities. This generative narratology has pointed to *possibilities* for political intervention that could mobilize and create new alliances for social change. Whether or not progressives will seize on these opportunities, and if they do whether or not these interventions will work, remains to be seen. Nevertheless, it is my goal to develop an approach toward understanding social movements that can actually be used by social justice activists and might provide new ideas for future political work. In addition, by claiming my intellectual space as an interested party in these movements, as one who has been involved in both Native activism and evangelical Christianity, I hope to take part in legitimating scholar activism both inside and outside the academy.

Highlighting the theoretical contributions of Native women activists, which have generally been ignored by social movement analysis, is central because they highlight the instabilities of political configurations often deemed "conservative" or "progressive." The struggles Native peoples face in fighting for sovereignty, however that is envisioned, are instructive for all those interested in social justice. Native women's struggles against sexism within Native activist circles point to the importance of not romanticizing social struggles and of constantly interrogating how progressive movements often reinscribe the sexism, racism, and other forms of oppression they ostensibly try to resist. Similarly, when investigating the progressive possibilities in conservative political projects, such as those found in this project's case studies, one cannot ignore the dangers of trying to mobilize these possibilities into more progressive political projects. I have attempted to critically assess not only the possibilities but also the pitfalls of forging these new alliances.

At the same time, Native women's political theory and practice affirm the thesis of this project—that even in politically conservative movements and constituencies potentially progressive elements can and have been mobilized for progressive political projects. Because the numbers of Native peoples in the United States is small, Native activists can seldom be under the illusion that they can achieve political victories by themselves. It is equally the case that no community can change the system of domination and exploitation on which the political and economic relationships of the world are based. Consequently, progressives do not have the luxury to dismiss entire sectors of society as potential coalition partners. Despite the dangers, it is imperative that we not foreclose our political possibilities when we so critically need new allies in order to create mass-based movements for social change. The success Native groups have had in doing so across the country suggests that such possibilities are not mere pipe dreams but realizable goals. These successes also demonstrate that Native sovereignty struggles are not simply the politics of small "interest groups" but are instructive for all peoples interested in social justice. The marginalization of Native peoples within social movement scholarship and activism is detrimental to everyone.

These prolineal genealogies of feminism, coalition building, and sovereignty can assist in some of the recent intellectual projects that call on Native peoples to "indigenize" or "decolonize" the academy (Mihesuah 1998; Mihesuah and Wilson 2004; Wilson 2005). These projects are critically important and have created a space for Native scholars to interrogate their position in the academy. The theorizing of Native women organizers about their vision of sovereignty and social change contributes to this conversation by demonstrating that "decolonization" is a political practice that is rooted in building mass-based movements for social change (Wilson 2005). As Sandy Grande asserts, decolonization cannot be separated from a struggle against imperialism and capitalism (2004, 6). The implications of decolonization projects, then, are that those in the academy interested in decolonization need to be part of or develop relationships of accountability with movement-building work. In addition, if we contemplate these more radical visions of sovereignty as part of a long-term vision, we might ask whether or not the current academic industrial complex is part of a long-term vision of sovereignty. As Justine Smith's work suggests, the academy is based on a capitalist notion of knowledge that can be commodified and bought and sold in the academic marketplace (2005). If the academy functions as an "ideological state apparatus" (Althusser 1971) that supports the current capitalist and nation-state form of governance, and we see that there are other visions of sovereignty not rooted in the nation-state or capitalism, then can a decolonized educational system exist within the current academic industrial complex at all? Does tenuring more Native scholars necessarily contribute to a decolonized academy or does it serve to further retrench a colonial academic system by multiculturalizing it? Does our position in the academy help our communities or does it enable us to engage in a process of secondary marginalization that creates an elite class that can oppress and police the rest of the members of our communities? If we see the need for such global movements for social justice, what should be the relationship of Native American scholars to these movements? Are good intentions on the part of scholars good enough or do we need formal relationships of accountability to these movements? Can we further social change when currently our only formal relationships of accountability are to tenure committees and other groups that represent those in power with no corresponding relationship of accountability to those we claim to represent? These questions are not easily answered, but continued dialogue between those in Native American studies and Native peoples involved in social justice movements is critical if we do not want Native American studies to fall into the trap Elizabeth Povinelli describes of adding social difference to the multicultural academy without adding social consequence (Povinelli 2002).

As mentioned previously, the contributions of Native activists recasts current debates within Native studies about "who stole Native American studies" (Cook-Lynn 1997). Many Native scholars have argued that Native studies has been co-opted by broader discourses such as those of ethnic or postcolonial studies (Cook-Lynn 1997; Stevenson 1998b). What the theories produced by Native activists suggest is that Native studies (as well as ethnic and postcolonial studies) have been co-opted primarily because they are not accountable to the movements for sovereignty and social justice that forced the academy to accept them in the first place. When Native studies is cut off from its source of power—people power and movement building—it is easily "stolen" and assimilated into the capitalist logic of the academy. Without this power, Native studies is not in a position to define the terms of the debate within the academy because without a base our demands become requests.

The response to the marginalization of Native studies in the academy is to call for increased autonomy, though sometimes this call for autonomy can read as a call for political and intellectual isolation, which further marginalizes Native studies. Thus, Native studies stands to benefit from the theories produced by Native women activists who differentiate autonomy from isolation. They point to the fact that it is easier to achieve political autonomy through political and intellectual engagement with others because we can then build sufficient political power to defend sovereignty *and* transform intellectual and political discourse and engagement. In this process, indigenous struggles can become centered rather than marginalized. Native studies, when it is accountable to movements for social justice, can develop autonomous, though not isolated, intellectual projects that are transformative not only for Native peoples but for the world.

Thus, the theoretical contributions of Native women activists demonstrate their commitment to building movements that are liberatory for all peoples rather than a commitment to national chauvinism and insularity, of which Native peoples are often accused. Their ideas have significance not only for people in Native American studies but for all those in academia. As Julie Star argues, "You can't win a revolution on your own, and I think we are about nothing short of revolution. Anything else is simply not worth our time."

Appendix 1

A Brief Map of Christian Right and

Native American Organizing

To provide some context for this project, I offer a brief overview of Christian Right and Native American organizing.

Christian Right Organizing

There are many definitions of the Christian Right in circulation. For the purposes of this book, I define the Christian Right as evangelical Christians who tend toward conservative politics (although they may disagree about the extent to which they believe they should engage in politics at all). I use the term *Christian Right* loosely, understanding that many evangelicals support conservative politics while not necessarily identifying with the label Christian Right (Guth 1983; Christian Smith 2000, 122–24; Zwier 1982, 91). The reason I use a less precise definition is because my object of study is more a community of discourse than discrete communities. While such a definition may be too loose for a more quantitative study of the characteristics of these communities, it speaks to communities of people who are in conversation with each other, even if this conversation involves violent disagreement.

There are several works that provide an extensive map of Christian evangelicalism, which I will not repeat here (Carpenter 1997; Dayton 1991; Dobson 1985; Fackre 1989; Fea 1993; Nash 1987; Ockenga 1968; Trollinger 1985). By "evangelical," I mean Protestants who generally subscribe to the five fundamentals of faith that have served as rallying points for evangelicalism: biblical inerrancy, the deity of Christ, substitutionary atonement, bodily resurrection, and the second coming of Christ. This definition includes Pentecostals and groups that do not trace their roots to the fundamentalist-modernist debates of the 1920s. I do not include the more explicitly racist Christian movements such as Christian Identity groups.

Within this community of discourse, there are two prominent strands: fundamentalists and neo-evangelicals; and Pentecostals and Charismatics.[1] While fundamentalism is commonly associated with the South, it actually began in the North around the turn of the century as a reaction to modernism and social dislocation brought on by industrialization. At its inception, it served as a counterpart to the social gospel. Both movements reacted to the social upheaval brought on by urbanization in the North. While the social gospel attempted to reform the social structures of the day, fundamentalism held out no hope that humans could change their inherently corrupt society. Fundamentalists believed that the only hope was for "salvation" on an individual rather than a societal level. In their view, "No longer was the goal to build a 'perfect society,' at best it was to restrain evil until the Lord returned" (Marsden 1980, 31).

George Marsden argues that there were two strands of fundamentalism (1980). One strand was the revivalist-pietist movement made popular by Dwight Moody, which stressed subordination of all other concerns to soul saving and practical Christianity. Part of Moody's legacy is the rise of extra-denominational agencies and Bible institutes in which fundamentalism later flourished.

Premillennial dispensationalist thought became prominent within this revivalist movement. Premillennialists argued that Christ's kingdom, far from being realized in this age or in the natural development of humanity, lay wholly in the future and was totally supernatural in origin. They stood in contrast to postmillennialists, who believed that in the present age the defeat of the Antichrist was taking place through a gradual process (Marsden 1980, 49).

Dispensationalism, a movement founded by John N. Darby of the Plymouth Brethren, arose from premillennialism. Darby divided history into periods or dispensations. God's rules for one dispensation were not necessarily applicable to another (e.g., while Christians may have spoken in tongues during the apostolic age, speaking in tongues is no longer applicable in the church age). Premillennial dispensationalism involved a complex rendering of history in which, after the current church age comes to an end, Christians would be "raptured" into heaven. This rapture would be followed by the Antichrist's

---

[1] As Donald Dayton notes, these strands do not exhaust the category of peoples who might identify with evangelicalism, such as non-charismatic groups that did not become involved in the fundamentalist-modernist controversies of the 1920s (1977, 1991).

reign on earth. Then Christ would come to the earth, defeat the Antichrist, and rule for a thousand years (Marsden 1980, 48–54).

A second strand of fundamentalism is rooted in an intellectual movement led by denominational conservatives in the Calvinist tradition (particularly at Princeton University). Princeton, through the works of B. B. Warfield, A. A. Hodge, and J. Gresham Machen, formed an intellectual fortress for biblical inerrancy and theological conservatism. In 1910, the Presbyterian General Assembly, in reaction to the suspected unorthodoxy of recent Union Theological Seminary graduates, adopted a five-point declaration of belief, which included biblical inerrancy, virgin birth, substitutionary atonement, bodily resurrection, and authenticity of miracles. This declaration later became a rallying point for fundamentalists, with the exception that belief in premillennialism was substituted for belief in miracles and belief in the deity of Christ was substituted for belief in the virgin birth (Marsden 1980, 117).

The fundamentalist intellectuals at Princeton, who were not premillennialists, had a number of disagreements with their revivalist counterparts. Machen, in fact, disliked the term *fundamentalist*. However, during the second decade of this century, they began to ally with each other in order to combat their mutual foe: liberalism. As Machen once stated, "I regret being called a fundamentalist . . . but in the presence of the real common foe, I have little time to be attacking my brethren who stand with me in the defense of the Word of God" (Dollar 1973, 182–83).

Formative in this alliance was *The Fundamentals*, which was published in twelve volumes between 1910 and 1915. These volumes contained writings from an array of conservative U.S. and British scholars, as well as a number of popular writers. This work served to unite the various strands of fundamentalism, as it stressed the points they agreed on and underplayed more controversial topics such as premillennialism (Marsden 1980, 118–19).

Fundamentalism today is generally associated with separatism (i.e., fundamentalists do not want to be associated with more liberal Christians much less non-Christians). However, as Marsden notes, fundamentalists were originally more central to their denominations in the North. Only when they lost their denominational battles did they separate from them (1980, 183).

Neo-evangelical refers to a specific group within conservative Christianity that split from the fundamentalist movement in the 1940s. After World War II, as fundamentalism became increasingly associated with dogmatism, anti-intellectualism, and social isolationism, a sector of the fundamentalist community attempted to break away from this label and its negative connotations and apply the name "evangelical" or "neo-evangelical" to themselves. Neo-evangelicalism did not question the basic doctrines of fundamentalism, the five fundamentals, but it rejected the separatist tendencies within fundamentalism, seeking to engage the broader world.

Since this split between neo-evangelicals and fundamentalists, however, militant fundamentalists (represented by groups and institutions such as Bob Jones University and the Plymouth Brethren) broke away from moderate fundamentalists, such as Jerry Falwell, who were beginning to cooperate with nonfundamentalists to further right-wing political goals (Nash 1987, 67). Meanwhile, neo-evangelicals were beginning to split into conservative, mainstream, and radical groups,[2] largely based on approaches to biblical inerrancy. Consequently, the boundaries between moderate fundamentalists and conservative neo-evangelicals became very vague (Dobson 1985, 4–10). Meanwhile, more radical neo-evangelicals became increasingly marginalized from mainstream evangelical discourse. This book engages radical evangelicals to the extent that they appear within what I am loosely defining as the community of Christian Right discourse.

Another strand of evangelicalism is Pentecostalism and Charismaticism (Anderson 2004; Eha 2005; Strang 1999). Pentecostalism emerged out of Methodism and the Holiness movement. John Wesley, the founder of Methodism, espoused the doctrine of a "second blessing," or sanctification, that occurs subsequent to conversion. Methodism stressed the emotional element of popular religion and the working of the Holy Spirit on a changed life. Eventually, a split occurred within Methodism between those who emphasized the teaching of sanctification, who eventually formed the Holiness movement, and those who did not and remained within mainstream Methodism. Some denominations that emerged out of the Holiness movement are the Church of God, the Christian and Missionary Alliance, and the Church of the Nazarene. As the Holiness movement developed, another sector arose, which connected the second blessing to worldwide revival, a "latter rain," which would precede the return of Christ. They spoke of a "third blessing" in which the baptism of the Holy Spirit would bestow spiritual gifts on the believer. A revival in 1896 in a group called the Christian Union in North Carolina was accompanied by healing and, according to some reports, speaking in tongues. The Church of God links this event to the emergence of its denomination. Another stream that gave rise to Pentecostalism was the Keswick movement, which emphasized Spirit baptism, not in terms of holiness but in terms of empowering believers for testimony and service. Thus, by the beginning of the twentieth century there were three distinct holiness groups: (1) the Wesleyan position, which held that sanctification was the second blessing or baptism of the Spirit; (2) the Keswick position, which held that the baptism of the Spirit empowered the believer for service; and (3) the third-blessing position, which subscribed to both the second blessing of sanctification and a third blessing of "baptism with fire," which empowered the believer for service.

A key figure in the development of Pentecostalism was Charles Parnham, a

---

[2] *Radical* is the term often used to describe politically progressive evangelicals such as Ron Sider and Jim Wallis.

white pastor of the early 1900s, who preached Spirit baptism, healings, and speaking in tongues. One difference between him and others who espoused speaking in tongues is that he thought people who did so were speaking authentic languages, which would enable them to proclaim the gospel message as part of a worldwide revival before the return of Christ. He also promoted Anglo-Israelism, the idea that European peoples were the lost tribes of Israel, and espoused racial segregation. Despite his racist teachings, William Joseph Seymour, an African American preacher who was able to listen to Parnham's lectures for a month through a half-opened door, founded a church on 312 Asuza Street in Los Angeles in part based on Parnham's teachings. At this Apostolic Faith Mission, followers began to speak in tongues as part of their Spirit baptism. At least twenty-six denominations trace their origins to this church, including the two largest Pentecostal denominations, the Church of God in Christ and the Assemblies of God. Originally, the leadership of the church was gender and race integrated. However, as more white people became involved in Pentecostalism, they challenged Seymour's leadership and began to build racially segregated churches. Two of his white workers stole his mailing list, which contained over fifty thousand names. Parnham, William Durham, and others tried to seize control of the denomination until, in 1912, it became a small black congregation.

William Durham, from Chicago, who tried to take over the Asuza Street Church, started preaching the "finished work" doctrine, which contended that there were not three blessings, as Seymour and Parnham maintained, but sanctification occurs with justification in the first blessing and the Spirit baptism occurs in the second. By 1914, 60 percent of North American Pentecostals embraced his positions, including his supporters who launched the Assemblies of God in 1914. This division also fell along racial lines, with some of the African American denominations supporting the third-blessing approach. Within the "finished work" camp, another division developed among those who supported the "oneness" movement. This movement holds that the trinity is not composed of three distinct persons but that all are manifestations of Jesus Christ. Consequently, churches within this movement hold that baptism must be performed in the name of Jesus Christ specifically (Grady 1997b). This Oneness movement contributed to the exodus of African American pastors from the Assemblies of God. In 1948, the Pentecostal Fellowship of North America was formed, which excluded African American Oneness Pentecostals. This fellowship was disbanded in Memphis in 1994 as part of the race reconciliation movement and was reformed into the racially integrated Pentecostal/Charismatic Churches of North America. This association does not include Oneness Pentecostals (Anderson 2004, 250). Recently there have been efforts made to heal the rift between the Oneness and Trinitarian Pentecostals (Grady 1997b, 2002).

Another split occurred in 1948, under the "Latter Rain" revival, in which several leading ministers resigned their posts to become part of a movement to restore the ministerial gifts of apostles and prophets to the church, emphasizing prophecy, challenging denominationalism, and promoting independence in the local church. Many independent Charismatic Churches today have their roots in the Latter Rain movement. The biggest Pentecostal Churches are the Church of God in Christ, Assemblies of God, Church of God (Cleveland), International Church of the Foursquare Gospel, International Pentecostal Holiness Church, United Pentecostal Church, and Pentecostal Church of God. The four rallying points of American Pentecostalism are (1) full gospel, which includes the doctrine of justification, sanctification for those following the third-blessing approach, healing, the second coming of Christ, and Spirit baptism evidenced in speaking in tongues; (2) latter rain (the restoration of the lost power of the Spirit as the culmination of salvation history); (3) apostolic faith (a New Testament model of the church based on the book of Acts), including gifts of spirit, signs and wonders, apostolic authority, gift ministries, prophets, evangelists, pastors, and teachers; and (4) Pentecost, in which Pentecostal experience is seen as the beginning of a new era for the church, focused on ecstatic experience and emotionalism (Anderson 2004). A driving force of Pentecostalism was the notion that fundamentalist churches were corrupt and in need of a spiritual revival. Fundamentalists such as B. B. Warfield, by contrast, saw Pentecostals as "the last vomit of Satan" (Anderson 2004, 62). While Pentecostals generally subscribed to premillennialism, some sectors of the fundamentalist and neo-evangelical strand contended that gifts of the Spirit had ended with the apostolic age and hence any apparent gifts of the Spirit today do not come from God. These sectors still exist, particularly in the militant fundamentalist strand. However, in 1942 the Assemblies of God joined the National Association of Evangelicals and became more identified with conservative neo-evangelicalism. Today the Evangelical Free Church, the Christian and Missionary Alliance, and the Church of God (Cleveland) belong to NAE, although few independent Charismatic churches do (Grady 1999). Still, there is an increasing rapprochement today between both of these strands of evangelicalism.

Emerging from Pentecostalism was the Charismatic movement of the 1960s. Within mainline Protestant Churches and the Roman Catholic Church, some congregations began to practice spiritual gifts, beginning with the Episcopalian Church in 1960 and the Roman Catholic Church in 1967 (Anderson 2004; Eha 2005). Some denominations, such as the Southern Baptist Convention and the Missouri Lutheran Synod, began to expel Charismatic congregations, although Charismatic Churches still exist within the Southern Baptist Convention (Owen 2002; Walker 1999).[3]

---

[3] For instance, the trustees for the SBC International Mission Board (IMB) have voted to bar new missionary candidates (the ban is not retroactive) who speak in

In the 1970s, a new independent, nondenominational Charismatic-Pentecostal movement developed, which emphasized house groups and "radical discipleship" (Eha 2005; Strang 1999). One sector of this movement was the discipleship movement, founded by the Fort Lauderdale Five (Charles Simpson, Derek Prince, Ern Baxter, Bob Mumford, and Don Basham). This movement emphasized submission to "shepherds," or church leaders, and was denounced by many evangelical leaders as exploitative. Its publishing arm produced *New Wine* magazine, which ceased publication in 1986 when the movement appeared to subside. Other movements include the Vineyard Church, which was founded by John Wimber, who taught a signs and wonders class at Fuller Seminary and also founded a church in Anaheim, California. Vineyard did not stress the "initial evidence" doctrine of tongues (which would hold that speaking in tongues is evidence of one's conversion, a doctrine supported by the Assemblies of God). John Wimber and others, including Jack Hayford of Foursquare Gospel, hold that speaking in tongues is "normal" but not "normative." The Vineyard Churches hold that Spirit baptism occurs at conversion and emphasizes gifts of the Spirit. In addition, it emphasizes cell or house churches within larger congregations to provide community and cohesion. A network of five hundred Vineyard Churches had emerged by 1998 (Anderson 2004; Maxwell, Johnson, and Geary 1998). The Calvary Church, which emphasizes developing ministries and services that blend with the culture of the people being ministered to, came out of the Jesus movement in the 1960s. The World of Faith movement, popularized by leaders such as Oral Roberts, Kenneth Copeland, and Frederick Price, which emphasized a health and prosperity gospel, also became popular. It holds that what a person confesses will happen, so if an individual wants to be healed that person must confess that he or she is healed regardless of the symptoms. Poverty is also seen as a curse. If believers do not receive what they confess, it can be due to unbelief. Some sectors of this movement do not believe in using medicine. Originally, the idea behind this movement was that these gifts were evidence that we were in the last days. However, as its adherents have become more affluent, they have deemphasized the last days aspects of this movement.

Two significant recent events in contemporary Pentecostal-Charismatic Christianity are the 1994 Toronto Blessing and the 1995 Brownsville Revival. In both places, revivals began that ended up attracting hundreds of thousands

---

tongues from serving in the mission field on November 15, 2005. Interestingly, the IMB president, Jerry Rankin, speaks in tongues (Alford 2006). Then the trustees of the IMB asked the convention to remove one of its trustees, Wade Burleson, who had criticized the board for its ban on missionary candidates who speak in tongues, as well for a requirement that candidates must be baptized in a church that practices baptism by immersion only (Pulliam and Hansen 2006; Richardson 2006). This decision was rescinded at the March 20–22 meeting of the IMB (News Briefs 2006).

of people. Both of these events were controversial, with some arguing that they were counterfeit revivals (Grady 1998). In fact, the Vineyard Church cut off its association with the Toronto Blessing, and the Brownsville Revival has gone from hundreds of thousands of visitors to a few hundred members (Grady 2006). These revivals were marked by phenomena such as "holy laughter" and people making strange animal noises (Stafford and Beverly 1997). Toronto and other revivals claim that people were being covered with gold dust or that the fillings in their teeth turned to gold (Gaines 1999; Henderson 1999; Stalcup 1999).

Aside from these strands of evangelical Christianity, the Christian Right also includes groups that are more explicitly political such as the Christian Coalition, Concerned Women for America, and the Traditional Values Coalition. Other groups may have right-wing tendencies but tend to focus more on evangelism and spirituality such as Promise Keepers and the National Association of Evangelicals (a group out of the neo-evangelical movement that formed as a counter to the National Council of Churches).

Native American Organizing

I will not repeat the more detailed analysis of contemporary Native American organizing found in other works but will provide a brief map of this organizing to contextualize the theories produced by Native women activists (Castle 2000; Cornell 1988; Deloria 1985; Johnson 1996; Olson and Wilson 1984; Steiner 1968; Warrior and Smith 1996; Weyler 1992). Many historians of pan-Indian organizing trace it to the relocation period of the 1950s when Native peoples were encouraged to relocate to urban areas. The rationale of this policy was that Native peoples would assimilate into the larger society if they were no longer tied to their land bases. Since Native peoples from diverse tribes were relocating to common urban areas, they began to forge links with Native peoples pan-tribally, helping to spark a pan-tribal consciousness. Ironically, a policy that was designed to assimilate Native peoples also contributed to the development of Native organizing that questioned the policies of assimilation (Castle 2000; Johnson 1996). Furthermore, as Renya Ramirez argues, in contrast to the prevailing narrative that urban Indians are necessarily estranged from their tribal communities, Native peoples in urban areas often retain strong links to their communities (1999). Consequently, the politics emerging from urban areas began to impact reservation areas (Crow Dog 1991; Deloria 1985; Warrior and Smith 1996).

There are many precursors of the Red Power movement. For instance, one early organizer was Wallace "Mad Bear" Anderson, who in the late fifties invaded the Department of the Interior with a group of Tuscarorans and attempted to place the secretary of the interior under citizen's arrest after he had seized part of the Tuscaroran land base and transferred it to the state of New York (Deloria 1985, 21). The black civil rights movement also inspired Native peoples to adopt some of its tactics to seek redress. About one hundred Native people participated in the Poor People's March and held a sit-in at the secretary of the interior's office (Deloria 1985, 33). The American Indian Chicago Conference and the Five County Cherokees both issued declarations in the 1960s calling for a mixture of civil rights and national self-determination (Moody 1988, 29–33). Clyde Bellecourt, a founder of the American Indian Movement, maintains that his organizing was first around civil rights for Indian people (Matthiessen 1991, 34). However, growing race consciousness among urban Indians encouraged them to reconnect with their land base so that even in the cities a politics based on nationalism largely supplanted a politics based on civil rights. As Bellecourt later realized, the "civil-rights struggle . . . was within the System, and the system had nothing to do with Indians" (40). Vine Deloria notes that civil rights language seemed like one more attempt to threaten the treaty status of Indian people and force them into the U.S. mainstream (1985, 23). Similar skepticism toward civil rights language animated Sam Kolbe's 1968 critique of Martin Luther King and civil rights: "Maybe they should create a NAACPAIL, National Association for the Advancement of Colored People and Indians Later" (1972, 97)! Consequently, the rhetoric of the Black Power movement, which focused on a land-based, national struggle, began to resonate with some Native activists. Vine Deloria was particularly influenced by Stokely Carmichael. "For many people," he writes, "particularly those Indian people who had supported self-determination a decade earlier, Stokely Carmichael was the first black who said anything significant" (1988, 182). In his poem "Sorry about That," Kenneth Kale (1972) wonders

. . . why BIA Zombies chose to pout
when it is evident we know all about
our red-skinned counterpart of Martin, Gregory, and Stokely rolled into one
Like an angry "Red Muslim" with work to be done . . .

One of the of the first invocations of the term *Red Power* in a public context occurred at the 1966 convention of the National Congress of American Indians (NCAI) (Witt and Steiner 1972, 225). Addressing the Congress, Vine Deloria Jr., then the director of the NCAI, announced, "Red Power means we want power over our own lives. . . . It frightens people I know to talk of Red Power, but we don't want to frighten them. We want to shock them into realizing how powerless the Indians have been. We feel that if we don't get Red Power— now—we may not be around much longer" (Steiner 1968, 269). In 1964, Clyde Warrior and other young Indian college graduates, calling themselves the Red Muslims, formed the National Indian Youth Council (NIYC) based on the framework of Red Power. At that time, Natives from the smaller tribes in

Washington state were being subjected to harassment, brutality, and arrest by state officials while exercising their treaty-protected right to fish. Under the auspices of the NIYC, Warrior, who had spent a summer working with the Student Nonviolent Coordinating Committee in Mississippi, helped organize "fish-ins" (modeled after sit-ins). The efforts of NIYC brought hundreds of Indians and non-Indians, including Dick Gregory and Marlon Brando, to stand in solidarity with the fishers (Olson and Wilson 1984; Steiner 1968, 39–64).

The American Indian Movement was formed in 1968 by urban Indians, many of whom came out of correctional facilities (Bellecourt 1990). In general, AIM patterned itself on the self-defense model of Huey Newton and Bobbie Seale's Black Panther Party. Its patrols monitored the streets of the Twin Cities, documenting and confronting police brutality directed against Native people. Chapters sprang up throughout the country (Weyler 1992, 36).

The Native people of the Bay Area also took cues from the Black Panthers, especially the nineteen Indian students who founded Indians of All Tribes and took over Alcatraz in an effort to turn it into an Indian cultural center. Three hundred Indians later joined them, and many non-Indian groups such as the Black Panthers lent their support (Mankiller 1993, 186–93). The events at Alcatraz inspired subsequent takeovers of federal poverty and even more militant direct action. When one of the leaders at Alcatraz, Richard Oakes, was killed in 1972, Native groups, spearheaded by AIM, organized a caravan to Washington, D.C., where they attempted to initiate a twenty-point treaty renegotiation program with the U.S. government. This protest ran less smoothly than the 1963 March after which it was modeled, and the participants, through various mishaps, ended up taking over the headquarters building of the Bureau of Indian Affairs (Deloria 1985, 46). In 1973, the Pine Ridge reservation erupted into conflict when AIM, in conjunction with certain community members of Pine Ridge, took over Wounded Knee to protest the actions of the tribal chair, Dick Wilson (Akwesasne Notes 1974; Warrior and Smith 1996).

According to Stan Steiner, these young activists saw themselves as challengers of the presumption that "Indians don't protest." Mel Thom (Paiute), a cofounder of NIYC, said, "The Indian had been stereotyped to act in certain ways; he was not supposed to take direct action, or to picket, or to demonstrate. People were curious to see if the Indians could do these things. So were the Indians" (1968, 54). Although Red Power began primarily among urban Indians, it soon became popular on the reservations and provided new models of protest for traditional people who heretofore had resisted the U.S. government only through nonparticipation. Government officials and conservative Indian leaders attempted to depict all Red Power proponents as urban misfits; however, fully 80 percent of the participants in the BIA building takeover were reservation based (Deloria 1985, 47). Summing up what Indians learned from Black Power and civil rights activists, Thom proposed that "The weakest link in the Indian's defense is his lack of understanding of this modern-type war. Indians have not been able to use political action, propaganda and power as well as their opponents" (1972).

As Native movements developed, they began to rely on increasingly confrontational tactics. Richard McKenzie, who led a raid on Alcatraz that was a precursor to the takeover, argued, "Kneel-Ins, Sit-Ins, Sleep-Ins, Eat-Ins, Pray-Ins like the Negroes do wouldn't help us. We would have to occupy the government buildings before things would change" (Steiner 1968, 45). Even at the fish-ins, participants started bringing guns to discourage police brutality (Council on Interracial Books for Children 1971). The student leader Clyde Warrior was no proponent of nonviolence. He argued, "What can you do when society tells you that you should be non-existent? As I look at it, the situation will not change unless really violent action comes about. If this country understands violence then that is the way to do. . . . The only thing we have left is our guns. Let's use them" (Steiner 1968, 68). Warrior's words were primarily rhetorical; he never embarked on a program of violent revolution. It was the "angry children of Clyde Warrior" who began to implement his vision. As he stated, "Five years ago those of us who started off the Youth Council were called the most radical of radicals. Those of us who headed the movement five years ago are now considered Uncle Tomahawks. There is a more and more angry bunch of kids coming up. Which I like" (Steiner 1968, 95).

Perhaps numerical scarcity also contributed to AIM's willingness to use violence at Wounded Knee and other places. Since Indians could not hope to draw crowds of thousands to mass protests in the style of Martin Luther King, they had to rely on more dramatic actions to get the attention of the media. It was argued by AIM that the real violence was perpetrated by white societies; its warriors were merely defending their nations (Akwesasne Notes 1974, 62). The embrace of armed self-defense began with a slew of Indian killings by white racists in the summer of 1972, particularly the killing of Raymond Yellow Thunder in Gordon, Nebraska. Bill Means states, "We realized that AIM could not allow Indian people to be murdered, that we would have to change tactics. It was a turning point. We could not just carry signs and protest, but we would have to be willing to die to protect our people" (Weyler 1992, 49).

Spirituality became an integral part of contemporary Native organizing. As Native peoples questioned the policies of assimilation, they began to reclaim the spirituality that was integral to Native cultures. For this reason, early AIM leaders visited Leonard Crow Dog, a spiritual leader from Rosebud, to find a spiritual compass for the movement. Thereafter AIM considered itself the primary agents of "the spiritual rebirth of our nation" (Akwesasne Notes 1974, 60). As Deloria notes, alienated urban Indians reconnected with traditionals through activism, becoming militant advocates of cultural and spiritual renewal. He also observes with irony that "the more educated Indians become, the more militant they are about preserving traditions and customs" (1974,

47). In addition, Native organizing often adopted an explicitly anti-Christian stance. As Grace Black Elk stated during the occupation of Wounded Knee, "So they want to convert us to Catholic, Episcopal, all that trash, and believe in the Bible. . . . So the Indian's supposed to lay down his weapons and be converted into Christian way. No more savage, he's gonna be Christian. But I don't see no wings on white people. All I see is horns on them. They are actually the devil . . . [and] they're just using the Bible as a mask. Every Sunday they go to church, and then Monday morning they stand in line making machine guns and tanks and H-bombs and nuclear heads and all that" (Akwesasne Notes 1974, 236). As was discussed in chapter 2, however, the model for understanding Native organizing as always being anti-Christian, oversimplifies religious and political practice in Native communities.

While much of the scholarship on Native organizing tends to stop with Wounded Knee, in fact it has continued in a variety of diverse forms. As discussed in chapter 3, as the focus in Native communities has shifted from activism based on short-term dramatic interventions to the long-term project of organizing Native communities, women have increasingly dominated this work. Women of All Red Nations, which was founded as a sister organization of AIM in 1978 by Madonna Thunder Hawk and Lorelei DeCora Means, has organized against environmental contamination in South Dakota Native communities. Its work helped to spark the current indigenous environmental movement. This movement was furthered by the work of Native Americans for a Clean Environment (Oklahoma), which led the successful campaign against Kerr McGee; the Indigenous Environmental Network, which emerged out of the 1991 People of Color Environmental Justice Summit; and many other groups. Women of All Red Nations also organized to protest sterilization abuses perpetrated against Native women in Indian Health Services, work that continues today in Native women's reproductive rights groups such as the Native American Women's Health Education Resource Center in South Dakota. Many women from WARN were involved in the founding of the Indigenous Women's Network in 1985.

Another critical area of indigenous organizing operates on the global scale. As Native organizing developed, Native peoples began to see a contradiction between asserting the sovereignty of indigenous nations on the one hand, and then seeking redress from their colonizer's government on the other. They concluded that if Indian nations wanted to articulate their independence they, too, could not continue to seek redress from the government domestically but had to seek recognition from other nations. As early as 1958, Mad Bear organized an Iroquoian delegation to Cuba to solicit sponsorship for admitting the Six Iroquois Nations into the UN as a sovereign nation (Steiner 1968, 281). In 1974, AIM organized the International Indian Treaty Council (IITC), which gained NGO observer status at the UN in 1977 (214). That same year it organized the International Conference on Discrimination against Indigenous Peoples in the Americas. Two recommendations from the conference were that the UN set up a Working Group on Indigenous Affairs (which it did) and a Committee on Transnational Corporations, which would investigate the depredations of multinational corporations on Indian lands. This latter committee never materialized (Steiner 1968, 61). In 2002, the United Nations held the first Permanent Forum on Indigenous Issues, which became another site where indigenous peoples could organize globally. Native peoples have also been involved in the various UN world conferences, such as the Beijing conference on women and the Durban conference on racism. In this work, Native women play a central role. To name but two, Mililani Trask, a leader in the Hawai'ian sovereignty movement, held a seat on the Permanent Forum. Tonya Gonnella-Frichner heads the American Indian Law Alliance, which facilitates the presence of indigenous peoples at the Permanent Forum, and was appointed to the Permanent Forum in 2007. Native women particularly mobilized for the Third Permanent Forum in 2004, which focused on the status of indigenous women.

Another key sector of Native women's organizing is the antiviolence movement. Some of the first Native battered women's shelters were the White Buffalo Calf Woman's Society, founded in 1977 in Mission, South Dakota, and the Women of Nations shelter of Saint Paul, Minnesota, which was formed in 1982. This movement gained critical momentum with the passage of the Violence against Women Act in 1994, which provided tribal set-aside funds for antiviolence programs. This movement is particularly significant in that it squarely addressed violence *within* Native communities, particularly gender violence. It demonstrated that it was not sufficient to organize against the oppression resulting from government or corporate practices; Native peoples, particularly Native men, had to be held accountable for the violence perpetrated against women and children within their communities. It further demonstrated that the violence perpetrated against Native communities was inextricably linked to violence committed within them (A. Smith 2005b). This movement had grown with the development of Clanstar, the Mending the Sacred Hoop Technical Assistance Project, Sacred Circle, and numerous other groups. Sarah Deer (Muscogee) and Bonnie Clairmont (Ho-Chunk), key leaders in this movement, wrote Amnesty International's report on sexual assault against Native Women, *Maze of Injustice* (2007). At the same time, the antiviolence movement has faced contradictions similar to those that its mainstream counterpart faces between trying to develop a holistic analysis of violence and obtaining most of its funding from the federal government. Ironically, Pat Robertson similarly commented, in March 2002, on the contradictions inherent in the fact that Christian groups receive federal monies through "faith based" initiatives: "It will be like a narcotic; then they can't free themselves later on" (Olsen 2002). In October, Robertson's Operation Blessing International received a grant of half a million dollars. Many Native activists, by contrast, argue that these funds are really owed to Native peoples and hence this funding should be seen less as federal grants and more as reparations owed by the U.S. government to tribal nations. The theory produced by the Native women activists in this book emerged from all these sectors of organizing.

Appendix 2

Interviewees and Dates of Interviews

This list includes interviewees' names, tribal affiliations, place of residence at the time of the interview, selected past and present organizational affiliations, and date of interview.

PAMELA ALFONSO (Menominee), Chicago. American Indian Movement, American Indian Economic Development Association, Metropolitan Tenants' Association, July 15, 2001.

YVONNE DENNIS (Cherokee), New York. Women of All Red Nations, June 11, 2001.

TONYA GONNELLA FRICHNER (Onondaga), New York. American Indian Law Alliance, June 16, 2001.

LAKOTA HARDEN (Lakota), Rapid City, South Dakota. Women of All Red Nations, Black Hills Alliance, July 13, 2001.

PAMELA KINGFISHER (Cherokee), Austin, Texas. Indigenous Women's Network, Native Americans for Clean Environment, June 16, 2001.

HEATHER MILTON (Ojibwe and Cree), Bemijdi, Minnesota. Native Youth Movement, Indigenous Environmental Network, July 12, 2001.

MONA RENCOUNTRE (Dakota), Wiconi Wawokiya, Fort Thompson, South Dakota. July 24, 2001.

LORETTA RIVERA (Seneca), Minnesota. Mending the Sacred Hoop, Stop Violence against American Indian Women Project, Women of All Red Nations, July 12, 2001.

LUANA ROSS (Salish), Seattle. American Indian Movement, Critical Resistance, December 26, 2001.

TONI SHEEHY (Blackfeet), Chicago. American Indian Movement, Domestic violence advocate, American Indian Business Association, July 15, 2001.

JULIE STAR* (southeastern tribe), midwestern city. Native treaty rights organization, December 27, 2001.

MADONNA THUNDER HAWK (Lakota), Cheyenne River reservation, South Dakota. American Indian Movement, Women of All Red Nations, July 14, 2001.

LISA THOMAS** (Muscogee), Chicago. Big Mountain Support Group, Women of All Red Nations, July 10, 2001.

SAMMY TOINEETA (Lakota), New York. American Indian Movement, National Council of Churches Racial Justice Working Group, March 15, 2001.

REBECCA VANVLACK (Lakota), New Haven, Connecticut. League of Indigenous Sovereign Nations, American Indian Movement, June 12, 2001.

SHERRY WILSON (Ho-Chunk), Black River Falls, Wisconsin. Women of All Red Nations, July 11, 2001.

* Name and identifying details have been changed.
** Name has been changed.

Bibliography

"Abortion: Common at Christian Colleges?" 1989. *Christianity Today*, July 14, 42–43.

"Abortion-Rights Marchers Crowd D.C." 2004. *Connecticut Post* (Bridgeport), April 26.

Abraham, Priya, John Dawson, Jamie Dean, and Lynn Vincent. 2005. "Criminals Next Door." *World*, June 18, 20–23.

Achtemier, Elizabeth. 1993. "Why God Is Not a Mother." *Christianity Today*, August 16, 17–23.

Aguayo, Anna Macias. 2005. "Navajos Override Gay Marriage Ban Veto." Gay.com.

Ahmanson, Howard. 1983. "Some Theological Considerations of Prison Ministry: What Prisoners Need to Know." *Journal of Christian Reconstruction* 9 (1–2): 89–90.

Aikman, David. 2000. "Changing America's Prisons." *Charisma*, October, 118.

——. 2005. "Resisting a Right to Kill." *Charisma*, May, 77.

Akwesasne Notes. 1974. *Voices from Wounded Knee*. Rooseveltown: Akwesasne Notes.

Aldred, Ray. 1997. "A Biblical Model for Reconciliation with Natives." *Faith Today*, September-October, 40–41.

——. 2000. "Justice: An Aboriginal View." *Faith Today*, September-October, 37–38.

Aldrich, Susan. 1987. "Forgiving the Killer." *Christian Herald*, November, 16–20.

Alexander, M. Jacqui, and Chandra Talpade Mohanty, eds. 1997. *Feminist Genealogies, Colonial Legacies, and Democratic Futures*. New York: Routledge.

Alexander, John, and Judy Alexander. 1975. "Who Cleans the Toilets?" *Eternity*, March, 38–39, 57.

Alford, Deann. 1999. "Prison Alpha Helps Women Recover Their Lost Hopes." *Christianity Today*, October 4, 29.

——. 2000. "A Throwaway Generation?" *Christianity Today*, April 24, 32.

Alford, Deann. 2004. "New Life in a Culture of Death." *Christianity Today*, February, 48–53.

——. 2005. "Mobs Expel 80 Christians." *Christianity Today*, November, 22.

——. 2006. "Tongues Tied." *Christianity Today*, February, 21.

——. 1999. *Peace, Power, Righteousness*. Oxford: Oxford University Press.

Alfred, Taiaike. 2005. *Wasáse: Indigenous Pathways of Action and Freedom*. Peterborough, ON: Broadview Press.

Allen, Paula Gunn. 1986. *The Sacred Hoop*. Boston: Beacon.

Alsdurf, James, and Phyllis Alsdurf. 1989a. "Battered into Submission." *Christianity Today*, June 16, 24–27.

——. 1989b. *Battered into Submission*. Downers Grove, Ill.: InterVarsity.

Althusser, Louis. 1971. *Lenin and Philosophy and Other Essays*. New York: Monthly Review Press.

Ammerman, Nancy. 1991. "Southern Baptists and the New Christian Right." *Review of Religious Research* 32 (3): 213–36.

——. 1993. *Bible Believers: Fundamentalists in the Modern World*. New Brunswick, N.J.: Rutgers University Press.

Amnesty International. 2007. *Maze of Injustice*. New York: Amnesty International. http://web.amnesty.org/library/Index/ENGAMR510352007.

Anderson, Allan. 2004. *Introduction to Pentecostalism*. Cambridge: Cambridge University Press.

Anderson, Joy. 1988. "Reaching Minorities Takes Cultural Acceptance." *Evangelical Missions Quarterly* 24 (July): 242–45.

Anderson, Karen. 1991. *Chain Her by One Foot*. New York: Routledge.

Andrescik, Robert. 2000a. "T. D. Jakes, the Man behind Manpower." *New Man*, November–December, 30–35.

——. 2000b. "Welcome to the New Men's Movement." *New Man*, September–October, 10.

——. 2003. "I'm No Hero." *New Man*, January–February, 34–35.

Andrews, Mark. 1989. "A Florida Couple, a Serial Killer, and God's Boundless Love." *Charisma*, April, 59–62.

Anishinabe Values/Social Law Regarding Wife Battering. N.d. *Indigenous Woman* 1 (3): 47, 49.

Ankerberg, John, and John Welson. 1996. *Encylopedia of New Age Beliefs*. Eugene: Harvest House.

Anonymous. 1992. "Now the Battle Had Begun!" *Indian Life*, November–December, 21.

Ansell, Amy Elizabeth. 1997. *New Right, New Racism*. New York: New York University Press.

Armistead, Frank. 2000. "Practices for Mind and Senses." *Charisma*, July-August, 40.

Asetoyer, Charon. 1995. "Health and Reproductive Rights." In *Indigenous*

Women Address the World, edited by Indigenous Women's Network, 31–42. Austin: Indigenous Women's Network.

——. 1996. "Population Controls." *Indigenous Woman* 2 (4): 10–12.

Associated Press. 1999. "2 Ex-Aides in Moral Majority Shun Politics." *Chicago Tribune*, March 19.

——. 2005. "Navajo Head Vetoes Gay Marriage Measure." *New York Times*, May 1.

Atwood, Thomas. 1990. "Through a Glass Darkly." *Policy Review* 54 (fall): 44–52.

Augspurger, Linda. 1995. "Bridge to the Navajos." *Evangelizing Today's Child*, March–April, 24–39.

Babbage, Stuart Barton. 1972. "C. S. Lewis and the Humanitarian Theory of Punishment." *Christian Scholar's Review* 2 (3): 224–35.

"Back to Prison . . . by Air." 2000. *PFI World*, November-December, 2.

Baker, Tamela. 1999. "Coming to New Convictions." *Inside Journal*, January–February, 8.

Baker, William. 1988. "Capital Punishment." *Fundamentalist Journal*, March, 59–62.

Baldridge, William. 1989. "Toward a Native American Theology." *American Baptist Quarterly* 8 (December): 227–38.

Balswick, Jack. 1989. "Toward a Social Theology of Punishment." *Perspectives on Science and Christian Faith* 41 (December) : 221–26.

Baly, Joseph. 1975. "Is a Husband a Hammer?" *Eternity*, March, 56–57.

Bandarage, Asoka. 1997. *Women, Population, and Global Crisis*. London: Zed.

Banks, Adelle. 2005. "Prisoners Secure Religious Freedom." *Christianity Today*, August, 19.

"Baptists Fire Missionaries." 2003. *Christianity Today*, July, 24.

Barker, Elizabeth. 1985. "The Paradox of Punishment." In *Abolitionism: Towards a Non-repressive Approach to Crime*, edited by Herman Bianchi and Rene van Swaaningen, 90–95. Amsterdam: Free University Press.

Barnes, Esther. 1989. "Native People Need Native Missionaries." *Faith Today*, May–June, 58–59.

Barnes, Rebecca. 2006. "The Rest of the Story." *Christianity Today*, January, 38–41.

Barr, James. 1977. *Fundamentalism*. London: SCM Press.

Barton, David. 1994. "The Shifting Paradigm: Where Will It End?" *Wall-Builder Report*, fall, 5.

Bauer, Susan Wise. 1999. "Re-imagining Women." *Christianity Today*, May 24, 66–67.

Bauman, Zygmunt. 1999. *In Search of Politics*. Stanford: Stanford University Press.

Bayly, David, and Susan Olasky. 1998. "Anti-Unisex Backlash." *World*, February 14, 20.

BDM. 1997. "Promise Keepers: Ecumenical Macho-Men for Christ." Biblical Discernment Ministries, April. http://www.rapidnet.com/jbeard//bdm/Psychology/pk/pk.htm

Beane, Becky. 1998a. "Battered . . . in Christ's Name." *Jubilee*, fall, 14–17.

——. 1998b. "Lessons from Dad." *Jubilee*, Fall, 20–21.

——. 1998c. "When Mommy Goes to Prison." *Jubilee*, summer, 6–12.

——. 2000a. "As for Me and My House." *Jubilee Extra*, August, 1–3.

——. 2000b. "Do Justice to the Afflicted." *Jubilee*, winter, 20–23.

——. 2000c. "The God of Restoration." *Jubilee Extra*, February, 1–3.

Beaucage, Marjorie. 1998. "Undermining the Innu at Voisey's Bay." *Indigenous Woman* 2 (5): 6–7.

Bee, Tom. 2001. "I Took the Gift and Ran." *Indian Life*, March–April, 7.

Beegle, Dewey. 1973. *Scripture, Tradition, and Infallibility*. Grand Rapids: Eerdmans.

Begin, Mark. 2005. "Beyond Stealth." *World*, January 29, 30–31.

"Beijing Declaration on Indigenous Women." N.d. *Indigenous Woman* 2 (3): 24–31.

Beisner, E. Calvin. 1993. "Are God's Resources Finite?" *World*, November 27, 10–13.

——. 1998. "Putting Kyoto on Ice." *World*, August 8, 12–16.

Bellecourt, Vernon. 1990. "Birth of AIM." In *Native American Testimony*, edited by Peter Nabokov, 372–76. New York: Penguin.

Bell-Jones, Jenny. 2001. "Oil Company Genocide." *Indigenous Woman* 4 (2): 16–19.

Belser, Ann. 2004. "Local Marchers Have Many Issues." *Pittsburgh Post-Gazette*, April 26.

Belz, Joel. 1999. "Wrong Again." *World*, October 23, 9.

——. 2004a. "Easy Target." *World*, March 13, 6.

——. 2004b. "No Preservatives." *World*, May 22, 8.

——. 2006a. "Handcuffing Prisons." *World*, August 12, 14–17.

——. 2006b. "Relativism at Fuller." *World*, July 1–8, 8.

Belz, Mindy. 1998a. "Monster by Day, Mother by Night." *World*, June 27, 12–16.

——. 1998b. "Slowing the Growth of Population Control." *World*, September 19, 36–38.

——. 1999a. "Blurred Vision." *World*, March 6, 20–21.

——. 1999b. "Ethnic Cleansing in a Pill." *World*, October 30, 23–24.

——. 1999c. "It Takes More than a Village to Depopulate One." *World*, February 20, 18–21.

——. 1999d. "People-Count Politics." *World*, October 9, 34–36.

——. 2004. "What Went Wrong?" *World*, August 14, 18–21.

Belz, Nat. 1998. "Who's Calling the Tune?" *World*, March 28, 19–21.

Bence, Evelyn. 1998. "Living Monuments to God's Grace." *Jubilee*, fall, 6–13.

Bender, Thornwald W. 1971. "Joint Heirs of Grace." *Eternity*, January, 27.

Bendroth, Margaret. 1984. "The Search for 'Women's Role' in American Evangelicalism, 1930–1980." In *Evangelicalism in Modern America*, edited by George Marsden, 122–34. Grand Rapids: Eerdmans.

——. 1993. *Fundamentalism and Gender, 1875–Present*. New Haven: Yale University Press.

Berger, Barry. N.d. "Some Tips to Remember in Introducing Your Jewish Friends to the Messiah." Scottsdale: Christian Jew Foundation.

Bergin, Mark. 2005a. "Black Gold Rush." *World*, November 26, 25.

——. 2005b. "Cell Blocked." *World*, November 19, 24–25.

——. 2005c. "Love Thy Neighbor, Love the Neighborhood." *World*, August 6, 22–23.

——. 2005d. "The New Pro-Choice." *World*, May 14, 25.

——. 2006a. "Greener Than Thou." *World*, April 22, 18–21.

——. 2006b. "Red Light, Green Light." *World*, February 25, 29.

Bergman, Jerry. 1986. "A Brief History of the Failure of American Corrections." *Journal of the American Scientific Affiliation* 38 (March): 27–37.

Bergner, Daniel. 1998. *God of the Rodeo*. New York: Crown.

Berkman, Patricia. 1999. "When God Took the Reservation by Storm." *Journal of Christian Nursing* 16 (fall): 22–27.

Bernal, Dick. N.d. *America's Spirituality Mapped*. San Jose: Jubilee Christian Center.

Bhabha, Homi. 1997. "Of Mimicry and Men." In *Tensions of Empire*, edited by Frederick Cooper and Ann Laura Stoler, 152–60. Berkeley: University of California Press.

Bianchi, Herman. 1985. "Pitfalls and Strategies of Abolition." In *Abolitionism: Towards a Non-repressive Approach to Crime*, edited by Herman Bianchi and Rene van Swaaningen, 147–55. Amsterdam: Free University Press.

Bible and Culture Collective. 1995. *The Postmodern Bible*. New Haven: Yale University Press.

"Bible Student Convicted of Murder." 1983. *Eternity*, April, 12.

Biddle, Calvin. 1973. "The Cross behind Prison Walls." *Moody Monthly*, June, 80–82.

Bilezikian, Gilbert. 1987. "Hierarchist and Egalitarian Inculturations." *Journal of the Evangelical Theological Society* 30 (4): 421–26.

Bill, Barbara. N.d. "Baskets Free to Dance . . . California Basketmakers." *Indigenous Woman* 1 (3): 42–45.

Billig, Michael. 1995. "Imagining Nationhood." In *Social Movements and Cultures*, edited by Hank Johnston and Bert Klandermans, 64–84. Minneapolis: University of Minnesota Press.

Bird, Brian. 1989a. "Christians Who Grow Coca." *Christianity Today*, September 8, 40–43.

———. 1989b. "Twenty Years after Helter Skelter." *Moody*, July–August, 24–30.

———. 1990. "Reclaiming the Urban War Zones." *Christianity Today*, January 15, 16–20.

Black, Joe. 2004. "Marchers Rally for Abortion Rights." *Houston Chronicle.* April 26.

Blackley, Don. 1993. "In Prison and Ye Visited Me." *Church Musician*, October–December, 77–79.

Blair-Mitchell, Lynette. 1997. "Prayer Targets Civil War Era Wounds." *Charisma*, February, 18–19.

Bledderus, Bill. 1997. "Canada Seen as a Leader in Native Reconciliation." *Faith Today*, January–February, 34–36.

"Blinded by Might?" 1999. *World*, 14, 21–24.

Bloesch, Donald. 1978. *Essentials of Evangelical Theology*. San Francisco: Harper and Row.

Blomberg, Craig. 2002. "Why I'm for the NIV." *Charisma*, November, 86, 108.

Blunt, Sheryl. 2003. "Saving Black Babies." *Christianity Today*, February, 21–23.

Bock, Darrell. 2005. "The Politics of the People of God." *Christianity Today*, September, 80–86.

Boggess, William. 1981. "Ex-inmate Asks: 'Why Was I Born?'" *Christian Life*, May, 71–77.

Boggs, Carl. 2000. *The End of Politics*. New York: Guilford.

Bomer, Norm. 1996. "The Anthropologists' 'Paradise.'" *World*, November 23, 20–21.

Bondy, David. 1998. "Deconstructing 'Canada': A Vision of Hope." *Media Development* 45 (3): 34–37.

Bonham, Chad. 2005. "Prayer Event Addresses Historic Injustice." *Charisma*, December, 27.

Boone, Katherine. 1989. *The Bible Tells Them So*. Albany: State University of New York Press.

Boone, Wellington. 1996. *Breaking Through*. Nashville: Broadman and Holman.

Boop, Betty. 1975. "It Seems to Me." *Moody*, July–August, 54–56.

Bourdieu, Pierre. 1998. *Outline of a Theory of Practice*. Cambridge: Cambridge University Press.

Bowman, Jim. 1994. "Is Male Headship Linked to Spousal Abuse?" *Christianity Today*, June 20, 62.

Box, Steve, and Chris Hale. 1982. "Economic Crisis and the Rising Prisoner Population in England and Wales." *Crime and Social Justice* 17:20–35.

Brasher, Brenda. 1998. *Godly Women: Fundamentalism and Female Power*. New Brunswick, N.J.: Rutgers University Press.

Brewer, Connie. 1991. *Escaping the Shadows, Seeking the Light: Christians in Recovery from Childhood Sexual Abuse*. San Francisco: Harper.

Brewer-Smyth, Kathleen. 2005. "Women behind Bars." *Journal of Christianity and Nursing* 22 (spring): 30–33.

Briner, Bob. 1996. *Deadly Detours*. Grand Rapids: Zondervan.

Brown, David, and Russell Hogg. 1985. "Abolition Reconsidered: Issues and Problems." *Australian Journal of Law and Society* 2 (2): 56–75.

Bruce, Billy. 1997a. "More Than Jailhouse Religion." *Charisma*, September, 52–59.

——. 1997b. "Standing on the Promises." *Charisma*, December, 48–54.

——. 1998a. "Prison Evangelist 'Chaplain Ray' Dies." *Charisma*, February, 27–28.

——. 1998b. "Promise Keepers Forced to Shut Down." *Charisma*, April, 35.

——. 2000. "Revival on Ice." *Charisma*, December, 46–55.

Bruce, Steve. 1988. *The Rise and Fall of the New Christian Right*. Oxford: Clarendon.

——. 1998. *Conservative Protestant Politics*. Oxford: Oxford University Press.

Bube, Richard. 1981. "Determinism and Free Will: Crime, Punishment, and Responsibility." *Journal of the American Scientific Affiliation* 33 (June): 105–12.

Bubna, Paul, and Jean Bubna. 1980. "Evangelicals and Feminism." *Alliance Witness*, February 20, 3–6.

Buckley, Jach. 1980. "Paul, Women, and the Church." *Eternity*, December, 30–35.

Bulletin Board. 2001. *New Man*, November–December, 12.

Bumiller, Elisabeth. 2003. "Evangelicals Sway White House on Human Rights Issues Abroad." *New York Times*, October 26.

Burkett, Elinor. 1998. *The Right Women*. New York: Touchstone.

Burlein, Ann. 2002. *Lift High the Cross*. Durham, N.C.: Duke University Press.

Burrow, Rufus. 1992. "Reflections on Some Theologico-Ethical Norms for Prison Ministry." *Asbury Theological Journal* 47 (fall): 78–91.

Bush, Rosaline. 1997. "Suffering for the Faith." *Family Voice*, August, 1–8.

Butcher, Andy. 2000. "Listen to the Children Crying." *Charisma*, June, 50–62.

Butler, Judith. 1990. *Gender Trouble: Feminism and the Subversion of Identity*. New York: Routledge.

——. 2004. *Precarious Life: The Powers of Mourning and Violence*. London: Verso.

Butterfield, Fox. 2000. "Study Shows a Racial Divide in Domestic Violence Cases." *New York Times*, May 18.

Cadbury, Deborah. 1995. "Human Laboratory." Video. Produced by the BBC.

Cagney, Mary. 1997. "Sexual Abuse in Churches Not Limited to Clergy." *Christianity Today*, October 6, 90.

Calhoun, Craig. 1994a. "Nationalism and Civil Society: Democracy, Diversity, and Self-Determination." In *Social Theory and the Politics of Identity*, edited by Craig Calhoun, 304–35. Malden: Blackwell.

——. 1994b. *Social Theory and the Politics of Identity*. Oxford: Blackwell.

——. 1996. *Critical Social Theory*. Oxford: Blackwell.

Careless, Sue. 2001. "God's Word in Languages of the Heart." *Indian Life*, May–June, 11.

Carlson, William G., and Margaret N. Barnhouse. 1975. "ERA: Fact or Fraud?" *Eternity*, November, 28–31.

Carnes, Tony. 1999. "The Anti-madams of Asia." *Christianity Today*, October 4, 26–27.

——. 2000. "Odd Couple Politics." *Christianity Today*, March 6, 24.

——. 2001. "Lost Common Cause." *Christianity Today*, July 9, 15–16.

Carothers, Merlin. 1970. *Prison to Praise*. Plainfield, N.J.: Logos International.

Carpenter, Joel. 1997. *Revive Us Again*. Oxford: Oxford University Press.

Carrasco, Rodopho. 1993. "Good News and Bad News." *World*, April 24, 10–12.

Carson, D. A. 1991. "Silent in the Churches." In *Recovering Biblical Manhood and Womanhood*, edited by Wayne Grudem and John Piper 144–53. Wheaton, Ill.: Crossway.

——. 1998. *The Inclusive Language Debate*. Grand Rapids: Baker.

Carter, Stephen. 2000. "The Freedom to Resist." *Christianity Today*, June 12, 58–62.

——. 2004. "Loving Military Enemies." *Christianity Today*, September, 84.

"The Case of the U'Wa vs. Oxy, 1999." *Indigenous Woman* 3 (1): 5–6.

Castells, Manuel. 1997. *The Power of Identity*. Malden: Blackwell.

Castillo, Rosalva Aida Hernandez. N.d. "Reinventing Tradition: The Women's Law in Chiapas." *Indigenous Woman* 2 (1): 4–7.

Castle, Elizabeth. 2000. "Black and Native American Women's Activism in the Black Panther Party and the American Indian Movement." PhD diss, Cambridge University.

Chacko, Mohan. 1995. "Reflections from India." *Rutherford*, March, 17.

Chandler, Russell. 1989. "Belief behind Bars." *Moody*, July–August, 28–30.

Charles, Daryl. 1995. "Crime, the Christian, and Capital Justice." *Journal of the Evangelical Theological Society* 38 (September): 429–41.

Charleston, Steve. 1996. "The Old Testament of North America." In *Native and Christian*, edited by James Treat, 68–80. Oxford: Oxford University Press.

Chiero, Kathy. 1998a. "Karla's Exclusive Final Interview." *The 700 Club*. First broadcast February 3, 1998, by the Christian Broadcasting Network. http://www.cbn.org/interviews/karla-final.asp (accessed January 19, 1999).

——. 1998b. "New Life on Death Row: The Karla Faye Tucker Story." *The 700 Club*. First broadcast January 30, 1998 by the Christian Broadcasting Network. http://www. cbn.org/news/stories/karla.faye.full.asp (accessed January 19, 1999).

"Child Sexual Abuse: A Problem for Our Nation and Our Church." 1990. *Christian Standard*, May 27, 8.

"Christian as Citizen." 1985. *Christianity Today*, April 19, 28.

"Christian Coalition Official Says Ending Sin Will End Racism." 1996. *Christian American*, November–December, 4.

"Christian Indigenous Peoples Gather to Worship the Greatest Chief." 1998. *Indian Life*, September–October,1, 8–9.

Christianity Today. 1998. "Promise Keepers Staff Lose Jobs." *Christianity Today*, April 6, 18.

——. 1999a. "Go Directly to Jail." *Christianity Today*, September 6, 41.

——. 1999b. "Just Saying 'No' Is Not Enough." *Christianity Today*, October 4, 50–55.

——. 2000a. "The Christian Divorce Culture." *Christianity Today*, September 4, 47.

——. 2000b. "Do Good Fences Make Good Baptists?" *Christianity Today*, August 7, 36–37.

——. 2000c. "Hang Ten?" *Christianity Today*, March 6, 36–37.

——. 2001. "Shaking Hands with Thugs." *Christianity Today*, December 3, 30–31.

——. 2002a. "A Preventable Tragedy." *Christianity Today*, April 22, 25.

——. 2002b. "Why the TNIV Draws Ire." *Christianity Today*, April 1, 36–37.

——. 2004. "The Evil in Us." *Christianity Today*, July, 22–23.

——. 2005a. "Fear Not the Disabled." *Christianity Today*, November, 28–29.

——. 2005b. "Gender Is No Disease." *Christianity Today*, February, 29.

——. 2006. "Sex Isn't a Spectator Sport." *Christianity Today*, July, 20–21.

"Christians for Biblical Equality Statement of Faith." 1994. *Priscilla Papers* 9 (spring): 19.

Churchill, Ward. 1993. *Struggle for the Land*. Monroe: Common Courage.

Churchill, Ward, and Winona LaDuke. 1992. "Native North America: The Political Economy of Radioactive Colonialism." In *The State of Native America*, edited by M. Annette Jaimes, 241–66. Cambridge, Mass.: South End.

Cienski, Jan. 2001. "Hard Time in 'Supermax' Jails." *Indian Life*, July–August, 10, 12–13.

Cizik, Richard. 2000. "The Real Christian Coalition." *Christianity Today*, June 12, 82–83.

Clapp, Rodney. 1989. "The Church Picnic Goes to Jail." *Christianity Today*, June 16, 14–15.

Clarkson, Frederick. 1996. "Righteous Brothers." *In These Times*, August 5, 14–17.

Claus, Tom. 1976. *On Eagles' Wings*. N.p.: Thunderbird Indian Company.

———. 1979. "Who's Giving What to the Indians?" *United Evangelical Action*, winter, 24–27.

Cleaver, Eldridge. 1977. "Soul on Grace: An Interview with Eldridge Cleaver." *Eternity*, May, 27–41.

Clough, Patricia. 1994. *Feminist Thought*. Malden: Blackwell.

Cochran, Pamela. 2005. *Evangelical Feminism*. New York: New York University Press.

Cohen, Cathy. 1999. *The Boundaries of Blackness*. Chicago: University of Chicago Press.

Cohen, Stanley. 1985. "Community Control: To Demystify or to Reaffirm?" In *Abolitionism: Towards a Non-repressive Approach to Crime*, edited by Herman Bianchi and Rene van Swaaningen, 127–32. Amsterdam: Free University Press.

Colson, Charles. 1977. "Who Will Help Penitents and Penitentiaries?" *Eternity*, May, 12–17, 34.

———. 1979. *Life Sentence*. Grand Rapids: Revell.

———. 1980a. "Prison Reform: Your Obligation as a Believer." *Christian Life*, April, 23–24; 50–56.

———. 1980b. "Sentenced for Life." *Moody*, February, 28–70.

———. 1983. "Why Charles Colson's Heart Is Still in Prison." *Christianity Today*, September 16, 12–14.

———. 1985. "God behind Bars." *Christian Life*, September, 28–32.

———. 1986. "What Easter Means to Me." *Decision*, March, 15–16.

———. 1987. "Of Mice and Men." *Eternity*, March, 11.

———. 1988. *Justice*. Washington, D.C.: Prison Fellowship.

———. 1989. *Changed Hearts*. Washington, D.C.: Prison Fellowship.

———. 1990. "Communities of Life." *Alliance Life*, May 23, 6–7.

———. 1992. "Dances with Wolves in Sheep's Clothing." *Christianity Today*, April 27, 72,

———. 1993. *Dance with Deception*. Dallas: Word.

———. 1994. "Being Salt." *Rutherford*, March, 11.

———. 1997. "Cleanliness Is Next to Crimelessness." *Christianity Today*, January 6, 80.

———. 1998. "A Pilgrim's Progress." Washington, D.C.: Prison Fellowship.

———. 1999. "What's Right about the Religious Right." *Christianity Today*, September 6, 58–59.

———. 2000. "A Worldview That Restores." *Jubilee*, winter, 5.

———. 2001a. "As the Dust Settles." Washington, D.C.: Prison Fellowship.

———. 2001b. "His Just Reward." *World*, June 16, 60.

———. 2001c. *Justice That Restores*. Wheaton, Ill.: Tyndale.

———. 2001d. "Prison Rape." *Jubilee Extra*, August, 7.

———. 2001e. "Sobering Statistics." *Indian Life*, July–August, 5–6.

———. 2001f. "Unalienable Rights." *Jubilee Extra*, September, 7.

———. 2002a. "A Clan of One's Own." *Christianity Today*, October 7, 156.

———. 2002b. "Just War in Iraq." *Christianity Today*, December 9, 72.

———. 2002c. "Patriotism in Two Kingdoms." *Jubilee*, winter, 15.

———. 2004. "Societal Suicide." *Christianity Today*, June, 72.

———. 2005. "What Is Justice?" *Christianity Today*, August, 80.

Colson, Charles, and Anne Morse. 2004. "The Moral Home Front." *Christianity Today*, October, 152.

———. 2006. "Bad Judgment." *Christianity Today*, August, 72.

Colson, Charles, and Nancy Pearcey. 1996. "Why Women Like Big Government." *Christianity Today*, November 11, 112.

Colson, Charles, and Daniel Van Ness. 1989. *Convicted*. Westchester, Ill.: Crossway.

Colson, Charles, and Ellen Vaughn. 1987. "What Prisoners Need Most." *Christian Herald*, November, 22–26.

Colter, Tiffany. 2004. "Robber-Turned-Reverend Reaches Inmates, Ex-Offenders for Christ." *Charisma*, April, 30–31.

Colvin, Mark. 1986. "Controlling the Surplus Population: The Latent Functions of Imprisonment and Welfare in Late U.S. Capitalism." In *The Political Economy of Crime*, edited by B. D. MacLean, 154–65. Scarborough: Prentice-Hall.

"Coming a Long Way." 1973. *His*, May, 6–18.

Conason, Joe, Alfred Ross, and Lee Cokorinos. 1996. "The Promise Keepers Are Coming." *Nation*, October 7, 11–19.

Conawa, Janelle. 1984. "Pastor Describes Brutal Conditions in Cuban Prisons." *Christianity Today*, August 10, 61–62.

Concerned Women for America. 1997. *Sisterhood or Liberalism?* Pamphlet. Washington, D.C., Concerned Women for America.

———. N.d. *Pro-Life Action Guide*. Washington, D.C.: Concerned Women for America.

Conn, Harvie. 1984. "Evangelical Feminism: Some Bibliographical Reflections on the Contemporary State of the Union." *Westminster Theological Review* 46:104–24.

———. 1994. "The City, Violence, and Jesus." *Urban Mission*, March, 3–5.

Connell, R. W. 1995. *Masculinities*. Berkeley: University of California Press.

"Controversy over Sterilization Pellet." 1994. *Political Environments* 1 (spring): 9.

Cook, Katsi. N.d. "Breastmilk, PCB's, and Motherhood." *Indigenous Woman* 1 (2): 1–4.

Cook-Lynn, Elizabeth. 1997. "Who Stole Native American Studies?" *Wicazo Sa Review* 12, no. 1 (spring): 9–28.

———. 1998a. "American Indian Intellectualism and the New Indian Story." In *Natives and Academics: Researching and Writing about American Indians*, edited by Devon Mihesuah, 111–38. Lincoln: University of Nebraska Press.

——. 1998b. *Why I Can't Read Wallace Stegner and Other Essays.* Madison: University of Wisconsin Press.

Cooperman, Alan. 2007. "Evangelical Body Stays Course on Warming." *Washington Post*, March 11.

Coote, Richard. 1972. "Rehabilitation: A Job for You." *Eternity*, March, 38.

"Coping with Crime." 1975. *Christianity Today*, June 6, 30–31.

Cornell, Stephen. 1988. *The Return of the Native: American Indian Political Resurgence.* New York: Oxford University Press.

Council on Biblical Sexual Ethics. 2001. *The Colorado Statement on Biblical Morality.* Colorado Springs: Focus on the Family.

Council on Interracial Books for Children. 1971. *Chronicles of American Indian Protest.* Greenwich, Conn.: Fawcett.

Courbat, Cindi. 1994. "Regent Produces *Prison to Praise.*" *Charisma*, October, 94.

Cowan, Len. 1991. "An Indigenous Church for Indigenous People." *Faith Today*, July–August, 23–26.

Cowley, Jack. 1999. Address given at the Justice Fellowship's Restorative Justice Forum, Washington, D.C., February 18–19.

Cox, Alison. 1990. "When Crime Hits Home." *Moody*, October, 12–16.

Cox, Kathryn. 2000. "The Valley of the Shadow of Death." *Salvation Army War Cry*, August 5, 4–7.

Crabb, Lawrence. 1976. "Should Lawbreakers Be Treated or Punished?" *Journal of the American Scientific Affiliation* 28 (June): 66–70.

Crenshaw, Kimberle. 1996. "Mapping the Margins: Intersectionality, Identity Politics, and Violence against Women of Color." In *Critical Race Theory*, edited by Kimberle Crenshaw, Neil Gotanda, Gary Peller, and Kendall Thomas, 357–83. New York: New Press.

"Crime and Consequences." 1990. *Moody*, October, 8.

"Critics Choice Awards." 1991. *Christianity Today*, April 8, 47.

Crouse, Janice. 2000. *Strategies for Reclaiming America's Culture.* Washington, D.C.: Beverly LaHaye Institute.

——. 2005. "Facing an Unwelcome Truth." *Christianity Today*, October, 87.

Crow Dog, Mary. 1991. *Lakota Woman.* San Francisco: Harper and Row.

Crow, Richard. 1973. "Not Caring Is Criminal." *Eternity*, September, 16–21.

Crum, Gary, and Thelma McCormack. 1992. *Abortion: Pro-choice or Pro-Life?* Washington, D.C.: American University Press.

Cryderman, Lyn. 1991. "Surviving the Street." *Campus Life*, November, 38–46.

Currie, Elliott. 1998. *Crime and Punishment in America.* New York: Metropolitan Books.

Curry, Dean. 1993. "Lawlessness and Disorder." *World*, April 24, 13.

Custer, Stewart. 1981. "The Critics' Corner." *Biblical Viewpoint* 15 (April): 67.

Cutrer, Corrie. 2001. "Witnesses Accused of Failing to Report Abuse." *Christianity Today*, December 3, 23–24.

——. 2002a. "Option for Alienated Baptist Missionaries." *Christianity Today*, November 18, 39.

——. 2002b. "A Time of Justice." *Christianity Today*, May 21, 19–20.

——. 2002c. "To Sign or Not to Sign?" *Christianity Today*, April 22, 20–21.

Daigle, Richard. 1999. "Mexican Woman Answers Call to Rescue Needy Mayan Orphans." *Charisma*, March, 28.

——. 2001. "Earl Paul Denies Sex-Abuse Charges." *Charisma*, July, 16–17.

"Daniel." 2001. "Thankful to Be Alive." *Indian Life*, July–August, 7.

Daniels, Kimberly. 2005. "Don't Be Fooled by Farrakhan." *Charisma*, November, 86–90, 122–23.

D'antonio, Michael. 1989. *Fall from Grace*. New York: Farrar, Straus and Giroux.

Dart, Bob. 2004. "Abortion-Rights Backers March." *Dayton Daily News*. April 26.

Dart, Bob, and Mary Lou Pickel. 2004. "Abortion Rights Supporters March." *Atlanta Journal-Constitution*. April 26.

Davids, Dorothy. N.d. "Powerful Women, Strong Willed Women." *Indigenous Woman* 1 (3): 56–58.

Davis, Angela. 1988. *Angela Davis: An Autobiography*. New York: International Publishers.

——. 2000. "Plenary Presentation." In *The Color of Violence: Violence against Women of Color*, edited by INCITE! Women of Color against Violence, 124. Conference proceedings. Santa Cruz: INCITE! Women of Color against Violence.

——. 2003. *Are Prisons Obsolete?* New York: Seven Stories.

——. N.d. "Crime and Punishment, Changing Attitudes Toward." Unpublished paper, copy in Andrea Smith's possession.

Davis, Stephen. 1977. *The Debate about the Bible*. Philadelphia: Westminster.

Dawson, John. 2005. "Stunted Intelligence." *World*, January 29, 26–27.

——. 2006. "Border War." *World*, April 1, 27.

Dayton, Donald. 1977. "The Social and Political Conservatism of Modern American Evangelicalism: A Preliminary Search for the Reasons." *Union Seminary Quarterly Review* 32 (winter): 71–78.

——. 1991. *The Variety of American Evangelicalism*. Knoxville: University of Tennessee Press.

Dean, Carolyn. 1999. *Inka Bodies and the Body of Christ*. Durham, N.C.: Duke University Press.

Dean, Jamie. 2005a. "Mission Impossible." *World*, October 29, 21.

——. 2005b. "Trail of Tears." *World*, April 2, 23.

——. 2006. "Forging Their Trespasses." *World*, April 1, 25–26.

Dearing, John. 1994. "The Priest and the Con Man." *Churchman* 108 (4): 357–64.

DeCastro, Bernie. 1998. "The Power to Change." *Decision*, November, 4–5.

———. N.d. "Letter from the Secretary." *Restorative Justice Journal* 1 (3): 4–5.

Degraffenred, Anna. 2004. "One Woman's Passion." *Fatherhood Today*, summer, 9–10.

Deloria, Philip. 1998. *Playing Indian*. New Haven: Yale University Press.

———. 2004. *Indians in Unexpected Places*. Lawrence: University of Kansas Press.

Deloria, Vine. 1985. *Behind the Trail of Broken Treaties*. Austin: University of Texas Press.

———. 1988. *Custer Died for Your Sins*. Norman: University of Oklahoma Press.

———. 1992. *God Is Red*. Golden, Colo.: North American Press.

———. 1999. *For This Land*. New York: Routledge.

———. 2000. "The "Vanishing" Americans." *Indian Life*, July–August, 12–13.

Deloria, Vine, Jr., 1974. *The Indian Affair*. New York: Friendship.

De Marco, John M. 1997. "*Native Wind* Reaches Forgotten People." *Charisma*, August, 28–31.

Denetdale, Jennifer. 2006. "Chairmen, Presidents, and Princesses: The Navajo Nation, Gender, and the Politics of Tradition." *Wicazo Sa Review* 21, no. 1 (spring): 9–28.

"Denominational Leaders Address Drug Crisis." 1990. *Christianity Today*, November 19, 58–59.

DeVore, Leigh. 2000. "New Gay Pentecostal Denomination Says Homosexuality Isn't Sinful." *Charisma*, January, 20–23.

DeYoung, Curtiss Paul, Michael Emerson, George Yancey, and Karen Chai Kim. 2003. *United by Faith*. Oxford: Oxford University Press.

Diamond, Billy. 1991. "Issues That Can't Wait." *Faith Today*, July–August, 27–28.

Diamond, Sara. 1989. *Spiritual Warfare*. Cambridge, Mass.: South End.

———. 1995. *Roads to Dominion*. New York: Guilford.

———. 1998. *Not by Politics Alone: The Enduring Influence of the Christian Right*. New York: Guilford.

Diemer, Tom. 2004. "Thousands Rally for Choice: 500,000 to 800,000 March in D.C. in Support of Abortion Rights." *Cleveland Plains Dealer*. April 26.

Di Leonardo, Micaela. 1998. *Exotics at Home*. Chicago: University of Chicago Press.

"A Different View of the Environment." 2000. *Faith and Freedom*, spring, 16.

Dilulio, John. 1999. "Two Million Prisoners Are Enough." *Wall Street Journal*. March 12.

Dixon, Herti. 2006. "Indigenous Christians Embrace Tradition." *Charisma*, April, 32–33.

Dixon, Richard, Roger Lowery, and Lloyd Jones. 1992. "The Fact and Form of

Born-Again Religious Conversions and Sociopolitical Conservativism." *Review of Religious Research* 34 (December): 117–31.

Dobson, Edward. 1985. "Standing Together on Absolutes." *United Evangelical Action*, September–October, 4–10.

Dobson, Edward, and Cal Thomas. 1999. *Blinded by Might*. Grand Rapids: Zondervan.

Dobson, James. 1999. "The New Cost of Discipleship." *Christianity Today*, September 6, 56–58.

"Dobson's Choice." 2002. *World*, April 20, 7.

Dollar, George. 1973. *A History of Fundamentalism in America*. Greenville: Bob Jones University Press.

Domigues, Patricia. 1994. "Women of the New Christian Right: Ideological Hegemony in Process." PhD diss. University of California, Riverside.

Donziger, Steven. 1996. *The Real War on Crime*. New York: HarperCollins.

Dorris, Michael. 1989. *The Broken Cord*. New York: Harper and Row.

Dorsch, Audrey. 1991. "The Book of Acts on James Bay." *Faith Today*, July–August, 18–22.

Doud, Guy Rice. 1991. "He Wore a Badge." *Moody*, June, 25–28.

Doyle, Barrie. 1974. "Jesus in Jail." *Christianity Today*, July 5, 44–46.

Duckworth, Marion. 1984. "Mark Winters: 'Jesus Tamed My Lions.'" *Christian Life*, March, 16–17.

Dunnet, Walter. 1975. Review of *All We're Meant to Be*. *Moody*, February, 74–75.

Eberly, Don. 1999. "We're Fighting the Wrong Battle." *Christianity Today*, September 6, 53–54.

Echohawk, Crystal. 1999. "Reflections on Sovereignty." *Indigenous Woman* 3 (1): 21–22.

"Economic Development in Bangladesh." 2000. *Population Research Institute*, January–February, 3, 13.

Edwards, James R. 1986. "Does God Really Want to Be Called Father?" *Christianity Today*, February 21, 27–30.

Edwards, Jonathan. 1998a. *The Works of Jonathan Edwards*. Peabody, Mass.: Hendrickson.

———. 1998b. *The Works of Jonathan Edwards*. Peabody, Mass.: Hendrickson.

Eghbal, Morry. 2005. "God Turned My Life to Good." *Decision*, February, 28–29.

Eha, Maureen. 2002. "She Will Not Remain Silent." *Charisma*, June, 36–47.

———. 2005. "Days of Thunder." *Charisma*, August, 68–78.

Eichstaedt, Peter. 1994. *If You Poison Us*. Santa Fe: Red Crane.

Eidsmoe, John. 1992. *Columbus and Cortez: Conquerors for Christ*. Green Forest, Ark.: New Leaf.

Ellisen, Stanley. 1972. "The Bible and the Death Penalty." *Moody*, June, 28–29, 102.

"Ending the Myth of Overpopulation." 1999. *Population Research Institute*, special edition, 1.

Enns, Aiden Schlichting. 2000. "Where the Spirit Lives." *Charisma*, July–August, 28–33.

Epstein, Barbara. 1995. "'Political Correctness' and Collective Powerlessness." In *Cultural Politics and Social Movements*, edited by Marcy Darnovsky, Barbara Epstein, and Richard Flacks, 3–19. Philadelphia: Temple University Press.

Erler, Bob, and John Souter. 1981. "The Catch Me Killer." *United Evangelical Action*, July–August, 38–40.

Etienne, Mavis. 2000. "The Importance of Community." *Charisma*, July–August, 33.

———. 2004. "A Mohawk Peace Maker." *Indian Life*, January–February, 8–9.

Evans, Alice. 1999. "Rediscovering Justice in, of All Places, Church." *Christianity Today*, August 9, 52–55.

Evans, Fred. 2000. "Courage to Fight Racism." *Charisma*, July–August, 32.

Evans, Tony. 1990. *America's Only Hope*. Chicago: Moody.

Evearitt, Daniel. 1993. *Rush Limbaugh and the Bible*. Camp Hill, Pa.: Horizon House.

Everton, Sean. 2001. "The Promise Keepers: Religious Revival or Third Wave of the Religious Right?" *Review of Religious Research* 43 (September): 51–69.

Ewen, Alex. 1996. "Dangerous Intersections: Feminist Perspectives on Immigration." Address delivered at "Population and the Environment," conference of the Committee on Women, Population, and the Environment, Union Theological Seminary, New York, October 26.

Fackre, Gabriel. 1989. "Evangelical Hermeneutics." *Interpretation* 43 (April): 117–29.

Fagan, Patrick. 1997. "The Real Root Cause of Violent Crime: The Breakdown of the Family." *Indian Life*, March–April, 5.

———. 2001. *How U.N. Conventions on Women and Children's Rights Undermine Family, Religion, and Sovereignty*. Washington, D.C.: Heritage Foundation.

Fager, Charles. 1982. "No Holds Barred." *Eternity*, April 1982, 20–24.

Falwell, Jerry. 1982. "Capital Punishment for Capital Crimes." *Fundamentalist Journal*, November, 8–9.

———. 1983. "Editor's Note." *Fundamentalist Journal*, November, 1.

———. 1999. "I'd Do It All Again." *Christianity Today*, September 6, 50–51.

Farhart, Scott. 2003. "For Better, and for Worse." *New Man*, May–June, 48–49.

Fea, John. 1993. "American Fundamentalism and Neo-evangelicalism: A Bibliographic Survey." *Evangelical Journal* 11:21–30.

Feedback. 2006a. *Charisma*, May, 10–12, 88.

——. 2006b. *Charisma*, February, 8–10, 74.

Feldmeth, Joanne Ross, and Midge Wallace Finley. 1990. *We Weep for Ourselves and Our Children*. San Francisco: Harper.

Feldt, Gloria. 2004. *The War on Choice*. New York: Bantam.

Felix, Paul. N.d. *The Hermeneutics of Evangelical Feminism*. Louisville: Council on Biblical Manhood and Womanhood.

Feminist Women's Health Centers. 1997. "Depo-Provera (The Shot)."http:/www.fwhc.org/bcdepo.htm.

Ferguson, Chris. 1998. "A Reflection on 'Culturally Sensitive Evangelism' from the United Church of Canada Tradition." *International Review of Mission* 87 (July): 381–87.

Fieguth, Debra. 2000a. "Fire and Ice." *Christianity Today*, October 23, 20–21.

——. 2000b. "Northern Christians Embrace the Faith." *Indian Life*, May–June, 1, 5–6.

——. 2000c. "What Can We Learn from Arctic Christians?" *Indian Life*, May–June, 6.

——. 2002a. "Arctic Revival." *Faith Today*, January–February, 18–22.

——. 2002b. "Prostitute Murders Spur Ministry." *Christianity Today*, November 18, 32–33.

"Field." 1996. *Family Voice*, August, 22.

Fiero, Charles. 1988. "The Ojibwe New Testament: It Sounds Good." *Alliance Life*, November 23, 22–23.

Fink, Chris. 2004. "Breaking into Prison." *Christianity Today*, May, 36–39.

Fiorenza, Elisabeth Schussler. 1984. *Bread Not Stone*. Boston: Beacon.

Fish, Stanley. 1994. *There's No Such Thing as Free Speech*. New York: Oxford University Press.

——. 2005. *Is There a Text in the Class?* Cambridge: Harvard University Press.

Fixico, Donald. 2003. *The American Indian Mind in a Linear World*. New York: Routledge.

Fledderus, Bill. 1999. "Native Speakers Get Scripture." *Charisma*, January–February, 15.

Forbes, Cheryl. 1982. "What Hope for America's Prisons?" *Christian Herald*, April, 32–40.

Fortune, Marie. 1983. *Sexual Violence: The Unmentionable Sin*. New York: Pilgrim.

——. 1989. *Is Nothing Sacred? When Sex Invades the Pastoral Relationship*. New York: Pilgrim.

Foucault, Michel. 1970. *The Order of Things*. New York: Vintage.

——. 1977a. *Discipline and Punish*. New York: Vintage.

——. 1977b. *Power/Knowledge*. New York: Pantheon.

——. 1980. *History of Sexuality*. New York: Vintage.

Frame, Randy. 1985. "News Media Takes High Profile in Well-Publicized Rape Case." *Christianity Today*, June 14, 58–64.

———. 1989. "The Theonomic Urge." *Christianity Today*, April 21, 38–40.

———. 1996. "Greening of the Gospel?" *Christianity Today*, November 11, 82–84.

———. 1997. "Helping the Poor Help Themselves." *Christianity Today*, February 3, 70–73.

———. 1999. "Reclaiming Feminism." *Christianity Today*, September 6, 102–3.

Francis, Vic. 1997. "Christians from 32 Countries Reclaim Native Customs." *Charisma*, April, 47–48.

Frank, Thomas. 2005. *What's the Matter with Kansas? How Conservatives Won the Heart of America*. New York: Owl.

Frankenburg, Ruth. 1993. *White Women, Race Matters: The Social Construction of Whiteness*. Minneapolis: University of Minnesota Press.

Freedman, Alix. 1999. "Why Teen-Age Girls Want." *Focus on the Family Citizen*, February, 6–9.

Freedman, Estelle. 1981. *Their Sisters' Keepers*. Ann Arbor: University of Michigan Press.

Frichner, Tonya Gonnella. 1999. "Haudenosaunee Law, Sovereignty and Governance." *Indigenous Woman* 2 (6): 34–36.

Fuller, Daniel. 1973. "On Relevation and Biblical Authority." *Journal of the Evangelical Theological Society* 2 (spring): 67–72.

Fuller, W. Harold. 1996. "Hurts Revealed, Hope Prevails." *Faith Today*, March–April, 14–16.

Gadoua, Renee. 2004. "A Woman Should Decide." *Post-Standard* (Syracuse), April 26.

Gaines, Adrienne. 1999. "Another Toronto Blessing? Pastors Say God Filled Teeth with Gold Says Arnott." *Charisma*, June, 38–40.

Gallagher, Sally. 2003. *Evangelical Identity and Gendered Family Life*. New Brunswick, N.J.: Rutgers University Press.

Gardner, Christine. 1998. "Caught between Cultures." *Christianity Today*, June 15, 14–15.

———. 1999. "Women Resist Abuse Globally." *Christianity Today*, April 26, 20.

Garland, Diana. 1985. "Volunteer Ministry to Families of Prisoners and the Christian Worker's Role." *Social Work and Christianity* 21 (spring): 13–25.

Garroutte, Eva. 2003. *Real Indians*. Berkeley: University of California Press.

Gedicks, Al. 1993. *The New Resource Wars*. Cambridge, Mass.: South End.

Geisler, Norman. 1987. "Inerrancy Leaders: Apply the Bible." *Eternity*, February, 25–28.

George, Timothy. 2005. "A Peace Plan for the Gender War." *Christianity Today*, November, 50–56.

Gibson, Gail. 2004. "Thousands Rally for Abortion Rights." *Baltimore Sun*. April 26.

Gil, Vincent. 1988. "In Thy Father's House: Self-Report Findings of Sexually

Abused Daughters from Conservative Christian Homes." *Journal of Psychology and Theology* 16 (2): 144–52.

Gilbreath, Edward. 2000. "The Jerry We Never Knew." *Christianity Today*, April 24, 113–14.

Giles, Thomas. 1993. "Coping with Sexual Misconduct in the Church." *Christianity Today*, January 11, 48–49.

Gilroy, Paul. 2001. *Against Race*. Cambridge: Harvard University Press.

Gitlin, Todd. 1994. "From Universality to Difference: Notes on the Fragmentation of the Idea of the Left." In *Social Theory and the Politics of Identity*, edited by Craig Calhoun, 151–74. Malden: Blackwell.

Glanco, Stephany. 1987. "A Tale of Two Children in the City." *Moody*, November, 94,

Gluck, Sherna Berger. 1998. "Whose Feminism, Whose History?" In *Community Activism and Feminist Politics*, edited by Nancy Naples, 31–56. New York: Routledge.

"God at the Wheel." 1999. *Jubilee Extra*, September, 1–2.

Gomez, Marsha. N.d.-a. "Dumping and Environmental Racism in Texas." *Indigenous Woman* 1 (4): 6–8.

———. N.d.-b. "IWN Honors: Interview with Janet McCloud." *Indigenous Women* 2 (3): 49–51.

Gomez, Reid. 2005. "The Storyteller's Escape: Sovereignty and Worldview." In *Reading Native American Women*, edited by Ines Hernandez-Avila, 145–70. Lanham, Md.: Altamira.

Gonzalez, Carlos. 1997. "Ministry of Reconciliation." *Alliance Life*, January 15, 11.

Goodwin, John. 1972. "Soledad Brother and the Crime of Punishment." *Eternity*, March, 14–15.

Goolsby, Bruce. 1999. "New Ministry in Nevada Aims to Reach Alienated Native Americans." *Charisma*, November, 39–40.

———. 2004. "Food for Hungry Hearts." *Charisma*, December, 52–54.

Gorcoff, Dennis. 1975. "It Seems to Me." *Moody*. July–August, 54–56.

Gorman, Michael. 2000. "Irreconcilable Differences." *Christianity Today*, March 6, 77–78.

Gowan, R. L. 1997. *Legends of the Trail*. Colorado Springs: IBS.

Grady, J. Lee. 1991. "Is the Future Safe for Our Children?" *Charisma*, January, 61–68.

———. 1994. "America's Forgotten People." *Charisma*, October, 25–32.

———. 1997a. "EPA Panel Rebukes World." *Christianity Today*, August 11, 58.

———. 1997b. "The Other Pentecostals." *Charisma*, June, 62–68.

———. 1998. "Toronto's Afterglow." *Charisma*, December, 70–78, 125.

———. 1999. "NAE Leader Wants to Build Bridges with Charismatics." *Charisma*, May, 23.

———. 2000a. "Let the Woman Preach!" *Charisma*, December, 56–61.

———. 2000b. "Native Americans Use Culture for Christ." *Charisma*, July, 22–23.

———. 2000c. "Out with Chauvanism." *Charisma*, December, 8.

———. 2001. "Control Freaks and the Women Who Love Them." *New Man*, January–February, 40–44.

———. 2002. "Stop the Feud." *Charisma*, July, 6.

———. 2004a. "Former Rock Musician Now Brings 'Native Praise' to Indian Communities." *Charisma*, November, 35.

———. 2004b. "Heretics among Us." *Charisma*, April, 6.

———. 2005. "It Was for Freedom." *Charisma*, April, 6.

———. 2006. "Don't Drop the Ark." *Charisma*, July, 6.

Graham, Billy. 1986. "Billy Graham Speaks Out on Jerry Falwell." *CALC Report*, December, 27.

Graham, John. 1987. "Confronting Your Teens about Drugs." *Fundamentalist Journal*, February, 29–32, 48.

Grande, Sandy. 2004. *Red Pedagogy*. Lanham: Rowman and Littlefield.

Greco, Sheila. 1997. "Revival Stirs Upstate New York." *Charisma*, December, 30–34.

Green, Rex. 1986. "Back to Jail." *World Christian*, September–October, 28–31.

Green, Ross Gordon. 1998. *Justice in Aboriginal Communities*. Saskatoon: Purich.

Greene, Bonnie. 1973. "These Christians Show the Way." *Eternity*, September, 16–21.

Greenway, Roger. 1989. "A Shift in the Global Center of Christianity." *United Evangelical Action*, November–December, 4–7.

Griffith, Lee. 1993. *The Fall of Prison*. Grand Rapids: Eerdmans.

Grinde, Donald, and Bruce Johansen. 1995. *Ecocide of Native America*. Santa Fe: Clear Light.

Groothius, Rebecca Merrill. 1999. "Sexuality, Spirituality, and Feminist Religion." Working paper, Christians for Biblical Equality.

———. 2001. "Religious Women Look at Feminism." *Priscilla Papers* 15 (summer): 20–21.

Grossman, Zoltan. 2002. "Unlikely Alliances: Treaty Conflicts and Environmental Cooperation between Native American and Rural White Communities." PhD diss., University of Wisconsin.

Grudem, Wayne. 1997. *What's Wrong with Gender-Neutral Bible Translations?* Libertyville, Ill.: Council on Biblical Manhood and Womanhood.

———. 2002. "Why I'm against the TNIV." *Charisma*, November, 87, 110.

Grudem, Wayne, and Grant Osborne. 1997. "Do Inclusive-Language Bibles Distort Scripture?" *Christianity Today*, October 27, 26–39.

Gruszka, Dennis. 1997. "God's Holy Fire." *Native Reflections*, winter, 2–3, 5.

Gumpert, Gary, and Susan Drucker. 1992. "Respect for Life Even at Public Executions." *Media Development* 39 (4): 17–18.

Gundry, Patricia. 1975. "Perhaps We Should Take Another Look." *Moody*, May, 61–64.

———. 1977. *Woman Be Free!* Grand Rapids: Zondervan.

———. 1988. "Mix at Our Own Risk." *Daughters of Sarah*, May–June, 14–15.

Gundry, Stanley. 1986. "Biblical Authority and the Issues in Question." In *Women, Authority, and the Bible*, edited by Alvera Mickelsen, 60–64. Downers Grove, Ill.: InterVarsity.

Guth, James. 1983. "Southern Baptist Clergy: Vanguard of the Christian Right?" In *The New Christian Right*, edited by Robert Liebman and Robert Wuthnow, 117–30. New York: Aldine.

———. 1996a. "The Bully Pulpit." In *Religion and the Culture Wars: Dispatches from the Front*, edited by John Green, James Guth, Corwin Smidt, and Lyman Kellstedt, 146–71. London: Rowman and Littlefield.

———. 1996b. "The Politics of the Christian Right." In *Religion and the Culture Wars: Dispatches from the Front*, edited by John Green, James Guth, Corwin Smidt, and Lyman Kellstedt, 7–29. London: Rowman and Littlefield.

Guthrie, Stan. 2003. "Life after 'Coach.'" *Christianity Today*, December, 25.

Haddan, Jeffrey. 1988. *Televangelism*. New York: Holt.

Hageman, Howard. 1988. "Colonial Outreach." *Reformed Journal* 38 (November): 6–7.

Hall, Charles. 1997. "The Christian Left: Who Are They and How Are They Different from the Christian Right?" *Review of Religious Research* 39 (September): 27–45.

Hall, Christopher, and John Sanders. 2001. "Does God Know Your Next Move?" *Christianity Today*, May 21, 38–45.

Hall, John. 1989. "The Thief." *Christian Herald*, November–December, 51.

Hall, Stuart. 1976. *Resistance through Ritual: Youth Subcultures in Post-war Britain*. New York: HarperCollins.

———. 1988. *The Hard Road to Renewal*. London: Verso.

———. 1996a. "Gramsci's Relevance for the Study of Race and Ethnicity." In *Critical Dialogues in Cultural Studies*, edited by David Morley and Kuan-Hsing Chen, 411–40. London: Routledge.

———. 1996b. "The Problem of Ideology: Marxism without Guarantees." In *Critical Dialogues in Cultural Studies*, edited by David Morley and Kuan-Hsing Chen, 25–45. London: Routledge.

Hall, Stuart, Chas Critcher, Tony Jefferson, John Clarke, and Brian Roberts. 1978. *Policing the Crisis*. New York: Homes and Meier.

Hamilton, A. C. 2001. "Working Towards Aboriginal Justice." *Indian Life*, July–August, 6–7.

Hammond, Phillip, and James Hunter. 1984. "On Maintaining Plausibility:

The Worldview of Evangelical College Students." *Journal for the Scientific Study of Religion* 23 (3): 221–38.

Han, Sora. 2006. "Bonds of Representation: Vision, Race, and Law in Post-civil-rights America." PhD diss., University of California, Santa Cruz.

Hancock, Barry, and Paul Sharp. 1994. "The Death Penalty and Christianity: A Conceptual Paradox." *Perspectives on Science and Christian Faith* 46 (March): 61–65.

Hanger, Donald. 1984. "The Battle for Inerrancy." *Reformed Journal* 34 (April): 19–22.

Hannah, Jeff. 1998. "Lessons from the Fall." *Focus on the Family*, October, 12–13.

Hansen, Jane. 1997. "Ending the Gender Wars." *Charisma*, December, 56–58.

Hanson, Allen. 1982. "Prison Ministry." *Alliance Witness*, July 21, 7–8.

———. 1985. "Witnessing in Jails and Prisons." *Alliance Witness*, February 27, 6–7.

Harawira, Makere. 1998. "Maori and the Multilateral Agreement on Investment: What Does It Mean?" *Indigenous Woman* 2 (5): 26–29.

Hardesty, Nancy. 1971. "Women: Second Class Citizens." *Eternity*, January, 14–29.

Hardt, Michael, and Antonio Negri. 2000. *Empire*. Cambridge: Harvard University Press.

Harjo, Joy, and Gloria Bird, eds. 1997. *Reinventing the Enemy's Language*. New York: Norton.

Harmon, Cedric. 1999. "Prayer Walk Revisits Cherokee Massacre Sites in Southern States." *Charisma*, October, 36.

———. 2002. "The Man and the Plan." *Charisma*, July, 46–53.

Harris, Lelan. 1995. "Battling for the Future of the World." *Rutherford*, March, 6–9.

Hart, Angie. 1983. "All's Not Wrong with Women's Rights." *Fundamentalist Journal*, November, 14–15.

Hartmann, Betsy. 1995. *Reproductive Rights and Wrongs: The Global Politics of Population Control*. Cambridge, Mass.: South End.

Hartsock, Nancy. 1990. "Foucault on Power: A Theory for Women?" In *Feminism and Postmodernism*, edited by Linda Nicholson, 157–75. New York: Routledge.

Harvey, Bob. 1997. "The Role of Churches in Native Reconciliation." *Faith Today*, April, 18–20.

———. 2000. "Christians and Crime." *Faith Today*, September–October, 30–36.

Hayford, Jack. 2003. "Men: Ordained to Lead?" *New Man*, November–December, 41.

Hearn, Virginia. 1993. "Meta Patriarchy Revisited." *Journal of Psychology and Theology* 21 (fall): 219.

Hebdige, Dick. 1979. *Subculture and the Meaning of Style*. London: Methuen.

Heggen, Carolyn. 1993. *Sexual Abuse in Christian Homes and Churches.* Scottsdale: Herald.

Hekman, Randall. 1985. "You Call This Justice?" *Moody*, May, 18–21.

Henderson, Lesa. 1999. "Charismatic Pastor Says God Is Sending Gold Miracles." *Charisma*, October, 33–34.

Henry, Carl F. H. 1975. "Battle of the Sexes." *Christianity Today*, July 4, 45–46.

———. 1984. "Conflict over Biblical Inerrancy." *Christianity Today*, May 7, 24–25.

Hentoff, Nat. 2003. "Conservatives Rise for the Bill of Rights!" *Village Voice.* April 25.

Herman, Didi. 1997. *The Anti-gay Agenda.* Chicago: University of Chicago Press.

Heystek, Al. 1996. "The War on Drugs." *Perspectives*, October, 5–8.

Heywood, Leslie, and Jennifer Drake, eds. 1997. *Third Wave Agenda: Being Feminist, Doing Feminism.* Minneapolis: University of Minnesota Press.

"Hidden Children." 1995. *Evangelizing Today's Child*, April, 12–14.

Highway, Marlene. N.d. "The Grassroots of the Reserve and the Strength of the Women." *Indigenous Woman* 2 (2): 22.

Himmelstein, Jerome. 1990. *To the Right.* Berkeley: University of California Press.

Hitt, Russel. 1986. "Crackdown on Crack." *Eternity*, November, 10.

Hobbs, Eric, and Walter Hobbs. 1983. "Contemporary Capital Punishment: Biblical Difficulties with the Biblically Permissible." *Christian Scholar's Review* 11 (3): 250–62.

Hodges, Louis Igou. 1994. "Evangelical Definitions of Inspiration: Critiques and a Suggested Definition." *Journal of the Evangelical Theological Society* 37 (March): 99–114.

Holloway, John. 2005. *Change the World without Taking Power.* London: Pluto.

hooks, bell. 1997. "Representing Whiteness in the Black Imagination." In *Displacing Whiteness*, edited by Ruth Frankenberg, 165–79. Durham, N.C.: Duke University Press.

Horner, S. Sue. 2002. "Trying to Be God in the World: The Story of the Evangelical Women's Caucus and the Crisis over Homosexuality." In *Gender, Ethnicity, and Religion*, edited by Rosemary Radford Ruether, 99–124. Minneapolis: Augsburg Fortress.

Horowitz, Michael. 2005. "How to Win Friends and Influence Culture." *Christianity Today*, September, 70–78.

House, Wayne H. 1979. "Paul, Women, and Contemporary Evangelical Feminism." *Bibliotecha Sacra* 136 (January–March): 40–53.

"How to Create a Woman." 1973. *His*, May, 6–18.

Hoyle, Lydia Huffman. 1994. "Elizabeth Morse: Missionary to American Indians." *Baptist History* 24 (January): 3–11.

Hubbard, David Allen. 1970. *What We Evangelicals Believe*. Pasadena: Fuller Theological Seminary.

Huckins, Kyle. 2000. "Potlatch Gospel." *Christianity Today*, June 12, 66–69.

Hudon, Eileen. 2000. "Organizing against Violence in Communities of Color." In *The Color of Violence: Violence against Women of Color*, edited by INCITE! Women of Color against Violence, 124. Conference proceedings. Santa Cruz: INCITE! Women of Color against Violence.

Hughes, Irfon. 2004. "The Remarkable John Eliot (1604–90), Missionary to the Indians." *Banner of Truth*, December, 1–6.

Humphreys, Fisher. 1987. "The Baptist Faith and Message and the Chicago Statement on Biblical Inerrancy." In *Proceedings of the Conference on Biblical Inerrancy*, 317–29. Nashville: Broadman.

Hunt, Angela, and Kay Raysar. 1988. "Reconciling the Forgotten." *Fundamentalist Journal*, March, 23–27.

Hunter, Joel. 2005. "8 Myths about Male Authority." *New Man*, November–December, 46–48.

Hutchinson, Mary. 2002a. "Joyce Meyer Leads Her Father to Faith." *Charisma*, May, 14–15.

———. 2002b. "Native Americans Believers Gather to Forgive 'White Man' of Injustice." *Charisma*, December, 18.

Hyatt, Susan. 2000. *Essential Elements of a Pentecostal/Charismatic Theology of Womanhood*. Dallas: Hyatt.

Ignatieff, Michael. 1978. *A Just Measure of Pain*. New York: Pantheon.

INCITE! Women of Color Against Violence, ed. 2006. *The Color of Violence: The INCITE! Anthology*. Cambridge, Mass.: South End.

———. 2007. *The Revolution Will Not Be Funded: Beyond the Non-Profit Industrial Complex*. Cambridge, Mass.: South End.

Indian Life. 1993. "Totem Poles," The Council Speaks. January–February, 16–17.

Indian Life Ministries. 1999. *The Council Speaks*. Winnipeg: Indian Life.

"Indians Hold Historic Crusade." 1988. *Christianity Today*, June 17, 72.

"Indigenous People's Statement from Seattle." 2001. *Indigenous Woman* 4 (2):44–46.

Indigenous Women's Network. 1995. *Indigenous Women Address the World*. Austin: Indigenous Women's Network.

———. N.d. "Summary of Issues Affecting Indigenous Women." *Indigenous Women* 2 (3):32–35.

Ingersoll, Julie. 2005. *Evangelical Christian Women*. New York: New York University Press.

"Inside—and Out—of the Miami Drug Cartel." 1998. *Inside Journal* 9 (8): 1, 7.

"In Theory." 1995. *C.C. Watch*, March, 7.

"Iowa IFI Program to Begin in September." 1998. *Jubilee*, summer, 15.

Isasi-Diaz, Ada-Maria. 1993. *En La Lucha*. Minneapolis: Augsburg.

Isitt, Larry. 1984. "Willie: Maximum Freedom in a Maximum Security Prison." *Christianity Today*, April 6, 22–25.

Iver, Martha Abele Mac. 1990. "Mirror Images? Conceptions of God and Political Duty on the Left and Right of the Evangelical Spectrum." *Sociological Analysis* 51 (3): 287–95.

Jackson, Dave. 1982. "Victims of Crime Turn the Other Cheek." *Christianity Today*, April 9, 33–35.

Jackson, Don. 1973. "A New Mission Opportunity with an Exciting Future." *Church Musician*, November, 32–39.

Jackson, Harry. 2004. "A Scandal in Iraq." *Charisma*, August, 18.

———. 2005a. "Church behind Bars." *Charisma*, June, 70.

———. 2005b. "The New American Dream." *Charisma*, February, 14.

———. 2006. "Seize the Moment." *Charisma*, May, 78.

Jacobs, Adrian. 2000a. "Drumming, Dancing, Chanting, and Other Christian Things." *Mission Frontiers*, September, 16–18.

———. 2000b. "New Songs and Ways of Worship." *Charisma*, July–August, 36.

Jacobs, Janet. 1984. "The Economy of Love in Religious Commitment: The Deconversion of Women from Nontraditional Religious Movements." *Journal for the Scientific Study of Religion* 23 (2): 155–71.

Jacobs, Sue-Ellen, Wesley Thomas, and Sabine Lang, eds. 1999. *Two-Spirit People*. Urbana: University of Illinois Press.

Jahoda, Gustav. 1999. *Images of Savages*. London: Routledge.

Jaimes, M. Annette, and Theresa Halsey. 1992. "American Indian Women: At the Center of Indigenous Resistance in North America." In *State of Native America*, edited by M. Annette Jaimes, 311–44. Cambridge, Mass.: South End.

James, Joy. 1999. *Shadowboxing*. New York: Palgrave.

Jankovic, Ivan. 1977. "Labour Market and Imprisonment." *Crime and Social Justice* 8:17–31.

Jasper, William. 2003. "Trading Freedom for Security." *New American*, May 5, 10–16.

Jennings, George. 1990. "Peyote: Its Appeal to Indian Christian Defectors." *Evangelical Missions Quarterly* 26 (January): 64–69.

Jeschke, Marlin. 1982. "Retribution or Restitution." *United Evangelical Action*, fall, 21–23.

"Jesus and Women." 1973. *His*, May, 6–18.

"Jesus Speaks Ojibway." 2002. *Indian Life*, January–February, 3.

Jewell, James. 2006. "A Corrupt Salvation." *Christianity Today*, March, 23–24.

Jewett, Paul. 1975. *Man and Male and Female*. Grand Rapids: Eerdmans.

Jewett, Paul, and Elisabeth Elliot. 1975. "Why I Favor the Ordination of Women, Why I Oppose the Ordination of Women." *Christianity Today*, June 6, 7–16.

Johnson Reagon, Bernice. 1983. "Coalition Politics: Turning the Century." In *Home Girls: A Black Feminist Anthology*, edited by Barbara Smith, 356–69. New York: Kitchen Table.

Johnson, Peter. 1998. "Forty on the Street Years." *Charisma*, February, 39–44, 96.

———. 1999. "The Salvation of a Serial Killer." *Charisma*, June, 66–70, 122.

———. 2002. "New York's Homeless Pastor." *Charisma*, December, 60–65.

Johnson, Troy. 1996. *Occupation of Alcatraz Island*. Berkeley: University of California Press.

Johnston, Robert. 1979. *Evangelicals at an Impasse*. Atlanta: John Know.

———. 1992. "Biblical Authority and Hermeneutics: The Growing Evangelical Dialogue." *Southwestern Journal of Theology* 34 (spring): 22–30.

Jones, Bob, IV. 1998. "Life Is Not a Party." *World*, October 3, 14–17.

Jones, Jim. 1998. "Unique Prison Program Serves as Boot Camp for Heaven." *Christianity Today*, February 9, 88–89.

Jones, Rufus. 1973. "Where Do We Go from Wounded Knee?" *Eternity*, August, 13, 26.

Jordan-Lake, Joy. 1992. "Conduct Unbecoming a Preacher." *Christianity Today*, February 19, 26–32.

Justice Fellowship. 1998. *1997 Criminal Justice Crime Index*. Washington, D.C.: Justice Fellowship.

———. 2002. *Justice e-Report*. Washington, D.C.: Justice Fellowship.

Justice, Nancy. 2000. "Amazon Tribe Still Responding to Gospel Years after Missionary Deaths." *Charisma*, August, 38–39.

Kadlecek, Jo. 1994. "The Other Face of Crime." *World*, March 12, 24.

Kale, Kenneth. 1972. "Sorry about That." In *The Way*, edited by Shirley Hill Witt and Stan Steiner, 143–44. New York: Random House.

Kamm, S. Richey. 1972. "Capital Punishment: Focus on the Issues." *Moody*, June, 26–28.

Kane, Donna, Sharon Cheston, and Joanne Greer. 1993. "Perceptions of God by Survivors of Childhood Sexual Abuse: An Exploratory Study in an Underresearched Area." *Journal of Psychology and Theology* 21:229–37.

Kaschak, Ellen, ed. 2001. *The Next Generation: The Third Wave of Feminist Psychotherapy*. Binghamton, N.Y.: Haworth.

Kassian, Nancy. 1992. *The Feminist Gospel*. Wheaton, Ill.: Crossway.

Kazanjian, David. 2003. *The Colonizing Trick*. Minneapolis: University of Minnesota Press.

Keiser, George. 1997. "The Critical Task." *Indian Life*, March–April, 5.

Kelley, Clint. 1984. "Unlocking Prisons of the Soul." *Moody*, June, 56–61.

Kelley, Robin. 1996. *Race Rebels*. New York: Free Press.

———. 1997. *Yo' Mama's Disfunktional*. Boston: Beacon.

Kellner, Mark. 2000. "Keeping Their Promises." *Christianity Today*, May 22, 21.

Kellogg, Miriam, and William Hunter. 1993. "Sexual Immorality in the Missions Community: Overtones of Incest." *Journal of Psychology and Theology* 21 (1): 45–53.

Kemadoo, Kamala. 2005. "Victims and Agents of Crime: The New Crusade against Trafficking." In *Global Lockdown*, edited by Julia Sudbury, 35–56. New York: Routledge.

Kendall, Glenn. 1988. "Missionaries Should Not Plant Churches." *Evangelical Missions Quarterly* 24 (July): 218–21.

Kennedy, Duncan. 1995. "A Cultural Pluralist Case for Affirmative Action in Legal Academia." In *Critical Race Theory*, edited by Kimberle Crenshaw, Neil Gotanda, Gary Peller, and Kendall Thomas, 159–76. New York: New Press.

Kennedy, John. 1994. "1.75 Million Paid to Abuse Victims." *Christianity Today*, June 20, 56.

———. 2002a. "From Trauma to Truth." *Christianity Today*, April 22, 16.

———. 2002b. "When Killers Become Christians." *New Man*, November–December, 34–38.

———. 2004. "The New Gambling Goliath." *Christianity Today*, April, 50–52.

Kersten, Katherine. 1994. "How the Feminist Establishment Hurts Women." *Christianity Today*, June 20, 20–25.

Kesselman, Amy, Lily McNair, and Nancy Schneidwind, eds. 1999. *Women: Images, and Realities*. Mountain View, Calif.: Mayfield.

Kikawa, Daniel. 1994. *Perpetuated in Righteousness*. Kane'ohe: Aloha Ke Akua.

King, Jeff. 1995. "The American Indian: The Invisible Man." In *We Stand Together*, edited by Rodney Cooper, 79–96. Chicago: Moody.

Klatch, Rebecca. 1999. *A Generation Divided*. Berkeley: University of California Press.

Kleiman, Mark. 2003. "Faith-Based Fudging." *Slate*, August 5. http://www.slate.com/id/2086617.

Knight, George, III. 1976. "Male and Female He Created Them." *Christianity Today*, April 2, 13–16.

Knippers, Diane. 2001. "Two Versions of Christian Unity." *Faith and Freedom*, spring–summer, 3.

Knopp, Fay. 1983. *Instead of Prisons*. Syracuse: Safer Society.

Kolbe, Sam. 1972. "Civil Rights and Indian Rights." In *The Way*, edited by Shirley Hill Witt and Stan Steiner, 96–97. New York: Random House.

Kolplen-Bugaj, Karen. 1988. "Dad Didn't Give up on Me." *Decision*, June, 7.

Kondo, Dorinne. 1997. *About Face*. New York: Routledge.

Kroeger, Catherine, and Mary Evans, eds. 2002. *The IVP Women's Bible Commentary*. Downers Grove, Ill.: InterVarsity.

Kroeger, Catherine, and Nancy Nason-Clark. 2001. *No Place for Abuse*. Downers Grove: InterVarsity.

Krust, Lin, and Charon Assetoyer. 1993. "A Study of the Use of Depo-Provera and Norplant by the Indian Health Services." Lake Andes, S.D.: Native American Women's Health Education Resource Center.

Kruzenga, Len, Dan Moal, and Debra Fieguth. 2000. "Mi'Kmaq Defiant in Fight over Fishing Rights." *Indian Life*, September–October, 1, 5.

Laclau, Ernesto, and Chantal Mouffe. 1996. *Hegemony and Socialist Strategy*. London: Verso.

LaDuke, Winona. 1993. "A Society Based on Conquest Cannot Be Sustained." In *Toxic Struggles*, edited by Richard Hofrichter, 98–106. Philadelphia: New Society.

———. 1995a. "Introduction." In *Indigenous Women Address the World*, edited by the Indigenous Women's Network, 4–9. Austin: Indigenous Women's Network.

———. 1995b. "Keynote Address, UN Conference on Women." *Circle*, October, 8.

———. 1996a. "Chiapas: A Bitter Harvest and a Hard Won Promise." *Indigenous Woman* 2 (4):41–45.

———. 1996b. "Don't Cheapen Sovereignty." *American Eagle*, May. http://www.alphacdc.com/eagle/op0596.html.

———. 1998. "Honoring the Earth." *Indigenous Woman* 2 (5): 3–5.

———. 1999. *All Our Relations*. Cambridge, Mass.: South End.

———. N.d. "Debbie Tewa: Building a Future with Her Community." *Indigenous Woman* 1 (4):1–3.

Laird, Rebecca. 2000. "What Has Gender Got to Do With It?" *Christianity Today*, September 4, 105–7.

Land, Richard. 1999. "Questioning Biblical Submission." *Light*, November–December, 2–3.

Larana, Enrique, Hank Johnston, and Joseph Gusfield. 1994. "Identities, Grievances, and New Social Movements." In *New Social Movements: From Ideology to Identity*, edited by Enrique Larana, Hank Johnston, and Joseph Gusfield, 1–35. Philadelphia: Temple University Press.

Laribee, Richard. 1976. "Eutychus and His Kin." *Christianity Today*, June 4, 20.

LaRocque, Emma. 1997. "Re-Examining Culturally Appropriate Models in Criminal Justice Applications." In *Aboriginal and Treaty Rights in Canada: Essays on Law, Equity, and Respect for Difference*, edited by Michael Asch, 75–96. Vancouver: University of British Columbia Press.

Larson, Bob. 1975. "Finding Freedom in Bilibid Prison." *World Vision*, October, 4–7.

Larson, Robert. 1989. *Larson's New Book of Cults*. Wheaton, Ill.: Tyndale Press.

Lawson, Steven. 2000. "Woman Evangelist Honored for Seven Decades of Jail Ministry." *Charisma*, April, 42–44.

———. 2004. "Christians Aim to Stop Child Sex Trade." *Charisma*, May, 20–21.

———. 2005. "Ministry Seeks to Stop Child Sex Tourism." *Charisma*, November, 30–31.

Lawton, Kim. 1988. "So What Should We Do with Prisoners." *Christianity Today*, November 4, 38–39.

———. 1991. "Churches Enlist in the War on Drugs." *Christianity Today*, February 11, 44–49.

———. 1998. "Saying No: One Church's War on Drugs." *Christianity Today*, October 7, 46.

"Leaders of the Christian Right Announce Their Next Step." 1985. *Christianity Today*, December 13, 65.

LeBlanc, Doug. 1997. "Hands Off My NIV!" *Christianity Today*, June 16, 52–55.

———. 2004. "Affectionate Patriarchs." *Christianity Today*, August 1, 44–46.

LeBlanc, Doug, and Steve Rabey. 1997. "Bible Translators Deny Gender Agenda." *Christianity Today*, July 14, 62–64.

LeBlanc, Terry. 1997. "A Native Canadian Question." *Faith Today*, November–December, 34–35.

———. 2000a. "Authentic Partnership Is a Long Haul." *Charisma*, July–August, 34.

———. 2000b. "Compassionate Community—or Unchecked Greed?" *Mission Frontiers*, September, 21.

Left Coaster. 2003. "Are True Conservatives Finally Riding to the Rescue of Their Country?" *Left Coaster*, November 24. http://www.theleftcoaster.com/archives/000811.php.

LePetre, Donna. 1999. "Life in Prison." *Indian Life*, May–June, 17.

"Lesson of Karla Faye Tucker." 1998. *Christianity Today*, April 6, 15–16.

Let the Prisoners Work. 1998. *Christianity Today*, February 9, 14–15.

Letham, Robert. 1990. "The Man-Woman Debate." *Westminster Theological Journal* 52:65–78.

Letters. 1986. *Christianity Today*, February 7, 10–11.

Letters. 1999a. *Charisma*, June, 10–14.

———. 1999b. *Charisma*, March, 10–14.

———. 2000. *Charisma*, April, 10–14.

———. 2004a. *Charisma*, August, 8–13.

———. 2004b. *Charisma*, July, 8–11.

Lewis, Bettye. 1998. "Violence in the Schools, Part 2." *Christian Conscience*, June, 14–22.

Lewis, Bonnie Sue. 2004. "The Dynamics and Dismantling of White Missionary Privilege." *Missiology* 32 (January): 34–45.

Lewis, C. S. 1970. *God in the Dock*. Grand Rapids: Eerdmans.

Liberty Prison Outreach. 1988. *Fundamentalist Journal*, March, 27–28.

Liberty Watch. 2005. *Charisma*, August, 34.

Lienesch, Michael. 1993. *Redeeming America*. Chapel Hill: University of North Carolina Press.

Lightner, Robert. 1978. *Neoevangelicalism Today*. Schaumburg, Ill.: Regular Baptist Press.

Lilienthal, Steve. 2001. *From the Free Congress Foundation*. Washington, D.C.: Free Congress.

Lindsell, Harold. 1976a. *Battle of the Bible*. Grand Rapids: Zondervan.

———. 1976b. "Egalitarianism and Scriptural Infallibility." *Christianity Today*, March 26, 45–56.

Liparulo, Robert. 2005. "A President's Son." *New Man*, May–June, 22–26.

Lister, Rob. 2001. "Overview of *The Gender-Neutral Bible Controversy*." *Journal for Biblical Manhood and Womanhood* 6 (spring): 31–34.

Litfin, Duane A. 1979. "Evangelical Feminism: Why Traditionalists Reject It." *Bibliotecha Sacra* 136 (July–September): 258–71.

Llewellyn, Dave. 1975. "Restoring the Death Penalty: Proceed with Caution." *Christianity Today*, May 23, 10–17.

Loconte, Joe. 1998. "Making Criminals Pay." *Policy Review* 87 (January–February): 26–31.

Lorentzen, Lois Ann. 1997. "Writing for Liberation: Prison Testimonials from El Salvador." In *Liberation Theologies, Postmodernity, and the Americas*, edited by David Batstone, Eduardo Mendietaardo, Lois Ann Lorentzen, and Dwight Hopkins, 128–47. London: Routledge.

Lovato, Michelle. 2005. "Pentecostal Pastor Seeks Clemency for Alleged Wrongful Imprisonment." *Charisma*, June, 22.

Lowe, Lisa. 1996. *Immigrant Acts*. Durham, N.C.: Duke University Press.

Lowe, Valerie. 1997. "Black Pentecostal Reaches out to American Indians in South Dakota." *Charisma*, February, 24–25.

———. 2000. "Shame in the Sanctuary." *Charisma*, May, 97–107.

———. 2005a. "God and the Gangsters." *Charisma*, May, 40–44.

———. 2005b. "MegaFest Draws Crowds, Criticism." *Charisma*, October, 27.

Lowe, Valerie, and J. Lee Grady. 2000. "Hanegraaff Accuses Jakes of Heresy." *Charisma*, April, 30–31.

Lupton, Bob. 1989. "How to Create a Ghetto." *World Vision*, October–November, 11.

Lutes, Chris. 1991. "Life on the Rez." *Campus Life*, October, 18–24.

Luthra, Rashmi. 1993. "Toward a Reconceptualization of 'Choice': Challenges at the Margins." *Feminist Issues* 13 (spring): 41–54.

Lynn, Barry. 1996. "The Right (and Wrong) of Religion and Politics." *Rutherford*, September, 11.

MacHarg, Kenneth. 2004. "Breaking Covenant." *Christianity Today*, November, 22.

Mack, Allen, and Steve Craft. N.d. "Restorative Justice: An Impossible Concept Apart from God." *Restorative Justice Journal* 1 (3):13.

Mackey, Lloyd. 1989. "In Toronto, Concerns about Police Racism." *Christianity Today*, April 7, 46.

Madigan, Erin. 2004. "Hundreds of Thousands March for Abortion Rights." *Milwaukee Journal Sentinel*. April 26.

Madsen, Nancy. 2006. "The Power of a Father's Blessing." *Christianity Today*, January, 48–50.

Maher, Lisa. 1990. "Criminalizing Pregnancy: The Downside of a Kinder, Gentler Nation?" *Social Justice* 17 (fall): 111–35.

Mahler, Mrs. John Candler. 1975. "It Seems to Me." *Moody*, July–August, 54–56.

Mailbag. 2002. *World*, April 27, M1–4.

Makkai, Valerie Becker. 2001. "Gendered Language and Bible Translation." *Journal for Biblical Manhood and Womanhood* 6 (spring): 27–30.

"Man Bites Dog." 1990. *Christianity Today*, April 23, 42.

Mancini, Michael. 1991. *One Dies, One Gets Another*. Columbia: University of South Carolina Press.

Mankiller, Wilma. 1993. *Mankiller*. New York: St. Martin's.

Mansfield, Stephen. 2005. "Men of the Year." *New Man*, November–December, 22–30.

Maracle, Lee. 1988. *I Am Woman*. North Vancouver: Write-On.

Maracle, Ross. 1991. "Passing by on the Other Side." *Faith Today*, July–August, 29.

"Marchers Say Bush Policies Harm Women." 2004. *Marin Independent Journal*. April 26.

Marcuse, Herbert. 1972. *Counterrevolution and Revolt*. Boston: Beacon.

Marinucci, Carla. 2004. "Hundreds of Thousands in D.C. Pledge to Take Fight to Polls." *San Francisco Chronicle*. April 26.

Marsden, George. 1980. *Fundamentalism and American Culture*. Oxford: Oxford University Press.

Martey, Emmanuel. 1994. *African Theology*. Maryknoll, N.Y.: Orbis.

Martin, Kent. 2002. *The Spirit of Annie Mae*. Montreal, National Film Board of Canada.

Martin, William. 1996. *With God on Our Side*. New York: Pantheon.

Martinez, Renilda. N.d. "Indigenous Women Facing the Ecological Crisis." *Indigenous Woman* 1 (3): 24–27.

Marty, Martin. 1987. *Religion and Republic*. Boston: Beacon.

Masterson, Mike, and Patricia Gutherie. 1986. "Taking the Shot." *Arizona Republic*. Pamphlet.

Mastris, Caris. 2001. "Intellectual Burqas." *World*, December 22, 27.

Mathews-Green, Frederica. 1998. "Wanted: A New Pro-life Strategy." *Christianity Today*, January 12, 26–30.

Matthiessen, Peter. 1991. *In the Spirit of Crazy Horse*. New York: Viking.

Mattingly, Terry. 2001. "The Culture of Co-opted Belief." *Christianity Today*, January 8, 88–89.

Maudlin, Michael. 1997a. "Inside CT." *Christianity Today*, July 14, 4.

———. 1997b. "Why We Need Feminism." *New Man*, November–December, 34–37.

Mauer, Marc. 1999. *Race to Incarcerate*. New York: New Press.

Maust, John. 1985. "The Land Where Spirits Thrive." *Christianity Today*, December 13, 48–50.

———. 1989. "Tensions in Miami." *Christianity Today*, February 17, 40.

———. 1992. "Keeping the Faithful." *Christianity Today*, April 6, 38.

———. 1993. "Hispanics Eye Mission Role." *Christianity Today*, October 25, 92.

Mawyer, Marin. 1982. "Muslim Growth in Prison." *Moody*, January, 30–32.

Maxwell, Carol, and Ted Jelen. 1995. "Commandos for Christ: Narratives of Male Pro-life Activists." *Review of Religious Research* 37 (December): 117–31.

Maxwell, Joe. 1991. "Getting out, Staying Out." *Christianity Today*, July 22, 34–36.

———. 1995. "PC Meets CC." *World*, April 29, 16–19.

———. 1997. "Will the Walls Fall Down?" *Christianity Today*, November 17, 62–65.

———. 2000. "MAB Men Are Back." *New Man*, September–October, 27–37.

Maxwell, Joe, Heather Johnson, and John Geary. 1998. "Vineyard Founder Wimber Dies." *Christianity Today*, January 12, 58.

Maynard, Roy. 1993a. "There's No Political Solution." *World*, October 16, 10–13.

———. 1993b. "The Valley of the Shadow of Death." *World*, September 25, 10–13.

———. 1994. "A Government Cure for Sin." *World*, February 26, 10–13.

———. 1995a. "The Hands That Rob the Cradle." *World*, March 11, 12–15.

———. 1995b. "Less Crime, More Punishment." *World*, January 28, 12–15.

———. 1996a. "By Man Shall His Blood Be Shed." *World*, March 16, 12–17.

———. 1996b. "We've Met the Enemy." *World*, October 19, 17.

———. 1997. "God and Man behind Bars." *World*, August 9–16, 14–17.

———. 1999. "The End of Innocence." *World*, January 30, 14–17.

McAdam, Doug. 1995. "Culture and Social Movements." In *New Social Movements: From Ideology to Identity*, edited by Enrique Larana, Hank Johnston, and Joseph Gusfield, 36–57. Philadelphia: Temple University Press.

McClintock, Anne. 1995. *Imperial Leather*. New York: Routledge.

McCloud, Janet. N.d. "The Backbone of Everything." *Indigenous Woman* 1 (3): 49–51.

McDowell, Josh. 1979. *Evidence That Demands a Verdict*. San Bernardino: Here's Life.

McGinnis, Ted. 1991. "I'm in Prison for Life." *Decision*, January, 4–5.

McGowen, Randall. 1995. "The Well-Ordered Prison." In *The Oxford History of the Prison*, edited by Norval Morris and David Rothman, 71–99. Oxford: Oxford University Press.

McGuire, Paul. 2000. "How to Light Her Fire." *New Man*, September–October, 58–61.

McKenna, David. 1971. "In the World." *United Evangelical Action*, winter, 6–7.

———. 1973. "In the World." *United Evangelical Action*, summer, 24–26.

McKinniss, Rick. 1986. " 'Christian America' Rest in Peace." *Christianity Today*, February 5, 10.

McLean, Gordon. 1993. "Is the Justice System Just?" In *Setting the Captives Free*, edited by Don Smarto, 157–61. Grand Rapids: Baker Book House.

McLoughlin, William. 1995. *Cherokees and Missionaries, 1789–1839*. Norman: University of Oklahoma Press.

McManus, Michael. 1994. "Coping with Sexual Misconduct in the Church." *Christianity Today*, April 25, 14–15.

McThenia, Sheila. 1995. "What Happened to the Dream." *Rutherford*, May, 6–9, 18.

McVicker, Gwen. 2001. *Discovering God's Heart for Suffering Women*. N.p.: Vision.

Medicine, Beatrice. 1993. "North American Indigenous Women and Cultural Domination." *American Indian Culture and Research Journal* 17 (3): 121–30.

———. 1996. "Bordertown, 1996." *Indigenous Woman* 2 (4): 38–39.

Meed, Marianne. 1990. "Crime and Punishment; or, Should That Be Justice?" *Faith Today*, November–December, 26–27.

Meers, Trevor. 2000. "Nebraska Pastor Builds Cultural Bridge." *Charisma*, December, 20–21.

Meeuwsen, Terry. 1998. *Karla Faye Tucker: From Prison to Praise*. Christian Broadcasting Network.

Melucci, Alberto. 1996. *Challenging Codes*. Cambridge: Cambridge University Press.

Meurer, Dave. 2004. "Great Moments in Guy History." *New Man*, July–August, 42–45.

Midgett, Linda. 1993. "Silent Screams." *Christianity Today*, July 19, 44–47.

Mihesuah, Devon. 2003. *Indigenous American Women*. Lincoln: University of Nebraska Press.

Mihesuah, Devon, ed. 1998. *Natives and Academics: Researching and Writing about American Indians*. Lincoln: University of Nebraska Press.

Mihesuah, Devon, and Angela Cavendar Wilson, eds. 2004. *Indigenizing the Academy*. Lincoln: University of Nebraska Press.

Mill, Manny. 1999. "No Prisons in Heaven." *New Man*, January–February, 74.

Miller, David. 1995. "Revival Behind Enemy Lines." *Charisma*, January, 40–47.

Miller, Donald E. 1997. *Reinventing American Protestantism: Christianity in the New Millennium*. Berkeley: University of California Press.

Miller, Sara, and Seth Stern. 2003. "Odd Bedfellows Fall in Line." *Christian Science Monitor*. October 29.

Mining and Indigenous Peoples Consultation. 1998. "Declaration." *Indigenous Woman* 2 (5): 46–47.

Mink, Gendolyn, ed. 1999. *Whose Welfare?* Ithaca: Cornell University Press.

Minter, Linda. 1997. "Putting Women in Their Place." *Charisma*, September, 67–69.

Moeller, Bob. 1993. "When Your Children Pay the Price." *Leadership*, spring, 87–94.

Mohler, Albert. 1998. "Revolutionary President." *World*, June 13, 24–25.

Mollenkott, Virginia. 1974. "The Women's Movement Challenges the Church and Three Responses." *Journal of Psychology and Theology* 2 (Fall): 298–321.

———. 1976. "A Challenge to Male Interpretation, Women and the Bible." *Sojourners*, February, 21–25.

———. 1977a. "Evangelicalism: A Feminist Perspective." *Union Seminary Quarterly Review* 32 (winter): 95–103.

———. 1977b. "What Is True Biblical Feminism?" *Christian Life*, September, 75–76.

———. 1977c. *Women, Men and the Bible*. Nashville: Abingdon.

———. 1980. *Speech, Silence, Action!* Nashville: Abingdon.

Monroe, Jemila. 2004. "Why I Apologized to Planned Parenthood." *Christianity Today*, November, 44–48.

Monture-Angus, Patricia. 1995. *Thunder in My Soul*. Halifax: Fernwood.

———. 1999. *Journeying Forward*. Halifax: Fernwood.

Moody, Roger, ed. 1988. *The Indigenous Voice*. London: Zed.

Moore, Art. 1997. "EPA Admits Ethics Probe Miscues." *Christianity Today*, September 1, 98.

Moore, John. 2002. "A Tender Warrior in South Dakota." *Charisma*, December, 65–66.

———. 2004. "Welcome to Lame Deer." *Charisma*, March, 42–49.

Moore, Michael. 2004. "Seventeen Reasons Not to Slit Your Wrists," November 5. http://www.michaelmoore.com/words/message/index.php?message Date=2004–11–05.

"More Wounds of Rape." 1992. *Christianity Today*, November 23, 6.

Moreland, Anita. 1982. "Six Years into a Life Sentence." *Christian Life*, July, 46–49.

Morgan, Timothy. 2002a. "Revised NIV Makes Its Debut." *Christianity Today*, February 4, 19.

———. 2002b. "TNIV Critics Blast Scripture 'Distortions.'" *Christianity Today*, April 1, 30.

——. 2004. "Healing Genocide." *Christianity Today*, April, 76–83.

Morley, Patrick. 2000. "The Next Christian Men's Movement." *Christianity Today*, September 4, 84–86.

Morris, Harold. 1988. "Today Is the Day to Love." *Fundamentalist Journal*, March, 29, 38.

Morrison, David. 2000a. "Resources and Recourses?" *Population Research Institute*, January–February, 5.

——. 2000b. "Tiahrt Violations!" *Population Research Institute*, January–February, 1, 6–7, 11–13.

Morse, Anne. 2001. "Brutality behind Bars." *World*, February 3, 21–23.

Mousseau, Marlin, and Karen Artichoker. N.d. *Violence against Oglala Woman Is Not a Lakota Tradition*. Pierre: Cangleska.

Mouw, Richard. 1991. "Preaching Christ or Packaging Jesus?" *Christianity Today*, February 11, 29–40.

——. 2001. "The Chosen People Puzzle." *Christianity Today*, March 5, 70–78.

Mumper, Sharon. 1986. "Where in the World Is the Church Growing?" *Christianity Today*, July 11, 17–21.

Nash, Ronald. 1987. *Evangelicals in America*. Nashville: Abingdon.

——. 1996. *Why the Left Is Not Right*. Grand Rapids: Zondervan.

National Association of Evangelicals. 2004. *Do the Prayers of Evangelicals Impact World Events?* Washington, D.C.: National Association of Evangelicals.

"Native Americans Find Peace in Promise Keepers." 1997. *Indian Life*, October–December, 1, 13.

Native Voices Public Television. 1995. *White Shamen, Plastic Medicine Men*. Bozeman: Montana State University.

Neff, David. 1991. "The Politics of Remembering." *Christianity Today*, October 7, 28–29.

——. 2004. "Creating Husbands and Fathers." *Christianity Today*, April, 55–56.

Neff, Miriam. 1980. "Why I Question the Feminist Movement." *Moody Monthly*, November, 36–38.

Nelles, Wendy. 1990a. "Justice for Victims." *Faith Today*, November–December, 28–30.

——. 1990b. "A Mother's Perspective." *Faith Today*, November–December, 29.

Nelson, Jennifer. 2003. *Women of Color and the Reproductive Rights Movement*. New York: New York University Press.

Nelson, Shirley. 1981. "Review of Speech, Silence, Action!" *Eternity*, December, 44.

Newman, Amy. 1976. "Evangelicals and Feminism." *Asbury Seminarian* 31 (July): 6–10.

Newman, Josie. 2003. "Former Prison Inmate Now Reaches Cons for Christ around the Globe." *Charisma*, October, 34–35.

———. 2004. "Pentecostal Pastor Reaches Inuit People in Canada's Arctic Circle." *Charisma*, February, 32.

———. 2005. "Predators in the Sanctuary." *Charisma*, July, 68–72.

Newman-Provost, Josie. 1997. "Reintegrating Sex Offenders." *Faith Today*, November–December, 37, 39.

News Briefs. 2006. *Charisma*, May, 38.

Nicholson, Linda. 1995. "Interpreting Gender." In *Social Postmodernism: Beyond Identity Politics*, edited by Linda Nicholson and Steven Seidman, 39–67. Cambridge: Cambridge University Press.

Nicholson, Linda, ed. 1997. *The Second Wave: A Reader in Feminist Theory*. New York: Routledge.

Nickell, Amy, and Johan Conrad. 1996. "Politics and Religion." *Rutherford*, September, 6–10.

Nielsen, Marianne, and Robert Silverman, eds. 1996. *Native Americans, Crime, and Justice*. Boulder: Westview.

Nikkel, Ronald. 1990. "A Passion for Justice." *Faith Today*, November–December, 25.

"NIV's Twisted Sister." 2002. *World*, February 9, 7.

Noble, Jomili. 2006. "Christians Issue Statement on Climate Change." *Charisma*, April, 27.

No Comment Zone. 1999. *World*, April 10, 11.

———. 1999. *World*, June 5, 12.

Nolan, Pat. 1999. "A Briefing from Pat Nolan." *Justice Report*, April, 1–2.

———. 2000. "Building on the Victory." *Justice Report*, September 13, 2–3.

———. 2003a. "Justice e-Report, April 2003." Justice Fellowship. http://www.justicefellowship.org/site—hmpg.asp.

———. 2003b. "Justice e-Report, August 2003." Justice Fellowship. http://www.justicefellowship.org/site—hmpg.asp.

———. 2003c. "Justice e-Report, July 2003." Justice Fellowship. http://www.justicefellowship.org/site—hmpg.asp.

———. 2003d. "Justice e-Report, May 2003." Justice Fellowship. http://www.justicefellowship.org/site—hmpg.asp.

———. 2003e. "Justice e-Report, October 2003." Justice Fellowship. http://www.justicefellowship.org/site—hmpg.asp.

———. 2003f. "Justice e-Report: Sniper Case Reveals Deficiencies in the U.S. Criminal Justice System." Justice Fellowship. http://www.justicefellowship.org/site—hmpg.asp.

———. 2003g. "Justice e-Report, Vol. 2, No. 1." Justice Fellowship. http://www.justicefellowship.org/site—hmpg.asp.

———. 2003h. "Justice e-Report: Muhammed Receives Death Sentence." Justice Fellowship. http://www.justicefellowship.org/site—hmpg.asp.

———. 2004a. "Justice e-Report: Angola Prison: Most Violent to Most Peaceful." Justice Fellowship. http://www.justicefellowship.org/site—hmpg.asp.

———. 2004b. "Justice e-Report: Florida Opens Faith-Based Prison." Justice Fellowship. http://www.justicefellowship.org/site—hmpg.asp.

———. 2004c. "Justice e-Report: Gates of Injustice." Justice Fellowship. http://www.justicefellowship.org/site—hmpg.asp.

———. 2004d. "Justice e-Report: Iraqi Prisoner Abuse and the Importance of Self-Restraint." Justice Fellowship. http://www.justicefellowship.org/site—hmpg.asp.

———. 2004e. "Justice e-Report: President Bush Supports Reentry Efforts." Justice Fellowship. http://www.justicefellowship.org/site—hmpg.asp.

———. 2004f. "Justice e-Report: Prison Rape Commissioners Appointed." Justice Fellowship. http://www.justicefellowship.org/site—hmpg.asp.

———. 2004g. "Justice e-Report: Prison Rape Victim Vindicated." Justice Fellowship. http://www.justicefellowship.org/site—hmpg.asp.

———. 2004h. "Justice e-Report: Prisoner Reentry Legislation Introduced." Justice Fellowship. http://www.justicefellowship.org/site—hmpg.asp.

———. 2004i. "Justice e-Report: Prisoner Reentry: Why We Should Care and How We Should Help." Justice Fellowship. http://www.justicefellowship.org/site—hmpg.asp.

———. 2004j. "Justice e-Report: Studies Investigate False Convictions." Justice Fellowship. http://www.justicefellowship.org/site—hmpg.asp.

———. 2004k. "Justice e-Report: Study Shows 'Neighborliness' Reduces Crime." Justice Fellowship. http://www.justicefellowship.org/site—hmpg.asp.

———. 2004l. "Justice e-Report: Study Shows 'Three Strikes' Laws Don't Reduce Violent Crime." Justice Fellowship. http://www.justicefellowship.org/site—hmpg.asp.

———. 2004m. "Justice e-Report: Two New Laws Provide Important Justice Reform." Justice Fellowship. http://www.justicefellowship.org/site—hmpg.asp.

———. 2004n. "Justice e-Report: U.S. Supreme Court Examines Sentencing Guidelines." Justice Fellowship. http://www.justicefellowship.org/site—hmpg.asp.

———. 2004o. "Justice e-Report: When Prisoners Return." Justice Fellowship. http://www.justicefellowship.org/site—hmpg.asp.

———. 2005a. "Justice e-Report: Violent Crime Slows, but Prisons Still Grow." Justice Fellowship. http://www.justicefellowship.org/site—hmpg.asp.

———. 2005b. "Justice e-Report: Why Are Some Prisons More Dangerous Than Others?" Justice Fellowship. http://www.justicefellowship.org/site—hmpg.asp.

———. 2006a. "Justice e-Report: 'Mandatory Sentences: Unjust and Unbiblical'." Justice Fellowship. http://www.justicefellowship.org/site—hmpg.asp.

———. 2006b. "Justice e-Report, June 21 2006." Justice Fellowship. http://www.justicefellowship.org/site—hmpg.asp.

Noll, Abigail. 2000. "Awakening to the Scandal of Sex Trafficking." *Faith and Freedom*, spring, 14.

Noll, Mark. 1984. "Evangelicals and the Study of the Bible." *Reformed Journal* 34 (April): 11–19.

Noll, Stephen. 1993. "Reading the Bible as the Word of God." *Churchman* 107:227–53.

"No More Broken Treaties." 1996. *Indian Life*, March–April, 8–9.

Norfolk, Marshall. 1975. "The Search for Gary." *Moody*, September, 114–16.

Norplant Linked to Strokes. 1995. *Rutherford*, May, 22.

Norris, Judy. 1979. "Paroled." *Moody*, November, 63–70.

Norsigian, Judy. 1996. "Quinacrine Update." *Political Environments* 3 (spring): 26–27.

Ockenga, Harold. 1968. "From Fundamentalism: through New Evangelicalism to Evangelicalism." In *Evangelical Roots*, edited by Kenneth Kantzer, 35–46. Nashville: Thomas Nelson.

O'Connor, James. 1998. *Natural Causes: Essays in Ecological Marxism*. New York: Guilford.

O'Connor, Lindsey. 2005. "Dying Smart." *Christianity Today*, August, 46–48.

Ogle, Barry. 1995. "Churches Helping Children with Incarcerated Parents." *Social Work and Christianity* 22 (fall):115–24.

Olasky, Marvin. 1998. "Jackson Day." *World*, March 14, 30.

——. 1999a. "Bible Cola." *World*, June 5, 34.

——. 1999b. "The Limits of Politics." *World*, May 15, 46.

——. 1999c. "Reasonable Risks." *World*, July 17, 34.

——. 2000. "Pro-life Priorities." *World*, January 15, 34.

——. 2004. "Finding IWD." *World*, March 6, 52.

Olasky, Susan. 1997. "Femme Fatale." *World*, March 29, 12–15.

——. 1999a. "Life on the Bible Beat." *World*, June 5, 20.

——. 1999b. "Regendering in Spanish?" *World*, June 5, 17–20.

——. 1999c. "There They Go Again." *World*, June 5, 14–16.

——. 1999d. "What's It All About?" *World*, June 5, 16–17.

——. 2002. "Five Days Early, Five Years Late." *World*, February 23, 18–24.

Oldfield, Duane. 1996. *The Right and the Righteous*. London: Rowman and Littlefield.

Olford, Stephen. 1982. "Nation or Ruination." *United Evangelical Action*, fall, 8.

Olsen, Ted. 1997. "Racial Reconciliation Emphasis Intensified." *Christianity Today*, January 6, 67.

——. 1998. "The Dragon Slayer." *Christianity Today*, December 7, 36–42.

——. 2002. "Quotation Marks." *Christianity Today*, November 18, 21.

——. 2004. "Grave Images." *Christianity Today*, June 1, 60.

——. 2006. "Peace, Peace." *Christianity Today*, May 1, 62.

Olson, James, and Raymond Wilson. 1984. *Native Americans in the Twentieth Century*. Urbana: University of Illinois Press.

"100 Things Churches Are Doing Right." 1997. *Christianity Today*, November 17, 13–42.

Opops'kan, and Limping Dog. 1991. *Dan Red Eagle and the Soul Catcher*. Winnipeg: Indian Life.

O'Rourke, Lawrence. 2004. "Thousands Rally for Abortion Rights." *Star Tribune* (Minneapolis), April 26.

Osborne, Grant. 1985. "Evangelical Interpretation of Scripture." In *The Bible in the Churches*. New York: Paulist.

Ostrowski, Julie. 2004. "Race versus Gender in the Court Room." *Africana*, May 4. http://www.africana.com/articles/daily/bw20040504domestic.asp.

Ottoson, Sheryl. 1992. "Mission to the Mapuches." *Alliance Witness*, March 18, 19.

"Overcoming a Past of Pain." 1998. *Jubilee*, summer, 13.

Owen, Mary. 2002. "Oregon Pastor Says Baptist Churches Are Embracing Charismatic Beliefs." *Charisma*, July, 20.

Owens, Chandler. 1998. "Risky Living among Atlanta's Drug Lords." *Charisma*, August, 48.

Owens, Terri. 1987. "Breaking the Cycle of Poverty." *World Vision*, October–November, 12–17.

Owens, Virginia. 1998. "Karla Faye's Last Stop." *Christianity Today*, July 13, 45–48.

Packer, J. I. 1986. "Understanding the Differences." In *Women, Authority, and the Bible*, edited by Alvera Mickelsen, 295–99. Downers Grove, Ill.: InterVarsity.

Padgett, Alan. 1987. "The Pauline Rationale for Submission: Biblical Feminism and the Hina Clauses of Titus 2:1–10." *Evangelical Quarterly* 59 (January): 39–52.

Padilla, Rene. 1991. "Come Holy Spirit: Renew the Whole Creation." *Transformation* 8 (October): 1–6.

Palau, Luis. 1990. "Evangelism: The Best Form of Social Action." *Christianity Today*, February 17, 51–52.

Parker, Shafer. 1999. "A Call for Prayer at the Birth of a Territory." *Faith Today*, March–April, 12–14.

Passantino, Gretchen. 1991. "Surviving in the City." *Moody*, September, 36–38.

Patchesky, Rosalind. 1990. *Abortion and Woman's Choice*. Boston: Northeastern University Press.

Patterson, Robert. 1992. "Spiritual Intimidation." *Christianity Today*, August 17, 56–57.

Patterson, Stephen. 1984. *Effective Prison Ministry*. Orlando: Review and Herald.

Peake, Connie. 2001. "God of the Covenant." *Indian Life*, November–December, 8.

Pearson-Wong, Pamela. 2000. "What Money Can't Buy." *Family Voice*, May–June, 14–19.

Peck, Jeff. 2000. "My People Will Live in Peaceful Dwelling Places." *Jubilee*, winter, 16–18.

Pederson, Duane. 1979. *How to Establish a Prison Ministry*. Nashville: Thomas Nelson.

Penemaker, Wesley. 2005. "How to Win the War on Terror." *New Man*, November–December, 50–53, 69.

Perdue, Theda. 1999. *Cherokee Women*. Lincoln: University of Nebraska Press.

"A Perilous Venture." 2006. *World*, March 18, 46–51.

Perrin, Robin, Paul Kennedy, and Donald Miller. 1997. "Examining the Sources of Conservative Church Growth: Where Are the New Evangelical Movements Getting Their Numbers?" *Journal for the Scientific Study of Religion* 36 (1): 71–90.

Perrin, Robin, and Armand Mauss. 1991. "Saints and Seekers: Sources of Recruitment to the Vineyard Christian Fellowship." *Review of Religious Research* 33 (December): 97–111.

"Peru's Forced Sterilization Campaign." 1999. *Population Research Institute*, special edition. Pamphlet.

Pesantubbee, Michelene. 2005. *Choctaw Women in a Chaotic World*. Albuquerque: University of New Mexico Press.

Peters, John. 1977. "Male Chauvinist in Retreat." *Christian Life*, October, 27–29, 42.

Petersen, Rodney. 2004. "Racism, Restorative Justice, and Reconciliation." *Missiology* 32 (January): 71–91.

Peterson, Daniel. 1999. "Tearing down the Iron Curtain." *Charisma*, May, 54–58.

Phelan, Shane. 1995. "The Space of Justice: Lesbians and Democratic Process." In *Social Postmodernism: Beyond Identity Politics*, edited by Linda Nicholson and Steven Seidman, 332–56. Cambridge: Cambridge University Press.

Phelps, Timothy. 2004. "Demonstration in D.C." *New York Newsday*. April 26.

Phipps, Neal, Glen Bradford, David Bosscher, and R. L. Gowan. 1973. "Wounded Knee Forum and the Future of Indian Missions." *Eternity*, August, 14–15, 23.

Phiri, Isaac. 2006. "Hope in the Heart of Darkness." *Christianity Today*, July, 23–31.

Pieterse, Jan Nederveen. 1992. "Christianity, Politics, and Gramscism of the Right." In *Christianity and Hegemony*, edited by Jan Nederveen Pieterse, 1–32. New York: Berg.

Pile, John. 1987. "To Live and Cry in L.A." *Christian Herald*, January, 18–22.

Pinnock, Clark. 1986. "Biblical Authority and the Issues in Question." In

Women, Authority, and the Bible, edited by Alvera Mickelsen, 51–58. Downers Grove, Ill.: InterVarsity.

Piper, John, and Wayne Grudem, eds. 1991. *Recovering Biblical Manhood and Womanhood: A Response to Evangelical Feminism*. Wheaton, Ill.: Crossway.

Piper, Noel. 2001. "Shaking off the Wigwam." *World*, November 24, 29.

Piven, Frances Fox, and Richard Cloward. 1979. *Poor People's Movements*. New York: Vintage.

Plowman, Edward. 1998a. "Gay Jihad in California." *World*, December 5, 23–24.

———. 1998b. "What Went Wrong?" *World*, March 21, 12–16.

Plowman, Edward, and Susan Olasky. 1998a. "Gender Neutralized." *World*, November 21, 20.

———. 1998b. "October Surprise." *World*, November 21, 16–19.

Pollitt, Katha. 2004. "Why America Hates Democrats: A Dialogue." *Slate*, November 5. http://www.slate.com/id/2109165.

Ponticelli, Christy. 1993. "Fundamentalist Ex-Gay Ministries: A Loving Approach to a Sinful Problem." PhD diss., University of California, Santa Cruz.

Population Research Institute. 1999. *The New Law of the Land*. Pamphlet.

Povinelli, Elizabeth. 2002. *The Cunning of Recognition*. Durham, N.C.: Duke University Press.

Powers, William. 1982. "A Policeman's Practical Perspective." *Christianity Today*, April 9, 37.

Poythress, Vern. 1998. "Searching Instead for an Agenda-Neutral Bible." *World*, November 21, 24–25.

Poythress, Vern, and Mark Strauss. 2002. "The TNIV Debate." *Christianity Today*, October 7, 36–45.

Preddy, Steven. 1983. "Just a Stupid Prank." *Campus Life*, September, 51–53.

Preschool in the Andes Highlands. 1987. *World Vision*, October–November, 15–17.

Previch, Chad. 2005. "Cherokee Council Bans Gay Unions." *The Oklahoman* (Oklahoma City), June 15.

PRI Staff. 2000. "False Premises of Population Control." *Population Research Institute*, January–February, 4, 10.

Price, Robert. 1986. "Neo-evangelicals and Scripture: A Forgotten Period of Ferment." *Christian Scholars Review* 15 (4): 315–30.

Prison Disfellowship. 1998. *World*, November 28, 10.

"Prisoners Showcase 2001." 2001. *Indian Life*, July–August, 8–9.

Prison Fellowship. 1998a. *Annual Report, 1997–1998*. Washington, D.C.: Prison Fellowship.

———. 1998b. *Portraits of Reconciliation*. Washington, D.C.: Prison Fellowship.

———. 2000. *Jubilee Extra*, February, 1–3.

"Prison Fellowship Moves Ahead on New Headquarters." 1985. *Christianity Today*, March 1, 40–41.

"Private Sins of Public Ministry." 1988. *Leadership*, winter, 14–23.

Prober, Rosalind. 1999. "Justice System Adds to Violation." *Indian Life*, September–October, 8–9.

"Promise Keepers Ministry Sweeps across Country." 1995. *C.C. Watch*, March, 8.

The Public Forum. 2000. *Population Research Institute*, January–February, 8–9.

Pulliam, Russ. 1987. "A Better Idea Than Prison." *Christian Herald*, November, 28–31.

Pulliam, Sarah, and Collin Hansen. 2006. "Costly Complaints." *Christianity Today*, March, 21–22.

Quebedeaux, Richard. 1974. *The Young Evangelicals*. New York: Harper and Row.

Quotation Marks. 2002. *Christianity Today*, August 5, 13.

Radmacher, Earl, and Robert Preus, eds. 1984. *Hermeneutics, Inerrancy, and the Bible*. Grand Rapids: Zondervan.

Rainwater, Lee. 1960. *And the Poor Get Children*. Chicago: Quadrangle.

Ramirez, Renya. 2007. *Native Hubs: Culture, Community, and Belonging in Silicon Valley and Beyond*. Durham, N.C.: Duke University Press.

Rascher, Leonard. 1995. "True Reconciliation." *Native Discipleship in the Americas* (November-December): 14–15.

Rausch, Arlie. 1976. "Eutychus and His Kin." *Christianity Today*, August 6, 22.

Readers Write. 2003. *Christianity Today*, July, 10–11.

——. 2004a. *Christianity Today*, August, 12–18.

——. 2004b. *Christianity Today*, September, 12–20.

——. 2004c. *Christianity Today*, October, 15.

——. 2005. *Christianity Today*, September, 14–21.

Redekop, John. 1990. "Canadian Justice: Is It Just?" *Faith Today*, November–December, 18–24.

Reed, Eric. 2002. "Southern Baptists Blast TNIV." *Christianity Today*, August 5, 17.

Reed, Ralph. 1990. *After the Revolution*. Dallas: Word.

——. 1999. "We Can't Stop Now." *Christianity Today*, September 6, 46–48.

Religious News Service. 1999. "Falwell Tames His Rhetoric." *Christianity Today*, December 6, 29.

——. 2003. "Suing Success." *Christianity Today*, April, 33.

Restoule, Jean-Paul. 1997. "Intercultural Communication in Aboriginal Sentencing Circles in Canada." *Media Development* 44 (3): 22–24.

Richardson, Suzy. 2004. "Faith-Based Prison Ministries Leave Legacies of Transformation." *Charisma*, March, 27–28.

——. 2005. "Foursquare Minister Seeks to Raise Awareness of Environmental Issues." *Charisma*, July, 19.

———. 2006. "Pastor Faces Removal for Tongues Challenge." *Charisma*, April, 28.

Richie, Beth. 1996. *Compelled to Crime: The Gender Entrapment of Black Battered Women.* New York: Routledge.

———. 2000. "Plenary Presentation." In *The Color of Violence: Violence against Women of Color*, edited by INCITE! Women of Color Against Violence, 124. Conference proceedings. Santa Cruz: INCITE! Women of Color against Violence.

Riggs, Charles. 1993. "Religious Diversity and the Christian Response." In *Setting the Captives Free*, edited by Don Smarto, 91–100. Grand Rapids: Baker Book House.

Riskind, Jonathan. 2004. "Supporters of Abortion Rights Seek Forefront." *Columbus Dispatch.* April 25.

Roberts, Dorothy. 1997. *Killing the Black Body.* New York: Pantheon.

Robertson, Pat. 1993. *The Turning Tide.* Dallas: Word.

———. 1998. *Pat Robertson's Perspectives.* Christian Broadcasting Network.

Rodriguez, Dylan. 2000a. "The Challenge of Prison Abolition." *Social Justice* 27 (fall): 212–18.

———. 2000b. "State Violence and the Logic of Prison Abolition: Beyond Resistance, toward Opposition." Unpublished paper, copy in Andrea Smith's possession.

———. 2005. *Forced Passages.* Minneapolis: University of Minnesota Press.

Rojas, Paula. 2007. "Are The Cops in Our Heads and Our Hearts?" In *The Revolution Will Not Be Funded: Beyond the Non-Profit Industrial Complex*, edited by INCITE! Women of Color Against Violence, 197–214. Cambridge, Mass.: South End Press.

Rosenberg, Ellen. 1984. *Southern Baptists: A Subculture in Transition.* Knoxville: University of Tennessee Press.

Ross, Loretta. 2000. "Plenary Presentation." In *The Color of Violence: Violence against Women of Color*, edited by INCITE! Women of Color against Violence. Conference proceedings. Santa Cruz: INCITE! Women of Color against Violence.

Ross, Luana. 1998a. *Inventing the Savage: The Social Construction of Native American Criminality.* Austin: University of Texas Press.

———. 1998b. "Native Women in Prison." Paper presented at the Critical Resistance conference, Berkeley, Calif., September 25–27, 1998.

———. 2000. "Plenary Presentation." In *The Color of Violence: Violence against Women of Color*, edited by INCITE! Women of Color against Violence, 124. Conference proceedings. Santa Cruz: INCITE! Women of Color against Violence.

Ross, Rupert. 1997. *Return to the Teachings.* London: Penguin.

Rotman, Edgardo. 1995. "The Failure of Reform." In *The Oxford History of the*

Prison, edited by Norval Morris and David Rothman, 149–77. Oxford: Oxford University Press.

Ruether, Rosemary Radford. 1985. *Woman Church*. San Francisco: Harper and Row.

Russel, Walt. 1992. "What It Means to Me." *Christianity Today*, October 26, 30–32.

Ryan, Joseph. 2004. "Abortion Rights Supporters Jump in to Rejuvenate Cause." *Chicago Daily Herald*, April 26.

Said, Edward. 1994. *Orientalism*. New York: Vintage.

Saint, Steve. 1998. "The Unfinished Mission to the Aucas." *Christianity Today*, March 2, 42–45.

Saletan, William. 1998. "Electoral Politics and Abortion." In *The Abortion Wars*, edited by Rickie Solinger, 111–23. Berkeley: University of California Press.

———. 2003. *Bearing Right*. Berkeley: University of California Press.

Salway, Craig. 1990. *The Lonely Search*. Winnipeg: Indian Life.

Sandlin, Andrew. 1997a. *The Creed of Christian Reconstruction*. Vallecito, Calif.: Chalcedon Foundation.

———. 1997b. *The Royal Race of the Redeemed*. Vallecito, Calif.: Chalcedon Foundation.

Sassoon, Anne Showstack, ed. 1982. *Approaches to Gramsci*. London: Writers and Readers.

Saxton, Martha. 1998. "Disability Rights." In *The Abortion Wars*, edited by Rickie Solinger, 374–93. Berkeley: University of California Press.

Scalberg, Daniel, and Joy Cordell. 1987. "A Savage with the Savages." *Moody*, April, 55–57.

Scanzoni, Letha, and Nancy Hardesty. 1993. *All We're Meant to Be*. Grand Rapids: Eerdmans.

Scanzoni, Letha, and Virginia Mollenkott. 1978. *Is the Homosexual My Neighbor?* San Francisco: Harper and Row.

Scarry, Donald. 1997. "A Passion for Prisons." *Alliance Life*, January 15, 8–9.

Scheff, Thomas. 1994. "Emotions and Identity: A Theory of Ethnic Nationalism." In *Social Theory and the Politics of Identity*, edited by Craig Calhoun, 277–303. Malden: Blackwell.

Schlossman, Steven. 1995. "Delinquent Children: The Juvenile Reform School." In *The Oxford History of the Prison*, edited by Norval Morris and David Rothman, 325–49. Oxford: Oxford University Press.

Schonmaker, Paul. 1978. *The Prison Connection*. Valley Forge: Judson.

Schreiner, Thomas. 1991. "Head Coverings, Prophecies, and the Trinity." In *Recovering Biblical Manhood and Womanhood*, edited by Wayne Grudem and John Piper, 124–39. Wheaton, Ill.: Crossway.

Scott, James. 1985. *Weapons of the Weak*. New Haven: Yale University Press.

———. 1990. *Domination and the Arts of Resistance*. New Haven: Yale University Press.

"The Secret Crime." 1988. *Eternity*, March, 36–63.

Seculow, Jay. N.d. "Religious Freedom Update: . . . and Nothing but the Truth." Washington D.C.: American Center for Law and Justice.

Segars, Melissa. 2004. "Rally for Women's Rights." *Capital Times* (Madison), April 26.

Seidman, Steven. 1997. *Difference Troubles*. Cambridge: Cambridge University Press.

———. 1998. *Contested Knowledges: Social Theory in the Postmodern Era*. Oxford: Blackwell.

Senogles, Renee. N.d. "Women of the Americas Conference." *Indigenous Woman* 1 (3): 28–30.

Senter, Ruth. 1973. "Dare to be Liberated." *Moody*, November, 81–84.

Settee, Priscilla. 1998. "Indigenous Peoples Uranium Speaking Tour." *Indigenous Woman* 2 (5): 30–34.

———. 1999. "8th Nuclear Free and Independent Pacific Conference." *Indigenous Woman* 3 (1): 26–27.

———. N.d. "World Trade Organization (WTO) Seattle Rally." *Indigenous Woman* 1 (3): 45–47.

Seu, Andree. 2004. "Significance of a Little Folly." *World*, May 29, 47.

"Sexual Abuse: Where's the Hope?" 1999. *Indian Life*, September-October, 5–6.

Shapiro, Joseph. 1995. "Heavenly Promises." *U.S. News and World Report*, October 2, 68–70.

Sheldon, Louis. 2001. *Ted Kennedy and Barney Frank Exploit Terrorist Attack!* Electronic newsletter. Washington, D.C.: Traditional Values Coalition.

Shelley, Bruce. 1999. "An On-Again, Off-Again Love Affair." *Christianity Today*, September 6, 54–55.

Shelley, Marshall. 1984. "The Death Penalty: Two Sides of a Growing Issue." *Christianity Today*, March 2, 14–17.

Shelton, John. 1991. "Free Indeed." *Charisma*, June, 58–67.

Shepard, Carol. 1998. " 'Jesus House' Gives Freed Inmates a Second Chance in Indianapolis." *Charisma*, September, 36–38.

Shepson, Bill. 2001. "Can Christians Be Gay?" *Charisma*, December, 38–44.

———. 2002. "Can Christians Be Gay?" *New Man*, January–February, 46–52.

Sherman, Amy. 1995. "A Young Life Is Spared." *World*, March 25, 15.

———. 1996. "STEP-ing out on Faith—and off Welfare." *Christianity Today*, June 17, 35–36.

Sherman, Bill. 2006. "Too Inclusive." *Christianity Today*, March, 24.

Shoemaker, Nancy, ed. 1995. *Negotiators of Change: Historical Perspectives on Native American Women*. New York: Routledge.

Shubin, Rusell. 2000. "That the Natives Might Lift Jesus Up." *Mission Frontiers*, September, 8–9.

Siddons, Philip. 1978. "Paul's View of Women." *Christianity Today*, February 19, 40–41.

Sider, Ronald. 1996. "Can God Use Democrats?" *Charisma*, October, 48–50.

———. 2001. "Putting Faith Back in Public Service." *Christianity Today*, June 11, 90–91.

Sigler, Mike. 1978. "PACE: Helping Prisoners Face Freedom." *Christian Life*, July, 30–34.

Sillars, Les. 1998. "At Death's Door." *World*, April 4, 13–15.

Silliman, Jael, and Ynestra King, eds. 1999. *Dangerous Intersections: Feminist Perspectives on Population, Environment, and Development*. Cambridge, Mass.: South End.

Silliman, Jael, Loretta Ross, Marlene Gerber Fried, and Elena Gutierrez. 2005. *Undivided Rights*. Cambridge, Mass.: South End.

Silva, Moises. 1988. "Old Princeton, Westminster, and Inerrancy." *Westminster Theological Journal* 50:65–80.

Simpson, Audra. 2003. *To the Reserve and Back Again: Kahnawake Mohawk Narratives of Self, Home, and Nation*. PhD diss., McGill University, Montreal.

Simpson, Sany. 2005. "A Call to the Nations?" Apologetics Coordination Team, April 28. http://www.deceptioninthechurch.com/acalltothenations.html.

Singleton, Jerry. 1984. "Captured!" *Decision*, December, 3.

Skeet, James. 2000. "From Brokenness to Reconciliation." *Trailblazer*, winter, n.p.

Skillen, James. 1990. *The Scattered Voice*. Grand Rapids: Zondervan.

———. 1993. "Cry for Justice, Hope for Shalom." In *Setting the Captives Free*, edited by Don Smarto, 129–39. Grand Rapids: Baker Book House.

Smarto, Don. 1990. "Behind the Bars." *Moody*, October, 19–20.

———, ed. 1993. *Setting the Captives Free*. Grand Rapids: Baker Book House.

Smeal, Eleanor. 1997. *Promise Keepers Hold No Promise for Women*. Press statement, October 2. Washington, D.C.: Fund for Feminist Majority.

Smedes, Lewis. 2002. "How to Deal with Criminals." *Christianity Today*, July 8, 59.

Smietana, Bob. 2004. "Mega Shepherd." *Christianity Today*, February, 28–35.

Smith, Andrea. 1997. "The Christian Right and Race Reconciliation." Master's thesis, Union Theological Seminary, New York.

———. 1999a. "The American Way and the Good Red Road: American Indians, the Christian Right, and the (De)Construction of American Religion." In *The Bible and the American Myth*, edited by Vincent Wimbush, 13–52. Macon: Mercer University Press.

———. 1999b. "Sexual Violence and American Indian Genocide." In *Remembering Conquest: Feminist/Womanist Perspectives on Religion, Colonization, and Sexual Violence*, edited by Nantawan Lewis and Marie Fortune, 31–52. Binghamton, N.Y.: Haworth.

———. 2001. " 'Better Dead Than Pregnant': The Colonization of Native Women's Health." In *Policing the National Body*, edited by Anannya Bhattacharjee and Jael Silliman, 123–46. Cambridge, Mass.: South End.

——. 2002. "Bible, Gender, and Nationalism in American Indian and Christian Right Activism." PhD diss., University of California, Santa Cruz.

——. 2005a. "Beyond Pro-choice Versus Pro-life: Women of Color and Reproductive Justice." *NWSA Journal* 17 (spring): 117–140.

——. 2005b. *Conquest, Sexual Violence, and American Indian Genocide.* Cambridge, Mass.: South End.

——. 2005c. "Domestic Violence, the State, and Social Change." In *Domestic Violence at the Margins: A Reader at the Intersections of Race, Class, and Gender*, edited by Natalie Sokolotf, 146–34. New Brunswick, N.J.: Rutgers University Press.

——. 2005d. "Native Feminism, Activism and Social Change." *Feminist Studies* 31 (1): 116–132.

——. 2006. " 'The One Who Would Not Break His Promises': Native Peoples in the Evangelical Race Reconciliation Movement." *American Behavioral Scientist* 50 (4): 478–509.

——. Forthcoming. *The Christian Right and Race Reconciliation.*

Smith, Barbara. 1982. *But Some of Us Are Brave.* Old Westbury, N.Y.: Feminist Press.

Smith, Christian, ed. 1996. *Disruptive Religion.* New York: Routledge.

——. 2000. *Christian America?* Berkeley: University of California Press.

Smith, Craig. 1997. *Whiteman's Gospel.* Winnipeg: Indian Life.

Smith, Dorothy. 1999. *Writing the Social.* Toronto: University of Toronto Press.

Smith, Eddie. 1999. "The Invisible Power of Prayer." *Charisma*, May, 46–51.

Smith, J. Alfred, and Ross Maracle. 1989. "Listening to America's Ethnic Churches." *Christianity Today*, March 3, 25–41.

Smith, Justine. 1996. "Custer Rides Again, This Time on the Exxon Valdez." In *Defending Mother Earth*, edited by Jace Weaver, 59–71. Maryknoll. N.Y.: Orbis.

——. 1999. "Native Sovereignty and Social Justice: Moving toward an Inclusive Social Justice Framework." In *Dangerous Intersections: Feminist Perspectives on Population, Environment, and Development*, edited by Jael Silliman and Ynestra King, 202–13. Cambridge, Mass.: South End.

——. 2000. "Resistance Disguised as Fundamentalism: Cherokee Nationalism, Racial Identity, and the Bible." Paper presented at the American Academy of Religion conference, Nashville, Tenn., November 19.

——. 2005. "Indigenous Performance and Aporetic Texts." *Union Seminary Quarterly Review* 59 (1–2): 114–24.

Smith, Linda Tuhiwai. 1999. *Decolonizing Methodologies.* London: Zed.

Smith, Marilyn B. 2000. *Gender or Giftedness.* Manila: World Evangelical Fellowship.

Smith, Tammie. 2004. "Marchers Call for 'A Choice' about Reproductive Rights." *Richmond Times Dispatch*, April 26.

Smith, Tom. 1992. "Are Conservative Churches Growing?" *Review of Religious Research* 33 (June): 305–29.

Sokoloff, Natalie, ed. 2005. *Domestic Violence at the Margins*. New Brunswick, N.J.: Rutgers University Press.

Solinger, Rickie. 2001. *Beggers and Choosers*. New York: Hill and Wang.

Solomon, Emmett. N.d. "Incarceration: Pros and Cons." *Restorative Justice Journal* 1 (3): 2.

Sound Off. 1998. *Charisma*, December, 18.

"Sovereignty." 1999. *Indigenous Woman* 3 (1): 18.

Spatt, Mindy. 1995. "Gay and Lesbian Experiences and Sensibilities in the Antiwar Movement." In *Cultural Politics and Social Movements*, edited by Marcy Darnovsky, Barbara Epstein, and Richard Flacks, 161–66. Philadelphia: Temple University Press.

Spencer, Aida Besancon. 1995. *The Goddess Revival*. Grand Rapids: Baker Book House.

Spivak, Gayatri. 1994. "Can the Subaltern Speak?" In *Colonial Discourse and Post-colonial Theory*, edited by Patrick Williams and Laura Chrisman, 66–111. New York: Columbia University Press.

———. 1999. *A Critique of Postcolonial Reason: Toward a History of the Vanishing Present*. Cambridge, Mass.: Harvard University Press.

Spoelstra, Watson. 1977. "God Turns Prisons Inside Out." *Christian Life*, September, 30–31, 68–69.

Spring, Beth. 1986. "Gay Rights Resolution Divides Membership of Evangelical Women's Caucus." *Christianity Today*, October 3, 40–43.

Stackhouse, John. 1998. "The Perils of Left and Right." *Christianity Today*, August 10, 58–59.

———. 1999a. "The Battle for the Inclusive Bible." *Christianity Today*, November 15, 83–84.

———. 1999b. "Finding a Home for Eve." *Christianity Today*, March 1, 60–61.

———. 2005. "Who's Afraid of Evangelicals." *Faith Today*, January–February, 29–31.

Stafford, Tim. 1989. "Angel of Light." *Christianity Today*, September 8, 19.

———. 1999. "The Criminologist Who Discovered America." *Christianity Today*, June 14, 35–39.

———. 2005. "Good Morning, Evangelicals." *Christianity Today*, November, 40–45.

Stafford, Tim, and James Beverly. 1997. "God's Wonder Worker." *Christianity Today*, July 14, 46–47.

Stafford, Wes. 2005. "One Child at a Time." *Christianity Today*, November, 80–81.

Stalcup, Elizabeth Moll. 1999. "When the Glory Comes Down." *Charisma*, November, 76–84.

Stammer, Larry. 2004. "Faith-Based Stance on Environment." *Los Angeles Times*, July 4.

Stanciu, T. L., and Nisha Mohammed. 1995. "People Are Never the Problem." *Rutherford*, March, 19–23.

Starkloff, Carl. 1985. "Religious Renewal in Native North America: The Contemporary Call to Mission." *Missiology* 13 (January): 81–102.

Startup, Kenneth Moore. 2002. "Red, White, and Gray." *Books and Culture*, July–August, 21.

Steiner, Stan. 1968. *The New Indians*. New York: Dell.

Steinken, Ken. 1998. "Native Christians Reclaim Worship." *Christianity Today*, October 26, 13.

Stentzel, Jim. 1979. "Called on the Evangelical Carpet." *Sojourners*, October, 9.

Stephen, Anil. 2001. "Muslim Leader Appeals to Evangelicals." *Christianity Today*, June 11, 24–25.

Stephenson, Kathy. 2004. "Utahns Take Part in D.C. and at Home." *Salt Lake Tribune*, April 26.

Stertzer, Carol Chapman. 2001. "When God Came to the Barrio." *Charisma*, August, 46–56.

Stevenson, Winona. 1998a. " 'Every Word Is a Bundle:' Cree Intellectual Traditions and History." Unpublished paper, copy in Andrea Smith's possession.

——. 1998b. " 'Ethnic' Assimilates 'Indigenous': A Study in Intellectual Neocolonialism." *Wicazo Sa Review* 13, no. 1 (spring): 33–51.

Stewart, Jimmy. 2000. "Native Praise." *Charisma*, November, 91.

Stewart, Tracy. 1985. "Jesus Walks among the Navajo." *World Christian*, July–August, 40–41.

Stoler, Ann. 1997. *Race and the Education of Desire*. Durham, N.C.: Duke University Press.

Strang, Heather, and John Braithwaite, eds. 2002. *Restorative Justice and Family Violence*. Cambridge: Cambridge University Press.

Strang, Stephen. 1995. "The Jesus Factor." *Charisma*, October, 116.

——. 1997. "Spiritual Trends." *Charisma*, January, 88.

——. 1999. "Pentecostal Trends." *Charisma*, July, 114.

Strauss, Mark. 1998. *Distorting Scripture*. Downers Grove, Ill.: InterVarsity.

Strom, Lisa. 2000. *Karla Faye Tucker Set Free*. Colorado Springs: Shaw.

Suffer, Austin, and George Knight III. 1981. "Ordination of Women, Yes; Ordination of Women, No." *Christianity Today*, February 20, 12–19.

Sullivan, Don. 1998. "Manitoba Forests." *Indigenous Woman* 2 (5): 43–44.

Summer, Sarah. 2005. "Bridging the Ephesian's Divide." *Christianity Today*, November, 59–61.

Suuqina. 2000. "Cultural Restoration: It's Time, It's Here." *Inuit Ministries International Newsletter*, February, 1, 3.

Swank, J. Grant. 1997. "My Son Is in Jail." *Alliance Life*, January 15, 12–13.

Sweeney, Annie. 2004. "Chicagoans Head to D.C. for Pro-choice March." *Chicago Sun-Times*, April 25.

Tailman Chavez, Valerie. N.d. "Native Americans Battle with Toxic Waste." *Indigenous Woman* 1 (2): 15–16.

Taliman, Valerie. N.d. "Stuck Holding the Waste." *Indigenous Woman* 1 (3): 5–7.

TallBear, Kimberley. 2001. "Racialising Tribal Identity and the Implications for Political and Cultural Development." In *Indigenous Peoples, Racism, and the United Nations*, edited by Martin Nakata, 163–74. Altona, Australia: Common Ground Publishing.

Tanis, Alta. 1996. *God's Warrior*. Winnipeg: Indian Life.

Tarr, Leslie. 1990. "Mediation Services." *Faith Today*, November–December, 24.

Tarro, Paul. 1992. "Wolves in Shepherds' Clothing." *Urban Mission*, March, 17–27.

Taylor, Clyde. 1974. "Capital Commentary." *United Evangelical Action*, spring, 8.

Taylor, LaTonya. 2002. "Falwell, ACLU Fight Church Restrictions." *Christianity Today*, June 10, 15.

Tbishkokeshigook, Judy DaSilva. 1998. "Asobpeeschoseewagong: One Voice." *Indigenous Woman* 2 (5): 19–22.

"Teen Sex: Black Youth Leaders for a Solution.' 1990. *Christianity Today*, September 10, 55.

Tennant, Agnieszka. 2002. "Classroom Corrections." *Christianity Today*, February 4, 62–63.

———. 2006. "What (Not All) Women Want." *Christianity Today*, August, 60.

Thielicke, Helmut. 1985. "The Great Temptation." *Christianity Today*, July 12, 26–31.

Thistlethwaite, Susan. 1985. "Every Two Minutes: Battered Women and Feminist Interpretation." In *Feminist Interpretation of the Bible*, edited by Letty Russell, 96–107. Philadelphia: Westminster Press.

Thom, Mel. 1972. "The New Indian Wars." In *The Way*, edited by Shirley Hill Witt and Stan Steiner, 102–7. New York: Random House.

Thomas, Cal. 1999a. "Have We Settled for Caesar?" *Christianity Today*, September, 48–49.

———. 1999b. "Let Them Eat Crude." *World*, November 6, 24.

Thompson, Barbara. 1984. "Back in Jail." *Christian Herald*, April, 36–38, 42.

———. 1995. "Working with the 'Dead Already.'" *World Vision*, August–September, 18–22.

Thompson, Fred. 1982. "The Glorification of Violence." *United Evangelical Action*, fall, 14–16.

Tiansay, Eric. 2002a. "The Battle for the Bible." *Charisma*, November, 82–85.

———. 2002b. "Pearson's Gospel of Inclusion Stirs Controversy." *Charisma*, May, 15.

——. 2003. "He Asked God for Nations." *Charisma*, September, 40–44, 84.

——. 2004. "T. D. Jakes Thrilled with Opening Box Office of New York." *Charisma*, December, 17.

——. 2005. "Arizona Pastors Say Reservation Has Become Wellspring of Revival." *Charisma*, June, 29.

"Till Death Do Us Part?" 2000. *New Man*, March–April, 21.

Tinker, George. 1993. *Missionary Conquest*. Minneapolis: Fortress.

——. 1998. "Jesus, Corn Mother, and Conquest." In *Unforgotten Gods: Native American Religious Identity*, edited by Jace Weaver, 134–54. Maryknoll, N.Y.: Orbis Press.

——. 2004. *Spirit and Resistance*. Minneapolis: Fortress.

Toner, Robin. 2004. "Abortion Rights Marchers Vow to Fight Another Bush Term." *New York Times*, April 26.

Touraine, Alain. 1977. *The Voice and the Eye*. Cambridge: Cambridge University Press.

Tousy, Sheila. N.d. "An Interview." *Indigenous Woman* 2 (1): 32–35.

Tracy, Steven. 2003. "Headship with a Heart." *Christianity Today*, February, 50–54.

Trask, Mililani. 1995. "Indigenous Women and Nation Building." In *Indigenous Women Address the World*, edited by the Indigenous Women's Network, 14–16. Austin: Indigenous Women's Network.

——. 2001. "IWN Sustainable Communities Gathering." *Indigenous Woman* 4 (2): 4–7.

——. N.d. "Indigenous Women Are the Mothers of Their Nations." *Indigenous Woman* 2 (2): 23–27.

Treat, James. 2003. *Around the Sacred Fire*. New York: Palgrave.

Treat, James, ed. 1996. *Native and Christian*. Oxford: Oxford University Press.

Trollinger, William. 1985. "How Should Evangelicals Understand Fundamentalism?" *United Evangelical Action*, September–October, 7–9.

Trouten, Doug. 2005. "Making Waves." *New Man*, March–April, 46–50.

Trunk, Tracy. 2000. "Holiday Fruitcakes . . ." *Population Research Institute*, January–February, 16.

Tunley, Roul. 1978. "Behind Steel Doors." *Campus Life*, October, 66–69.

Turner, Dale. 2006. *This Is Not a Peace Pipe*. Toronto: University of Toronto Press.

Turner, Ralph. 1995. "Ideology and Utopia after Socialism." In *New Social Movements: From Ideology to Identity*, edited by Enrique Larana, Hank Johnston, and Joseph Gusfield, 79–100. Philadelphia: Temple University Press.

Twiss, Richard. 1996. *Culture, Christ, and the Kingdom Seminar*. Vancouver, Wash.: Wiconi International.

——. 1998. *Sanctification, Syncretism, and Worship*. Vancouver, Wash.: Wiconi International.

———. 1999. "The Bleeding Heart of Native America." *Charisma*, April, 82–91.

———. 2000a. "Can I Call You Gringo?" *Charisma*, December, 44.

———. 2000b. "Indian Uprising." *Charisma*, October, 51.

———. 2000c. "Out of Sight, out of Mind." *Mission Frontiers*, September, 12–13.

———2001. "A Prophetic Destiny." *Charisma*, December, 72.

———. 2002. *Culture, Christ & the Kingdom: Presenting Biblical Principles for Native Ministry that Honor God, His People, and His Creation*. Rev. ed. Vancouver, Wash.: privately printed.

Umbreit, Mark. 1982. "Victim-Offender Reconciliation Is Ultimately Practical." *Christianity Today*, April 9, 33–36.

"Update: The Wheels Turn Slowly for an Appeal in the Linscott Case." 1983. *Christianity Today*, November 11, 71, 73.

Uttley, Jim. 1999. "The Crime That Won't Go Away." *Indian Life*, September–October, 4.

———. 2001. "'Men without Chests' Need Moral Reformation." *Indian Life*, July–August, 4.

———. 2004a. "Native Americans Highlighted in Conference." *Indian Life*, January–February, 1, 3.

———. 2004b. "Native Leaders Say Land Restitution Is Result of Reconciliation Gathering." *Charisma*, October, 24, 26.

———. 2005. "Partnership Encourages Theological Training for First Nations Leaders." *Charisma*, June, 23–24.

Valaskakis, Gail Guthrie. 2005. *Indian Country*. Waterloo, Ont.: Wilfrid Laurier University Press.

Vander Broek, Lyle. 1984. "Review of the Divine Feminine." *Reformed Journal* 34 (February): 22–25.

Van Domelen, Bob. 2000. "Profile of a Perpetrator." *Charisma*, May, 99.

Van Leeuwen, Mary Stewart. 1991. *Gender and Grace*. Downers Grove, Ill.: InterVarsity.

———. 1997. "Servanthood or Soft Patriarchy? A Christian Feminist Looks at the Promise Keepers Movement." *Priscilla Papers* 11 (spring): 28–39.

Van Loon, Michelle. 2006. "'Equality Ride' Targets Christian Colleges." *Charisma*, June, 20–21.

Van Ness, Daniel. 1985. "The Crisis of Crowded Prisons." *Eternity*, April, 33–37.

———. 1986. *Crime and Its Victims*. Downers Grove, Ill.: InterVarsity.

———. 1987a. "Punishable by Death." *Christianity Today*, July 10, 24–27.

———. 1987b. "Restoring Crime's Victims." *Eternity*, March, 8–14.

———. 1993. "The Ministry of Justice." In *Setting the Captives Free*, edited by Don Smarto, 73–81. Grand Rapids: Baker Book House.

———. 2001. "Forgiveness and Terrorism." *PFI World*, September–October, 3–4.

Varoqua, Eman. 2004. "N.J. Supporters Form Large Column for Rights." *The Record* (Bergen County, N.J.), April 26.

Vaughn, S. 1985. "The Surprising Results of Prison Ministry." *Moody*, May, 22–26.

Veenker, Jody. 1999. "How to Heal a Broken Church." *Christianity Today*, August 9, 21.

——. 2000. "Prison Fellowship Downsizing." *Christianity Today*, November 13, 23.

Veith, Gene Edward. 1996. "Heroin Chic." *World*, November 9, 12–15.

——. 1999a. "Academic Icon Exposed." *World*, February 13, 25.

——. 1999b. "Bible Belt Breakups." *World*, November 27, 30–31.

——. 1999c. "Feminist Misogyny." *World*, January 9, 26–27.

——. 1999d. "Ministry or Vocation?" *World*, January 23, 24.

——. 2004a. "The Image War." *World*, May 22, 30–35.

——. 2004b. "Natural Allies." *World*, March 6, 33.

——. 2005a. "Friendliest Book in the World." *World*, November 12, 32.

——. 2005b. "No Arms, No Legs, No Problem." *World*, September 3, 10.

——. 2005c. "Practicing What They Protest." *World*, June 4, 30.

——. 2006a. "Radical Tactic." *World*, January 21, 36.

——. 2006b. "To Protect and Conserve." *World*, May 20, 30.

Venne, Sharon. 1998. "Mining and Indigenous Peoples." *Indigenous Woman* 2 (5): 23–25.

——. 1999. "The Meaning of Sovereignty." *Indigenous Woman* 2 (6): 27–30.

Vernon, Robert. 1991. "L.A. Cop: Robert Vernon." *Christianity Today*, April 29, 42–43.

Vincent, James. 1987. "Faith and a Badge." *Moody*, December, 73.

Vincent, Lynn. 2002a. "Breaking Faith." *World*, March 30, 18–23.

——. 2002b. "Breaking Faith Update." *World*, April 13, 12.

——. 2004. "Preserving Habitat." *World*, December 18, 21.

——. 2005. "Tookie's Victims." *World*, December 24, 21.

——. 2006a. "Drawing Blood." *World*, April 22, 32–36.

——. 2006b. "Justice and Mercy." *World*, April 8, 30–31.

Visweswaran, Kamala. 1994. *Fictions of Feminist Ethnography*. Minneapolis: University of Minnesota Press.

Vizenor, Gerald. 1994. *Manifest Manners: Postindian Warriors of Survivance*. Hanover, N.H.: University Press of New England.

Walker, Ken. 1998. "T. D. Jakes Takes Gospel behind Bars." *Charisma*, April, 24–26.

——. 1999. "Shaking the Southern Baptist Tradition." *Charisma*, March, 68–76; 116.

——. 2003. "Time to Decide." *Christianity Today*, April, 36–37.

——. 2004. "Breaking the Chains." *Charisma*, December, 44–46.

Walker, Samuel. 1998. *Sense and Nonsense about Crime*. Belmont, Calif.: Wadsworth.

Wall, Robert. 1988. "Wifely Submission in the Context of Ephesians." *Christian Scholar's Review* 17: 272–85.

Wallis, Jim. 1994. *Who Speaks for God?* New York: Delacourte.

"Wanted: Black Leadership." 1991. *Christianity Today*, July 22, 36.

Ward, Marianne Meed. 1995. "The Seventh Fire: From Paternalism to Partnership." *Faith Today*, September–October, 28–31.

———. 2000. "Why Should Christians Care?" *Faith Today*, July–August, 36–40.

Ward, Mark. 1994. *The Conquering Indian*. Winnipeg: Indian Life.

Warrior, Robert. 1991. "Canaanites, Cowboys, and Indians." In *Voices from the Margin*, edited by R. S. Sugirtharajah, 294–95. Maryknoll, N.Y.: Orbis.

———. 1994. *Tribal Secrets*. Minneapolis: University of Minnesota Press.

———. 2005. *The People and the Word*. Minneapolis: University of Minnesota Press.

Warrior, Robert, and Paul Chaat Smith. 1996. *Like a Hurricane*. New York: New Press.

Warriors for Christ. 1996. "Dance a Good Dance." Hungry Horse, Mont.: Warriors for Christ.

Washinawatok, Ingrid. 1995a. "Our Responsibility." In *Indigenous Women Address the World*, edited by the Indigenous Women's Network, 17–19. Austin: Indigenous Women's Network.

———. 1995b. "Sovereignty as a Birthright." In *Indigenous Women Address the World*, edited by the Indigenous Women's Network, 12–13. Austin: Indigenous Women's Network.

———. 1999a. "An Interview with Ingrid: Health Solutions for Sustainable Communities Gathering, 1997." *Indigenous Woman* 3 (1): 13–16.

———. 1999b. "Sovereignty Is More Than Just Power." *Indigenous Woman* 2 (6): 23–24.

Weaver, Jace. 1996a. "A Biblical Paradigm for Native Liberation." In *Native and Christian*, edited by James Treat, 103–4. Oxford: Oxford University Press.

———. 1997. *That the People Might Live*. Oxford: Oxford University Press.

———, ed. 1996b. *Defending Mother Earth*. Maryknoll, N.Y.: Orbis.

Weaver-Zercher, Valerie. 2000. "God's Crime Bill." *Christianity Today*, April 24, 100–104.

Webb, Lee. 1999. "Faith behind Bars." January 6. http://159.26.240.64/News/stories/990106.asp?text=1 (accessed January 6, 1999).

Wennberg, Robert. 1973. "Legal Punishment and Its Justification." *Christian Scholar's Review* 3:99–112.

"We're in This Together." 1998. *World*, February 28, 7.

West, Cornel, and bell hooks. 1991. *Breaking Bread*. Cambridge, Mass.: South End.

Weyler, Rex. 1992. *Blood of the Land*. Philadelphia: New Society.

Weyrich, Paul. 1999. "The Moral Minority." *Christianity Today*, September 6, 44–45.

Whaley, Rick, and Walt Bresette. 1994. *Walleye Warriors*. Philadelphia: New Society.

Whalin, Terry. 1997. "Murdered But Not Defeated." *Charisma*, May, 79–82.

"What Can Christians Do to Fight Crime?" 1973. *Eternity*, September, 15.

White Hat, Annie. 1999. "Sovereignty." *Indigenous Woman* 3 (1): 20.

White, Janelle. 2004. "Our Silence Will Not Protect Us: Black Women Confronting Sexual and Domestic Violence." PhD diss., University of Michigan.

White, Lavina. N.d. "Listening to Our Elders." *Indigenous Woman* 1 (2): 13–14.

"White Liberals on the Warpath." 2005. *Focus on the Family Citizen,* November, 14.

Whitehead, John. 1994. "Christ Was Controversial and Dogmatic." *Rutherford*, March, 6–7.

——. 1995. "Death Control." *Rutherford*, March, 11.

——. 1996. "Is Religion Just Another Tool in the Politician's Toolbox?" *Rutherford*, September, 12–13.

Whitt, Laurie Anne. 1998. "Cultural Imperialism and the Marketing of Native America." In *Natives and Academics: Researching and Writing about American Indians*, edited by Devon Mihesuah, 139–71. Lincoln: University of Nebraska Press.

"Who Are the 'Indian Givers'?" 1973. *Eternity*, August, 8–9.

Wiconi International. 2001. *First Nations Ministry Report*. Vancouver, Wash.: Wiconi International.

Wilcox, Clyde. 1987. "Popular Backing for the Old Christian Right: Explaining Support for the Christian Anti-communism Crusade." *Journal of Social History* 21 (fall): 117–32.

Wilcox, Clyde, and Leopoldo Gomez. 1990. "The Christian Right and the Pro-Life Movement: An Analysis of the Sources of Political Support." *Review of Religious Research* 31 (June): 380–89.

Wilcox, Clyde, Ted Jelen, and Sharon Linzey. 1995. "Rethinking the Reasonableness of the Religious Right." *Review of Religious Research* 36 (March): 263–76.

Wilcox, Clyde, Sharon Linzey, and Ted Jelen. 1991. "Reluctant Warrior: Premillennialism and Politics in the Moral Majority." *Journal for the Scientific Study of Religion* 30 (3): 245–58.

Wilcox, Clyde, Mark Rozell, and Roland Gunn. 1996. "Religious Coalitions in the New Christian Right." *Social Science Quarterly* 77 (September): 546–56.

Wiley, Norbert. 1994. "The Politics of Identity in American History." In *Social Theory and the Politics of Identity*, edited by Craig Calhoun, 130–49. Malden: Blackwell.

Williams, Frederick. 1982. "Opinion." *Biblical Viewpoint* 16 (November): 175.

Williams, J. Christopher. 1993. "Christianity Not a Whiteman's Religion." *Indian Life*, January–February, 8–9.

Williams, Raymond. 1991. "Base and Superstructure in Marxist Cultural Theory." In *Rethinking Popular Culture*, edited by Chandra Mukerji and Michael Schudson, 407–23. Berkeley: University of California Press.

Williams, Russ. 1980. "Truth . . . and Consequences: How Pat Gundry Discovered Biblical Feminism." *The Other Side*, October, 15–19.

Williams, Susan, and Kathryn M. Hoover. 1999. "Assaults on Tribal Sovereignty: Signs of a New Era in Federal Indian Policy?" *Indigenous Woman* 2 (6): 31–33.

Williamson, Parker. 1998–99. "Hearing the 'Heartbeat of Mother Earth.'" *Faith and Freedom*, winter, 11.

Willoughby, Karen. 1999. "Ministerial Oversight?" *World*, November 6, 20–22.

Wilson, Bill. 1996. "Why I Chose to Live in Hell." *Charisma*, October, 55–62.

Wilson, Earl. 1988. "Ministering to Victims of Incest." *Leadership*, winter, 127–29.

Wilson, E. R. 1975. "Letters." *Moody*, June, 4.

Wilson, Ron. 1971. "High on the Campus." *Moody*, March, 83–85.

Wilson, Waziyatawin Angela. 2005. *Remember This!* Lincoln: University of Nebraska Press.

Winger, Mell. 1998. "The Miracle of Almolonga." *Charisma*, September, 66–72.

Wink, Walter. 1996. "Getting off Drugs: The Legalization Option." *Friends Journal* (February): 13–16.

Winn, Pete. 2002. "Rightly Divided?" *Focus on the Family Citizen*, May, 28–29.

Winner, Lauren. 2000a. "The Man behind the Megachurch." *Christianity Today*, November 13, 56–60.

——. 2000b. "T. D. Jakes Feels Your Pain." *Christianity Today*, February 7, 52–59.

——. 2005. "Sex in the Body of Christ." *Christianity Today*, May, 28–33.

Witt, Shirley Hill, and Stan Steiner. eds. 1972. *The Way: An Anthology of American Indian Literature*. New York: Random House.

Wolfe, Elizabeth. 2004. "Rights March Packs Mall." *The Commercial Appeal* (Memphis), April 26.

Womack, Craig. 1999. *Red on Red*. Minneapolis: University of Minnesota Press.

"Women's Role in Church and Family." 1985. *Christianity Today*, February 21, 10–11.

Wood, Gail. 2003. "Former Football Pro Has Taken the Gospel into Hundreds of U.S. Prisons." *Charisma*, October, 42–44.

——. 2005. "On Sacred Ground." *Charisma*, May, 58–63.

Wood, Rick. 2000. "Games of Chance." *Mission Frontiers*, September, 22–24.

Woodbridge, John. 1995. "Why Words Matter." *Christianity Today*, June 19, 31.

Wooding, Dan. 1994. "God's Wake up Call." *Charisma*, July, 29.

Woodley, Randy. 2000. "Putting it to the Test." *Mission Frontiers*, September, 18–19.

———. 2001. *Living in Color*. Downers Grove, Ill.: InterVarsity.

World Mailbag. 1998. *World*, December 19, 4–6.

Wright, Dorothy. 1999. "Changed Forever." *Indian Life*, September–October, 8.

Wynn, Kelli. 2004. "Hundreds Go to D.C. for March Today." *Dayton Daily News*, April 25.

Yamashita, Jeff. 1987. "Hawaii Cop." *Decision*, November, 4–5.

Yancey, Philip. 1976a. "Paper Chains." *Campus Life*, February, 22–25.

———. 1976b. "Window to a Murderer." *Campus Life*, February, 26.

———. 1988. "Holy Subversion." *Christianity Today*, February 5, 14–19.

Yapi, Sota Iya Ye. 2000. "Legal Procedures Hinder Justice for Indian Youth." *Indian Life*, September–October, 1, 3.

Yarbrough, Richard. 1991. "Retreating Authority: Evangelical-Liberal Rapprochement." *Christian Scholar's Review* 19 (2): 149–62.

Yates, Douglas. 2001. "Protest March Calls Attention to Criminal Justice System." *Indian Life*, July–August, 10.

Yazzie, Esther. N.d. "Leetso: The Powerful Yellow Monster." *Indigenous Woman* 2 (1): 24–27.

Young, J. Terry. 1987. "The Relationship between Biblical Inerrancy and Biblical Authority." In *The Proceedings of the Conference on Biblical Inerrancy* 391–409. Nashville: Broadman.

Zald, Mayer. 1987. "The Future of Social Movements." In *Social Movements in an Organizational Society*, edited by Mayer Zald and John McCarthy, 319–36. New Brunswick, N.J.: Transaction.

Zedner, Lucia. 1995. "Wayward Sisters: The Prison for Women." In *The Oxford History of the Prison*, edited by Norval Morris and David Rothman, 295–324. Oxford: Oxford University Press.

Zoba, Wendy Murray. 1997. "Your Sins Shall Be White as Yucca." *Christianity Today*, October 27, 18–25.

———. 1999. "Daring to Discipline America." *Christianity Today*, March 1, 31–38.

———. 2000a. "Take a Little Time Out." *Christianity Today*, February 7, 86.

———. 2000b. "A Woman's Place." *Christianity Today*, August 7, 40–48.

———. 2001. "The Legacy of Prisoner 23226." *Christianity Today*, July 9, 28–35.

———. 2003. "The Hidden Slavery." *Christianity Today*, November, 68–74.

Zoscher, Paul. 1976. "Eutychus and His Kin." *Christianity Today*, June 4, 20.

Zwier, Robert. 1982. *Born-Again Politics*. Downers Grove, Ill.: InterVarsity Press.

Index

Andrea Smith is an assistant professor of American Culture and women's studies at the University of Michigan, Ann Arbor. She is the author of *Conquest: Sexual Violence and American Indian Genocide* (South End, 2005).

Library of Congress Cataloging-in-Publication Data
Smith, Andrea.
Native Americans and the Christian right : the gendered politics
of unlikely alliances / Andrea Smith.
p. cm.
Includes bibliographical references and index.
ISBN 978-0-8223-4140-6 (cloth : alk. paper)
ISBN 978-0-8223-4163-5 (pbk. : alk. paper)
1. Indians of North America—Religion. 2. Indians of North America
—Social conditions. 3. Fundamentalism—United States. 4. Evangelical-
ism—United States. 5. Social justice—United States. 6. Social justice
—Religious aspects—Christianity. I. Title.
E98.R3S54 2008
299.7—dc22   2007033634